# ONE HUNDRED YEARS OF CATHOLIC EDUCATION:

Historical Essays in Honor of the
Centennial of the
National Catholic Educational Association

Edited by
*John Augenstein*
*Christopher J. Kauffman*
*Robert J. Wister*

NCEA

ISBN No.    1-55833-296-0
PART No.    RES-15-1279

# CONTENTS

# FOREWORD:
## CONTEXTS AND CONTENTS

*Christopher J. Kauffman*

W hat a splendid collection of essays; the reader is treated to well-researched and neatly crafted chapters, each with its own unifying principle of organization. The chapters logically fall into four thematic parts: Leadership, Church and State, Ethos and Charism, and Ethnicity. The reader will note that the section, "Contributors," represents the interdisciplinary character of this work: historians, theologians, social scientists, education specialists, and some authors who combine teaching and administration. In an attempt to capture the meanings of this book, this brief foreword will be an exploration of its contexts and an overview of its contents.

## CONTEXTS

The National Catholic Educational Association (originally, the Catholic Educational Association) was founded in 1903-04 during a period characterized by a strong organizational impulse. Other national Catholic organizations were established during this period: The Federation of Catholic Societies (1901), The National Association of Catholic Charities (1910), and The National Hospital Association (1915). Following a pattern developed by non-religious associations during the last two decades of the nineteenth century, these Catholic associations represent new stages in the modernization of institutions and the professional life of their personnel. Schools, orphanages, welfare agencies, and hospitals were required by accrediting agencies to achieve increasingly higher standards and teachers, social workers, nurses, and administrators in each of these areas were required to achieve a level of competence symbolized by their experience in higher-education diploma or certificate programs.

NCEA sponsored national meetings that featured sessions on topics related to curricular development, pedagogy, the need of public funding, administrative strategies, the Catholic theory of education, religious education, the religious ethos of the schools, and, in general, the cultivation of American and Catholic identities. As education became more complex, NCEA's departments expanded and proliferated. Over the years, the association developed several departments beyond its original three divisions: seminaries, colleges, and parish schools.

The immigrant-Catholic character at the foundation of parish schools in the nineteenth-century was perceived by the leaders of the host society as inherently "papist," opposed to republicanism and the bible. For nativists, American public education, symbolized by the "little red school-house" icon of Americanism, was considered to be the pillar of patriotism. Nativism and anti-Catholicism were currents in mainstream American society, symbolized by church and convent burnings, by caricatures in the popular press depicting the rowdy immigrants, tyrannical bishops, and the pope as the anti-Christ. The anti-Catholic animus achieved almost hysterical proportions in the 1920s. During the decade of "the tribal twenties" the KKK joined forces with other groups in attempts to prohibit students from attending Catholics schools by adopting laws mandating students to attend public schools. Anti-Catholicism lingers in several spheres of influence and is particularly effective among those who are opposed to any form of aid to parochial schools.

Historians trace displays of Catholic loyalty to the nation as a force of integration within the Catholic separatist subculture, which functioned as a source of sustenance for the cultivation of Catholic values, for organizations and societies that parallel their non-religious counterparts, i.e., NCEA to the NEA. Catholic devotional life, identified with sodalities, confraternities, and other pious societies were nurtured in the subculture. Middle-class men and women were integrated in American society but they simultaneously asserted their abiding Catholic identity in the subculture, particularly in its devotional and association aspects.

The term, "ethnos," means particular; America-Catholic ethnic groups formed their own separate organizations within the larger subculture. African-American Catholics were separated by discrimination; Latinos frequently devolved from insiders to outsiders by the forces of Anglo-Saxon dominance. While Latinos have continued to cultivate forms of popular or lived religion, Vietnamese Catholics tend to cling to a pre-Vatican II culture as a source of Catholic identity in a pluralist Church and society.

# Contents

The leadership of NCEA is explored explicitly in Part One, but its historical significance is recognized in many chapters. A glance at the endnotes reveals many references to speeches by various leaders of the association, as well as its many publications. Indeed, the presence of the association in American Catholic education appears pervasive in policy formation, as well as acting as an agency representing the needs of its members.

The leadership of the bishops is paramount on both the national and local levels. The association and the bishops' dwell in a symbiosis as the NCEA has bishops on its board, and the bishops conference provides another strong voice in articulating priorities in various spheres of education, particularly in religious education.

A chapter on the historical role of women religious could have been placed in more than one part in this book, but their leadership is most evident. Though they have been staffing parochial schools for nearly two hundred years, sisters have been at the forefront of leadership on the diocesan and national levels. They have understood first hand the scope of the challenges and could provide that experiential leadership so important to the vitality of the school system.

The historians of Part Two elucidate the complexity of Church-State issues with an abundance of insight. To consider the problems in this area from the period of Bishop John Hughes to that of Cardinal Francis Spellman requires narrative and analytical skills that can only come from many years of professional experience as an historian and theologian. The treatment of the issue from Richard Nixon to George W. Bush entails a command of the literature of religion and politics complemented by expertise in the relevant court decisions. Both scholars rely upon their publications for presenting clear and cogent ideas that are easily accessible to the general reader.

The three chapters on the Catholic ethos and charism represent diverse methodologies. They open with the history of Christian humanism and education, a chapter that could only be written by a scholar of religion and culture, and a committed intellectual of uncommon breadth of interest and depth of experience. Despite its two-thousand-year study, the author's thesis is abundantly clear throughout the essay.

The chapter on the ethos of the school, with a focus on the organizations that contribute to students' Catholic sensibility by participating in various associations and societies, is neatly woven into significant patterns. A blend of historical and religious research is evident throughout the chapter. This study reveals the insight of a scholar of global Christianity who can draw vital relationships among the events in the Church, society, and the academy and the articulation of a Catholic ethos. These are the insights of a seasoned scholar and an experienced teacher.

The focus on Catholic education in World-War-II Baltimore is in contrast an in-depth analysis of the relationship between the influence of wartime patriotism on the progress of assimilation and the decline of traditional religious and racial hostilities. This chapter is based upon a wide range of primary sources, including the views of participants in the events of the times derived from oral interviews. The result is a fine blend of narrative and analysis of the cultural developments with a thesis that is well grounded and could be neatly applicable to other urban areas during this significant period

The chapters constituting the fourth part relate to the education of African Americans, Latinos, and European ethnic groups. The reader encounters the Catholic complicity with discrimination against people of color. Separate parish schools for black students were generally not equal to the white schools, but despite this status, they did foster a sense of ownership and Catholic identity that drew many converts during the twentieth century. Indeed, the author notes that her most rewarding experience was not related to her scholarship and her teaching but her student life in a black Catholic parish school.

Latino Catholic education, originating in the colonial era, encompasses many distinctive periods. A glance at the endnotes reveals the authors' command of the sources related to the many topics considered in their chapter. Their thesis is that only when the Latinos are free from the imposition of the Americanization process and other forms of discrimination will they be free to blend their culture with the good news of the Gospels, i.e. inculturaltion. Readers will discover a clear and cogent narrative and analysis of a complex story of the development of Latino culture and Catholic education.

To have sewn together the several threads of many distinctive Catholic ethnic groups into patterns of parochial education is the principal achievement of the author of the final chapter of the book. He not only demonstrates his expertise in immigration history, but also his sorting out the significant differences of how the Catholic school functioned for these groups. The historian informs us of the importance of neighborhood parish and school to the formation, development, negotiation and re-negotiation of American-Catholic-ethnic identities.

The final chapter is a fitting way to conclude a book on historical essays to honor the Centennial of NCEA. The association's own identity becomes more vital by allowing the past to influence its direction toward another century of service.

# PART I
# NATIONAL LEADERSHIP

## CHAPTER 1

# NCEA'S FIRST CENTURY—AN OVERVIEW

>~~~

*John Augenstein*

I n its earliest days about 200 individuals belonged to the association. By 1910 that had become nearly 1500 and it grew to about 5000 in 1950 and to over 12,000 in 1960. Today, the National Catholic Educational Association (NCEA) has more than 24,000 members, a combination of individual and institutional memberships serving over 200,000 Catholic educators. As the Association grew so did its budget. In 1910 it was barely $5,000 and that grew gradually to $50,000 by 1950. Ten years later it had increased to $200,000+ and to more than a half million in 1967. Currently it is more $5,000,000. The original staff was Father Francis Howard, Secretary General, and a clerk. That had become a staff of 18 in 1960; there are 50 in 2002.

In its 100 years, the association has had five homes. The first was in Columbus, Ohio, where Father Howard resided. The second was 1312 Massachusetts Avenue in Washington, home of the National Catholic Welfare Conference (NCWC), followed in 1951 by offices in the American Council on Education (ACE) a few blocks from the NCWC. When ACE moved to a new facility at One Dupont Circle in 1967, NCEA followed. In 1983 the association purchased the first floor of James Place condominium in Georgetown, which continues to serve as its headquarters.

## BISHOP CONATY'S VISION

NCEA's beginning was the outgrowth of one man's vision. Two years after becoming rector of The Catholic University (1898), Monsignor Thomas J. Conaty, a man with a vision for Catholic education, convened a gathering of representatives of seminary faculties. In 1899 he followed up with a conference of representatives of Catholic colleges and universities. Two weeksbefore the 1902 Catholic college meeting in Chicago, he wrote inviting the bishops of the country to send a representative of their "parochial school system"[1] to the college confer- ence. Eight dioceses attended. In 1903 he issued another invitation to the bishops but this time with more advance notice. Twenty-five dioceses were represented in 1903. In March of that year before the groups' meeting, Conaty was appointed bishop of Monterey-Los Angeles. In January 1904, representatives of the colleges, seminaries, and schools met in the Archdiocese of New York where they prepared a draft of organizational bylaws. The following summer the Educational Confer- ence of Seminary Faculties, the Association of Catholic Colleges, and the Parish School Conference met in St. Louis and formed the Catholic Educational Asso- ciation of the United States (CEA). Although the original bylaws included "na- tional" in its title, it was dropped at the St. Louis meeting and not incorporated until 1927. The original Constitution explained its *raison d'etre.*

> The object of this association shall be to keep in the minds of the people the necessity of religious instruction and training as the basis of morality and sound education; and to promote the principles and safeguard the interests of Catholic education, in all its departments.[2]

> To advance the general interests of Catholic education, to encourage the spirit of co-operation and mutual helpfulness among Catholic educators, to promote by study, conference and discussion the thor- oughness of Catholic educational work in the United States.[3]

> To help the cause of Catholic education by the publication and circu- lation of such matter as shall further these ends.[4]

## A Century of Leadership

### Secretary Generals

The day-to-day operation leader was first called Secretary General and then in 1956 became Executive Secretary and finally in 1969 President. NCEA has had eight CEO's. The first Secretary General (1904-1929) was Father Francis W. Howard, later Bishop of Covington, Kentucky. He was among the eight parish school representatives at the 1902 Chicago meeting and was there because of his membership on the Diocese of Columbus school board.

During his term, these diverse Catholic educational groups were unified, a constitution adopted, and the association attained its autonomy from the bishops.

4

Howard established and maintained the association's office in Columbus, Ohio.

Bishop Howard was succeeded by Monsignor George Johnson (1929-1944), then Executive Secretary of the NCWC Education Department. Johnson was an advocate of curricular reform and expanded NCEA's relationships by developing partnerships with other American educators and agencies. Early in his term the association office was moved from Columbus, Ohio, to the NCWC offices in Washington, DC.

Monsignor Frederick G. Hochwalt (1944-1966), a student of Johnson's at The Catholic University, took over after Johnson's sudden death during his commencement address at Trinity College. Hochwalt, too, headed the NCWC Education Department and NCEA. During his time the Special Education Department, Sister Formation Section, and Adult Education Commission were initiated and there was remarkable growth in the membership, staff, services and financial base.

Following the enrollment peak when Catholic school student numbers began to decline and schools were closing and consolidating rapidly, Reverend C. Albert Koob, O. Praem., Secondary Department Associate Secretary, was selected Executive Secretary. He faced the crisis of decline and made it a time of professional growth by calling a Symposium on Catholic Education to address the challenges of Vatican II. The symposium resulted in a rewritten constitution establishing a broadly representative governing board and changing the Executive Secretary's title to President. It also established a Department of Religious Education, the National Forum of Religious Educators, and the National Association of Boards of Education (NABE). The superintendents' department became the Chief Administrators of Catholic Education (CACE). In 1972 Koob was severely injured in an accident and Monsignor John F. Meyers, Executive Director of CACE, was appointed Acting President.

In 1974, Meyers became the first President and fifth executive and served until 1986. Under his leadership, a second symposium on Catholic Education was held and new services were initiated including the National Forum of Catholic Parent Organizations, the curriculum project, Vision and Values, Religious Education Outcomes Inventory and the Knights of Columbus McGivney Fund for New Initiatives in Catholic Education. He also addressed the need to continue serving the poor and minorities and promoted development as another school and association income source.

Sister Catherine McNamee, CSJ, succeeded Meyers and emphasized collaborative efforts in the educational community which lead NCEA to establish partnerships with the National Federation of Priests Councils, American Forum on Global Education, and the Catholic Health Association. In her tenure the association held its first international convention in Toronto. Finally, she continued NCEA's involvement in the Inter-American and International Catholic Educational Associations.

In 1996, Dr. Leonard DeFiore assumed the leadership of the organization succeeding Sr. Catherine. Dr. DeFiore had previously served as Superintendent of Schools for the Diocese of Metuchen and the Archdiocese of Washington. Between the two he served in the Reagan Administration. In an initial address, he emphasized some association challenges, namely, preparation of lay leadership, school finance, the choice/voucher issue, and the incorporation of both intellectual and moral formation in Catholic higher education.

The eighth NCEA head, Michael Guerra, moved to the leadership position in 2001. Guerra was the long-time Secondary Department Executive Director. Early in his presidency, in an interview with *NCEA Notes*, he highlighted selected issues facing the association in the 21st century. These included the need for Catholic schools to continue their high standards and to serve new communities, for NCEA to help the members address "the critical issues of teacher recruitment and retention,"[5] and to continue efforts in the public forum in support of educational choice. Last, he noted "the need to make sure that we maintain a sensitive and sensible balance between local interests and the larger needs of the educational ministry."[6]

## *Governing Board*

From its inception, NCEA has been governed by a board of directors chaired by a bishop who was first titled President General (1904-1968) and later Chairman of the Board (1969-present). The first to serve as President General was Bishop Denis J. O'Connell, Rector of The Catholic University. In 2002 the board chair is Bishop Gregory M. Aymond. Included in its historical roster are Cardinals Ritter (St. Louis), Meyer (Chicago), Dearden (Detroit), Cody (Chicago), and Bernadin (Chicago).

When Howard stepped down as Secretary General he became President General (1929-1936). In his final convention address in that role he enunciated the principles of Catholic education and their application to economic, political, and social life as well as opposition to the absolute state control of education. He concluded with his and the association's long standing position on parental rights stating: "The natural right of the parent to give his child the education he sees fit to give is protected by the organic law of the country."[7]

The board was originally composed of the President General, Secretary General, and departmental representatives. When it developed a new Constitution in 1969, it began to include at-large members including non-educator laity.

The board has always served as the policy-making body and included in its responsibilities the selection of the president, budget approval, and planning the association's future. Like other governing groups it utilized standing and ad hoc committees. Early on, an Advisory Committee in which "there was little difference between the executive committee and [it]"[8] was established and remained active until Bishop Howard's death in 1944. That was followed by the Washington Committee and the Problems and Plans Committee. These were standing committees that played significant roles in the association. More recently, like other organizations, it adopted a mission statement and established initiatives derived from that statement. Selected Mission 2000 initiatives were leadership development and renewal, responding to a multi-ethnic Church and society, and creating innovative ways to collaborate at all levels, including international, in Catholic educational ministry.

## Serving the Membership

### *Organizational Development*

The association was organized to serve those involved in the many facets of Catholic education. Its original constituencies were Catholic colleges, seminaries, and parish schools that were also the original departments. Its members included college presidents, seminary rectors and faculty, pastors, principals, school board members, and teachers. As education became more sophisticated and complex and as the issues diversified, NCEA expanded and refined its organization to serve those challenges.

Its principal structural components were and still are departments. But when a department's membership requires more specific delineation, a section is developed to serve those unique needs. For example, the original Parish School Department incorporated many school constituencies, among them diocesan superintendents and male religious communities' school inspectors. That segment of the department's membership began meeting separately and informally in 1906, then petitioned the Board and in 1908 became a section of the Parish School Department. It acquired full department status in 1935. Secondary Schools were initially part of the College Department but became their own department in 1929. The Parish School Department was renamed Department of Elementary Schools. Presently, the Departments include Chief Administrators of Catholic Education, Elementary Schools, Secondary Schools, Religious Education, Seminary, and Boards/Councils and Commissions. In 2002, the Association of Catholic Colleges and Universities changed its status from that of an NCEA department to that of an affiliate member.

Over the years other groups have sought and secured affiliated status. Among those were the National Catholic Music Educators and the Catholic

Audiovisual Educators. Because of the numerous requests the Board considered a proposal, "Affiliation of Other Organizations with NCEA" (1963) that addressed types of organizations, admissions procedure, criteria, annual fees, advantages to affiliates and NCEA, and general provisions.[9]

## The Staff

For nearly forty years the staff consisted of the Secretary General, a secretary, and a clerk. It was only under the leadership of Monsignor Hochwalt that the association staff began to grow. The first professional position created in 1946 was that filled by James Cummings, Convention Manager and Secretary for Publications. In 1954 the Board approved associate secretaries for Seminary, Secondary, Superintendents, and Elementary departments

As the association grew its fulltime staff, many names became synonymous with NCEA, e.g., Joseph O'Donnell (1958-1978) vice president for business affairs and convention manager; Wilma Roberts bookkeeper for 30 years; and Nancy Brewer (1953-1999) who began as secretary to Monsignor Hochwalt and ended her service at NCEA as Convention and Exposition Director. The departmental and section executives for many years were drawn from religious communities of women and men as well as diocesan clergy, but have been succeeded by capable lay persons who emerged from school, college, and diocesan leadership ranks.

## Membership Services

NCEA has served its membership in many ways, but first and foremost through its annual convention. The first was its founding in St. Louis (July 12-14, 1904). St. Louis hosted the 75th in 1978 and will welcome the association's 100th in 2003. The convention was cancelled only twice, 1940 and 1942, the World War II period. Beginning in 1947, each gathering has had a theme and that year it was "The Role of Catholic Education in the Post-War World." The theme for the opening of the centennial year is "Dream by the River: Faithful Past–Faith-Filled Future." Commercial exhibits were first noted in 1930 but the first formal opening of exhibits was held in 1953 when John N. Gibney was serving as President of the Catholic Exhibitors Association. A plenary session with a nationally recognized speaker was established in 1963 when Dr. Hans Kung, Professor of Theology at Tubingen, Germany and Vatican II *peritus,* spoke on "The Church and Freedom." He was followed the next year by Senator Abraham Ribicoff. Other General Session presenters included Harold Howe II, U.S. Commissioner of Education, Mother Teresa of Calcutta, India, Senator Patrick Moynihan, Sr. Helen Prejean, CSJ, Sr. Joan Chittister, OSB, and Alan L. Keyes, former U.S. Ambassador to the United Nations Economic and Social Council.

The attendance in recent years has ranged from 10-15,000.

Maintaining one of its original purposes, "To help the cause of Catholic education by the publication and circulation of such matter as shall further these ends,"[10] publications have been another staple of service to the membership. Its first and long-running publication was its annual proceedings that became a quarterly in 1908 and ended in 1966. A proposal for a monthly magazine was accepted in 1959 and it first appeared a year later as the *National Catholic Educational Monthly*. For the past thirty-three years it has appeared as *Momentum*. Departments have also published newsletters and journals[11] as well as special topic books/booklets, e.g., *Evaluative Criteria for Elementary Schools* (1965) and *Catholic Schools Make a Difference: Twenty-Five Years of Research* (1992). As media and technology advanced, NCEA made audio and videotapes available as well as CD's and it is now utilizing the Internet for correspondence, newsletters, etc. and satellite conferences.[12]

## Organizational Relationships

### *NCWC/USCC*

The association has always connected with the bishops through its President General/Chairman of the Board and conducted its annual meetings under the authority of the local bishop where the convention was held. It had a relationship with the Bishops' conference since the conference's founding in 1919. Father Howard was approached to serve as the first director of the Conference's Bureau of Education but he declined. However, in November 1928 Monsignor Johnson, a professor at The Catholic University of America (CUA), accepted the directorship and the next June took on the NCEA Secretary General's position. From then and through most of Monsignor Hochwalt's term (1944-1965) the head of NCEA was also the head of the Bishops' Education Department. After the "one person two hats" ceased, there have been several ad hoc committees convened to study and clarify the NCEA/USCC relationship and responsibilities. The first was established in the mid 1960s and was followed with others in years such as 1972, 1980-81, 1989, and 1991. The 1981 document prepared by Archbishop Bernadin and Father Meyers representing NCEA and Bishop Pilarczyk and Father Gallagher representing NCCB/USCC enumerated the key issues.

- NCEA elects a bishop as Board Chair.
- NCEA President is an ex officio non-voting member of the USCC Committee on Education.
- USCC Education Secretary is an ex officio voting member on the NCEA Board.

- NCEA is a membership organization.
- USCC relates to dioceses.
- NCEA relates to institutions, individuals, and diocesan offices.
- USCC Department of Education, Office of Government Liaison, and Office of General Counsel are responsible for planning, lobbying, and implementing federal aid in consultation with NCEA.
- USCC Department of Education is primarily responsible for policy recommendations to the bishops.

### Government

For more than fifty years the association's relationship with the federal government and its agencies was minimal. It always favored parental rights in education and until the 1960s opposed federal aid and a federal department of education. Under Hochwalt there was discussion about the disposal of surplus property after World War II and in 1950 some NCEA staff began serving on U.S. Office of Education committees.

Occasionally government officials would send greetings or a message to NCEA during its convention. The first was sent by P.P. Claxton, U.S. Commissioner of Education (1912). Later several Presidents sent messages as well including Roosevelt, Truman, Eisenhower, Kennedy, and Johnson. President Reagan made a visit at the 1982 Convention in Chicago where he spoke at a general session. In recent years, NCEA officials were invited to the White House for discussion of aid to nonpublic school parents and children. Such was the case when in December 1989 President Bush met with NCEA officials and the "Big Ten" superintendents (from the ten largest dioceses).

### International Education

It was in the Hochwalt era that the association reached out to educators on the international stage. NCEA was invited to send a representative to a meeting of private schools in Bogotá, Colombia (1945) and a year later a committee was created to consider assisting Catholic educational institutions in postwar Europe. Hochwalt was part of the U.S. delegation at the UNESCO meeting in Paris (1947). In that same year Father Felix Newton Pitt of the Archdiocese of Louisville was part of the U.S. Education Mission to Germany. The association was represented at the 1947 Inter American Conference on Catholic Education and continues its participation today. It has also worked with the Catholic International Education office. Finally as the times and culture changed, the association established contacts with the National Education Association (NEA), American Association of School Administrators (AASA), as well as church school (not Catholic) associations, e.g., Hebrew Day Schools, Episcopal schools.

## Focal Issues

Throughout its first century the association addressed many topics directly or indirectly affecting Catholic education but those affecting elementary/secondary schools, seminaries, and Catholic higher education are woven throughout. Catholic schools topics address teachers and administrators, curriculum, religious education, parents and their rights, pastors, and public education. The education of minorities and the place of women in the association are addressed briefly.

## Elementary/Secondary Schools

Although Catholic and public schools warranted attention, the former received the 'lion's share' in the association's first 50 years. Working with the goal of 'every Catholic child in a Catholic school,' much time and effort was devoted to Catholic schools. Conventions included paper presentations and discussions related to teachers, administrators, curriculum, religious education, parents, and pastors.

## Teachers/Administrators

Early on there was concern about the preparation of teachers for the classroom and coupled with that who should prepare them. Well-trained teachers were critical. However, it was felt that state universities were not the "fitting places" for such preparation; rather teachers should be trained in Catholic institutions where they were encouraged to learn more about pedagogy.

The concern for adequate preparation continued because it was important to be able to say to both the parish and civic communities that Catholic school teachers were as well prepared as any others. Immediately after World War II concern was raised over the teacher shortage. The preparation issue surfaced strongly again in the 1950s and '60s "baby boom era" when enrollments and schools were expanding so rapidly that securing fully prepared teachers was not always achievable. Although lay teachers were found in 19th century Catholic schools, it was in this boom period that their need was great and their numbers increased dramatically.[13] Among the resolutions at the 1960 Chicago convention was

> that every possible means be utilized to encourage our lay teachers now
> in the schools, and to attract new ones, through benefits such as tenure,
> retirement, and health programs, adequate salaries, participation in
> curriculum planning, and policy making, and by giving them appro-
> priate professional status.[14]

Because of their growing numbers, the association authorized meetings specifically for lay teachers in the '60s and a general session paper "The Lay Teacher in

Catholic Education," was presented by Dr. William H. Conley, Assistant to the President of Marquette University. But the goal has always been to put into the classroom those who are prepared educationally, professionally, and religiously.

As the percentage of lay teachers increased they began to raise the issue of salary and benefit gaps between elementary and high school teachers as well as between Catholic and public schools. Like their public school counterparts they began to organize into collective bargaining units. John Reilly of Philadelphia promoted the founding of and then led the National Association of Catholic School Teachers (NACST). Under Father Meyers' presidency a workshop on unions was held to provide a forum for discussion of the unionization of Catholic school teachers. It was hailed for its willingness to address the topic and assailed because its invitees were primarily administrators.

As the numbers of religious declined, their numbers in the principalship also diminished and the Association became an advocate for well prepared lay principals. Particularly in the fourth quarter of its history, NCEA became the source of papers, workshops, and publications focused on administrator preparation.

## *Curriculum*

The schools' curriculum was often a topic for papers. Father Howard presented a paper at a 1913 general session "The Problem of the Curriculum" in which he stated:

> The purpose of this paper is not to propose an "ideal" curriculum for general or for partial adoption. Its aim is to invite our educators to a study of actual conditions and to inquire into the causes that have produced the present state of confusion in the educational work of the entire country...to take a comprehensive view of the situation as a whole, to the end that a workable plan for the cooperative study of this problem may be suggested to the Catholic educators of the United States.[15]

Although Howard maintained that he was not proposing a standard curriculum, standardization appeared in the program in 1921, 1922, and 1928.[16]

Six years later (1920) Father William J. Fitzgerald, Hartford Superintendent of Parish Schools, discussed "Differentiation in the Curriculum of the Grammar Grades: Viewpoint of Junior High Schools" in which he was promoting the addition of ninth grade. As he was concluding, he explained:

> To add one more year to the seventh and eighth grades, and to organize the work on a reasonable high school plan would not mean very great

hardship in our parish schools. It would mean a great blessing of retaining our young people an additional year in a Catholic atmosphere, and might be a further incentive to the erection of central Catholic high schools.[17]

He was followed by Brother Bernardine, FSC, Cathedral High School, Duluth, Minnesota, whose paper addressed "Differentiation of Studies in the Seventh and Eighth Grades: Viewpoint of Vocational Preparation." Vocational education was in the forefront because of the passage of the Smith-Hughes Act in 1917 that provided monies for vocational education below college. Thus, Bernardine had been asked to present a paper on the topic. At the outset he noted:

> ...I have felt some misgiving as to whether my position on the matter...would gain or lose in strength by challenging the opinions of those among us who are opposed to making any concession to the vocational propaganda on the ground that if it finds its way into our Catholic schools it will disarrange our scholastic program, and perhaps prove a serious menace to the integrity of Catholic educational ideals. After having maturely reflected on the matter...I resolved to take the risk of losing the support of the conscientious objector to the vocational idea by appealing to the logic of the facts upon which it rests...[18]

General sessions through the mid 1960s would focus periodically on curricular topics, e.g., Latin American Studies (1943), Music in Education (1952). As the departments were staffed with full-time directors, they took on curriculum issues appropriate to their membership, i.e., elementary and secondary.

### Religious Education

As the original Constitution, Article II, Section 1 stated:

> The object of this Association shall be to keep in the minds of the people the necessity of religious instruction and training as the basis of morality and sound education;[19]

From that time to this religious education has been prominent in its meetings and publications. Concern for and emphasis of religious education was found first through convention paper presentations in both general and departmental sessions.

At the first convention a paper, "The Teaching of Catechism and Bible History," was read in the Parish School Department session. General session audiences heard "The Catholic School and Social Morality," "Religious Education and American Democracy," and "The Value of an Enlightened Conscience for the Proper Performance of Civic Duties." Four years later, Father Cavanaugh, University of Notre Dame president, discussed "Religious Instruction, the Basis of Morality" in which he stated that "The most powerful force in the world is religion"[20] and a short time later, "Is it any wonder , therefore, that religion, which enters into every aspect of human life, should be so large an element in the training of youth?"[21] That was followed in 1911 with a general session paper, "Religion and Education," by Father Edward A. Pace of the Catholic University of America in which he declared:

> The whole work of this Association culminates in this one result, namely, that religion shall not be an appendix or addition to the studies of the school, but religion shall pulsate like a vital stream through every part of our course of education, and shall vitalize every element there;[22]

"Religion was seen as the core of the school's curriculum around which all other subjects revolved. It was expected to permeate the curriculum. It was not just 'education in religion,' which meant presenting information, but 'religious education' which was intellectual but whose purpose was to influence life."[23]

Finally, in the 1960s a Department of Religious Education was formed to serve the needs of teachers of religion in schools, catechists in parishes, and diocesan directors of religious education. Among its accomplishments have been the assistance provided schools and parishes in the discussion and implementation of Vatican II documents, e.g., *Declaration on Christian Education*, and the development and use of *Religious Education Outcomes Inventory* (REOI) which has been in use since 1976. It continues collaboration with the Elementary and Secondary Departments as well as the Chief Administrators (CACE).

### *Parents and Their Rights*

Parents, their rights and obligations, have been recognized and supported throughout the association's history. Parental rights to educate their children were acknowledged in papers but equally importantly in general session resolutions. For example, one 1921 resolution stated:

> The authority of the parent over the education of his child is a natural and fundamental right. Catholic parents have the obligation of providing for the proper education of their children through the medium of Catholic schools.[24]

14

Again in the early 1930s the rights of parents and the Church were reaffirmed.

> We take this occasion to emphasize the right and duty of parents to
> control the education of their offspring and the pre-eminent right of
> the Church by virtue of her supernatural mission to conduct her own
> schools unhampered by any unreasonable interference on the part of
> secular authorities.[25]

The theme for the 1958 Philadelphia convention was "The Right to
Educate – The Role of Parents, Church, State."

The association's position on parental rights continues today in the
voucher and choice legislation debate. Just as parental rights were affirmed,
enrolling their children in Catholic schools was also stressed. Archbishop Ireland
in his sermon to the 1915 convention delegates declared: "The Sunday School
taking the place of the regular school of five days in the week, is not to be thought
of among Catholics."

Among the 1917 resolutions, one reads:

> In these days of materialistic tendencies and weakening of faith the
> need of keeping before us the idea – "Every Catholic child in a Catholic
> School" – cannot be stated too strongly. As far as human wisdom can
> foresee, the preservation and spread of the Catholic Church in this
> country depend upon the adoption by priests and people of a vigorous
> policy in support of the parish school.[26]

Four years later it was noted that bishops had not enforced penalties on parents
who did not send their children to the parish school. Today, Catholic schools, no
longer relying on that demand, have developed some sophisticated marketing and
recruitment plans. The focal time is Catholic Schools Week co-sponsored by
NCEA and USCC Department of Education held in early February. They stress
the quality of education as well as the value-permeated curriculum.

As the laity and particularly parents became more educated and sophisticated, they wanted to have more involvement in their children's education.
Although diocesan school boards had been around since the Third Plenary
Council of Baltimore, their memberships were primarily clerical. In the mid
1960s the association through its Superintendent's Department supported the
development of parish boards with parental participation and it also promoted
lay involvement in diocesan boards. Today NCEA houses a Commission for the
National Association of Boards of Education with its own Executive Director.

## *Pastors*

The original Parish School Department included pastors among its members. An early acknowledgement of the pastor's role is found among the 1906 Resolutions.

> "Resolved, that we approve the system of the pastor as director of the parish school, together with a principal whose duty it is to regulate, unify and supervise the work of the grades."[27]

A few years later (1910) they were asked to expand their support to secondary and higher education.

The lead general session paper in Detroit given by Monsignor Thomas J. Shahan, Rector of The Catholic University, spoke to "The Pastor and Education." He notes early "…the bearing of the pastor's activity upon the whole system of Catholic education."[28] Shahan commends pastors for inspiring and strengthening teachers and encouraging others to enter the profession. His aim is to encourage pastors to "extend to the whole Catholic system the care which he directly feels for the organization of his school…[so that] there will also result a system of Christian education in the true sense of the word."[29]

Father Francis T. Moran, a Cleveland pastor and CEA Treasurer General (1906-1929), reflected on "The Pastor and Education." He reviewed the many roles and responsibilities of a pastor including securing the land and overseeing the construction of the school as well as its finances, and the work of raising funds for its operation. Considering the time and effort required of the pastor for the school, Moran asks:

> Has the Catholic school justified the trouble and expense? This question can no longer be asked…now that the question has been threshed out and that the happy results are so plain, only someone who had wandered into the mountains and had been wrapped in a Rip Van Winkle slumber would ever dream of asking it.[30]

As he reaches the paper's end he explains: "He knows the value of the educated layman. In the last analysis the pastor deals both with the raw material and the finished product."[31]

As years went on and teachers and administrators became professionals, pastors' roles and responsibilities changed. They were delegating the school's operation as well as other parish services to the professionals. This, coupled with increasing demands by other parishioners to meet their needs, resulted in the school becoming one among several priorities in his life that included adult education, religious education of a growing number of school-age children in public schools, parish council, and parish school board. Pastors needed a forum where they could discuss and learn about new possibilities in the broad spectrum of Catholic education where they had become like chairmen of the board overseeing a multifaceted operation. To help meet that need NCEA reached out and initiated Pastors' Day at its annual conventions and worked hard to provide programming that would attract them. Today it publishes quarterly the *NCEA Pastor Education Digest*.

### Public Education

For many years public schools and public education appear as the "other system" from which Catholic schools were to be preserved from contamination. As a 1928 convention resolution noted: "Men true to themselves, to their country and to God cannot be reared in institutions that choose to know nothing of God…"[32] That feeling covered not only elementary and secondary schools but higher education institutions as well.

Often the earlier existence of Catholic schools would be cited and such was the case in a 1923 resolution that bragged:

> Even before the establishment of our Republic Catholics had already built schools and laid the foundations of the existing widespread system of parish schools. The parish school system thus antedates the State-supported public school system.[33]

In the association's efforts to promote tax support of nonpublic schools and children, the substantial investment of tax dollars for public education was periodically criticized. The 1923 assemblage supported a resolution stating that "They (Catholic parishioners) pay a double educational tax – part for the education of their children and part for the upkeep of the public schools."[34]

When threatened with the possibility that only attendance at public schools would meet state compulsory attendance laws such as the Oregon law[35] and a similar one in Michigan, in 1923 the association took a strong stand in opposition.

> Legislative measures to prohibit attendance at schools other than public schools, strike at fundamental rights of Catholics as men and citizens. Such measures would render practically impossible the instruction and training of Catholic children in their faith and in accordance with their parents' obligations. This would be religious persecution.[36]

However, when enrollments in large city public elementary schools exceeded their capacity, the association came to their aid, condemning the treatment of these children.

> In many of our large cities, there is a great lack of accommodations for the children of the elementary public schools, so that much overcrowding in classrooms results and, moreover, large numbers of the children are able to get only half-time at school; in spite of this condition, the municipalities continue the policy of spending enormous sums of public money on large and extravagantly equipped high schools, and even colleges, We reprobate this as a crime against the children of the common people, who need full time and proper accommodations during their few years of schooling. The municipalities have no right to favor the privileged few at the expense of the many...[37]

Even though the association invested much of its efforts in Catholic education at all levels, it recognized early on that there was a problem, namely, Catholic training of Catholic children in public schools especially where no Catholic school existed. It was supportive of the Confraternity of Christian Doctrine (CCD) programs for Catholic children in public schools.

In the 1950s the NCEA's Board considered but took no action on a proposed Catholic Teachers' Guild for Catholic teachers in public schools. A decade later the Superintendents' Department requested and received $2500 to study moral and spiritual values for public school teachers. Also at that same time (1964) the Board authorized the updating of the Fr. Neil McCluskey, S.J., "Guidelines to the Catholic Church in the Public School." Following the "baby boom," Vatican II, and with more Catholic children in public schools as well as the recently formed Department of Religious Education, more of the Association's efforts were directed toward those children.

## WOMEN AND MINORITIES

Although not focal issues, it is important to discuss briefly the education of minorities and the place of women in the association.

### *Education of Minorities*

From 1919 through 1922 there was a Catholic Negro Education Section of the Parish School Department. In only one of those years (1920) were paper presentation topics listed. Father J. T. Bustin addressed "Primary Education Among the Colored People" and Father Timothy B. Moroney, SSJ, discussed

"Catholic Secondary Education for Negroes." In the remaining years only the proceedings were found.

The education of minorities surfaced again in 1956 when support was given to the integration of Negro and white children. Four years later concern is expressed for those who are the victims of nationality, race, and religious discrimination and support was provided to the American bishops' position on racial discrimination and segregation.

In the early 1970s the board approved the establishment of a minority concerns committee that later recommended the hiring of a staff person to begin such an office. As the years progressed, the association broadened its focus to include among others Native Americans, Hispanics,[38] and Asians.

## *The Place of Women*

Through the years the majority of association members have been women – religious women early on and then both religious and lay in more recent years. Their place in the association parallels the role and place of women in society and the Church over these last 100 years.

Among the resolutions of the 1906 convention in Cleveland one read "we deplore that in the past not so much attention has been paid to the higher education of our boys, as to that of the girls;"[39] This was likely a follow-up to the paper addressing Catholic high schools for boys. Catholic women's colleges were first a section of the College Department. Several years later the Sister Formation Section was also attached to the College and University Department. Other indicators of gender differences in the Howard and Johnson administrations were the separate provisions for convention lunches with the clergy lunch courtesy of the commercial exhibitors and convention receptions for visiting priests and brothers but no mention of such for religious women.

In the Hochwalt era, women began to have their own place in the association. In 1951 a meeting of Catholic school supervisors and administrators of women's colleges was convened. A few years later the Sister Formation Conference was formed under NCEA. A formal group for diocesan school office supervisors, the majority of whom were women, was authorized in 1961 but not attached to the Superintendents Department which then permitted only brothers' and priests' supervisors. This group ultimately became the Supervision, Personnel, and Curriculum (SPC) Section of the present Schools Division of the Chief Administrators' (CACE) Department.

Finally, the first woman to lead the Association was Sister Catherine McNamee, CSJ, 1986-1996.

## The Association's Future

Over its nearly 100 years, NCEA has adapted and met the needs of the times and its membership. It has been the professional arm of the Church's work in education and is likely to continue its emphases, which have been:

- support for professionally and religiously prepared staff and leadership,
- curriculum development reflecting the ever-growing knowledge base,
- collaboration among colleges and universities, elementary and secondary schools, and seminaries,
- protection of parental rights and promotion of their sharing in the public education tax dollar, and
- connecting with the broader educational community at the national and international levels.

Using a variation on a Clark Kerr statement, the Association will continue "to be educator, wielder of power...caretaker...consensus seeker, [and] persuader."[40]

### Endnotes

[1] *Report of Proceedings and Addresses of the First Annual Meeting of the Catholic Educational Association*, St. Louis, MO, July 12, 13, and 14, 1904, (Columbus, OH, 1904), 18. (Hereafter referred to as *Proceedings* [Year])

[2] *CEA Membership, Object, Constitution, Article II, Section 1,* Vatican Archives 105/1 1907-09, Department of Archives and Manuscripts, The Catholic University of America, Washington, DC. (Hereafter cited as ACUA)

[3] Ibid., *Section 2.*

[4] Ibid., *Section 3.*

[5] *NCEA Notes, A Newsletter for Catholic Schools,* (Washington, DC, NCEA, Vol. 34, No. 1, September 2001): 1.

[6] Ibid., 1.

[7] *Proceedings 1936*, 70-71.

[8] Howard Collection, paper entitled "Historical Evolution of the Advisory Committee", 1. ACUA

[9] *National Catholic Educational Association Bulletin August 1963*, 9. (Hereafter cited as Bulletin [Month, Year] Are located in the NCEA Papers, ACUA).

[10] *Constitution, Article II, Section 3.*

11 Among the current newsletters and journals are *Department of Religious Education News, Development Sharings, News for Catholic School Parent Leaders, NCEA Notes, The Seminary Journal*, and *Current Issues in Catholic Higher Education*. Since 1970 the association has published an annual statistical report on schools, enrollment, and staffing.

12 *Serve Our Schools and Parishes The Cyberspace Connection Training Catholic Teachers* is a live satellite interactive course on Catholic faith.

13 The influx of lay teachers to all or nearly all religious dominated faculties posed the challenge of integrating the religious/lay faculties. This, too, was addressed at conventions between 1958 and 1968.

14 *Bulletin, (June 1960):* 33.

15 *Proceedings, 1913,* 132.

16 Rev. Austin G. Schmidt, SJ, "The Philosophy of Standardization" (1921), Rev. George J. Johnson, "Principles of Standardization" (1922), and Rev. Henry Woods, SJ, "Standardization and Its Abuse" (1928)

17 *Proceedings, 1919.* 113.

18 *Proceedings, 1919,* 115.

19 CEA Membership, Object, Constitution, Vatican Archives 105/1 1907-09, Department of Archives and Manuscripts, The Catholic University of America, Washington, DC.

20 Proceedings, 1908, 85.

21 Ibid., 86.

22 *Proceedings*, 1911, 86.

23 John J. Augenstein, *Lighting the Way 1908-1935 The Early Years of Catholic School Superintendency,* (Washington, DC: National Catholic Educational Association, 1996), 52.

24 *Proceedings, 1921,* 51.

25 *Proceedings, 1932,* 55.

26 *Proceedings, 917,* 51-52.

27 *Proceedings, 1906,* 34.

28 *Proceedings, 1910,* 47.

29 *Proceedings, 1910,* 59.

30 *Proceedings, 1915,* 62.

31 *Ibid.,* 65.

32 *Proceedings,* 1928, 42.

33 *Proceedings,* 1923, 39.

34 *Proceedings,* 1923, 39.

35 This culminated in the 1925 benchmark nonpublic school US Supreme Court decision, *Pierce v. Society of Sisters.*

36 *Proceedings,* 1923, 39.

[37] *Proceedings*, 1916, 46.

[38] Included among its publications is *Integral Education: A Response to the Hispanic Presence* (1987).

[39] *Proceedings*, 1960, 33.

[40] Clark Kerr, "The Uses of the University," *Godkin Lectures at Harvard University*, (Cambridge: Harvard University Press, 1963).

## CHAPTER 2

# THE SEMINARIES AND NCEA

$\gamma\!\!\sim$

## *Robert J. Wister*

T he Seminary Department of the National Catholic Educational Association (NCEA)[1], established four years before the association itself, originated as a small conference of seminary rectors seeking to strengthen the relationship between seminaries and universities.[2] Today, an integral component of the total Catholic educational system in the United States, it has experienced, in microcosm, many of the twentieth century's challenges to the larger Church. For more than a century, the department consistently has endeavored to balance certitude with questioning, the sacred with the professional, and Church tradition with cultural change.

## SEMINARIES

Catholic seminaries[3] are often perceived as a part of a very well organized, even monolithic, system, each part of which relates to and is coordinated with others. The reality is not so simple. Seminaries are divided into those whose principal mission is the spiritual, intellectual and pastoral formation of diocesan priests who will serve the parishes of the various dioceses throughout the United States, and those whose principal mission is the formation of priests who are members of the many religious orders. The origins of these institutions are as diverse as are the institutions themselves. Seminaries founded to train diocesan priests owe their existence to the initiative of an individual bishop such as James Roosevelt Bayley in Newark; to the Sulpicians or Vincentians, religious communities whose mission includes the training of diocesan priests; to Benedictine monasteries such as St. Meinrad in Indiana, which have chosen the training of diocesan priests as their particular apostolate; to groups of priests who took over from the Sulpicians Mount St. Mary's in Emmitsburg, Maryland, in 1826; as well as to individual priests such as Father Joseph Jessing who founded the Pontifical College Josephinum. The characteristics of the individual foundations contributed to the particular institution's "ethos" or "spirit," which in many instances perdures to this day.

The seminaries of religious communities owe their existence to similar pioneering spirits. Each order has a unique spirit or "charism," as well as one or more specific apostolates. The American Jesuits and Dominicans, as well as the Augustinians and others, are dedicated primarily to education. The Franciscans, in the spirit of their founder, focus on the witness of poverty, while not neglecting educational enterprises. The Benedictines are monks linked to a particular monastery, primarily devoted to the *lectio divina*, but also involved in educational apostolates, with a particular emphasis on liturgy. The Sulpicians are exclusively involved in seminary education, which also forms a significant part of the work of the Vincentians. Almost all religious communities are involved to some degree in parish ministry. These diverse apostolates necessitated individual and separate seminaries in which the candidates would not only be trained for the work of the order but also, very importantly, imbued with the spirit, the "charism" of the order. This would, of course, lead to a multiplication of institutions, in many instances, very small and weak ones. Recent years have seen their amalgamation into a variety of "theological unions."

While the foundation of these seminaries was in many ways haphazard, in fact entrepreneurial in some cases, the majority benefited from a system in place within the Church. They followed the outline of a course of studies and a basic philosophy of education and formation that evolved from the sixteenth century Council of Trent for the diocesan clergy, and from the particular religious communities for their own members. Initially, diocesan seminarians and no one else went to seminaries established for them. Jesuit seminarians went to Jesuit seminaries; Franciscans went to their seminaries, and so on.

From the foundation of St. Mary's Seminary in Baltimore, Maryland, in 1791, "seminary leaders...(implemented) the received tradition of clerical formation for a developing Catholic Church in the United States."[4] Some thrived, some survived, many disappeared after a few years. In 1884, the Third Plenary Council of Baltimore legislated basic norms for the conduct of American seminaries. Five years later, the founding of The Catholic University of America provided the nation with a central institution dedicated to excellence in theological education as well as graduate programs in the sacred sciences.

The directives of the Third Plenary Council of Baltimore provided a national benchmark against which seminaries could begin to measure their programs. This, in turn, provided a basis for discussions among seminary officials that they did not before possess. Catholic University sought to attract from across the country the most gifted of the seminarians for its programs. These two factors established a basis for national conversations.

## *Origins*

On May 25, 1898, under the leadership of and in response to a call from Monsignor Thomas J. Conaty, Rector of The Catholic University of America, rectors from ten seminaries convened at St. Joseph's Seminary, Dunwoodie, New York, to form "The Educational Conference of Seminary Faculties," which would later become the Seminary Department of the NCEA. The group's charter membership included St. Mary's Seminary, Baltimore; St. John's Seminary (Brighton), Boston; St. John's Seminary, Brooklyn; Mount St. Mary's Seminary of the West, Cincinnati; Mt. St. Mary's Seminary, Emmitsburg, Maryland; St. Joseph's Seminary (Dunwoodie), New York; Our Lady of the Angels Seminary, Niagara, New York; St. Charles Seminary (Overbrook), Philadelphia; St. Patrick's Seminary (Menlo Park), San Francisco; and Immaculate Conception Seminary (Seton Hall), South Orange, New Jersey. The heads of St. Meinrad Seminary, St. Meinrad, Indiana; Christ the King Seminary, Allegheny, New York; St. Mary's Seminary, Cleveland, Ohio; Kenrick Seminary, St. Louis, Missouri; and The Saint Paul Seminary, St. Paul, Minnesota, were unable to attend this first meeting but sent letters of endorsement for the endeavor.[5] "The Rochester and Milwaukee seminaries, disdaining the university and all its works, were not represented."[6]

Monsignor Conaty, Rector of The Catholic University from 1897 - 1903 and subsequently appointed Bishop of Monterey-Los Angeles, issued this invitation as a response to a growing concern about the inadequate preparation and insufficient numbers of seminary students who were sent to the university. Although conference participants agreed to meet a second time in Philadelphia in 1899, they lapsed into inactivity. They did not gather again until the first convention of the Catholic Educational Association (CEA) in St. Louis in 1904. The reasons for the lapse into inactivity seem to have included the poor health of the first president of the conference, Reverend Alphonse L. Magnien, S.S. In addition, some may have believed, however falsely, that the Seminary Conference had been established primarily for the benefit of Catholic University. Also, some seminary rectors participated in the Association of Catholic Colleges, founded by Monsignor Conaty in 1899, and a number of them might have preferred instead to join this organization, which welcomed fifty-three college representatives at its first meeting. However, the seminary educators decided that there should be a seminary component in the embryonic CEA. As a result of this decision, the Seminary Department henceforth would become part the NCEA, and would meet annually during the organization's conventions, with the exception of the war years of 1943 and 1945.[7]

## Curriculum and Professionalization

The legislation of the Third Plenary Council of Baltimore was soon enhanced by regulations from Rome providing universal norms for seminary training. The Sacred Congregation of Seminaries and Universities (since 1967 the Congregation for Catholic Education), established in 1915, would provide a series of decrees affecting seminary formation. In addition, the Code of Canon Law, promulgated in 1917, contained several canons regarding seminaries. The application of these regulations and related issues stimulated discussions within the seminary community. However, these were very incomplete, often conflicting directives. The code and the decrees of the congregation did not establish a precise plan of studies to be followed in Catholic seminaries. While the code listed the courses to be offered in the major seminary course of six years, it did not provide details regarding the number of classes per week or their sequencing.

Throughout more than the first half of the twentieth century, "isolation characterized the seminary at several levels: seminarians were isolated from secular activities; the seminary was separated from the life of the local church; and the seminary had limited contact with contemporary educational standards. Furthermore seminaries were greatly isolated from each in the absence of formal direction to cooperate... The annual meetings of seminary educators at the ... convention provided the forum for seminary educators to express (their) views."[8] As a strictly voluntary organization with no official role, the Seminary Department's resolutions had no binding effect. Its major service to seminaries was to serve as an arena for the exchange of views. At the annual convention, the Seminary Department discussed issues ranging from the qualifications considered necessary and desirable for admission into seminaries to questions of appropriate pedagogy and curriculum. These issues were debated through the presentation of papers and lengthy discussions. Although only a fraction of the country's seminaries were represented at these meetings, published *Proceedings* of the meetings served to disseminate the reflections of the most professionally active seminary educators.

In 1919, because of the many issues unique to the minor seminary, a separate Minor Seminary Department was organized. From that time on, members met in their own sessions to hear papers and discuss topics relevant to the studies and internal life of the preparatory seminary, such as curriculum, boarding and day school needs, and discipline. For decades the minor seminary remained an educational anomaly in United States education. Organized to offer a six-year course of studies, they were modeled on the European model of a *gymnasium* or *lycée*, corresponding to the American system of four years of high school and two years of junior college. Although as early as 1919 some seminary educators, such as Reverend Charles Schrantz, S. S., were arguing for change,[9] the 1921 meeting of the minor seminary department passed a resolution in favor of retaining the six-year system.[10]

Of primary importance during discussions at early department meetings of both major and minor seminary personnel was the seminarian's spiritual formation. Although intellectual ability remained a pivotal criterion for admission and advancement, it was considered secondary to "character, tendencies, and religious spirit."[11] Specific practices such as frequent communion and spiritual reading, both public and private, were emphasized, and the consultation of every seminary faculty member concerning those who were to be called to Orders was encouraged.

With regard to the major seminaries, the ambiguity deriving from sketchy rules set the stage for discussions that demonstrated the differences between the advocates of a strictly uniform curriculum and uniform course content for all seminaries, those desirous of preserving local autonomy, those who sought to innovate and to apply contemporary pedagogical principles to seminary education, and those who wished to bring seminaries into greater conformity with American educational structures. These issues would be debated at departmental meetings along with the perennial demands to add specific courses beyond the theological curriculum. Apart from these basics, discussion during these early years reflected concern about seminarians' knowledge of ecclesiastical art and architecture, their appreciation of liturgical symbols and liturgical ideals, and their instruction and skills in Gregorian chant.[12]

Not surprisingly, given the wider context of the organization, a particular emphasis, as early as 1905, was placed on the importance of priests' responsibilities to the Catholic school system in the United States. Seminary instructors were urged to form their students in "true pedagogical principles and methods, in view of the needs of parochial schools and diocesan high schools,"[13] to impress upon them the importance of Catholic schools and the duties of priests to take an active interest in them, and to be certain that classes in church history include the history of education. The priest's mission as teacher was to be kept in mind by every seminary professor, and the seminary was to be viewed as the "training school for the highest—teaching—profession."[14]

Seminary students, according to the resolutions at department meetings during these early years, were to be specifically trained for catechetical instruction, preferably through the mentoring of skilled and experienced priests. Support was expressed for summer vacation activities that encouraged seminarians to participate in such pastoral activities as visiting the sick and imprisoned, and to engage in practice sermon writing, book analysis, and physical fitness.[15]

Beginning in 1913, department meetings devoted considerable attention to issues of the seminary curriculum. Members debated the need for curricular readjustment to avoid repetition, appropriate course sequencing, and the standardization of content across seminaries. In particular, moral theology, dogmatic theology, Canon Law, homiletics, and the natural sciences were to receive sufficient and significant attention. There was considerable disagreement concerning how this was to be accomplished.

That same year, 1913, for example, Herman Heuser, a German-born Philadelphia priest, editor of *The American Ecclesiastical Review,* considered one of the most influential seminary figures of his time, called into serious question the current methods for teaching and learning dogmatic theology. In particular, he raised doubts about the traditional apologetic approach, observing, "Textbooks used in class are loaded down with arguments that are often purely artificial, and—to make a bold but true statement—are sometimes hurtful to the sense of honesty and truth. Deductions from Scripture and the Fathers which are unsound because they rest upon a defective and imaginary exegesis; illustrations appealing to supposed historical facts that are in reality legends…are features of our present textbooks."[16] He recommended the coordination of various subjects to avoid repetition and loss of time, the elimination of information that had been valuable once but had lost meaning over time, such as the refutations of heresies and the rehearsing of controversies that were no longer controversial, and the coordination of content.

Father Heuser renewed his theme in 1914, arguing that Scripture studies should precede theological studies.[17] "Heuser's audience expressed qualified approval for his views, but there was slight interest in implementing them."[18] His opinions are noteworthy in that he was speaking in a time when Church authorities sought increasing conformity in theological discussion within and outside of the seminary. It was the era of the "manuals," summary texts that organized theological and philosophical studies into compact volumes. Joseph White, in *The Diocesan Seminary in the United States,* notes that in the early decades of the twentieth century, "The use of Latin textbooks in dogma and moral theology remained a major characteristic of seminary learning."[19] In 1925 the Seminary Department surveyed seminary studies and found the textbooks defective, noting in particular that they did not address contemporary questions and issues.[20] Proposals for reform garnered scant support and the status quo had its defenders. "The many papers delivered at annual meetings in which educators described how they taught their subjects attest to the loyalty to the traditional divisions of subject matter. It was unlikely that a rearrangement of course offerings was possible, though the question had been raised."[21] By the 1930s a consensus had formed around one dogmatic author, Alphonse Tanquerey. The favorite moral theology manual was that of James Noldin and A. Schmitt.[22] The age of manual theology would not end until the 1960s, by which time J. M. Hervé had replaced Tanquerey as the favorite dogmatic manual.[23]

In addition to curriculum, social problems and seminary professionalism held a central place in Seminary Department papers and discussions, and were cited frequently in department meeting resolutions from the late 1920s to mid-century. In addition to maintaining loyalty to such Church documents as *Studiorum Ducem* by Pius XI and to the works of St. Thomas Aquinas as a master guide in theological and philosophical studies, members were urged toward a more careful study of the theology of Eastern Churches in accordance with *Rerum Orientalium Studiis* of 1931. It was suggested that superior students, moreover, could be given the opportunity to pursue Oriental languages as a preparation for teaching.

While a traditional stress on Canon Law and apologetics was preserved, an emphasis on homiletics, Sacred Scripture, and curricular evaluation was intensified. Professors in various branches of theology, for example, were encouraged to point out possible sermon lines in their classes, to promote the incorporation of Sacred Scripture in the teaching of homiletics, and to "constantly reexamine apologetics" to determine whether it was in keeping with the "special questions and problems of the times."[24]

Social concerns, including missionary activity at home and abroad, entered department discussions in 1925 and remained a significant theme into the mid-1940s. Members were urged to acquire special training in social and economic sciences, study principles of justice, charity and other social action guides, be well instructed in the importance of their work regarding the Negro [sic] and rural populations, and adapt teachings, especially in moral theology, to the "fast-changing conditions in…social life."[25] While members discussed the importance of "bringing in converts," they also recognized the need to have a personal acquaintance with both exponents of scholasticism and those "antagonistic schools and systems"[26] whose influence was felt in their intellectual world. In short, priests were implored to face, both as intellectuals and as problem-solvers, the importance of applying moral and pastoral theological principles to contemporary social situations.[27]

A sign of concern about the professional character of seminaries, the importance of seminary libraries surfaced in 1926 in department discussions and resolutions. Seminary administrators, specifically, were urged to hire competent librarians, support more extensive use of library resources for research, consider establishing a seminary periodical in order to stimulate a greater interest in the study and production of Catholic literature, endorse the Catholic Periodical Index, encourage "collateral reading" to supplement classroom teaching of dogmatic theology, and foster the publication of research by seminarians, particularly in the field of American Church History.[28]

Other issues of seminary professionalism, including the awarding of academic degrees and meeting the standards for external accreditation, continued to be discussed through the 1920s and throughout the department's history. In 1929, the topic was launched into a passionate debate by the Very Reverend Thomas W. Plassmann, O.F.M., President of St. Bonaventure's Ecclesiastical Seminary in Allegheny, New York. In his "A Protest Against Seminary Standardization," he decried such efforts by asserting, "Degrees have no place in the seminary. It seems like sewing a cheap button on a rich vestment. Humility is the basis of the spiritual life. The only degrees (a seminarian) needs are the seven degrees of Holy Orders."[29] Others recognized the advantages and supported the values that would accrue to students from such positive relations between the seminaries and government and accrediting agencies. They supported accreditation without allowing the "poison of secularism to infiltrate" programs and pledged "sedulously to safeguard the sacred and unchanging traditions of Christian Education" which only the Church possesses.[30] Lack of accreditation meant that seminaries had an uncertain standing in the world of education.

Although regional accreditation agencies, in particular the North Central Association of Colleges and Universities, encouraged seminaries to seek accreditation, progress was very slow. "The lack of any national Catholic authority in seminary matters or formulation of a national policy by the bishops meant that there would not be a concerted movement among seminaries to seek accreditation."[31] In 1928, the National Catholic Welfare Conference (NCWC) formed a committee on seminaries. Archbishop James T. McNicholas, chair of the committee, soon discovered that there was precious little information on seminaries across the nation upon which to base any informed discussion. In 1931, McNicholas asked the NCEA Seminary Department to formulate recommendations to ensure quality seminary education. Due to the negative character of these recommendations, which noted "mediocrity of teaching" and "interference of higher ecclesiastical authority," the archbishop did not pass them on to the bishops.[32]

After World War II, this issue assumed greater significance, particularly in light of the G.I. Bill. Some returning veterans sought admission to Catholic seminaries and applied for educational benefits from the federal government. The government required a list of approved institutions and turned to NCEA, but it was not an accrediting body. The accreditation issue would not go away. When it celebrated its golden jubilee in 1948, the Seminary Department encompassed 140 colleges, 68 freestanding and 72 combined colleges and high schools, and 141 theologates. Of these theologates, 55 were freestanding, and 86 included theology and two years of philosophy. Excluding high school enrollments, the total number of seminarians at this time was 22,920.[33]

## Transformation and Leadership

As the Catholic population grew, new dioceses and new seminaries were established at an astounding rate. Particularly influential in leading the reform of Catholic seminaries in the middle of the twentieth century was Reverend J. Cyril Dukehart, S.S., appointed in 1958 as the first full-time Associate Secretary for the Seminary Department. Although he served in this capacity for less than two years, dying of a heart attack in 1960, his perceptions, communications, and concerns were both practical and visionary in nature.

Father Dukehart's appointment was a result of the assumption of NCEA leadership by Monsignor Frederick Hochwalt, who became General Secretary in 1944. The leading statesman of American Catholic education in the postwar era, Monsignor Hochwalt "oversaw the expansion of services of his association with the appointment of full-time associate general secretaries for each level of Catholic education from elementary schools to universities."[34] The presence of a full time Executive Secretary heralded a new era of service and leadership for the seminaries by the NCEA. The Executive Secretary could now devote all of his efforts to the post.

Considered an advocate of measures to minimize the seminary's isolation from the rest of the educational community, Father Dukehart urged seminary accreditation through the formation of an "American Association of Roman Catholic Theological Seminaries," to be similar to the Protestant seminaries' American Association of Theological Schools (the present Association of Theological Schools of the United States and Canada - ATS). He strove to improve seminary standards and professionalism, and suggested specific ways to resolve the acute problem of more than 150 minor and major seminaries with an enrollment of fewer than 50 students.[35] Father Dukehart pointed out another basic problem affecting the quality of seminaries, the rapid pace of seminary foundations. In 1959, there were 381 seminaries, 131 of which had been opened since 1945, or a 53 percent increase since World War II.

The triumphal catalogue of institutional expansion had not been welcomed by all. Reverend John Tracy Ellis, the dean of historians of American Catholicism, lamented, "The dismal procession of numerous small and weak seminaries continued to appear in every part of the land."[36] Throughout the 1950s and early 1960s, the Catholic critique of the seminaries focused on their physical and intellectual isolation and called for more involvement in pastoral life and greater efforts to achieve academic excellence.[37] This discussion was summed up by Stafford Poole in *Seminary in Crisis* and by James Lee and Louis Putz in *Seminary Education in a Time of Change*.[38] While the post-World War II growth took place without any central planning, attention to academic excellence and to pastoral preparation was not neglected. An increasing number of faculty obtained doctoral degrees and serious discussion of the need for professional accreditation had begun.[39]

Father Dukehart proposed arranging regional meetings of seminary administrators and personnel; publishing at least biannually a "Directory of Seminaries" with the inclusion of meaningful statistics; pursuing research on specific problems such as testing, mortality rates, curriculum, and teacher training; and regularly publishing a newsletter as an effective means of communication among seminaries. His words to department members at the 1959 NCEA Convention seem equally appropriate today. "You yourselves, the educators of our diocesan and regular clergy, would be the last to admit that there is no room for improvement. You realize better than anyone else that our seminaries...should be models in the educational world: staffed by the very best talent that can be mustered, governed in keeping with the highest standard of school administration, with physical facilities adequate for their purposes and in keeping with their dignity. The education of the clergy should be the chief concern of the Church in our country, and it may well be that the establishment of our office in the NCEA was really a result of this conviction."[40]

Although issues such as curriculum and spiritual formation in seminaries continued to concern department members in the 1950s and 1960s, seminarians who sought to participate in the G.I. Bill brought the need for seminary accreditation to a head.[41] In the first issue of the *Seminary Newsletter*, published in October 1959 by Father Dukehart, the question was raised about why so few seminaries (31) were accredited. Concern was also expressed at that time about the fact that only 40 percent of the United States major seminaries and 41 percent of the minor seminaries had institutional memberships in the Seminary Department.[42] From its earliest issues, the *Seminary Newsletter* provided a persuasive voice in promoting the adaptation of seminaries to contemporary cultural needs. Practical issues such as professional accreditation, educational television and technology, and the advantages of a "4 - 4 - 4" seminary arrangement for high school, college, and theology instead of the traditional "6 - 6" were discussed. Resources for assisting seminaries in these areas were also included.

## THE SECOND VATICAN COUNCIL

As in other areas of Church life, the Second Vatican Council gave a powerful impetus to a seminary renewal already in progress. The implications of the goals set by the council were not all immediately evident. The structure of the renewal was local, national and international. On an official level, the renewal consisted in the implementation of various "norms" established by the council, by the Congregation for Seminaries and Universities, and by the National

Conference of Catholic Bishops (NCCB; in 2001 the NCCB became the United States Conference of Catholic Bishops). This renewal was both orderly and chaotic, its direction sometimes was clear, at other times obscure. The direction of renewal often produced agreement, but conflict was not unknown. Often, conflict would occur when there were contradictory interpretations of the mind of the Second Vatican Council and the needs of the Church. Very significantly, the renewal also was driven by completely unforeseen forces outside the control of the seminaries.

Although the Roman Catholic seminaries still appeared to many to be isolated in "monastic fastness," this was no longer true. The currents affecting religious, social, political and cultural change had enormous impact in the years following the council. Some would prove to be positive, some otherwise.

These years were highlighted by growing secularism throughout Western society. Sin began to disappear and was replaced by psychological explanations of behavior. The "me generation" was born in America. In the United States, the civil rights and women's movements began. The assassinations of Martin Luther King and Robert Kennedy contributed to growing disillusionment fired by the Vietnam War. Watergate signaled erosion and a mistrust of authority in all forms. The drug culture began to emerge and spread throughout the country. A human person walked on the moon. The technological and information age had begun.

The Roman Catholic Church worshipped in the language of its people for the first time in a millennium and a half. Ecumenism was welcomed with enthusiasm; onetime heretics became separated brethren. Synods of bishops began to meet in Rome and the Roman Curia was internationalized. Pope Paul VI's encyclical, *Humanae Vitae*, reaffirming the traditional Church teaching on artificial birth control, was followed by a growing dissent within the Church among both laity and clergy. Marriage and family life declined, divorce increased. The abortion controversy began to emerge. A phenomenal number of priests began to leave the active ministry; seminary enrollments plummeted. Burgeoning numbers of psychologists and other social workers developed as a class of secular healing professionals. All of these currents would impact on the seminaries and NCEA would engage in addressing them. The focus of Seminary Department meetings and activities would include cultural and social issues affecting the seminaries as well as the traditional issues of structure and academics. The Seminary Department would facilitate discussion and planning among bishops and seminary leadership. The changing context would demand many changes within the Department.

On December 8, 1965, Pope Paul VI solemnly closed the Second Vatican Council. In its *Decree on Priestly Training (Optatum totius)*, the council called for a renewal of seminary studies. Four years later, the Congregation for Catholic Education published the *Basic Plan for Priestly Formation (Ratio Fundamentalis)*. The *Basic Plan* called on each nation to adapt the plan to its own exigencies. Within the United States, the direction of this renewal was assumed by the Bishops' Committee for Priestly Formation (BCPF), established in 1966 by the NCCB. For the first time, the national bishops' conference had a standing committee charged to serve the seminaries. This oversight was limited. The committee did not control the seminaries or endorse their programs. Direct oversight of the individual institutions remained in the hands of the bishops and superiors. A major role of this committee was the drafting of the *Program of Priestly Formation*.

In 1971, the Congregation for Catholic Education gave final approval to the *Program of Priestly Formation* formulated by the NCCB after a lengthy consultation with the seminaries. The conciliar decrees, the *Basic Plan* and the *Program*, together with subsequent decrees from the Congregation for Catholic Education, would form the foundation blocks of the renewal of Catholic seminaries. The *Program* was the most immediately influential for it contained "principles according to which seminaries at every level should be conducted."[43]

The first statistical study and directory of American Catholic Seminaries appeared in 1966. "Catholic Seminaries in the United States 1966," provided an exhaustive and precise portrait of the institutions in that year. Ironically, the statistics reflected the previous year, the year of the highest seminary enrollments in history. It reported 149 major seminaries, 216 minor seminaries and 89 seminaries with both major and minor sections, a total of 454 institutions. There were 32,796 seminarians in high schools, junior colleges and novitiates; 6,290 in philosophy; 8,916 in theology; 1,144 in scholasticates, and 811 studying abroad; for a total of 49,957 seminarians. Changing methods of reporting make it difficult to accurately translate these statistics, but the final numbers are impressive.

The department responded to the needs of the changing seminary scene. In 1968, a new series of seminary newsletters was initiated under Associate Secretary, Rev. Eugene I. Antwerp. Beginning in 1967, the seminaries formed regional groupings such as the Midwest Association of Theological Schools (MATS), and a variety of organizations of rectors and deans of high school and college seminaries and theologates. The Executive Secretaries maintained contact with these organizations, attended their meetings, and engaged them in fruitful collaboration, sharing their local insights and research with the seminaries throughout the nation.

Reverend David M. Murphy became Executive Secretary in 1972 and outlined what he considered to be the most pressing problems confronting seminaries at the outset of his term as executive secretary in the post-Vatican II Seminary Department. He stressed the need for long-range planning, amalgamation and cooperative arrangements among seminaries, an examination of patterns for awarding degrees, support for contextual learning, and the relationship between religious and diocesan seminaries. He further cautioned, in 1973, against what he termed "the five-pound" bag problem: trying to squeeze ten pounds of material into a five-pound bag—or pressuring the seminary curriculum to take on more and more.[44]

Because of these concerns and reduced resources, evaluation—of institutions, programs, students, and faculty—became a major theme over the next 25 years. Significant attention was given, for example, at both department meetings and in various related writings, to psychological and religious evaluations of seminarians and to trends in seminary enrollments, costs, and facilities. Pursuant to the 1974 Buckley Amendment on the Rights and Privacy of Students and other governmental legislation, issues such as confidentiality, due process, copyright restrictions, and handicapped regulations required further adaptation and change. In addition, over the next decades, seminaries became increasingly attuned to the role of permanent deacons and lay ministers. Convention programs addressed these questions as well as the needs of Hispanics and other minority groups, the evolution of the Rite of Christian Initiation for Adults (R.C.I.A.) as a model for formation, the principles and challenges of collaboration, and a variety of psychosexual considerations.[45] Clearly, seminaries are "influenced by factors extraneous to their own internal life and even the life of the Church."[46]

In 1976, the Executive Secretary became the Executive Director as NCEA changed the title of its department heads. The first Executive Director was Reverend James Sullivan, who succeeded Father Murphy in 1976. Throughout the 1970s seminaries were "under siege." Closings of institutions, particularly high [47] school seminaries and small religious order seminaries were noted in the *Seminary Newsletter*.[48] The "quality" of incoming seminarians was criticized. Father Sullivan reacted to this, writing "Perhaps the time has come for some serious soul-searching by seminary folk. Archbishop Bernardin and Frs. Creedon and Fogarty fault the seminarians; Fr. Fox rails against the seminaries. Is there really something wrong in Camelot?" These remarks provoked a spirited debate in *Seminary Newsletter*. The seminaries did not ignore these criticisms and the department continued to address the changing seminary scene at convention and in its publications. Convention sessions included "Areas of Theological Competence for Priestly Ordination," "The Woman in the Theologate: Teacher, Learner, Director," " The Role of the Theologate in Preparation for non-Sacerdotal Ministries,"[49] "The Seminarian: Consumer or Ascetic," "Relationships: The Third

Dimension of the College Seminary."[50]  The department sponsored workshops on "Justice and Peace Formation in the Seminary" and on the relationship between the seminaries and the psychological sciences.  The papers of the latter workshop were published in 1978 as *Seminaries and Psychology*.

## THE MISSION EXPANDS

Beginning in 1980, Reverend William Baumgaertner, as Executive Director of the Seminary Department, sought to foster even greater communication among seminaries and to sponsor programs, research, and collaboration for strengthening and improving educational and formational programs.  At this time the department settled its present configuration of theologates, college seminaries and high school seminaries, each represented on the departmental executive committee.  Seminaries were trying to respond in different ways to the directives of Vatican II as well as to the impact of far-reaching changes in the American culture.  It became clear that major steps would have to be taken for training administrative officers to work with governing boards and to understand an emerging pattern of financing quite different from what had prevailed for almost a century.  The demand was for solid longer-range planning.  Responding to changing Church needs would place heavy demands on programs and personnel as well.  An increasingly diversified student body constituted another factor.  The experience of prior generations was history.  As the needs of the seminaries changed, so did the department.

To strengthen the governance of seminaries, the Seminary Department collaborated actively with the Association of Governing Boards of Colleges and Universities (AGB) to adapt their materials to the special needs of theological schools.  This yielded several publications, including *The Good Servant* in 1983, which were broadly used by Catholic schools to respond to the changing and expanded demands placed on their boards.

By the 1980s, most seminaries had been accredited by the Association of Theological Schools of the United States and Canada (ATS) and by regional agencies as well.  The Seminary Department cooperated with ATS to generate a series of extended programs to train presidents and other senior officers in an understanding of current executive management skills.  This was done in collaboration with the Graduate School of Management of Columbia University.  Under Father Baumgaertner, the Seminary Department began a relationship with the Lilly Endowment that led to a series of studies, consultations, and publications that continue to this day.  Over the last twenty years the Lilly Endowment, with the constant collaboration of Fred Hofheinz of the Religion Department of the Endowment, has made a series of grants to the Seminary Department totaling almost $1.5 million dollars.[51] The Lilly Endowment underwrote the principal costs of the great majority of department activities over the last quarter century and greatly enhanced the effectiveness and services of the department.[52]

In collaboration with the NCCB Office for Christian-Jewish Relations, the department published a book on the teaching of the history of Christian-Jewish relations in theological seminaries. NCEA's Seminary Department likewise collaborated with the Office of Priestly Formation of the NCCB in facilitating the conduct of the Papal Visitation of United States Catholic seminaries.

Funded by the Lilly Endowment, a major statistical study of program and revenue costing for all programs in theological seminaries was conducted by Rev. Francis K. Sheets, O.S.C., of the Center for Applied Research in the Apostolate (CARA) together with the director of the Seminary Department. The results were published in *Planning for the Future*. The study was conducted with the assistance of the New York office of the auditing firm Peat, Marwick and Mitchell.

A major project of the Department was its leadership in the convocation of the 1983 Assembly of Rectors and Ordinaries. This meeting, for the first time, brought together rectors, bishops and religious superiors for three days of discussion. The issues it surfaced reflected the rapidly changing world of the seminary. The topics highlighted were: Formation Programs for Multicultural Candidates; Formation Programs to Prepare Candidates to Serve in Multicultural Ministries; Ecclesiology, different understandings of the Church and its mission resulting in tension on rectors; Equity in Seminary Funding; Relationship of Priest and Lay Formation Programs; Planning for Regional/National Formation Programs; Screening and Selection of Candidates and Establishment of Regional Screening Centers; Better Data on Seminaries and Seminarians; and Development of an Effective Collaborative Process for Education/Formation after Ordination. Many of these matters had been germinating for two decades and would be addressed by the NCCB and the NCEA in the following years.

Reverend Charles M. Kavanagh took the helm of the Seminary Department in 1985. Father Kavanagh was a consultant to the Papal Visitation of Seminaries and participated in many of the visitations.[53] Thanks to Lilly Endowment funding, the department continued to expand the body of research in the area of seminary formation. NCEA published the first national study on the attitudes of American seminarians by Reverend Raymond Potvin, a study on the academic profile of our theological schools by Reverend Edward B. Rosinski, and two major studies on the American seminarian by Reverend Eugene Hemrick and Dr. Dean Hoge. In collaboration with the NCCB, the department was also involved in the work of preparation of the Fourth Edition of the *Program of Priestly Formation* and the Catholic Education Futures Project.

These years also saw the Second Assembly of Ordinaries and Rectors, held at Seton Hall University in June 1987. This was the largest gathering in history of bishops, rectors and religious superiors involved in priestly formation. A joint effort of the Bishops Committee on Priestly Formation, The Conference of Major Superiors of Men and the NCEA, this meeting provided a rich opportunity for open dialogue, information sharing, and planning for the future. Four major areas of concern surfaced: the theology of priesthood, the relationship between diocesan and religious programs of formation, collaborative ministry, and scholarship and academic freedom.

Reverend Robert J. Wister succeeded Father Kavanagh in June 1988. Shortly thereafter, he directed the merger of the department's two publications *Seminary News* and *Seminaries in Dialogue*. The major task of the department in the following years involved collaboration with the Bishops Committee on Priestly Formation (BCPF) in the revision of the PPF and its implementation. Once again, funding for all of the various activities of this collaboration was provided by the Lilly Endowment. In 1989, the publication, *Theology of Priesthood and Seminary Formation: Issues of Assembly II*, addressed all of the issues the assembly raised and asked to be discussed in preparation for the new PPF. The major issue of Assembly II, theology of priesthood, was the subject of a series of colloquia that engaged prominent scholars Donald Senior, Agnes Cunningham, Peter Fink, John O'Malley and Robert Schwartz. Its outcomes were edited by Father Wister and published as *Priests: Identity and Ministry* in 1990, and included additional reflections by Cardinal William Baum, Archbishop J. Francis Stafford and Bishop Daniel Buechlein, O.S.B. The convention programs were devoted to the discussion of the revision of the PPF that was issued by the NCCB in November 1992. The director of the Seminary Department and Reverend Howard Bleichner, S.S., served as editors of the new PPF.

Shortly thereafter, in early 1993, the department sponsored a meeting of rectors of college seminaries and theologates to discuss "Pre-Theology," which had been mandated by the new formation program. The summary of the conference was published in May 1993 as *Report on Pre-Theology*.

The many meetings surrounding the revision of the formation program, as well as convention presentations and discussions, brought the issue of psychological testing and counseling in seminaries to the fore. The department conducted a series of discussions and sponsored papers that were published in August 1993 as *Psychology, Counseling and the Seminarian*, edited by Father Wister. This volume included chapters on psychosexual maturity, spiritual direction and psychotherapy, the use of counseling in vocational discernment, addictions, legal issues and ethnic issues in counseling. The demand for this book necessitated a second printing in March 1994.

Other significant publications of this period exemplify the questions raised by the seminaries and the bishops. *A Survey of Priests Ordained Five to Nine Years* (1991), with the collaboration of Father Hemrick, studied the effectiveness of programs from the perspective of recently ordained priests as well as their satisfaction with ministry. *The Recruitment and Retention of Faculty in Roman Catholic Theological Seminaries* (1992), also with the collaboration of Father Hemrick, addressed changes in methods of faculty recruitment, the changing profile of faculty, and problems caused by the declining number of priests. Father Hemrick also contributed to *Readiness for Theological Studies: A Study of Faculty Perceptions on the Readiness of Seminarians* (1993). All of these activities and publications were the product of the collaborative efforts of seminary personnel and experts in the field.

Reverend James Walsh became executive director in 1993. He replaced *Seminary News* with an entirely new publication, *Seminary Journal.* Its purpose was to provide an opportunity to share ideas and practices in the field and to enable NCEA to continue to be a resource to all seminaries. Articles in *Seminary Journal* include such varied topics as "Fire in the Belly: From Experience to Imagination to Passion" by Reverend Walter Burghardt, S.J., ""Speaking in a Different Tongue: Spiritual Direction in a Multicultural Church" by Reverend Peter Phan, and "What Will and Won't Change in the Future Parish" by Archbishop Daniel Pilarczyk. The journal has developed an excellent following throughout North America and in English-speaking countries such as The United Kingdom and Australia.

The Department was involved in the development of biennial Institutes for Formation Staff and Advisors in collaboration with the Society of St. Sulpice. These weeklong institutes provide seminaries a way to do "in service" training for their formation staffs. The department was a major contributor to the "Keystone Project," a five-year program for faculty development in 20 Catholic theologates with the goal of enhancing the quality of teaching and learning. Father Walsh also implemented a strategy for the NCEA Seminary Department to provide consultation to seminary rector/presidents regarding governance, board development, strategic planning, working with foundations and preparation for reaccreditation.[54]

A major effort of Father Walsh was *Grace Under Pressure: What Gives Life to American Priests.* This is the all time NCEA best seller with over 15,000 copies sold. It recounts interviews with 36 priests of different ages, backgrounds and regions of the United States. In it they tell where they find life in the priesthood, how they deal with controversies in the Church, how they feel about being a man in today's society, and what advice they would give to seminary staffs. Other publications include *Ripe for the Harvest*, a collection of articles on various aspects of priestly formation, and *Formation for Priestly Celibacy*, by Reverend Thomas

Krenik, a resource for all charged with this ministry in the seminary.

In light of the observance of the NCEA centennial, it seems appropriate to return to the first meeting of the Seminary Department as part of the CEA in 1903. Rev. P.R. Heffron, President of the St. Paul Seminary, St. Paul, Minnesota, cogently reminded participants that their "seminaries need no apologist. They are doing their work nobly and thoroughly. Often laboring under difficulties and with scanty means, the results are simply marvelous."[55]

## ENDNOTES

[1] This chapter draws on research and publications of Angeline K. Cepelka. Angeline K. Cepelka, "NCEA Seminary Department at 100 Years," in *Momentum*, October/November 1998, 48-51; "NCEA Seminary Department: 100 Years of Transitions and Transformation," in *Seminary Journal*, 4, n. 2, (Fall 1998): 30-36.

[2] Joseph M. White, The Diocesan Seminary in the United States: A History from the 1780s to the Present (Notre Dame: University of Notre Dame Press, 1989), 202 - 203.

[3] Robert J. Wister, "The Effects of Institutional Change on the Office of Rector and President in the Catholic Theological Seminaries," in *Theological Education*, XXXII, (Supplement I, Autumn 1995): 51-52.

[4] Joseph M. White, "Leadership in the American Diocesan Seminary: Contexts, Institutions, and Personalities – 1791 to 1965," in *Theological Education*, XXXII, Supplement I, 1995, 5.

[5] "History of the Educational Conference of Seminary Faculties," in *Report of the Proceedings of the First Annual Meeting* (Columbus, Ohio: Catholic Educational Association, 1904), 25 - 27.

[6] White, *The Diocesan Seminary in the United States*, 203.

[7] Edgar P. McCarren, "The History of the Seminary Department of the NCEA," in *The National Catholic Educational Association Bulletin* (Washington, D.C.: NCEA, 1953), 107 - 113.

[8] White, *The Diocesan Seminary in the United States*, 388-389.

[9] *Catholic Educational Association Proceedings* (1919), 19-31. (hereafter, *Proceedings*)

[10] *Proceedings* (1921), 589.

[11] *Proceedings* (1917), 477.

[12] "Seminary Department," *Catholic Educational Association Proceedings* (1905, 1920, 1921, 1923).

[11] *Proceedings* (1920), 211-212.

[14] *Proceedings* (1920), 520.

[15] *Proceedings* (1916), 456.

[16] White, *The Diocesan Seminary in the United States*, 361.

[17] *Proceedings* (1914), 378-389.

[18] White, *The Diocesan Seminary in the United States*, 362.

[19] White, *The Diocesan Seminary in the United States*, 366.
[20] *Proceedings* (1925), 585-587; 589-600.
[21] White, *The Diocesan Seminary in the United States*, 363.
[22] Ibid, 366-367.
[23] Ibid, 379.
[24] "Seminary Department," *Proceedings* (1924 - 1926); Seminary Department Proceedings," *The National Catholic Educational Association Bulletin* (1927, 1929, 1931, 1938, 1940).
[25] "Seminary Department Proceedings," *The National Catholic Association Bulletin* (1925, 1926, 1928, 1931 - 1934, 1936, 1938, 1940, 1941, 1944).
[26] *The National Catholic Educational Association Bulletin* (1926), 499.
[27] *The National Catholic Educational Association Bulletin* (1942), 608.
[28] "Seminary Department Proceedings," *The National Catholic Educational Association Bulletin* (1926, 1928, 1930, 1931, 1940).
[29] Thomas W. Plassmann, "A Protest Against Seminary Standardization," *The National Catholic Educational Association Bulletin* (1930), 596.
[30] *The National Catholic Educational Association Bulletin* (1946), 66.
[31] White, *The Diocesan Seminary in the United States*, 393.
[32] Ibid, 393-394.
[33] Rev. James J. Walsh, Seminary Department Executive Director, telephone interview with author, 4 March 1998.
[34] White, "Leadership in the American Diocesan Seminary: Contexts, Institutions, and Personalities – 1791 to 1965, in *Theological Education*, XXXII, Supplement I, (Autumn 1995): 40.
[35] Katarina Schuth, *Reason for the Hope: The Future of Roman Catholic Theologates* (Wilmington, Delaware, 1989), 27.
[36] John Tracy Ellis, "The Formation of the American Priest: An Historical Perspective," in *The Catholic Priest in the United States: Historical Investigations* (Collegeville, MN: St. John's University Press, 1971), 54.
[37] White. *The Diocesan Seminary in the United States*, see especially 405-430.
[38] Stafford Poole, *Seminary in Crisis*, (New York: Herder and Herder, 1966), and James Michael Lee and Louis J. Putz, eds. *Seminary Education in a Time of Change*, (Notre Dame, IN: Fides, 1965.
[39] White. *The Diocesan Seminary in the United States*, 396, 398, 422.
[40] J. Cyril Dukehart, "Our Seminaries: Their Commitments and Resources," *The National Catholic Educational Association Bulletin*, (1959), 73 - 76.
[41] Lee and Putz, eds., *Seminary Education in a Time of Change*, 101-105.
[42] *Seminary Newsletter*, 1 (October 1959): 1-7.
[43] *Program of Priestly Formation*, 1971, xii.
[44] David M. Murphy, "The Five Pound Bag," *Seminary Newsletter* 12 (December 1973): 1.
[45] *Seminary News* 19-33, September 1980-Winter 1994; *Seminaries in Dialogue*, December 1980-Spring 1991; *Seminary Journal* 1-3, Spring 1995-Spring 1997.
[46] Steven M. Avella, ed., *St. Francis Seminary Sesquicentennial Essays* (St. Francis Seminary, St. Francis, Wisconsin, 1997), 48.
[47] *Seminary Newsletter*, vol. 18, (September 1979): 1.
[48] *Seminary Newsletter*, vol. 15, (December 1976): 2; vol. 16, (June 1978): 3.

[49] *Seminary Newsletter,* vol. 17, (December 1978): 2.

[50] *Seminary Newsletter,* vol. 18, ( December 1979): 2.

[51] Fred Hofheinz, July 27, 2001. Telephone interview by Robert J. Wister.

[52] William Baumgaertner, February 7, 2001. Letter to Robert J. Wister.

[53] Charles Kavanagh, "NCEA Report 2001," undated report to Robert J. Wister.

[54] James Walsh, "Developments in NCEA Seminary Department 1993-2000, undated report to Robert J. Wister.

[55] P.R. Heffron, "Qualifications Necessary and Desirable for Entrance into the Seminary," *Catholic Educational Association Proceedings* (1904), 169.

## CHAPTER 3

# ONE HUNDRED YEARS: THE ASSOCIATION OF CATHOLIC COLLEGES AND UNIVERSITIES[1]

✎

### Kathleen A. Mahoney

I n 1898 The Catholic University of America Rector Msgr. Thomas Conaty (1895-1903) sent ninety-five Catholic college educators Christmas greetings and a query: had they interest in a conference for "exchanging [of] views" that might result in "increasing efficiency" and "raising standards"? In April 1899 fifty-three representatives of Catholic men's colleges met in Chicago for a two-day conference.[2] After a "beautiful" Solemn High Mass, they discussed eight papers and voted to establish an association. The proceedings summarize neatly: "Four sessions were held, a permanent organization was effected, and it was resolved that this organization be known as The Association of Catholic Colleges of the United States" (ACCUS). It is now known as the Association of Catholic Colleges and Universities (ACCU).[3]

Conaty's plans to unify, improve, and systematize American Catholic education were prodigious. Nearly a thousand institutions offered some sort of "higher" education, including universities (10), seminaries (109), colleges for boys (178) and academies for girls (662). Some, by virtue of the curriculum and age of students, were colleges only in name; others, by virtue of the same, were colleges in everything but name. Scores of religious orders, with their own traditions and little enthusiasm for cooperation with other orders, complicated the scene. In 1895 Catholic higher education was "almost chaotic," according to Georgetown President J. Havens Richards, S.J. (1888-1898).[4]

In 1904 the ACCUS joined with representatives of parochial schools and the seminaries to form the Catholic Educational Association (which became the

National Catholic Educational Association in 1927). With affiliation, the ACCUS assumed a new name: the College Department (which will, for the sake of clarity, be used throughout most of this chapter). Subsequent name changes reflect shifts in the College Department's self-understanding, relation to other departments, and locus within the NCEA. In 1918 the College Department became the Department of Colleges and Secondary Schools; eleven years later, after the college and high school representatives went separate ways, the earlier name, "The College Department," came back into vogue until 1935 when the College Department matured into the College and University Department. In 1978 the college group reverted to a permutation of its original name, becoming the Association of Catholic Colleges and Universities.

For a century the ACCU has worked to improve Catholic higher education and represent its interests before other constituencies. During its first two decades the College Department worked primarily from the "inside-out," focusing on the nature, purpose, and structure of their institutions. With World War I, the department's attention turned more outward, with the impetus for improvement coming more frequently from the "outside-in." In this the College Department became the corporate face of American Catholic higher education within the three primary contexts: on the American scene (especially as represented by the federal government), amid the larger academic community, and within the Catholic Church. Through the work of the College Department in this period, we see Catholic higher education coming of age, joining the academic mainstream. The final period began in the mid-1960s: the ACCU became the primary forum for Catholic colleges and universities to explore and negotiate the meanings and tensions inherent in being institutions devoted to the public good, committed to the academic and professional mores of the American academy, and devoted to the Church and its missions.[5]

## Early Years, Difficult Times

"Shall we have a university?" American Catholics debated the issue for many years before the establishment of The Catholic University of America in 1889. Initially, advocates argued for a center to educate clerical and lay elites. In time, they expanded that idea; not only would it educate individuals, but it would educate corporately, functioning as "a great intellectual centre of Catholic intelligence and influence" and a "crown of honor and a focus of light for our schools, colleges, and seminaries."[6] Through 1897 Conaty's plans involved a program of affiliation between the colleges and CUA. (Under one variant, graduates of Catholic colleges deemed academically respectable gained *de facto* admission to the university for advanced studies.) In 1898 Conaty adopted a new tactic. Announcing that "educational conventions" were the "order of the day," and that "organized effort, not isolation," was the "secret of success," Conaty convened the first conference.[7] His success is especially notable given the historic lack of cooperation between religious orders and skepticism about the university in some quarters. The case of the Jesuits of St. Louis University is illustrative. They were likely among those forwarding an "extremely favorable" response to Conaty's initial query; in actuality, they were unenthusiastic. In discussing Conaty's proposal, the community's consultors voted in the affirmative because they did not want to "place [themselves] in a position of apparent antagonism to any effort of Catholic colleges." Loss of autonomy concerned others. Eight years after their first meeting, John Conway, S.J. (then president of the College Department) recalled fears that educational standards "might be imposed." It took several years for "this feeling of unrest and suspicion to die out."[8]

At annual meetings the college men listened to Conaty, ecclesiastical guests, and their peers. Here again is evidence of Conaty's acumen; he picked timely topics and speakers from various religious orders. The topics were substantive: the religious and moral foundations of education, subject matter and pedagogy, entrance requirements, the elective system, the relationship between high schools and colleges, educational legislation, and Catholic attendance at non-Catholic schools. Largely thoughtful and critical, the papers often inspired animated conversation—revealing the college men to be, as one commentator put it, "united in the faith and little else."[9] This was an ideologically and temperamentally eclectic group, variously conservative and progressive, with some clearly at home in modern America and others railing against the world in which they lived.

The press regularly depicted the conferences as successful. But the "secret of success" proved elusive. For instance, an early attempt to establish common entrance requirements failed after years of work. This voluntary association of representatives from different religious orders, each with distinct educational traditions and market interests, could find neither common ground nor means of enforcement. More pointedly, their work became increasingly superfluous as membership waned. Fifty-two delegates attended the conferences in 1899 and 1900; in 1901 the number dropped to forty-two. In 1903 only thirty-one delegates arrived for the annual conference. By 1904 the ACCUS was, in Conway's words, on the verge of "failure and collapse," saved by affiliation with the CEA. With the school and seminary departments, the College Department benefited from the strong leadership of Rev. Francis W. Howard, secretary general of the CEA (1904-1929), and James Burns, C.S.C., future Notre Dame president, who together "largely shaped the activities of the Association for the first fifteen years of its existence."[10]

But the College Department still languished. Some members chafed at their place in the newly created CEA. Moreover the colleges were "catching it badly," sometimes from those from whom support might be expected. Case in point: at the 1905 conference, Archbishop John Farley of New York publicly humiliated the colleges, claiming that they would gain the "confidence of the people" only when they raised their standards.[11] By 1906 Burns mused that the "college men need a stirring up" but "nothing short of an earthquake" would move some of them. He counseled patience, noting—in the wake of the San Francisco calamity—that earthquakes were becoming more common.[12] The wait was short. In 1907 and 1908 a metaphorical earthquake and strong aftershock hit the College Department, in the form of two reports documenting Catholic student demographics.

In 1907 the College Department heard from Harvard chaplain, Rev. John Farrell, on the number of Catholic collegians at non-Catholic colleges. The college men had discussed the issue at every conference to date, but few would have guessed the extent of the "drift" toward non-Catholic colleges. Farrell estimated the number at 8,671. The following year another survey found only 4,232 collegians in Catholic colleges. The results were so dismal that the leadership debated keeping the information private—*subjecta oculis fidelibus*—"for the scrutiny of the faithful." They compromised, printing the report, but kept it out of the *Proceedings* and the CEA *Bulletin*.[13]

In light of paltry enrollments, the College Department made an unusual move. Wary of external interference—civil or ecclesiastical—they decided to traverse the "great abyss" that kept them "divided from the hierarchy and the hierarchy from them." Approaching the archbishops with a "Memorial on Catholic College Education," they requested "a little encouragement" and "zeal" on behalf of Catholic colleges. Deferentially refraining from specific suggestions, they clearly wanted the hierarchy to direct Catholics to Catholic colleges just as they directed Catholic parents to send their children to parochial schools. Support was not forthcoming. Though the archbishops seemed sympathetic, a subsequent meeting came to naught.[14] Without episcopal support, the college men had two means to raise enrollments: persuasion and the perceived merits of their colleges. In the free market of higher education, a deficit in terms of the latter with its adverse effects on enrollments eventually motivated the college men to improve and modernize their colleges.

The rebuff from the hierarchy marked a turning point: the college men abandoned their crisis mentality. Their meetings assumed a predictable rhythm, their energies devoted primarily to curricular matters. Early standardization efforts and the popularity of the high schools also taxed them, forcing them to define what they meant by a "standard college." Increasingly the College Department worked along disciplinary lines, with sections devoted to Latin and Greek, science and mathematics, the modern languages, etc. Occasionally they rallied. In the early 1910s the College Department first used a public, common voice, distributing 25,000 pamphlets by Catholic educational apologist Timothy Brosnahan, S.J., assailing the Carnegie Foundation's refusal to provide retirement funds to sectarian colleges.[15]

In the 1910s the "feminine element" joined the College Department, with sisters delivering papers, primarily in the modern language section. It was strenuous work by Mary Molloy, Ph.D., of St. Teresa's College in Minnesota that won inclusion of the women's colleges in the College Department. The women's colleges first met in 1916, with formation of a Section on Catholic Colleges for Women realized in 1917.[16] Catholic educators "do not seem to value the 'get together' idea and spirit as much as outsiders do, 'probably' due to our training and traditions," claimed Albert Fox, S.J., in 1917.[17] The get together idea and spirit only came gradually, but it came. Some efforts failed, yet the department assumed an important role. It served as a forum for members to discuss common concerns and a means to foster professionalism. It provided a platform for the best and brightest—such as Burns, Howard, Molloy and Fox—to exercise leadership. And by the 1920s the College Department proved valuable as Catholic colleges increasingly had to deal with those whom Fox described as "outsiders."

## "Splendid Isolation is Fraught with . . . Embarrassments and Dangers"

In 1900, in the midst of a "spirited discussion," Conaty weighed in with the progressives: "splendid isolation" from the educational currents of the day was "fraught with grave embarrassments and dangers."[18] During its first two decades the College Department operated in *relative* isolation. This is not to suggest that it was moribund or reactionary; the college men and women were certainly aware of the issues of the day. Yet the College Department was primarily *intramural*. This changed. The First World War meant increased involvement with the federal government, while accreditation pressures eroded parochialism. The stakes and consequences for Catholic colleges were tremendous. Amid these changes the College Department's *intermural* role sharpened: it came to represent the community's interests before the government and larger academic community while it helped member institutions negotiate educational challenges.

World War I dissolved Americans' isolationist tendencies, engendered a national sense of the "get together idea and spirit," and led to unprecedented involvement of the federal government in many aspects of American life. The declaration of war mobilized—rhetorically—America's "academic chieftains" who placed the "great army of students and teachers" at the nation's service. But their initial assurances of support assumed a different demeanor in 1918 when the draft age was lowered from twenty-one to eighteen, shrinking enrollment pools. Colleges suddenly became keenly interested in the Student Army Training Corps program whereby the government issued contracts to colleges and universities for the "subsistence, quarter, and military and academic instruction" of aspiring cadet officers.[19] Forty-two of 525 contracts went to Catholic colleges which quickly changed into quasi-military posts. The experience proved an important object lesson. Many Catholic colleges suffered because small enrollments rendered them ineligible to participate in war-time programs. More importantly, in working with government agencies and educational associations, it became clear that the work of the CEA "should be made strictly professional" if Catholic colleges were to be vital players.[20]

American Catholics eagerly supported the War effort. Toward that end, the hierarchy established the National Catholic War Council that coordinated chaplains' work, supported servicemen and their families, and organized Catholic colleges' war-time efforts. Having demonstrated its usefulness, after the armistice the War Council became the National Catholic Welfare Council, complete with a Department of Education. Cognizant of the CEA's work, the NCWC allowed the CEA to function as its Department of Education with an interlocking directorate of officers.[21]

The arrangement struck between the NCWC and CEA raised concerns, especially about "episcopal interference." Some deemed voluntarism, versus canonical status, the key to the Association's success. Yet the need for an official presence in Washington to represent Catholic interests was clear. In the post-War years, the country seemed to be moving toward federalized education, a shift clearly threatening to private and religious schools. Lobbying by the NCWC made clear the value of formalized relations with the hierarchy whereby Catholic educators could speak officially on behalf of their schools.[22]

Concurrently, the College Department entered the accreditation arena. The CEA became a member of the American Council on Education, an umbrella group of higher education organizations. Its formation during the War marked the culmination of an "Age of Standards," a period between 1895 and 1920 when colleges and universities sought improvement through implementation of standards. Accreditation, the "authentication of an educational unit by an external authority as meeting certain standards," put teeth in the process. By 1919 seventy-five organizations were devoted to the cause—including the College Department.[23]

From its inception the ACCUS discussed standards. Conaty wisely arranged for papers on "College Entrance Requirements" and "Requirements for

College Degrees" at the first conference. In the 1910s, the college men discussed "The Standard College" at length, trying to define the boundary between preparatory and collegiate level work. But there was little action during the first dozen years. With little reason to embrace communal norms, many religious orders clung to their own traditions. Many colleges were reluctant to divide their six- and seven-year "colleges" into high schools and colleges. Others resisted measuring the value of education quantitatively. Nonetheless, in 1915 the College Department "unanimously adopted" a "number of conditions . . . essential to the standard college." Modeled after those of their non-Catholic counterparts, their standards included a high school program of sixteen units, a college graduation requirement of 128 semester hours, and minimums pertaining to the number of departments, educational attainments of the faculty, holdings for the library, and resources for the laboratories.[24] Having adopted these standards, the more serious task remained: enforcement.

Enforcing standards entailed development of a plan "broad enough to include every institution that is worthy of the name of College" yet "restrictive enough to exclude those that should not be so designated." Critics considered standards a "great mistake," antithetical to the nature of a *voluntary* association.[25] On the other hand, Burns considered it "imperative," for "[i]f we do not do it, others will do it for us—others who do not sympathize with us and may do us harm." Some Catholic colleges had secured accreditation from agencies and states, yet Catholic colleges generally fared poorly on standards-based lists.[26]

The College Department tried to straddle the tension between inclusiveness and restrictive standards by offering "all possible assistance to institutions that aspire to the rank of a standard college."[27] Meanwhile the College Department published its first list of accredited colleges in 1918, comprised of 14 women's and 38 men's colleges meeting its definition of a "standard college." No doubt, accreditation encouraged Catholic colleges to adopt higher standards. It also resulted in institutional inclusion on other lists; e.g., that of the Middle States Association and the U.S. Bureau of Education. Moreover, the College Department and CEA leadership gained entrée into ACE, giving Catholics "a share in fixing the Standards" and "enhanced . . . stature and prestige of Catholic educators as a group."[28]

The College Department's accreditation system was not perfect; reporting and enforcement proved troublesome for years. But ultimately it helped improve Catholic higher education. In 1923 College Department President Albert Fox, S.J., could report that the "last five years have proved to all of us what can be accomplished when the Catholic colleges get together and work together."[29] Fox's satisfaction with the results of "getting together" (of which he despaired a few years earlier) was justified. But some of the most difficult work lay ahead. Having worked diligently on *collegiate* education for twenty years, the College Department would spend much of the next twenty grappling with *graduate* education. At the heart of their future conversations were the issues of the nature and purpose of higher education and the viability of American Catholic higher education.

## Resetting the Compass

With the nineteenth-century emergence of the high school, the American educational ladder assumed an eight-plus-four-plus-four year pattern. The change proved especially problematic for Catholic men's colleges with highly-structured European-styled programs spanning six or seven years. (Saddled with less tradition, the nascent women's colleges adapted more easily.)[30] The public and the Catholic systems began and ended at different points, creating articulation problems for students moving between systems and enrollment and retention problems for Catholic colleges. New diocesan high schools created a Catholic path to a terminal degree, exacerbating the problem. Ultimately, Catholic educators had to accept the American innovation, but resistance lingered well into the 1910s because the survival of the college often depended on the enrollment of students who tended to be more heavily concentrated in the early years of the program.[31]

Conversations about the "high school problem" became more intense with the creation of the CEA. A year rarely passed without a conference paper on articulation and the educational ladder. Over time the college men reluctantly conceded that the high school was an educational fact of life; even so, in 1911 they voted to keep representatives of the high schools and colleges together within the College Department. In 1918 the College Department actually changed its name to the Department of Colleges and Secondary Schools, though representatives of the two began meeting in separate sections in 1923. The establishment of a separate Department of Secondary Schools in 1929 marked Catholic educators' belated acquiescence to the American educational ladder.

Severing their ties with secondary schools, the college men and women turned their attention toward graduate-level and professional studies. Once almost entirely devoted to preparatory and collegiate work, Catholic higher education enthusiastically expanded its academic repertoire upward, responding to the vocational and professional aspirations of Catholics, accreditation pressures to equip faculty with advanced degrees, and a desire to respond to the needs of the day and contribute to the intellectual life and mission of the Catholic Church.[32]

Burns first broached the issue of graduate studies in 1920 with an address, urging Catholics to recognize the role graduate studies and research played in the "new intellectual order."[33] In 1927, a watershed year, the College Department established a Committee on Graduate Studies. Thereafter the Committee issued reports, and talks on graduate and professional education regularly graced the program, including "How We Can Secure More and Better Students for Our Graduate Schools" (1929) and "The Future of Graduate Work in Our Catholic Women's Colleges" (1930). Indicative of the new direction, in 1935 the College Department changed its name to the College and University Department.

In terms of advanced studies, the College and University Department became an important forum to examine "many problems in that field which we have never considered very carefully"—problems keenly felt in the 1930s. An article in *America* reminded readers that "only a generation ago the list of accredited Catholic colleges could have been written on a calling card. If we are in a strong position today, it may be largely traced to the leadership furnished by the College Department of the N.C.E.A."[34] Indeed, between 1930 and 1938 the percentage of Catholic institutions meeting regional accreditation requirements rose from approximately 40 to 76 percent. Yet the Department's accreditation endeavors could not stave off debacles, especially in graduate and professional studies. Too slow in abandoning secondary-level work, Catholic higher education was too quick in embracing graduate and professional studies. Programs folded; others lost or could not secure accreditation. In 1934 ACE issued a particularly devastating report; among Catholic institutions only CUA and Notre Dame were deemed qualified to offer doctoral degrees.[35]

Challenges confronting Catholic colleges in the 1930s mirrored increasing national dissatisfaction with accreditation; a "mood of counterreformation" set in. The process, its critics complained, relied too heavily on quantitative data that failed to capture the "real worth of colleges." By the end of the 1930s accreditation agencies had retooled themselves, more frequently relying on a college's own institutional goals as benchmarks for evaluation and starting points for recommendations. [36]

Noting that accreditation efforts seemed to be falling into "disfavor," by 1935 two basic questions were on the table: "Whether the College Section . . . should continue its policy of accrediting. . ." and "What shall be the relation to (or the attitude of) the College Section . . . regarding the various other accrediting agencies?"[37] Intense debate resolved in 1938 with two decisions: to abandon the accreditation program begun twenty years prior and to promote "friendly cooperation" with accrediting agencies. The decision stemmed from recognition that the department's process was "too largely imitative of the ordinary procedures of the regional standardization bodies" and relied on quantitative measures failing to promote "educational improvement." Furthermore, the department's tendency toward leniency was, as one commentator put it, "getting us nowhere." But the

College and University Department did not dismiss standards altogether. It made accreditation by an outside agency requisite for full institutional membership. Furthermore, the department refocused its attention on the *Catholic* dimensions of college and university life, developing religious standards for member institutions.[38]

In 1926 Burns wrote, "We have abandoned much of our Catholic tradition and have adopted the ideals of the big secular colleges in almost all matters outside religion." He argued, "we ought to take stock of our situation" and "thresh the matter out." Emerging from a "taken-for-granted" period vis-à-vis religious identity and entering a time of heightened consciousness, his peers needed little encouragement. As Philip Gleason has so ably described, Burns and friends were on the cusp of the Catholic Renaissance, a period between 1920 and 1960 characterized by the belief that Catholicism had much to offer intellectually, aesthetically, morally, and socially to a world gone astray. It was a time of self-confidence, of innocence, of being "so certain and set apart." Such certainty did not, however, translate automatically into self-evident propositions regarding the practice and teaching of Catholicism.[39]

The department spent significant energies considering how religion should be taught. Until the 1920s Catholic colleges did not, as a rule, teach theology (a subject reserved for seminarians). Most undergraduates were taught the tenets of their faith in catechetical sessions outside the formal curriculum, reflecting belief that piety achieved through prayer and moral discipline was more important that "intellectual mastery of doctrine."[40] Beginning in the 1920s, Catholic educators quickly shifted to an academic approach whereby religion achieved curricular prominence. Its growing prestige was mirrored by its frequent appearance as a topic for the department's annual meeting, e.g., "A College Course in Religion" (1927) and "An Argument for Teaching Theology in the Catholic College" (1946).

In the 1940s offering courses in religion and scholastic philosophy became requisites for membership in the College Department. Concerned that a "few of our so-called Catholic colleges" offered "only a minimum of religion courses" and "little or no scholastic philosophy," the secretary of the Department implemented a survey as "some sort of semi-self-educative process" to help colleges stay "on their toes." Without religious standards, he argued, the College Department would devolve into an "Educational Rotary Club with everybody back-patting everybody else and each going its own sweet way." Full membership was eventually limited to institutions requiring eight semester hours in religion and twelve semester hours in philosophy.[41]

Concern for Catholicity extended beyond the curriculum. In the 1940s the department collected information on Mass attendance requirements, chaplain availability, religious clubs, retreats, and "provisions . . . for fostering vocations." In 1952 the committee on membership published a lengthy study on *Catholic Colleges of the United States of America at the Middle of the Twentieth Century,* with information on religion courses, texts, extracurricular affairs, religious discipline, and the number of non-Catholic faculty.[42]   Concern for the extracurricular surfaced at the annual conferences and in the quarterly *College Newsletter* (established 1937) which regularly reported on sodalities, the Catholic Action movement, participation in "present day youth movements," and the Catholicity of library holdings.

## Reorganization

During the 1930s, as it focused on religious identity and institutional quality, the College Department underwent restructuring and established new affiliations. In this, 1934 proved a pivotal year. The Depression made the annual meeting of the membership impossible, but the leadership met. Their substantive decisions marked an increasingly executive orientation within the College Department. Moreover, the establishment of standing committees (educational policy, accreditation, organization, and financing) under the Committee on Committees signaled greater interest in activism and legislation in order to solve the more important problems involved in Catholic college education.

Creation of regional units counterbalanced the move toward a stronger executive. Though some faltered, the establishment of units in the East, Midwest, South, and West in 1935 (with a New England unit added a few years later) breathed new life into the department, with the NCEA secretary general reporting, "it is very apparent that . . . there is really more interest in the Association than there was before." Geographically-proximate meetings bolstered attendance and created additional opportunities for leadership, even among women.[43]

The membership began to meet in sub-groups based on special lines of work. Sessions devoted to the interests of specific audiences came to dominate the annual programs. The days of a few dozen men discussing eight or nine papers were gone. In 1949, for instance, there were sessions on graduate study, the community college, and public relations, and panels for registrars, deans, and teacher educators.

In the 1930s the College Department established stronger ties with other educational associations. The department remained wary of the NCEA, urging Catholics participating in it to a stance of "cautious cooperation." On the other hand, the department developed friendly ties with the Association of American Colleges (established 1915), an association with close ties to the Protestant Council of Church Boards of Education. With some Catholics already active in the AAC, in 1934 the Executive Committee decided to hold its regular winter meeting in conjunction with the AAC annual meeting. The move signaled less defensiveness and greater willingness to engage the larger academic community.[44]

The College Department's collegial overture to the AAC stands in sharp relief to its treatment of sisters and women within the Department. In 1934 the male Executive Committee voted that representatives of women's colleges were to meet separately; they were no longer welcome at the annual meeting. The women's meeting was to be held in the same locale, following the men's meeting, allowing the NCEA's male leadership to attend the men's meeting and oversee the women's. Further, the women were to stay in local convents and hold their meetings in local seminaries. Ostensibly the rationale was to provide women time "to discuss their specific problems and to give full expression to their points of view." Two factors actually drove the decision to exclude the women. Some high-ranking clerics deemed it inappropriate for sisters to stay in hotels. Others resented the sisters' voting power. Were it not for advocacy by some of the men (who feared that the women would form an independent association), women would not have been allowed to participate in the department's newly-established committees. And the women? They were "seething" and in 1936 voted that "the Women's College Section of the College and University Department of the National Catholic Educational Association discontinue its separate meetings for the present."[45]

## THE SECOND WORLD WAR AND THE FEDERAL GOVERNMENT

Like the first great War, World War II impinged on the College and University Department. Originally scheduled for San Francisco, the 1942 meeting was moved to Chicago for fear of "Japanese bombs." And following a directive from the Office of Defense Transportation that "no conventions be held . . . except such that contribute directly to the shortening of the war," the 1943 and 1944 conventions were cancelled.[46]

Meanwhile the leadership worked on critical war-related issues. They exhorted the Catholic educational community to service with articles and addresses, including "The Catholic College and National Defense" (1941) and "The Services That Catholic Women's Colleges are Rendering in the Existent Emergency" (1942). The *College Newsletter* advanced the cause by reporting on particular efforts: Ursuline College in Kentucky introduced a defense course stressing first aid, health, and safety; St. Norbert's College in Wisconsin taught courses in radio and military science and tactics; and Webster College in Missouri developed courses in wartime nutrition and meal planning.[47]

The executive committee also dealt with critical issues facing its constituency. When the draft age was lowered to eighteen, Catholic educators (like non-Catholics) drew up plans to maintain enrollments, including academically accelerated programs. One plan called for a collegiate course comprised of two years of the liberal arts followed by two years of military science.[48] The Department also sought contracts for military training programs. Department representatives convinced the Joint Army-Navy Board to pay clergy-educators involved in military programs "on the same basis as average salaries actually paid to comparable lay teachers in the same institution for similar work." In 1943 the Executive Committee fretted over rumors that the proposed G.I. Bill would provide returning servicemen and women tuition solely for use at public institutions or for vocational programs, a policy that would have weakened Catholic higher education. (Fr. P. A. Roy, S.J., reported hearing that some "persons in Washington" considered liberal arts education a "country club education" for "playboys"; the government had no plans to pay for their "useless and expensive education.") Convinced of the "advisability of doing something to keep before the minds of the American people the essential place of the liberal arts education in our civilization," they convened a committee to issue a statement on the value of liberal arts education in American society.[49] In the war's wake, many in the country were sympathetic to the need for an ennobling education that fostered a sense of human dignity and common culture.

The Department's interest in the liberal arts pre-dated the war. In 1934 it established a committee on the liberal arts, with William McGucken, S.J., voicing a commonly held view that Catholicism in a liberal arts college must be more than "a creed, a code, or a cult." Rather, he proposed, "Catholicism must be seen as a culture."[50] This approach imbued the entire curriculum with religious significance. Unfortunately, the committee collapsed in three years, unable to reach consensus on the role of liberal arts in the Catholic college. Tellingly, that same year University of Chicago President Robert Hutchins chastised Catholic educators at the Midwest Regional Meeting, alleging they had abandoned the best of their tradition, namely the classics, and emulated the worst features of the American educational scene, including vocationalism and athleticism.

The 1930s foreshadowed the 1940s. The war-time committee on the liberal arts also failed to issue a statement; it was "no easy task to make a composite of the disparate points of view on what constitutes liberal education in Catholic colleges." On the other hand, the AAC issued a report on the liberal arts in 1943, and the famous Harvard Report, *General Education in a Free Society*, was published in 1946. Given that the liberal arts were considered the special purview of Catholic higher education, it is ironic that Catholic educators were unable to make a statement on the subject at this historic juncture.[51]

In the post-war years, Catholic educators continued working with government agencies. GIs and their tuition dollars made their way to Catholic campuses, swelling enrollments; federal dollars also made their way to campus, supporting research. Msgr. Frederick Hochwalt (secretary general of the NCEA, 1944-67) convinced his Catholic colleagues of the value of UNESCO, a U.N. organization devoted to rebuilding war-torn Europe. With a resolution from the Department in its support, Hochwalt secured Catholic representation.[52] Hochwalt also sat on the presidential commission that produced *Higher Education for American Democracy* (1947), a milestone report in American higher education. The Catholic community also spoke on the topic, issuing "A Democratic Plan for National Defense" in 1945. Sent to Congress and the Senate, it indicated willingness to serve the country's defense needs, but strong opposition to universal military training in peacetime. In 1946 the Executive Committee described universal military training in wartime as a "necessary evil," justified in peacetime only insofar as its absence jeopardized national security.[53]

Catholics were ambivalent about benefits of war-related programs and the dollars that came with them. Compounding long-time concerns that federal involvement jeopardized private education, the war had taught an important lesson: "Government subsidy during the war . . . determined Government power to direct an institution's program." Yet Catholic educators increasingly turned to external funding to support research during the post-war years. Cognizant that their viability as research institutions required military and industrial contracts, Catholic colleges moved cautiously, enabling some to develop respectable research programs. As one contemporary put it, working with the National Science Foundation was a "venial sin" forgivable "in view of the good which it might do."[54]

## SIGNS OF THE TIMES: GENDER AND RACE

"After considerable needling by interested women's college administrators I succumbed to the temptation to provide a conference for them and their special problems during these days of emergency . . ." So wrote a chagrined Hochwalt in 1951, embarrassed by a fellow priest's criticism that arranging special meetings for women constituted a violation of the by-laws. (Note: no questions surfaced about the by-laws for men's meetings.) The same critic noted that the problems of the women's colleges rarely differed from those of the men's, making separate meetings unnecessary. The "needling" women would have sharply disagreed. While women resented imposed separatism in 1934, they adopted it as a strategy in the 1950s to work out their "peculiar" problems. Indeed, in the early 1950s the women considered the men's colleges one of their most difficult challenges.[55]

Growing enthusiasm for coeducation deeply concerned the women. Opening the doors of men's colleges to women was clearly market-driven; GIs swelling enrollments in the late 1940s had disappeared, while the Korean conflict threatened to deplete their pool of students. In their favor, the sisters had tradition and a papal encyclical spelling out the dangers of coeducation, but the latter held little sway over the men who, in more than a few cases, had been admitting women for many years, primarily to professional, evening, and summer programs. A contemporary recalled a "heated discussion" at the 1953 conference: "practically all the Priests" lined up "favoring Catholic Co-Educational schools and their increase in number" while "all the Sisters did their best to hold their own in favor of the now struggling Women's Colleges." It was, he thought, "an unequal and unfair combat," as the sisters' vigorous defense was tempered by the "deference they felt they should show the clergy." Not surprisingly a paper from the female-dominated Special Committee on the Separate Colleges for Women reported, "It was felt by most present that very few men understand women's education."[56]

Despite second-class treatment, participation in the College Department advanced the cause of sisters and their colleges in significant ways. It provided a platform for notable women religious to exercise national leadership, including Sr. Madeleva Wolff, C.S.C., of St. Mary's College, Indiana, Mother Grace Damman, R.S.C.J., of Manhattanville College, and Sr. Mary Aloysius Molloy, O.S.F., (formerly Mary Molloy) of St. Teresa's College (who served as president of the College and University Department in 1948 and 1949). These women worked within the department to advance the cause of the women's colleges; their efforts, for example, resulted in the establishment of a teacher education section in 1948 and a nursing committee in 1952, important initiatives for the sisters, their students, and their colleges.

More importantly, the Sister Formation Movement—a highly successful venture in religious and intellectual formation to prepare sisters *as sisters* for their work—sprang from seeds planted at annual meetings. Talks by their peers, such as Sr. Madeleva's famous 1949 address, "The Education of Sister Lucy," on the training of a hypothetical devoted young nun, galvanized women religious who started advocating for more thorough, timely, and professional training. Emboldened by a 1951 papal address to sisters worldwide on the need for solid education, women's orders established the Sister Formation Conference to achieve what they claimed as a mandate: better and thorough formation.[57] It was fantastically popular. The sisters developed curricula, training programs, published a popular newsletter, and established colleges for sisters. Attending college and securing a degree in a timely manner became accepted practice among sisters, who had often gone without a degree or spread their studies over exceedingly long periods of time. Although many of the Sister Formation colleges were soon recognized as weak, the push for academic excellence marked a sea-change in convent practice and ethos. The colorful writing of Sr. Bertrande Meyers speaks to the challenges and the significance of the work: 'With string and bow I shall try and kill, or, at least to maim, the fear that Sisters have in common with the American laity . . . The idea that one cannot be "good and holy" and at the same time live on a high intellectual plane is an anathema to my heart.'[58]

Though the Sister Formation Conference still held sessions at the annual meetings through 1974, in 1964 it migrated from the College and University Department to the Conference of Major Superiors of Women, whose leaders felt that the formation of sisters fell under their purview. Concern for the special needs of women's colleges in the department  resurfaced in a new form at that point. A bequest to the NCEA to support the formation of sisters was used to establish the Neylan Fund; it later supported the "Neylan Colleges," a consortium of Catholic colleges founded by women religious.[59]

Racial tensions also surfaced in the 1950s. Journalists described the 1950 NCEA convention in New Orleans as a "distinct event in the fight for better understanding among the races in the United States." The NCEA took up the fight publicly, inviting citizens to a municipally-owned auditorium "to hear and see . . . as Negro children joined their voices with white children to sing the Mass." A bishop from Uganda "occupied a place of honor on the stage" while "Negroes took their places where they desired in the vast congregation." Speakers preached the gospel of integration and members passed a resolution enjoining Catholic colleges to "join in with and possibly spearhead movements to remove inequality of educational opportunities by opening their doors to students regardless of their race, color, or national origin." Days later colleges in Louisville (Nazareth, Ursuline, and Bellarmine) announced they would accept "Negroes as students in all departments." Unfortunately, integrative efforts only created counterpoint to patterns of racial segregation practiced formally and informally at many Catholic colleges. Sadly, enthusiasm evident in 1950 was short-lived; the College and University Department did not thereafter make race an important issue.[60]

## More Signs of the Times: Vatican II

In retrospect, theological progenitors of Vatican Council II (1962-65) become apparent: Karl Rahner, Hans Küng, Yves Congar, and John Courtney Murray laid much of the theological groundwork. Antecedent glimpses of Vatican II-styled ecclesiology surface in the Sister Formation Movement with its emphasis on mission, orientation toward formation, and enthusiasm for ecumenism. But what is evident in retrospect was not clear to contemporaries who experienced the council as an unanticipated, ecclesiastical revolution. The Church, once set so firmly and triumphantly over and against  the world, now embraced the modern world with a commitment to service and an uncharacteristic openness.

In March of 1964, as the revolutionary nature of Vatican II captured Catholics' attention, the College and University Department took up a series of critical questions:  "What specific responses must American Catholic education at all levels make to the Age of Vatican II?  How can our schools, colleges, and seminaries at all levels serve as more adequate instruments for the communication and interpretation of the spirit and decrees of the council?[61]  Catholic educators were, in these early days, clearly committed to advancing the renewal of the Church at large through the service of their colleges and universities.  But that commitment to a renewed vision of the Church was immediately overshadowed by a more fundamental project: a renewed vision of the Catholic university.  The issue provoked deep conversation about what it meant to be a Catholic university in the twentieth century.

With the council's seminal document "The Church in the Modern World" setting the tone, Catholic educators internationally looked to develop a statement on the Catholic university in the modern world.  Two documents from this period proved critical to American Catholic higher education.  In advance of a meeting of the International Federation of Catholic Universities (IFCU), in 1967 Notre Dame president and IFCU leader Rev. Theodore Hesburgh, C.S.C., convened twenty-six leading Catholics to draft a position paper on "The Nature of the Catholic University."  Their work culminated in a "symbolic manifesto," known as the Land O'Lakes Statement, that opened with a revolutionary assertion: "To perform its teaching and research functions effectively the Catholic university must have true autonomy and academic freedom in the face of authority of whatever kind, lay or clerical, external to the academic community itself."  In 1972, the work of the IFCU resulted in "The Catholic University in the Modern World," spelling out the necessity of institutional autonomy and academic freedom: "A university can render its own specific service to the community only if it is able to follow the imperatives which flow from its very nature, primary among which is the pursuit and transmission of truth.  From this flows its autonomy, its freedom in teaching and research. . . . Any limitation imposed on it which would clash with this unconditioned attitude for pursuing truth would be intolerable and contrary to the very nature of the university."[62]

Catholic educators had clearly embraced the professional and intellectual norms of the larger academic community.  Vatican II, with its openness to the modern world, provided the immediate setting, but the Land O'Lakes statement and "The Catholic University in the Modern World" must be understood in light of conversations about academic excellence dating from the mid-1950s.  Msgr. John Tracy Ellis fired the first salvo in his 1955 address, "American Catholics and the Intellectual Life," wherein he faulted American Catholics for their failure to make a significant contribution to matters intellectual. It fostered resolve among many Catholic educators to improve academic standards and strive toward excellence.[63]

The confident tone of the Land O'Lakes statement and "The Catholic University in the Modern World" is thrown into relief by the records of conversations within the College and University Department. The Land O'Lakes statement defined a Catholic university as a "community of learners or a community of scholars" in which "Catholicism is perceptibly present and effectively operative." Yet as early as 1962 members of the College Department wondered, "How Catholic are our schools? Is the spirit of secularism infiltrating our schools . . . under the guise of emphasis on 'intellectual development?'" Though both documents claimed autonomy and academic freedom as conditions making service to the Church and the world possible, some—including Vatican officials—found such claims problematic insofar as they seemed to undermine the Church's role as arbiter of orthodoxy.[64]

In 1969, the executive secretary of the College and University Department wrote, ". . . Catholic higher education lives in two worlds: the world of the Catholic Church/community and the world of American higher education." After Vatican II, the College and University Department (later as the ACCU) continued the work undertaken seven decades previous on behalf of its constituency. It served as the public, corporate face of Catholic higher education within American politics, the academy, and the Church. Increasingly the College and University Department/ACCU negotiated the competing, sometimes contradictory demands arising from participation in these three contexts. If "splendid isolation" was, as Conaty claimed, "fraught with . . . embarrassment and dangers," being a Catholic university in the modern world was fraught with critical challenges. Financial viability, academic integrity, and religious identity were all at stake.[65]

## The Juridical Matters

Federal aid played an immense role in American higher education after World War II. The GI Bill, research grants, student aid, and monies for facilities propelled phenomenal growth. But federal aid also made American higher education dependent upon federal support. For some institutions, it determined institutional prestige or survival.

In the 1950s and 1960s Catholic educators adopted a new tactic: historically opposed to federal aid, Catholic educators now sought it, provided funds came with few strings. They argued that Catholic schools and colleges served the public good and should, therefore, be eligible for financial aid to achieve goals not linked to the religious mission of their institutions. In 1961, for instance, Msgr. Hochwalt vocally argued that the 1958 National Defense Education Act should be amended to make private schools eligible for loans and "the same benefits of equipment and teaching materials in science, mathematics, languages and other subjects deemed critical to the national defense by Congress."[66]

Securing federal aid strengthened Catholic higher education in the 1960s. But it created legal quagmires and thus a new role for the College and University Department: providing legal assistance.[67]  They provided advice to Catholic colleges and advocated for them before the courts and regulatory agencies.  The most valuable legal work involved a case in Connecticut with critical implications: four Catholic colleges faced the prospect of losing funds granted under the 1963 Higher Education Facilities Act if plaintiffs could prove that funding church-related colleges violated the First Amendment principle of separation of church and state. The College Department came to their aid, garnering assistance from the AAC and ACE who filed *amicus curiae* briefs on their behalf. The department also solicited funds from Catholic colleges and the hierarchy to help the colleges in question defray daunting legal fees. The case was resolved in 1971 when the Supreme Court narrowly ruled in favor of the Catholic colleges' position in *Tilton v. Richardson.*

During this period an important legal principle emerged: church-related colleges were eligible for federal funds provided they were not "pervasively sectarian." To appear less sectarian and acting in the spirit of Vatican II, in the 1960s and 70s Catholic colleges shifted from boards of trustees mainly comprised of clergy or religious, to boards largely comprised of lay persons. Again the College Department provided assistance through years of committee work on the complex legal issues surrounding ownership of Catholic colleges.  Most notably, the College and University Department asked Msgr. John McGrath, a canon lawyer, to report on the subject. His work, known as the McGrath thesis, was not without critics; nonetheless, it became the generally accepted justification for the transfer of ownership and governance from religious communities to predominately lay boards of trustees.[68]

Academic freedom also emerged as a central concern in the 1960s, most immediately in terms of "pervasive sectarianism," and more broadly, as Catholic educators wrestled with tensions between academic freedom and the Church's magisterium.  Gleason is correct:  until the 60s, "academic freedom had never been a major concern for Catholic educators." Not so thereafter.[69] In 1963 CUA barred theologian Hans Küng, with three others, from speaking on grounds of liberalism; the ban rendered him a celebrity at other colleges and the NCEA convention.  In 1965 St. John's University in New York summarily dismissed thirty-one faculty members without due process, almost prompting the AAUP "to invent a supergrade of censure." Months later a handful of faculty at the University of Dayton faced allegations of heresy leveled by a few conservative faculty members; the local archbishop's involvement in the matter raised thorny academic freedom issues. Soon after, Rev. Charles Curran faced his first employment challenge at CUA when, over the unanimous faculty recommendation for promotion and tenure, trustees voted to dismiss him. Amid these crises the College and University Department established a Committee on Academic Freedom in 1966. Two years later, after the Land O'Lakes Statement, the Executive Committee passed a motion recommending that "each member institution include the AAUP 1940 Statement on Academic Freedom and Tenure in its faculty handbook" and "establish and publish the mechanism and procedures by which claims of violations of academic freedom are to be studied and adjudicated."[70]

Successful resolution of the court cases involving federal aid and eventual adoption of academic freedom as a norm made Catholic higher education financially and academically viable. But juridical concerns were far from resolved. The most consuming question lay ahead: what makes a Catholic college or university a *Catholic* institution? Given the revolutionary nature of Vatican Council II, Catholic colleges and universities understandably wrestled with the issue. Not surprisingly, the executive director of the College Department described his work in 1968 as a "venture into troubled seas." But few could have imagined how troubled those seas would be. Nor could they have foreseen that the issue of religious identity would dominate Catholic higher education for thirty-plus years and prove immensely problematic insofar as an undesirable juridical resolution might risk federal funds, academic integrity, and ability to "fulfill the mission" of Catholic higher education.[71]

As noted by Alice Gallin, O.S.U., (executive director of the ACCU, 1980-93), conversations about religious identity in Catholic higher education after Vatican II era fall into four sets. As discussed above, the IFCU was at the center of conversations (1965-72) about the nature of Catholic higher education culminating in "The Catholic University in the Modern World." This document precipitated the second set of conversations (1972-80). The Sacred Congregation for Education in Rome approved "The Catholic University in the Modern World," with reservations, claiming it "needed improvement," relative to affirmation and monitoring of Catholic identity by colleges. The third set of conversations (1977-83) preceded the publication of the revised Code of Canon Law; it was of special interest to American educators concerned that Rome would expand the scope of canon law to Catholic colleges and universities, including those operating in the U.S. under charters granted by civil authorities. The fourth set of conversations (1985-90) preceded promulgation of John Paul II's letter on

Catholic higher education, *Ex Corde Ecclesiae*.[72] To Gallin's list, a fifth set of conversations (1991) is added: discussions stemming from Rome's directions that norms for implementation of *Ex Corde* and the new code of canon law (including canons 810 and 812 dealing with episcopal appointment and oversight of theologians) be developed within national conferences to fit local circumstances.

ACCU's role in these conversations deserves more attention than the summary provided here. By 1974, as the conversations became more formal and official, ACCU surfaced as the recognized representative of 220-plus institutions. Because the U.S. has far more Catholic colleges than any other country, the ACCU became an important voice in the dialogues. Throughout the ACCU sought to advance two convictions: Catholic colleges in the U.S. were and wished to remain Catholic institutions. Second, the type of juridical norms proposed by Rome endangered American Catholic higher education, particularly as such norms might render Catholic institutions ineligible for federal funds and undercut Catholic higher education's reputation in the larger academic community vis-à-vis the issue of academic freedom.

Highlights of the multi-faceted dialogue include the establishment of the Bishops and Presidents Committee (1974), with members appointed by the National Catholic Conference of Catholic Bishops and the ACCU. Described as the "first instance in the history of the U.S." that the hierarchy and colleges had "established a structured relationship," it became a valued, sympathetic one.[73] Responding to Rome's concerns about "The Catholic University in the Modern World," in 1976 the Association issued "Relations of American Catholic Colleges and Universities with the Church." The ACCU solicited criticism of early drafts of the new Code of Canon Law by canonists, which it then forwarded to Rome. In 1986 Gallin synthesized the responses of the college presidents to the first draft of what became known as *Ex Corde* to forward to Rome, while the ACCU Board submitted its own response. In 1989 it assumed responsibility for naming eighteen delegates to an international gathering in Rome convened in advance of the promulgation of *Ex Corde*. American educators' response to *Ex Corde Ecclesiae* were generally positive; they were both pleased and relieved that its approach was non-juridical.

Since the publication of *Ex Corde*, representatives of the ACCU have worked with the U.S. bishops to create a set of norms for implementation in the U.S. The first set of proposals, approved in 1996 by the U.S. bishops by a vote of 224-6 (claimed to be the largest voting margin ever recorded in that episcopal conference),[74] were deemed unsatisfactory by Rome and returned for revisions. A second set, more juridical in tone, were subsequently developed; these were approved by Rome and the U.S. bishops.

## Where Catholicism is Perceptibly Present and Effectively Operative

Promulgation of *Ex Corde Ecclesiae* and the revised Code of Canon Law provoked serious concerns, but they also fostered fruitful dialogue about the religious character of Catholic colleges and universities, in the places where, in the words of the Land O'Lakes Statement, Catholicism is "perceptibly present and effectively operative." Since 1990 the ACCU's "most important on-going service" to its membership has been "providing opportunities for collective dialogue." But the ACCU's role in fostering discussion during this time of soul-searching was preceded by a period of soul-searching within the association about its purpose, relationships with the NCEA and other educational associations, even its existence. Greater autonomy and redefined relationships resulted.

In the early 1970s a question arose: what was the purpose of the College and University Department? Given the existence of the AAC and the National Association of Independent Colleges and Universities, was a specifically *Catholic* higher education association warranted? Should the department join one of these organizations as a section? (A "marriage proposal" from the AAC partly prompted the discussion.)[75] Given that much of the department's energies were spent on issues common to other private colleges and universities, the issue warranted serious attention. Ultimately the department resolved in favor of its own ongoing existence, its efforts directed toward matters pertaining to Catholic colleges and universities as *Catholic* institutions. With *Ex Corde* on the horizon, the Department's agenda along these lines would be full for years to come.

But continued existence did not mean business as usual. In 1966 the Department urged the NCEA to "re-examine itself in the spirit of Vatican II." The result was a division of the NCEA into two divisions: Fundamental Education and Higher Education. The organizational emphasis on *higher* education foreshadowed the future. Wishing to operate as a higher education association among other such associations, the Department sought a significant degree of independence within the larger NCEA organization. By 1978, the College and University Department had a new name: The Association of Catholic Colleges and Universities. While continuing as a department of NCEA, it changed the description of its elected leadership from that of an executive committee to a governing board. Although ACCU operated with a greater degree of autonomy than other departments of NCEA, the elected leadership periodically raised the issue of whether or not ACCU would be better served if it established itself an independent organization. Here, concern about federal legislation and various court cases played a role. Catholic K-12 education was considered sectarian and thus ineligible for government funds, while Catholic higher education was deemed less sectarian and was, therefore, eligible for the same. Organizational separatism was adopted, in part, to reinforce the distinction. In 1999-2000, with approval from the NCEA Board of Directors, ACCU established itself as an independent association with separate incorporation and affiliate membership in NCEA.[76]

While the ACCU tended to ongoing concerns such as federal regulation, it marshaled its efforts around religious concerns and endeavors. Issues of justice and peace surfaced around 1975 as a serious concern, with committee work and conferences devoted to the topic in the following years. Committees also addressed student life, taking up, for instance, campus ministry and some of the more difficult aspects of student affairs. The association disseminated research on these and other topics in its journal, *Current Issues in Catholic Higher Education* (1980-). In 1982 the Association established the Hesburgh Award to recognize leaders in Catholic education and the Presidents Award in 1994 to honor benefactors of American Catholic higher education.

The ACCU primarily serves college presidents and senior administrators, but occasionally assists others laboring in the field of Catholic higher education. It has held programs for trustees, workshops for faculty, and co-sponsored an institute at John Carroll University for student affairs professionals who work at Catholic colleges. During a 1995 conference, "Catholic Higher Education: Practice and Promise" (co-sponsored by the University of St. Thomas) presidents, administrators, faculty and staff socialized, prayed, and attended presentations on Catholic intellectual life, models of faculty engagement, student affairs and Catholic identity, the importance of the liberal arts tradition, community service, and campus ministry.

## Conclusion

Over one hundred years ago Msgr. Thomas Conaty convened representatives of the country's Catholic colleges to create an association that would assist and improve Catholic higher education. Like other associations, its efficacy was tempered by its *voluntary* nature; as a Catholic association, its efforts were further tempered by scores of religious orders with their own traditions and constituencies. Nonetheless, Catholic higher education benefited from the Association. It became the single most important forum in which Catholic educators discussed common concerns and, on occasion, hammered out solutions. The association also exposed members to a greater diversity of educational philosophies and academic practices, an important service to those in religious life.

The ACCU became the corporate face of Catholic higher education. Within the boundaries of religious communities, colleges enjoyed autonomy; Catholic colleges, like others in the United States, were fiercely independent. Yet through participation, members ceded to the association the right to represent their interests as a group. It has provided important assistance insofar as the association has mediated between the Catholic higher education and the government, the academy, and the Church. Today the association stands on the shoulders of those who, like Conaty, sought to improve, protect, and advance American Catholic higher education. It faces the twenty-first century with resolve.

## Endnotes

[1] A longer version of this paper appeared in *Current Issues in Catholic Higher Education* 19 (1999): 3-46.

[2] Conaty's invitational query has not been located; information about it is gleaned from the minutes of the January 2, 1899 meeting of the consultors of St. Louis University, who met in special session to discuss his proposal (St. Louis University Archives). Rector's Report to the Senate, January 10, 1899 and March 14, 1899 (Archives of the Catholic University of America [henceforth, ACUA]). Unless otherwise indicated, all primary source materials are located in the NCEA files located at Catholic University of America. The NCEA materials are uncataloged; they will, therefore, be cited by box number and file name when possible. The author thanks the archivists of St. Louis University, the University of Notre Dame, and Georgetown University their assistance. Special thanks is forwarded to the staff of Department of Archives and Manuscripts at Catholic University of America. The author also acknowledges the contributions of doctoral students who participated in a seminar on the history of Catholic higher education at Boston College who helped with the preparation of this paper: Rev. John Chen, Andrew Simmons, Karen Pellegrino, and Peter Harrington. Thanks, too, to Philip Gleason, Mary Oates, and Jack Augenstein who offered thoughtful comments on this paper.

[3] "Catholic Education," *Pittsburgh Catholic*, April 19, 1899 (Georgetown University Archives, CEA, box 5, folder 102); *Proceedings of the First Annual Meeting of the Association of Catholic Colleges and Universities of the United States* (Washington, DC: Catholic University Press, 1899), 200. James Howard Plough, "Catholic Colleges and the Catholic Educational Association: The Foundation and Early Years of the CEA, 1899-1919" (Ph.D. diss., Univ. of Notre Dame, 1967), 75-80; Peter E. Hogan, *The Catholic University of America, 1896-1903: The Rectorship of Thomas J. Conaty* (Washington, DC: Catholic University of America Press, 1949), 69-72.

[4] Philip Gleason, *Contending with Modernity: Catholic Higher Education in the Twentieth Century* (New York: Oxford University Press, 1995), 3; J. Havens Richards to Conaty, August 5, 1897 (ACUA, rector files, box 3, folder 9). Also see Edward J. Power, *A History of Catholic Higher Education in the United States* (Milwaukee: The Bruce Publishing Company, 1958), and *Catholic Higher Education in America: A History* (New York: Appleton-Century, 1972).

[5] This periodization mirrors that found in Gleason's *Contending with Modernity*. The three-fold contexts construct is drawn from the work of David O'Brien. The author is grateful for his participation in a seminar held at Boston College for those working on the history of the ACCU.

[6] "Shall We Have a University," *American Catholic Quarterly Review* (April, 1876): 230-53; John Tracy Ellis, *The Formative Years of the Catholic University of America* (Washington, DC: The American Catholic Historical Association, Catholic University Press, 1946); C. Joseph Nuesse, *The Catholic University of America: A Centennial History* (Washington, DC: The Catholic University of America Press, 1990), 3-64; *An Appeal to the Catholics of the United States on Behalf of the University Which the Late Council of Baltimore Resolved to Create* (New York: 1885), 5, cited in Plough, "Catholic Colleges," 56. The final quote is from a draft of a letter from Conaty to Leo XIII, ca. 1900 (rector files, box 3, folder 10, Roman Correspondence, 1896-1901 ACUA).

[7] Rector's Report to the Faculty Senate, April 7, 1897, June 3, 1897, October 18, 1897 and January 10, 1899; The Ninth Annual Report of the Rector, 1898 (ACUA, rector files). "The Association of Catholic Colleges," *Catholic University Bulletin* 5 (1899): 357.

[8] Minutes of St. Louis University consultors, *op. cit.*; John A. Conway, "Conference of Catholic Colleges," *Woodstock Letters* 36 (1907): 257-58.

[9] Plough, "Catholic Colleges," 82.

[10] The number of delegates is drawn from the *Proceedings* of the first five conferences, which list the participants. Conway, "Conference," 259; Gleason, *Contending with Modernity*, 46.

[11] James Burns to Francis Howard, August 5, 1905. Archives of the University of Notre Dame [henceforth AUND], CBUR, Msgr. Howard), Archbishop Wants Better Colleges," *New York Times*, July 12, 1905 (box 75).

[12] Burns to Howard, May 7, 1906 (AUND, CBUR, Msgr. Howard).

[13] John Farrell, "The Catholic Chaplain at the Secular University," *The Catholic Educational Association: Report of the Proceedings and Addresses of the Fourth Annual Meeting* (Columbus, OH: published by the Association, 1907): 150-80; "Report on the Statistics of Catholic Colleges of the United States" (Columbus, OH: CEA, 1908), (box 3, Secret Vatican Archives 105/1). Records labeled "Secret Vatican Archives" consist of photocopies of documents from Rome available at the ACUA. Burns to Howard, February 29, 1908, (AUND, CBUR, Howard, Rev. Francis); John A. Conway to Howard, March 15, 1908 (AUND, CBUR, Msgr. Howard).

[14] Denis O'Connell to Howard, January 26, 1907 (box 2, O'Connell); "Memorial on Catholic College Education Presented by the Standing Committee of the Catholic Colleges of the United States to the Archbishops of the United States, April 11, 1907" (box three, Secret Vatican Archives, 105/1). Gleason, *Contending with Modernity*, 22-25; Plough, 216-35, 252-56; John Whitney Evans, *The Newman Movement: Roman Catholics in American Higher Education, 1883-1971* (Notre Dame: University of Notre Dame Press, 1980), 32-36.

[15] Howard to John O'Mahoney, July 25, 1911 (box 2, O'Mahoney).

[16] On the "feminine element," Francis X. Heiermann to Howard, April 14, 1911, cited in Plough, 287-88. Papers delivered by sisters are as follows: in 1910, "A Beginner's Year in French," A Sister of St. Joseph, "Should Another Modern Language Be Substituted for French or German in Our School Curriculum?," A Sister of St. Joseph; "The Claims of Greek to a Place in the College Course," Sister Marie José, "Outline of a Course in French," A Sister of St. Joseph, "The Influence and the Teaching of French in the High Classes," A Sister of Holy Cross; in 1916, "How

Much and How Shall We Study the History of Literature with the Author," Mary Aloysia Molloy. Mary Molloy to Howard, March 2, March 13, and April 26, 1915 (box 2, Mary Molloy).

[17]

[18] Albert Fox to Howard, December 28, 1917 (box 1, Fox).

Conaty, in discussion following James Burns, "The Elective System," *Report of the Second Annual Conference of the Association of Catholic Colleges and Universities* (Washington, DC: Catholic University Press, 1900): 60, 59.

[19] David M. Kennedy, *Over Here: The First World War and American Society* (New York: Oxford University Press, 1980), 57-59; Hawkins, *Banding Together,* 141; John S. Brubacher and Willis Rudy, *Higher Education in Transition: A History of American Colleges and Universities,* 4th ed. (1958; New Brunswick: Transaction Publishers, 1997), 225.

[20] Gleason, *Contending with Modernity,* 72-78; Minutes of the Advisory Committee of the CEA, February 23, 1920 (ACUA, Pace papers, cited in Gleason, *Contending,* 78).

[21] Douglas J. Slawson, *The Foundation and First Decade of the National Catholic Welfare Council* (Washington, DC: The Catholic University of America Press, 1992); Gleason, *Contending with Modernity,* 63-69; Plough, 490-91.

[22] O'Connell to Howard, June 11, 1907 (box 2, O'Connell); Dennis J. Dougherty to Howard, July 3, 1917 (box 1, Dougherty); Louis Walsh to Howard, March 19, 1918 and June 12, 1918 (box 3, Walsh); Gleason, *Contending,* 66-69.

[23] Edward Pace to Howard, January 3, 1921 (box 2, Pace); Hawkins, 78, 90.

[24] Circular letter from Matthew Schumacher to College Presidents, May 9, 1916 (AUND, CBUR, Howard, Rev. Francis). Minutes, *Catholic Educational Association Bulletin* [henceforth *CEAB* or *NCEAB*] (1915): 159.

[25] O'Mahoney to Howard, September 27, 1916 (box 2, O'Mahoney); R. H. Tierney (editor of *America*) to Howard, July 3, 1916 (box 2, Tierney).

[26] Schumacher to College Presidents, *op. cit.*; Burns to Howard, March 10, 1917 (AUND, CBUR, Msgr. Howard); Howard to Shahan, June 30, 1917 (box 2, Burns). One gets a taste for the concern of Catholic educators in the following excerpt of a letter from H. S. Spalding, SJ to Howard, March 20, 1914 (box 2, Spalding). "As I informed you in my last letter the Council of the Amer. Medical Association is doing all it can to injure us. Ohio is one of to the few states where they can injure us, and I am anxious to prevent the Ohio State Board from taking any action against us. . . I would not ask you to put yourself to too much trouble. But if you could learn from some friendly doctor who are [sic] on the board you might be able to put in a good word for us. . . . It would be impossible to state all the circumstaces [sic] of this attack You can simply say that . . . the Ohio Medical Board is going to consider whether it will give Loyola <u>Full recognition</u> and we are most anxious to have the vote in our favor."

[27] Minutes, *CEAB* (1918), 125.

[28] Minutes, *CEAB* (1918), 133-35. Circular letters from Fox to college presidents, May 5, 1922 (AUND, CBUR, Howard, Rev. Francis) and May 1, 1923 (box 2, circulars). Gleason, *Contending,* 70-71.

[29] Fox to Presidents of Colleges and Directors of Secondary Schools, May 1, 1923 (box 1, circulars).

[30] William J. Reese, *The Origins of the American High School* (New Haven, CT: Yale

[31] University Press, 1995).
O'Mahoney to Howard, July 21, 1911 (box 2, O'Mahoney). O'Mahoney addressed one of his most pressing concerns: "The first I think is the classification of our institutions which are colleges and which claim to be colleges. We are afraid of this question because there are so many colleges that give a course scarcely better than that of an ordinary High School. I received a catalogue a few days ago from an institution which passes as a college. Out of a large enrollment it had less than fifty taking the classical course and these were scattered over five Latin Classes with two students in the fifth year."

[32] Gleason, *Contending with Modernity,* 221, 175.

[33] Burns, quoted in Gleason, *Contending with Modernity,* 171.

[34] Johnson to Howard, December 4, 1929 (box 3, Howard 1929-1933). Also see *America* (May 21, 1932): 164.

[35] Gleason, *Contending with Modernity,* 182, 184-88, 198-200; William P. Leahy, *Adapting to America: Catholics, Jesuits, and Higher Education in the Twentieth Century* (Washington, DC: Georgetown University Press, 1991): 36-48; Hawkins, *Banding Together,* 91; Lester F. Goodchild, "The Turning Point in American Jesuit Higher Education: The Standardization Controversy between the Jesuits and the North Central Association, 1915-1940," *History of Higher Education Annual* 6 (1986), reprinted in *The History of Higher Education,* 2nd ed., ASHE Reader Series, Lester F. Goodchild and Harold S. Wechsler, eds. (Needham Heights, MA: Simon & Schuster Custom Publishing, 1997): 528-50.

[36] Hawkins, *Banding Together,* 93, 95.

[37] Howard to Johnson, February 24, 1930 (box 3, Howard 1929-1933). "Report of the Committee on College Accreditation," *NCEAB* (1935), 75.

[38] "Report of the Committee on Educational Problems," *NCEAB* (1939), 145.

[39] Burns to Howard, February 10, 1926 (AUND, CBUR, Msgr. Howard). Gleason, *Contending with Modernity,* 105-166; William M. Halsey, *The Survival of American Innocence: Catholicism in an Era of Disillusionment, 1920-1940* (Notre Dame: University of Notre Dame Press, 1980); James Hennesey, "So Certain and Set Apart," in *American Catholics: A History of the Roman Catholic Community in the United States* (New York: Oxford University Press, 1981).

[40] Gleason, *Contending with Modernity,* 142. Also see Gleason's essay, "Catholic Higher Education as Historical Context for Theological Education," and other related topics in *Theological Education in the Catholic Tradition,* Patrick W. Carey and Earl C. Muller, eds. (New York: Crossroad Publishing Company, 1997).

[41] Anselm Keefe to Johnson, December 2, 1940; Keefe to John Hagan, April 17, 1940 (box 3, Hagen). For a sample membership form, see *NCEAB* 43 (August, 1946): 164-67.

[42] *NCEAB* 43 (August, 1946): 164-67; James F. Whelan, *Catholic Colleges of the United States of America at the Middle of the Twentieth Century* (New Orleans: Loyola University, 1952), 132.

[43] Johnson to John B. Peterson, April 1, 1939 (box 4, Peterson); *NCEAB* (1941): 80.

[44] Frederick Hochwalt to William A. Scully, chair of NCWC, October 3, 1949 (AUND, CHOC, Relations with NEA); Johnson to Howard, August 23, 1934 (box 3, Howard 1934-38). On the AAC, see Hawkins, especially at pp. 16-20.

[45] NCWC News Service, June 11, 1934 (box 75); Johnson to Howard, August 22, 1934

(box 3, Howard 1934-38); *NCEAB* (1936): 107.     Gleason, *Contending with Modernity,* 188-190.

46

W. Union Telegram, January 13, 1943 (box 3, Circulars, Executive Board 1930-44).

47

"Defense Courses," *College Newsletter* 5 (March 1942): 2.

48

"Report of Progress of The National Catholic Educational Association Committee on The Reorganization of the School System" (Washington, DC: Office of the Secretary General, 1943). Also see Gleason, *Contending with Modernity,* 211-15.

49

Johnson to Cunningham, October 26, 1942 (box 3, committee on reorganization).

50

*NCEAB* 32 (November, 1935): 70-71.

51

Julius Haun to Hochwalt, April 29, 1946 (box 8, committee on the liberal arts); Hochwalt to Samuel K. Wilson, January 30, 1945 (box 7 ). William Cunningham, CSC eventually published some of the work of the committee on liberal arts in *General Education and the Liberal Arts College* (St. Louis: B. Herder, 1953).

52

Hochwalt to College Presidents and Executive Board, October 26, 1945 (box 7, circulars-general); *NCEAB* (1946), 138-39. Also see Hochwalt to executive board, February 15, 1946 (box 7, circulars, general).

53

Hochwalt to Congressmen and Senators and Executive Board, September 14, 1945 (box 7, circulars—national defense); Statement of the college and university department committee, January 9, 1946  (box 5, "c" miscellaneous).

54

Hochwalt to Roy, July 12, 1944 and July 28, 1944 (box 7, circulars, federal aid, 1944-49); Gleason, *Contending with Modernity,* 217.

55

Hochwalt to Bill Dunne, March 15, 1951, March 13, 1951; Meade to Hochwalt, March 13, 1951  (box 7, committee on coeducation).

56

Thomas Bolduc to Hochwalt, January 9, 1954 (box 5, B-3);  "Report of Meeting of the Special Committee on the Separate Colleges for Women, Washington, D.C., January 7, 1951" (box 7, committee on coeducation).   Leahy, *Adapting to America,* 67-92.

57

Sr. Bertrande  Meyers to Hochwalt, December 4, 1959 (box 5, B-2); Sister Madeleva's talk about Sr. Lucy was published as "The Education of Our Young Religious Teachers," *NCEAB* 46 (August 1949): 253-56."   On the history of the Sister Formation Movement, see Marjorie Noterman Beane, *From Framework to Freedom: A History of the Sister Formation Conference* (New York: University Press of America, 1993).

58

Sr. Annette to Hochwalt, August 30, 1961 (box 17, sister formation [5]); Sr. Bertrande to Hochwalt, March 3, 1960 (box 5, B-2).

59

There is extensive documentation on the Sister Formation Conference in the NCEA files at ACUA.  For the events described here, see materials from Executive Committee minutes, April 1957, page 7 (box 54).  Also see correspondence dated October 28, 1961, October 18, 1963, March 20, 1964, March 21, 1964, September 25, 1964, November 6, 1974 (box 17, sister formation).

60

NCWC News Service press release, April 17, 1950; *NCEAB* (1950), 145.  Equivocal feelings on race are evident in minutes of the Program and Plans Committee minutes: "What definite action (if there is to be any) should be taken in our schools on all levels with respect to the race problem?"  (October 15, 1963).

61

Suggested Items for Problems and Plans Committee Agenda, March 10, 1964 (box 8, Problems and Plans, agendas, 1949-63).

62

Gleason, *Contending with Modernity,* 317.  The "Land O'Lakes Statement: The

Nature of a Contemporary Catholic University," and "The Church in the Modern World," can be found in Alice Gallin, ed., *American Catholic Higher Education: Essential Documents, 1967-1990* (Notre Dame: University of Notre Dame Press, 1992), and Joseph M. O'Keefe, ed., *Catholic Higher Education at the Turn of the New Century* (Boston: published for the Center for International Higher Education at Boston College by Garland Publishing, 1997).

63 John Tracy Ellis, "American Catholics and the Intellectual Life," *Thought* 30 (Autumn 1955): 351-88.

64 "Land O'Lakes Statement," in Gallin, 7. Problems and Plans Committee, March 13, 1962 (box 8, problems and plans).

65 Friedman to Dr. Richard A. Matre, February 24, 1969 (box 61, executive committee [1]).

66 NCWC News Service, "Bishops' Spokesman Asks End to NDEA 'Inequities,' Suggests Long-term Building Loans for Private Schools," June 5, 1961 (box 20, U.S. Office of Education/National Defense Act [1]).

67 For an excellent review of legal issues and the ACCU, see Peter J. Harrington, "Civil and Canon Law Issues Affecting American Catholic Higher Education 1948-1998: An Overview and the ACCU Perspective," *The Journal of College and University Law* 26 (1999): 67-105.

68 On the transition to lay boards of trustees, see Alice Gallin, *Independence and a New Partnership in Catholic Higher Education* (Notre Dame: University of Notre Dame Press, 1996).

69 Gleason, *Contending with Modernity*, 309.

70 Friedman to presidents, October 24, 1968. In response to the academic freedom debacles in Catholic universities, in 1967 the AAUP issued a statement, "Academic Freedom and Tenure in Church-Related Colleges and Universities," *AAUP Bulletin* 53 (winter 1967): 570-71.

71 "Statement of Presidents of Leading Catholic Universities of North America on the Schema for the Proposed Document on the Catholic University" (June 1986), in Gallin, 279.

72 Gallin, *American Catholic Higher Education.*

73 "Bishops Set Up Group for Dialogue with Colleges," NC News Service, December 20, 1974 (box 59, Bishops and Presidents 1974 [1]).

74 "The State of the *Ex Corde Ecclesiae* Implementation Process," *Update: Association of Catholic Colleges and Universities* 24 (July/August 1997): 1.

75 Memo to the executive committee from Rev. Msgr. John F. Murphy, February 26, 1975 (box 64, Executive Committee Memos ).

76 Federal legislation and various court cases played a role in the separation. Catholic K-12 education was considered more sectarian and thus ineligible for funds, while Catholic higher education was deemed less sectarian and was therefore eligible for the same. Organizational separatism was adopted, in part, to reinforce the distinction. Interview with Jeanne Knoerle, SP, Indianapolis, IN, April 14, 1998.

## CHAPTER 4

# LEADERSHIP OF WOMEN RELIGIOUS

*Karen M. Kennelly, CSJ*

T he leadership of women religious has intertwined itself with the NCEA from its inception. Congregations of women laid the groundwork for the association in the nineteenth century by taking the lead in establishing Catholic schools in every region of the country, schools that multiplied and achieved high standards of quality in the twentieth century largely owing to the efforts of women's congregations. Leadership exercised by individual women religious, within the association but even more conspicuously outside its formal structure, enhanced the reputation of Catholic education and, with it, the ability of the NCEA to fulfill its mission.

## PIONEER LEADERSHIP
Religious congregations of women began contributing to the formation of the Catholic school system in the United States when nine Ursuline nuns came to French colonial New Orleans in 1727.[1] They set a pattern for later congregations by opening an academy for girls, a free school for Blacks and Indians, and an orphanage. Prior to American Independence, hostility toward Catholics and restrictive laws inhibited religious congregations from establishing themselves in the British colonies. Anglo-Catholic families in Maryland often sent their daughters to be educated in convent schools in France and Belgium: convent archives name thirty-six nuns from Maryland families as of the 1780s. Among the Americans in the Carmelite priory in Hoogstraeten, Belgium, were Ann Matthew and two nieces. This trio introduced religious life for women into the newly formed United States in 1790 by establishing a Carmelite monastery in Port

Tobacco, Maryland.

The Carmelites declined to make use of a papal permission to open schools, an approval Bishop John Carroll had secured for them in hopes of giving the nuns a way to demonstrate their usefulness in a mostly Protestant society with a long history of virulent anti-Catholicism. With only 30,000 Catholics in a population of 3.9 million, families able and likely to endow or give alms to a cloistered community of women were few and potential critics were many. Moreover, there was an urgent need for schools among the Catholic families in the former colony of Maryland. This need began to be met when a group of three "pious ladies" came to Georgetown from Philadelphia in the mid-1790s to teach for another recently founded cloistered group, the Poor Clares. Visitation Academy for girls, the first of its kind in what was then territorial U.S., was born when the Poor Clares departed and the three teachers stayed to form a community following the rule of the semi-cloistered Visitation order.

A fresh impetus for the establishment of Catholic schools came when the convert and widow, Elizabeth Bayley Seton, came from New York to Baltimore, Maryland in 1808 and then settled in Emmitsburg, Maryland, the following year. Seton and the four women who accompanied her found support for an active apostolate in the rule Vincent de Paul and Louise de Marillac had devised for the Daughters of Charity. They opened an academy and a free school and took in orphans as their initial work. Conditions were primitive but more women soon joined them, and income from the academy helped support free schooling for children unable to pay anything. Within less than a decade they had sent sisters to Philadelphia and New York City to engage in similar work.

The women who formed the next several congregations to be founded in the U.S., Sisters of Loretto, Sisters of Charity of Nazareth, and Sisters of the Third Order of St. Dominic, all in the frontier territory of Kentucky between 1812 and 1822, embraced the vocation of teaching as a primary apostolate.[2] Extension of schooling further penetrated the frontier when Mother Rose Philippine Duchesne and four companions introduced the Society of the Sacred Heart to America. They established themselves in St. Louis in 1818 and immediately opened an academy for girls. By the time of Duchesne's death in 1852 the Society was responsible for six schools in the lower Mississippi Valley; an academy and parish school in St. Louis; and a mission among the Potawatomi Indians in Kansas.

It was in the late 1820s that Elizabeth Lange, an Afro-Caribbean immigrant to Baltimore from San Domingo, gathered two Haitian women about her for the purpose of teaching African American children. Maryland public schools were legally prohibited from accepting slave children and no exceptions were made for free people of color. Lange and her companions took up this cause with little support from the Catholic community in Maryland and at considerable personal danger. In 1829 they professed vows as Oblate Sisters of Providence, adapting the rule of the Oblates of St. Frances of Rome and began a ministry of educating African-American girls.

From this point on to mid-century the pioneer core of women's congregations increased by sixteen new foundations with a corresponding number of academies and free or parochial schools dispersed throughout the country. American-born women and recent immigrants from Ireland formed the Sisters of Charity of Our Lady of Mercy; the African-American Sisters of the Holy Family; the Sisters of Charity of the Blessed Virgin Mary; Sisters, Servants of the Immaculate Heart of Mary; and Sisters of the Third Order of St. Dominic. Eleven groups came as missionaries from Europe: Sisters of St. Joseph, Sisters of Providence, Sisters of the Good Shepherd, and the Congregation of the Holy Cross from France; Sisters of Notre Dame de Namur from Belgium; School Sisters of Notre Dame, Franciscans, and Dominicans from Germany; Sisters of Mercy from Ireland; and Sisters of the Precious Blood from Switzerland.

By the close of the Civil War an additional thirty congregations, plus offshoots of the earlier groups, had given a definitive character to Catholic education in the U.S. as a rapidly growing network, initiated and maintained primarily through the efforts of women religious, that kept pace with the westward movement of the frontier and the elaboration of diocesan and parish structures. Although the massive waves of immigration that were to transform the American church had yet to come, the arrival of large numbers of Irish and German Catholics during the middle third of the nineteenth century presaged the future. Women religious proved equal to the task of providing schools for America's new Catholics, thanks to their leadership, zeal, and dynamic increase in membership. The number of sisters grew from around 1,300 in 1850 to over 40,000 by 1900.[3]

The letters of Mother Caroline Friess of the School Sisters of Notre Dame give us a unique insight into lives of nineteenth-century religious educators.[4] Written by a gifted and dedicated leader over the forty-four year period between her arrival in America in 1848 and her death in 1892, this correspondence alternately shocks, entertains, and inspires the reader with its graphic descriptions of conditions confronting the classroom teacher as with this description of scenes encountered in rural Pennsylvania: "My God, how I pitied the children! Completely neglected, they sat near a herd of swine or among geese and looked so shy and frightened as though they feared the daylight!" and in urban Baltimore where the children "seem to be prone to an inordinate love of all freedom from birth. Little girls only nine or ten years old resent any admonition . . . They would pack their books and, in English, grumble very rude and insulting expressions thinking that the German Sisters could not understand them" (Letter of June 18, 1850).

Conditions in the sisters' New York schools were even worse: "The majority of the children have bugs not only in their hair but also in their clothes . . . Some children are clad only in rags." Children often ran the streets for days at a time rather than attending class: "Equipped with a basket and an iron rod, they collect rags, bones, coal and old iron and sell these things for money" which they were bound to turn in to parents "who used it for alcoholic drink" (Letter of November 12, 1853). Keenly aware of these challenges and sensitive to the needs of the sisters as human beings, Friess went about the country encouraging each local community and its leadership; assessing prospects for new schools; negotiating with pastors for humane working conditions; and talking with women interested in joining the congregation, personally receiving the vows of some 2,000 women.

Although few left behind so voluminous and lively a correspondence, Mother Caroline had many counterparts in the building up of congregations and schools. A selective roster of outstanding leaders would include Mother Theodore Guerin, of the Sisters of Providence in Indiana; Mother St. John Fournier of the Sisters of St. Joseph in Missouri, Minnesota, and Pennsylvania; Mother Joseph Periseau of the Sisters of Providence in the Pacific Northwest; and Mother Austin Carroll of the Sisters of Mercy in the South.[5] They and the women who associated themselves with them prepared the way for the flourishing Catholic educational system of the twentieth century not only through the schools they founded but also through attending to the sick.

Health care, teaching, and social services of all kinds were virtually inseparable in the pioneer, pre-professional era. The same women who taught during the day often lived with and cared for orphans at night, turned schools into hospitals in time of need, and volunteered their services as nurses during the Civil War. Many a Protestant unlearned bigotry and learned to respect Catholicism when cared for by sisters during recurrent epidemics of yellow fever and cholera or in the aftermath of battle. The ministry of teaching and nursing was all one in the mind of the sisters and the general public. As Mother Caroline Friess described the situation, "We have more than 4,000 children who are taught and cared for by the mission Sisters (the Order numbers 84 members) in 18 schools and four orphanages. . . . Last summer when cholera reigned almost everywhere, our orphanage and schoolhouse in [St. Mary], Detroit, was turned into a hospital for children. The Sisters of Mercy were crowded with so many sick people that they had to put them even in the corridors" (Letter of March 15, 1856).

Mother Austin Carroll's correspondence told a similar story as she recounted the experiences of the Sisters of Mercy in the South, as in this letter from the 1880s: "The epidemic must be my excuse for not writing sooner . . . the dreadful times are over for the present, and for a long time I hope. The state of things in poor Pensacola is simply appalling. Over one-third of the population was attacked, all business suspended, and the well-to-do people fled. . . . our poor sisters are the heroines of the hour. Day or night they never left the patients who had none to nurse them, or the hospital, but relieved each other as appointed."[6] Not surprisingly, "men who swore they believed in no God . . . looked upon the sisters as angels and spoke of us as such." (Letter of 15, 1856).

A substantial number of sisters, 617 from 21 congregations, ministered to the sick and injured of both the Union and the Confederacy during the Civil War, with the largest number coming from the Daughters of Charity. That congregation was the first in the country to organize care for the sick in hospitals.[7] In all, 479 hospitals had been founded by sisters as of World War I, 58 by the Daughters. Sisters of Mercy had founded 79 hospitals by then; the various Franciscan congregations, 57. Sisters of Providence were especially prominent in this work in the West and Northwest; the Sisters of Mercy, Daughters of Charity, and Sisters of the Incarnate Word, in the South. The connection between health care and education endured well into the era of greater professionalizing of both fields as sisters conducted hospital-based nursing education.

Still other women's congregations addressed immigrants' need for health care as well as schooling. Various branches of the Franciscans established hospitals among Germans in such cities as Baltimore, Philadelphia, Cincinnati, St. Louis, Milwaukee, and Cleveland; Felician sisters among immigrants from Poland in Chicago and Manitowoc, Wisconsin; and Mother Cabrini's Missionary Sisters of the Sacred Heart among Italians in New York City, Chicago, and Seattle. Others, such as the Dominican Servants of Relief for Incurable Cancer, founded by convert Rose Hawthorne Lathrop in 1899, dedicated themselves to caring for the sick poor. Most of those the sisters cared for in hospitals, as well as children attending the free schools, were so poor as to require great ingenuity on the sisters' part to cover expenses.[8]

Impressive as was the work of the Catholic sisterhoods in health care, and critical for defusing bigotry, no activity equaled that of education in its importance for the Church in America. American bishops recognized the vital importance of providing schools as early as their 1829 gathering for the First Provincial Council. Recognition of the indispensable role of sisters in meeting educational needs surfaced as the bishops continued discussing the subject at the plenary councils of 1852 and 1866, but was much more explicit in the mandate passed at the Third Plenary Council of Baltimore in 1884, requiring establishment of a school in every parish. It was an ambitious goal, inconceivable but for the partial system of parochial or free schools in place by then as a result of the sisters' leadership. By the time of the Civil War, sisters were responsible for some 200 academies, income from which helped meet the expense of conducting nearly

1,500 free schools. Post-war growth was explosive, with an average increment by decade from 1870 – 1900 of over 100 parochial schools and nearly 40,000 pupils.

The Third Plenary Council also concerned itself with the need to comply with teacher certification standards if parochial schooling was to compete successfully with public education, again turning to the sisterhoods for practical solutions. Having pledged themselves in rather simplistic fashion to facilitate the establishment of normal schools, the bishops agreed to confer with superiors of congregations regarding implementation of this provision. Their praiseworthy if naive concern was not backed up by resources, with the result that it was left to the women to devise practical means whereby sister-teachers' credentials could be up-graded. They accomplished this by incorporating teacher training courses in novitiate programs, by arranging for members to attend classes in secular normal schools and universities, and by creating their own post-secondary institutions inasmuch as the few Catholic universities then in existence were closed to women.

Catholic women's colleges were the most enduring and unique phenomenon to emerge from the sisters' desire not only to elevate teacher education standards but also, and more fundamentally, to meet women's need for education beyond the secondary level.[9] Beginning in the last quarter of the nineteenth century a handful of women's congregations anticipated the extension of academy curricula into a baccalaureate level by securing charters granting them the right to award college degrees. The School Sisters of Notre Dame in Maryland; Ursulines in Ohio; Sisters of the Holy Cross in Indiana; Sisters of Charity in New Jersey; and Sisters of Notre Dame de Namur in Washington, D.C., had all taken this step by the turn of the century.

Others followed suit, until by the time the Catholic Educational Association first included Catholic women's colleges on its list of accredited institutions (1918), institutions founded by ten more congregations were acknowledged: Sisters of St. Joseph and Franciscans, in Minnesota; Dominicans in Wisconsin; Sisters of Charity of the Blessed Virgin Mary in Iowa; Sisters, Servants of the Immaculate Heart of Mary in Michigan; Ursulines and Gray Nuns in New York; Sisters of Mercy in New Jersey; and Religious of the Sacred Heart in Ohio.

The Sisters of the Blessed Sacrament for Indians and Colored People, founded in 1891 by the Philadelphia heiress Katherine Drexel worked alongside older congregations to extend the Church's presence among Indians and African Americans. As of Drexel's death in 1955, sixty-nine schools for Indians and African Americans, established or supported by her, were serving 15,000 pupils. Xavier University, begun by Drexel in 1915 to afford African Americans access to Catholic higher education and particularly to prepare teachers, gained accreditation in the 1920s and continues to flourish today as the only institution of its kind in America.

The enormity of the task confronting congregations determined to advance sister-teacher education is suggested by the action of the Sisters of Charity of the Blessed Virgin Mary of Dubuque, Iowa. The sum of $6,000 their council agreed to budget for six sisters' full-time baccalaureate study in 1911 equaled the accumulated annual stipends paid by parishes to thirty teaching sisters![10]

Undaunted by the scarcity of financial resources, or by the opposition of those bishops who felt women had no need for a higher education,[11] the sisters were courageous and quick to act on their perceptions of the broader implications of rising certification standards and expanding opportunities for women. It would be difficult to overestimate the positive effects of their action for the nation's Catholic schools at the elementary and secondary levels, directly in the stimulus given to better teacher education, and indirectly in the cultivation of Catholic women's leadership in American society.

## Leadership for the Twentieth Century

Some of the women religious whose leadership built up the reputation of Catholic education in the period before and after the creation of the NCEA are well enough known as not to require further commentary here. Published biographical materials for persons such as Mary Molloy,[12] distinguished educator, co-founder of the College of St. Teresa in Winona, Minnesota, and cogent critic of the Catholic college system in speeches delivered at NCEA meetings, are readily available. Others in this same category include Antonia McHugh,[13] founder of the College of St. Catherine in St. Paul, Minnesota, admired educator and fund raiser, avid promoter of women's higher education, and strategist par excellence who secured for her faculty a chapter of the nation's most prestigious honor society, Phi Beta Kappa, years before any other Catholic college or university gained such distinction. Madeleva Wolff brought St. Mary's in South Bend, Indiana, to the forefront of higher education, spearheaded establishment of the country's first graduate program in theology open to women, and was instrumental in initiating the Sister Formation Movement besides finding time to write her autobiography.[14]

The vast majority of women religious through whose efforts the parochial school system came into being are anonymous, a regrettable situation several women in Minnesota have helped rectify through a collaborative research project that resulted in *They Came to Teach, the Story of Sisters Who Taught in Parochial Schools and Their Contribution to Elementary Education in Minnesota*.[15] Focusing their study on nine Minnesota-based congregations who staffed schools in parishes throughout this mid-western state, the authors list the names of 7,219 women, a few of whom are profiled here by way of illustrating the impressive examples of leadership waiting to be discovered throughout the country.

Each of these women gives abiding witness to the extraordinary potential released in otherwise ordinary individuals by the power of education. Each gained a stature that was bigger than life, as it were, by reason of membership in religious congregations that recognized their gifts. Each of them, along with the thousands not profiled here, contributed her part in helping the church fulfill the Third Plenary Council's mandate to establish a school in every parish. They and others like them have given the NCEA the inspiration and means for attaining high standards of excellence.

Celestine (Ellen) Howard (1842 – 1915), born in Ireland and orphaned during the potato famine, came when she was ten years old to St. Paul with the Richard Ireland family.[16]   She and her cousin, Ellen Ireland, got to know the Sisters of St. Joseph as students at St. Joseph Academy.   Both entered the congregation after they graduated in 1858 and went on to form an unusual family partnership in the furtherance of Catholic education in the Upper Midwest.

One week after receiving the habit, Sister Celestine was sent to teach at the sisters' school in Minneapolis.  Appointment as principal of other newly opened parochial schools in both Minneapolis and St. Paul followed, and then service as directress of her alma mater.  We get a glimpse into the evolution of teacher education during this period from Sister Celestine's 1879 designation as supervisor of parochial schools in the St. Paul Province.  A directress of studies for the novitiate was appointed at the same time; Sister Celestine in her capacity of school supervisor was regarded as "highest common directress" of studies whose duties included developing and presiding over annual summer institutes for teachers and novices.

"Mother" Celestine as she came to be called owing to a succession of appointments as superior of local houses beginning in 1884, conceived of her most original idea, the creation of St. Agatha's Conservatory, because of tight financial resources and a housing shortage.  Sister-teachers in the numerous parochial schools established in St. Paul from 1860 to 1885 had run out of convenient convent space, having outgrown accommodations at St. Joseph Academy and Hospital. Struggling young parishes could not afford to build convents simultaneously with schools; the religious congregation could not afford to pay its debts, provide for the daily expenses of its members and their education, and cover the cost of constructing convents on the small stipends paid to teachers.

Mother Celestine suggested a solution for the dilemma. St. Agatha's convent where she had recently been appointed superior could be relocated to a larger building and transformed into a combined convent-conservatory where parochial school sisters could live while other sisters could offer music, drama and art lessons for a fee.[17] Money earned from such lessons would meet the expenses of the grade-school teachers and help retire debt. During peak years, as many as 100 sisters set forth daily to their respective schools from the centrally located six-story building. A combination of sisters' stipends (as low as $10 per month in 1901, but set at $25 by diocesan policy as of 1912) and fees paid by students taking private lessons enabled house bookkeepers to balance the books for house expenses, and to make contributions ranging from $4,500 to $26,792 to the St. Paul province provincial house from 1904 to 1914.

Unique in the country for its time, the multi-purpose conservatory was extremely successful, serving as a home and a place of study for teachers in downtown St. Paul parochial schools; affording hundreds of students opportunities to study the fine arts (a 1912 advertisement listed 817 students enrolled in classes in music, speech, languages, and the plastic arts); and generating badly needed income for the congregation.

The anonymous author of Mother Celestine's obituary emphasized her roles as a highly disciplined and effective educator and administrator. Another contemporary described her keen interest "in whatever tended to promote the welfare of Catholic schools from a material, religious and intellectual standpoint," noting that Mother Celestine habitually "did all in her power to inspire the Sisters of her community and unceasingly labored to improve the conditions of the schools under her care by introducing the best approved methods of Catholic pedagogy."[18]

One of the young women who enrolled in art classes at St. Agatha's Conservatory was Caroline Hanggi (1875 – 1968) better known as Sister Carmela, founder of the School Police program of national and international fame.[19] Her Swiss-German parents had emigrated from Europe to St. Louis, Missouri, where they were married in 1860. The outbreak of the Civil War prompted a move upriver to St. Paul where Josef Hanggi became co-founder of St. Paul Furniture Company and contributed his wood carving and designer skills to the embellishment of numerous private homes, public buildings and churches in the area. He and his family were firmly rooted in Catholicism, while the mother had been raised as a Lutheran but converted to Catholicism before Caroline's birth.

Carrie, as she was affectionately known to family and neighborhood friends, was taught by Sisters of St. Joseph at Cathedral School, St. Joseph's Academy, and, as already mentioned, St. Agatha's Conservatory where she pursued her love for German language, poetry and music for several years before entering the Sisters of St. Joseph just a few months shy of her twenty-first birthday. Her novitiate program was followed by a long and innovative teaching career during which she served as teacher or principal in several urban and rural parochial schools and academies. A hymnbook she edited for congregational singing, the *St. Paul Hymnal* (1915), was widely used throughout the Northwest as part of a movement to foster more active participation in the liturgy.

As principal of Cathedral School in St. Paul in the 1920s, Sister Carmela became concerned for student safety on heavily trafficked city streets near the school. Meanwhile, preparation for assuming the Sisters of St. Joseph school supervisor role had taken her to the East Coast where she observed a school-crossing monitoring program in New Jersey. Putting the need and the remedy together, she conceived the idea of having the local police department authorize elementary school children as "police" trained to safeguard youngsters crossing streets to and from school. The idea became a reality when St. Paul and Minnesota state patrol officers supported it and the Minnesota legislature passed laws delegating appropriate authority to the young patrols. The School Patrol program created by Sister Carmela soon spread to other states and is still operative throughout the U.S. and many other countries.

With Mary Leon (Sophie) Smykalski (1911 —) we pick up the threads of Mother Caroline Friess and the schools established by the School Sisters of Notre Dame. It was Friess who sent sisters to Mankato, Minnesota, in 1865 in response to the petition of a pastor and a delegation of German immigrant parishioners. Sophie, born to first-generation Polish immigrant parents on a farm in Silver Lake, Minnesota, grew up helping her brother and sister and her widowed mother with farm chores such as milking and feeding the family's small herd of cows and harvesting grain.[20] She attended a two-room country school house for the early grades, but when the School Sisters of Notre Dame opened a parish school in Silver Lake in 1923, her mother arranged for Sophie and her brother to stay in town so they could finish grade school there. Sophie was much attracted to the sisters, and after graduating from eighth grade she enrolled as an aspirant or member of the sisters' pre-novitiate program at the Academy of Good Counsel in Mankato. The Mankato province accepted her as a candidate before she completed her senior year.

Her teaching career began in December of her senior year at the Academy when she was sent to teach first and second grade in Minneapolis as a substitute for a sick sister. She finished the academic year and returned to Mankato where she graduated from the academy and, after a three-month interlude, accepted her second teaching assignment, grades three and four in the southeastern Minnesota city of Winona. There the superior-principal took her under her wing and guided her in effective teaching methods without the formality of a structured practice teaching program. Reception of the habit a year later was followed by a year's novitiate, following which she resumed a teaching career marked by versatility, compassion, and keen insight into students' character and needs.

During her eleven year assignment in Winona, Sister Mary Leon taught grades six, seven, and eight at various times, as well as training 75 to 100 mass servers each year, coaching seventh-and eighth-grade girls in volleyball, and serving as moderator for the Young Ladies Sodality and the Junior Holy Name Society. Summer vacations found her and other sisters teaching religion to students from Winona public schools. During the school year, she used her spare time to instruct immigrants preparing to apply for citizenship. As World War II engulfed Europe and affected the School Sisters of Notre Dame along with the general populace in Germany, England, and Poland, she organized local Boy Scouts to package and send foodstuffs and warm clothing abroad for distribution to the needy. At home, she and the sisters with whom she taught were good at spotting children who came from poor families and did all they could to alleviate their hunger by giving them bread and other foodstuffs. They also distributed clothing and waived tuition for children from the neediest families.

Sister Mary Leon's path to higher education typified that of many an elementary school teacher. She earned her first credits applicable toward a baccalaureate degree by taking courses most Saturdays and occasionally after school at the institution Mary Molloy and the Sisters of St. Francis had founded in Winona, the College of St. Teresa. Assigned in the 1940s to SSND schools in St. Paul, she joined sisters from many other Minnesota-based congregations for classes at the Diocesan Teachers College,[21] and finally earned a Bachelor of Arts degree in 1944 with a major in education and a minor in history from the SSND's Mount Mary College in Milwaukee, Wisconsin. Subsequent study earned her a master's degree in history from Creighton University in Omaha, Nebraska.

Appointment in 1950 as provincial coordinator of the annual SSND Educational Conference acquainted sisters beyond the Mankato province with her leadership qualities and afforded her an opportunity to promote the educational activities of the School Sisters throughout North America, with the result that she was chosen executive chairperson for the inter-provincial committee of the SSND Educational Conference on Elementary Education, a position she filled with distinction from 1955 to1960.

Mary Thomas (Anna Helen) Egan (1910 —) had completed her elementary and secondary education and teachers' training, and had taught in a rural school for five years before entering the Benedictines of Crookston, Minnesota. Born in Summit Township, Richland County, North Dakota, the ninth of eleven children, to first-generation immigrant Irish parents, her interest in education expressed itself in her youthful pursuit of studies and in her evident love of teaching in later years—"her whole personality radiates in such a way as to affect all the people around her . . . she loves to teach!"[22] Sister Mary Thomas spent most of her teaching career in high school classrooms, but her single most notable contribution to education in Minnesota came about in her capacity as diocesan supervisor of schools for the Sisters of St. Benedict from 1967 to 1979. A human relations course she developed during that time was approved by the Minnesota Department of Education and continues to be taken today by teachers in fulfillment of requirements for teaching certification in the state. As a diocesan supervisor, she planned innumerable diocesan and parish programs, organized workshops and training sessions, identified policy needs for efficient operation of the Catholic school system within the Crookston diocese, and collected data that enabled her to contribute effectively to basic educational philosophy and curriculum. Human relations programs were introduced in the diocese along with a variety of continuing education programs for teachers. Diocesan school boards came into being as a result of her leadership. Hers was an extraordinary exercise of leadership that earned for her the National Catholic Educational Association's Presidential Award in 1975.

Marilyn (Mary) Micke (1918 —) also built on her own classroom teaching experience to assist other teachers in a supervisory capacity. Born in Wisconsin and raised in the small towns of northern Minnesota, she attended a one-room country school as a first and second grader, after which another family move enabled her to complete her elementary education in a parochial school staffed by Benedictine sisters from Duluth, Minnesota. Her attraction to that community was nurtured by attendance at Villa Sancta Scholastica Academy in Duluth as an aspirant, and solidified by a two-year novitiate experience following her graduation. Her twenty-one year teaching career began at age twenty with her assignment to a parochial school in northern Minnesota. Her leadership as young teacher and principal took many forms—a former student characterized it as resourcefulness in meeting the daily challenge of managing a double-grade classroom as well as an entire school with seeming ease and very little by way of support staff: "she faithfully met the day-to-day challenge of fulfilling the role of principal, teacher, mother, doctor, janitor, referee, psychologist, counselor, fund raiser . . . not only to the students in our seventh and eighth grade but to all the students in St. Rose School."[23] Appointed diocesan supervisor of schools in 1959, and diocesan superintendent of schools ten years later, Micke earned the nickname of "Mafiette" in professional circles by breaking into the all-male club of superintendents known as the "Minnesota Mafia." Her thorough knowledge of the educational process, developed through firsthand experience and years of supervising education for Catholic schools located from the Canadian border to Chicago, gave her a special empathy for troubled youth and an appreciation for creative ideas that might help them learn. Approached in 1976 by a young man with an intriguing theory on youth crime prevention, Micke collaborated with him and a small group of Duluth principals to initiate what later became known as Operation Aware.

Based on the principle that negative peer pressure is the primary reason for criminal behavior among youth, Operation Aware empowers teachers and students to establish and maintain a positive peer culture. Piloted in a handful of Duluth Catholic schools in 1976-1977, the sixth-grade Operation Aware program quickly became a mandatory part of the regular curriculum in all Duluth schools. Sister Marilyn played a decisive role in the incorporation of Operation Aware into middle-school curricula beyond Duluth first as a part-time administrator of the program while still superintendent of schools, and later as its full-time executive director. As of 1990, usage had spread to 28 states, to 8 provinces of Canada, and beyond North America to Australia and Taiwan.

Celestine Howard, Carmela Hanggi, Mary Leon Smykalski, Mary Thomas Egan, Marilyn Micke, and the 7,214 other sisters identified with the parochial schools in Minnesota from its inception in 1851 to 1990, claim our admiration and appreciation as the NCEA celebrates its first hundred years. Perhaps the centennial can serve as an incentive to develop more state-by-state monographs on the sisters and the religious congregations that have played such a crucial role in the development of the Catholic educational system and, with it, the National Catholic Educational Association.[24]

## ENDNOTES

[1] For background on the history of women religious in the United States, see Karen M. Kennelly, C.S.J., "Historical Perspectives on the Experience of Religious Life in the American Church," in *Religious Life in the U.S. Church: The New Dialogue*, ed. Robert J. Daly, S.J., and others (New York: 1984), 79-97; and "Women Religious in American Catholic History: Religious Life for Women in the United States," in *The Encyclopedia of American Catholic History* (Collegeville, MN: 1997).

[2] Barbara Misner, S.C.S.C., *Highly Respected and Accomplished Ladies, Catholic Women Religious in America* (New York: 1988) traces the history of the first seven women's congregations; themes pertinent to nineteenth-century developments are explored in depth by Mary Ewens, O.P., *The Role of the Nun in Nineteenth Century America* (New York, 1978).

[3] The most reliable Sister-population statistics are those compiled by Catherine Ann Curry, P.V.B.M., using the *Official Catholic Directory* and other sources; see George C. Stewart, Jr., *Marvels of Charity* (Huntington, Indiana: 1994), Appendix F.

[4] Quotations here are taken are from the complete edition and translation of the Friess correspondence by Barbara Brumleve, S.S.N.D., *The Letters of Mother Caroline Friess* (Winona, Minnesota: 1991); extended quotations are also included in *Gender Identities in American Catholicism*, ed. Paula Kane, James Kennelly, and Karen M. Kennelly, C.S.J. (New York: 2001), Parts 1, 2, and 6.

[5] For brief profiles of these and other pioneer religious, see Mary Ewens, O.P., "Women

in the Convent," in *American Catholic Women: A Historical Exploration*, ed. Karen
M. Kennelly, C.S.J. (New York: 1989), 17-47.

[6] Carroll to Mother Gonzaga, R.S.M., Archives, Sisters of Mercy of Manchester.
Carroll's biography by Hermenia Muldrey, R.S.M. should be consulted for the full
context of this correspondence: *Abounding in Mercy, Mother Austin Carroll* (New
Orleans: 1988).

[7] Christopher J. Kauffman, *Ministry and Meaning: A Religious History of Catholic
Health Care in the United States* (New York: 1995), especially Part I, Formation of
Catholic Identities, 11-28. See also Mary Denis Maher, C.S.A., *To Bind Up the
Wounds: Catholic Nursing Sisters in the Civil War* (Westport, CT: 1989).

[8] Mary J. Oates, C.S.J., *The Catholic Philanthropic Tradition in America* (Bloomington,
IN: 1995), provides a comprehensive analysis of the financial contributions of the
sisterhoods, concluding that they were critical for the survival of parochial schools
as well as for hospitals, orphanages, and other charitable works.

[9] See *Catholic Women's Colleges in America*, ed. by Tracy Schier and Cynthia Russett
(Baltimore: 2002) and works cited there.

[10] Incident cited by M. Jane Coogan, B.V.M., *The Price of Our Heritage* (2 vols.,
Dubuque, IA: 1975-1978), vol. II: 1869-1920.

[11] The range of attitudes adopted by bishops relative to women's higher education is
described by Karen M. Kennelly, C.S.J., " Ideals of American Catholic Woman-
hood," in *American Catholic Women: A Historical Exploration*, ed. by Kennelly (New
York: 1989), 1-16. For excerpts from bishops' declarations on the subject, see Paula
Kane, James Kenneally, and Karen M. Kennelly, C.S.J., eds., *Gender Identities in
American Catholicism* (Maryknoll, N.Y. 2001).

[12] Kennelly, "Mary Molloy: Women's College Founder," *Women of Minnesota: Selected
Biographical Essays*, ed. by Barbara Stuhler and Gretchen Kreuter (St. Paul, MN: rev.
ed. 1998), 116-135..

[13] Kennelly, "The Dynamic Sister Antonia and the College of St. Catherine," *Ramsey
County History*, 14:1 (Fall/Winter 1978), 3-18.

[14] Madeleva Wolff, C.S.C., *My First Seventy Years* (New York: 1959); for a succinct
biography of Wolff , see Kennelly, "Madeleva Wolff," in *Notable American Women*,
Vol. IV (Cambridge, MA: 1980).

[15] Ed. by Annabelle Raiche, C.S.J., and Ann Marie Biermaier, O.S.B. (St. Cloud, MN:
1994). Data contributed by 22 other congregations whose members served in Minnesota schools without having a province or general motherhouse in the state are also
included in this account. Additional biographical studies have been done by Ann
Thomasine Sampson, C.S.J., *Seeds on Good Ground: Biographies of 16 Pioneer Sisters
of St. Joseph* (Minneapolis, MN: 2000)..

[16] Helen Angela Hurley, C.S.J., *On Good Ground* (Minneapolis, MN: 1951); and
Sampson, *Seeds On Good Ground*, pp. 159-169.

[17] Ann Thomasine Sampson, C.S.J., "St. Agatha's Conservatory and the Pursuit of
Excellence," *Ramsey County History* 24:1 [Fall/Winter 1988], 3-19. The Conservatory remained open until 1962.

[18] Quotations from obituary and tribute in the local historical journal, *Acta et Dicta*,
as cited by Sampson in *Seeds on Good Ground*, 166.

[19] Profile by John Christine Wolkerstorfer, C.S.J., *They Came to Teach*, 147-149.

[20] Profile by Marjorie Myers, S.S.N.D., *They Came to Teach*, 151-154.

[21] On the contribution of this institution to teacher education in Minnesota, see Annabelle Raiche, C.S.J., *A Home Becomes a College: St. Paul Diocesan Teachers College, 30 Years in the James J. Hill Mansion* (St. Paul, MN: 2000).

[22] Cited in profile by Laurian Lasha, O.S.B., *They Came to Teach*, 163-164.

[23] Biographical details and quotation as cited in profile by Timothy Kirby, O.S.B., *They Came to Teach*, 159-161.

[24] No treatment of parishes, sisters, and education would be complete without reference to the groundbreaking work by Jay P. Dolan, R. Scott Appleby, Patricia Byrne, and Debra Campbell, *Transforming Parish Ministry: The Changing Roles of Catholic Clergy, Laity, and Women Religious*
(New York: 1989). Byrne's analysis of the changing role of sisters in parishes from 1930 to the 1970s is a helpful complement to my treatment here of sisters' leadership.

CHAPTER 5

# BEING GOOD SHEPHERDS:
# THE CONTOURS OF AMERICAN CATHOLIC
# EDUCATIONAL LEADERSHIP

*Timothy Walch*

"I am the good shepherd," Christ proclaims in John 10:14-16, "I know my own and my own know me, just as the Father knows me and I know the Father; and I lay down my life for my sheep. And there are other sheep I have that are not of this fold and these I have to lead as well. They too will listen to my voice and there will be only one flock and one shepherd." Certainly the good shepherd was the role model that the Catholic Church intended for her educational leadership. The challenge, of course, was to convince the American Catholic people to act as one flock in the education of their children.

Unfortunately, the changing contours of American Catholicism over the past two centuries taxed even the most dynamic educational leaders. In the eighteenth century, American Catholicism struggled to survive in a hostile land. But by the middle of the nineteenth century, growing numbers of immigrants overwhelmed the Church and made the native-born population uneasy about "the Popish religion." The first half of the twentieth century saw American Catholicism abandon its ethnic cultural traditions and become a vigorous denomination with its own unique identity. But in the second half of the century, American Catholics abandoned many of the traditions so lovingly preserved by their ancestors. The leadership of American Catholic education was shaped by these changing social dimensions.[1]

## SEEKING ONE VOICE, 1790-1840

The earliest efforts to assert national leadership in Catholic education came during years of struggle. Indeed, from the initial establishment of the Church in Maryland in 1634 to the appointment of John Carroll as the first Catholic bishop of the United States in 1789, there were few efforts to provide direction for Catholic schools. Catholic education in the United States in the years before the nineteenth century functioned exclusively on the local level.

To be sure, Archbishop Carroll did make efforts to instruct his flock on the importance of education, but he faced far too many other problems to do much about the establishment of Catholic schools. In the years after the American Revolution, American Catholics wanted to fit in, to be inconspicuous, to accept the dominant Protestant culture in all things but religious beliefs. With these goals in mind, most Catholics were not inclined to support a separate system of schools.

But the changing social composition of the American Catholic community brought about by immigration forced education to the forefront. As early as 1790, tens of thousands of Catholics from Ireland, France, and Germany came to the United States, thereby reinforcing a powerful American prejudice that Catholicism was a foreign religion. Carroll and his episcopal successors faced the complicated task of Americanizing these foreign-born Catholics without compromising their religious faith. To a large extent the bishops relied on education to achieve this goal.

Carroll's initial campaign for parish schools was motivated by a simple concern. Without Catholic schools or some similar social institution, untold numbers of Catholics would be lost to the Church. In his first pastoral letter to the American Church, Carroll emphasized the importance of Christian education as a means of instilling principles that would preserve religious faith. He called on parents to educate their children while they retained "their native docility and their hearts are uncorrupted by vice."[2]

Carroll acknowledged that the expense of Catholics schools would be great and that many parents would have to sacrifice if these institutions were to succeed. What surprised and dismayed Carroll was that Catholic parents wanted a role in how these schools were administered. Through elected trustees, Catholic parents pooled their funds, built parish schools, hired Catholic teachers, and decided on the curriculum. Trustees saw no reason to consult the parish priest about educational matters.

When Archbishop Carroll and his priests attempted to control parish schools as specified in canon law, the laity rebelled. During the years from 1815 until the late 1830s, trustees in Norfolk, Charleston, Philadelphia, New York City and elsewhere fought with priests and bishops over the appointment of pastors and the financing of churches and schools. "Trusteeism," as it was called, proved to be the most significant educational conflict within the American Church in the years before the public school movement.[3]

But struggles with the laity were not the only problems faced by the bishops in their effort to guide the development of Catholic education. Beginning in the 1830s, Catholic bishops were forced to address the public call for common schooling for children of all religious denominations. Children of all faiths were to be mixed together with liberal doses of deference, patriotism, Christianity, and the good moral example of a righteous teacher, and the end result would be "Americanized" children. Common school advocates were quite clear in their argument that Americanization and education were the responsibility of the state.

Catholic bishops challenged both of these arguments. They accused common schoolmen of incorporating large doses of Protestant doctrine into the "non-sectarian" common school curriculum. Catholics further accused common schoolmen of a subtle campaign to win the allegiance of Catholic children and at the same time to denigrate the Catholic Church. The end result, noted Catholic leaders, was a generational conflict between these "Americanized" children and their immigrant Catholic parents. It was clear to the bishops and many Catholic parents that the common school was not acceptable for the education of Catholic children.[4]

The Church also disputed the claim that the state had a primary role in the education of children. For hundreds of years, indeed during the formative years of the American Republic, education had been a private matter, handled by the churches in consultation with parents. The state had no role in the education of children, the Church argued; the establishment of common schools was a usurpation of the right of parents to choose schools that reflected their own moral code and culture.

In defining their position on the question of common schools, Catholic bishops consistently turned to the newly emerging Catholic press for assistance in spreading their message. Catholic editors obliged by giving statements on Catholic education prominent display on the front pages of their publications. In fact, Catholic newspapers and pamphlets were the main means of contact for immigrants with the world outside the ghetto. Catholic bishops used these newspapers to speak to their flocks on the issues of the day and no one issue was more important than the education of the young.

## THE CAMPAIGN FOR CONTROL, 1830-1880

The bishops also spoke to the Catholic population through pastoral letters that were issued at the close of periodic provincial and plenary councils. Beginning in 1829 and continuing until 1884, the Catholic hierarchy met periodically to discuss the issues affecting the Catholic Church in America. The resulting pastoral letters were meant to guide both the temporal and the spiritual lives of American Catholics. As was the custom in such letters, the advice was very general, reflecting the bishops' concern for various social problems, but offering no specific solutions. It remained for the Catholic press to interpret what the bishops wanted done.[5]

The pastoral letters on education warned Catholic parents about the dangers of public schooling. "In placing [your children] at school," noted the bishops in 1829, "seek for those teachers who will cultivate the seeds which you have sown; for of what avail will it be, that you have done so much, if the germs which begin to put forth shall now be stifled or eradicated; . . ."[6] Throughout the 1830s, the messages from the councils were very similar; in 1833, and again in 1837, the bishops reminded the laity of their duties as parents and implied that their only possible choice was Catholic education.[7]

The bishops were less than pleased with the response of the laity and they were particularly alarmed at the large number of Catholic children who attended public schools or no schools at all. But the bishops were not so much concerned with illiteracy as they were denominational loyalty. "The great evil," they concluded in 1840, "is the danger to which [the children] are exposed, of having their faith undermined, the imperfect instruction which they receive, if they get any, upon the most important subject of religion, the nearly total abandonment of their religious practices and their exposure in their tender youth to the fatal influence of shame which generally arises from the mockery of the superciliousness of those who undervalue their creed."[8]

The message of this and other pastoral letters was filtered through the pens of Catholic editors to the laity. The letters served as the justification for the seemingly endless editorials in favor of Catholic education that appeared in the Catholic press. Were the pastoral letters and the subsequent editorials effective tools in rallying the support of the Catholic population? The answer has to be a qualified "yes," for without the strong support of the hierarchy, there would have been few parish schools. But the influence of the bishops was limited; even with all their cajoling, only about half of all Catholic children ever attended Catholic schools.

Even though the bishops had only limited influence as a group, they did have substantial influence as individual leaders of specific dioceses. Some bishops—Benedict Fenwick of Boston, for example—chose to minimize their involvement in educational matters. Others were able to do very little because ethnic conflict and poverty had created far larger problems than the establishment of parish schools. Still other bishops were tireless advocates of parochial education, and in their dioceses, their word was Church doctrine. Two of these men—Francis

Kenrick of Philadelphia and John Hughes of New York—were so forceful as to become national leaders of the Catholic school movement.[9]

Of the two, Kenrick was considered a moderate. No less an advocate of parochial schools than Hughes or his brother bishops, Kenrick saw no value in dramatic confrontations. He saw no need to rally his flock against Protestant or "infidel" common school reformers. From the time of his arrival in Philadelphia in 1830 until his death as Archbishop of Baltimore in 1863, Kenrick quietly and consistently stressed the need for parish schools.[10]

Kenrick counseled moderation and compromise on all issues. His regular consultations with the priests of his diocese minimized misunderstandings within the diocese and the weekly publication of the *Catholic Herald* provided guidance and instruction to the laity. His moderate policies led to an agreement with public school officials that permitted Catholic children to use the Douay Version of the Bible in the common schools. In fact, it was Kenrick's counsel of moderation that minimized the retaliatory violence of the Catholic population of Philadelphia after the horrible anti-Catholic riots of the spring and summer of 1844. And it was Kenrick's quiet but persistent resolve, rather than confrontation or polemics that led to the establishment of a parochial school system in Philadelphia in the early 1850s.

Kenrick's moderation was in sharp contrast to the confrontational style of John Hughes of New York. In January of 1838, the Pope had selected Hughes to assist and eventually succeed John Dubois, the aging bishop of New York. Hughes' combative style and unwillingness to compromise made it inevitable that he would clash with city leaders over public education. In fact, the bishop's campaign against the Public School Society between 1840 and 1842 received national attention in the press and it is often considered by historians to be a turning point in the Church's effort to establish parish schools.

Hughes self image was that of a protector; it was a mode of social behavior that would predominate among the American hierarchy for the next century. "I had to stand up among them as their bishop and chief," Hughes wrote in his memoirs, "to warn them against the dangers that surrounded them; to contend for their rights as a religious community; to repel the spirit of faction among them; to encourage the timid and sometimes to restrain the impetuous; in short to knead them into dough, to be leavened by the spirit of the Catholic faith and of Catholic union."[11] Hughes articulated and typified the ghetto mentality that dominated American Catholicism throughout the nineteenth century.

The bitter violence and confrontation of the 1840s gave way to relative calm a decade later. Surprisingly, it was John Hughes who changed the debate. "How are we to provide for the Catholic education of our children?" he wrote in the *Freeman's Journal* in 1850. "I answer: Not by agitating the question on constitutionality, legality, or expediency of state schools. Let us leave these points to be settled by the politicians ...let us leave the public schools to themselves."[12] At the First Plenary Council of Baltimore (1852) the bishops endorsed the resolve shown by Hughes. It was an important event for the American Church. Growth in the number of communicants and growth in the number of dioceses and provinces meant that American Catholicism was truly national—from the Archdiocese of Baltimore in the East to the Archdiocese of Oregon City in the West. The pronouncements of this first national council had a more substantial impact than the previous pastoral letters of the provincial councils.[13]

One message that certainly came through clearly was the firm resolution of all the bishops to support and establish parochial schools. "Listen not to those who would persuade you that religion can be separated from secular instruction," the bishops warned. "Listen to our voice, which tells you to walk in ancient paths; to bring up your children as you yourselves were brought up by your pious parents; to make religion the foundation of the happiness you wish to secure for those whom you love so tenderly.... Encourage the establishment and support of Catholic schools; make every sacrifice which may be necessary for this object."[14] The words of the bishops encouraged Catholic school advocates to redouble their efforts to establish a Catholic school in every parish.

The next thirty years were a time of persistent tension in Catholic education.[15] The leaders of the American Church struggled to refine and articulate a philosophy of education that would win over the hearts and minds of their co-religionists. Most Catholic leaders were generally pleased with the rapid growth of parish schools, but some Catholics — conservatives for the most part —were not satisfied. In fact, conservatives were appalled with the large number of Catholic parents who continued to send their children to public schools in spite of papal instruction to the contrary. They looked for a way to force reluctant pastors to build more schools and require recalcitrant Catholic parents to send their children to these schools.[16] Public school advocates worked just as hard to attract Catholic parents to their cause.

## THE SEARCH FOR ORDER, 1870-1930

Much of the discussion of parochial schools in the 1870s and 1880s was tactical. How can we convince the laity of the vital importance of parish schools? Should the bishops take a clear-cut stand and require pastors to build parish schools?[17] Should they require recalcitrant parents, under the pain of sin, to send their children to parish schools?[18] It was clear to all the bishops present that the tone of their message would be as important as the content.

The result was an effort to take the middle ground at the Third Plenary

Council of Baltimore of 1884. The pastoral letter on the "education of youth" was gentle. "No parish is complete," concluded the letter, "till it has schools adequate to meet the needs of its children and the pastor and the people of such a parish should feel that they have not accomplished their entire duty until the want is supplied." There were no harsh words in the pastoral concerning pastors and parents who did not agree with the bishops or follow their advice.[19]

The decrees of the Council were another matter, however, and reflected a firm commitment to the belief that every Catholic child belonged to a Catholic school.[20] They were a setback for the liberal prelates who wanted to encourage Catholic parents to send their children to parish schools, but stop short of imposing sanctions on those parents who chose not to follow. But the conservatives had argued persuasively that decades of "encouragement" had not stopped the tide of Catholic children from attending public schools. It was time, the conservatives argued, to require these fair-weather Catholics and recalcitrant pastors to build and support parish schools.

Yet there was a vast chasm between this new policy and its implementation, and the education decrees had only limited impact on the pattern and rate of parochial school development during the balance of the century. The education decrees of the Third Plenary Council failed to face the clear fact that the American Church lacked the economic resources to provide a Catholic education for every child.

However, the decrees did have a significant impact on the organizational structure of parochial schools. For more than a century, the Catholic schools had been administered at the parish level by pastors and trustees. Most dioceses were patchworks of semi-autonomous parish schools as different from one another as the cultures that made up American Catholicism itself. But the educational discussions of the Third Plenary Council gave momentum to an effort to coordinate parish schools through diocesan school boards and superintendents. The establishment of boards and the appointment of superintendents in most dioceses in the years from 1885 to 1930 was the first major step in the long campaign to standardize and establish diocesan control over parochial schools.[21]

In fact, this search for order led many Catholic schoolmen to enthusiastically support school boards in general and superintendents in particular as vital to the future success of any diocesan school system in the new century. But at the turn of the century, less than ten percent of the American dioceses had school superintendents and it was not clear that bishops would willingly transfer their authority over parochial schools to superintendents.

But these bishops were realists and implicitly understood that school boards and superintendents would improve the quality of educational leadership at the diocesan level. By 1910, more than 55 percent of American dioceses had established boards and a surprising 17 percent of these dioceses had appointed superintendents. Writing in 1911, in the recently published *Catholic Encyclopedia*, James A. Burns summarized the progress of the supervision movement. "The board system," he concluded, "represented an important advance in the work of Catholic school organization, and had everywhere a quickening effect. It soon became evident, however, that the system was far from perfect. ... There was a need, it was seen, of an executive officer of the central board who would be specifically qualified for the work of inspection and supervision, and who should devote his entire time to the task."[22] Burns and his colleagues urged the bishops of smaller dioceses to follow the example of the archbishops and appoint school superintendents.

It is doubtful that Burns or any other Catholic educator in 1910 could have anticipated how rapidly the bishops would respond to the call to appoint these superintendents. Over the twenty years from 1910 to 1930, the percentage of dioceses with superintendents nearly quadrupled. By the end of the 1920s, it was clear to a majority of Catholics that the appointment of school superintendent was vital to ensure the continued development of Catholic education in any diocese.[23]

Diocesan school supervision was not without problems, however. There were serious concerns about who was to serve on these school boards and for how long. There also were calls for more extensive training for diocesan school superintendents. Perhaps most explosive of all, however, was a call by a few educators for the centralized control of school funds. There was a wide range of ideas on what should be done, but few Catholic educators were willing to speak openly about their problems; perhaps there was concern that such frank discussion would cause scandal among the laity.[24]

But the laity was not consulted about their schools. The decisions to establish boards and appoint superintendents were made by bishops acting as individuals and their decisions when to centralize control of their parochial schools were affected by many different factors. This pattern of school-board development varied substantially from one region of the country to the next. The varying response to the school-board movement across the country underscored the fact that the bishops did not move in unison on matters concerning parochial education. Boards and superintendents were appointed early in those dioceses where the local bishops were interested in modern methods of school supervision. In other dioceses, where the local bishops were protective of their control over the schools, school boards and superintendents did not come until much later.

In spite of all the differences, however, there was one common element in the response to the supervision movement. All American bishops sought more order in the administration of the parochial schools in the first three decades of the twentieth century. By 1930, over sixty percent of the bishops in the United States had established school boards and appointed superintendents. The trend toward improving the management of parochial schools was clear.[25]

## THE MOVE TO NATIONAL ORGANIZATIONS, 1900-1930

In addition to supporting centralized management of the parochial schools, Catholic educators in the early decades of the twentieth century also established national organizations to encourage professional communication among and between teachers, school administrators, and bishops on the issues affecting parochial schools. The result was two organizations: the Catholic Educational Association founded in 1904 and the Education Department of the National Catholic Welfare Council founded in 1919. Even though these organizations shared many goals and many leaders, they served different functions within the parochial school movement.[26]

The Catholic Educational Association — renamed the National Catholic Educational Association in 1928 — was founded in St. Louis in July 1904. The new association was a hybrid organization, the merger of three separate and distinct Catholic educational associations: the Educational Conference of Seminary Faculties, the Association of Catholic Colleges, and the Parish School Conference. After the merger, these associations became departments in the CEA.

The driving force behind the establishment of the CEA was Thomas J. Conaty, the rector of the Catholic University of America. Conaty's determination, initiative, and credibility gave momentum to the efforts of other Catholics to establish a national association devoted to Catholic education. "Many Catholic educators saw the need for a national Catholic educational association that would do for the Catholic schools what the National Education Association was doing for public schools," notes historian Donald Horrigan. "By July of 1902, Conaty had the components for such an organization nearly in place."[27]

The task of implementing Conaty's plan fell to Francis Howard. The new secretary of the CEA was a former chairman of the diocesan school board in his native diocese of Columbus where he acquired the reputation as a skilled negotiator. For Howard, educational reform was the result and reward for extensive discussion, debate, experimentation, and finally, widespread implementation.

Experience had taught Howard that change could never be forced on parish schools. It was not surprising, therefore, that Howard resisted efforts by the bishops to take over the new association. The CEA was to be a forum for the exchange of educational methods and ideas, not an episcopal policy-making agency.

Yet Howard was "equally committed to the achievement of national unity in Catholic education." Howard's concern for achieving unity while preserving individual freedom was the hallmark of the guidance he gave the CEA."[28] The depth of Howard's commitment to this goal in general and to the CEA in particular is symbolized by his willingness to serve as secretary for a quarter of a century.

The task for the consensus-oriented Howard was not an easy one. During his tenure as secretary, progressive CEA members clashed with traditional members on a number of educational issues. It was Howard's job to keep the peace and he sought ways of allowing both sides to be heard. "To achieve a consensus," noted historian Donald Horrigan, "he established an advisory committee modeled after the NEA's national council to study various aspects of controversial issues as they arose and to direct the Association's policy."[29]

In establishing an advisory committee that represented all views on the issues, Howard was able to move disagreements out of the CEA's public meetings into closed committee rooms. "The Catholic Educational Association is an expression of the unity of principle that unites all Catholic educators," wrote Howard in a brief article published in 1911. He had conviction and the influence to give truth to this statement.[30]

Just as the NCEA became the voice of Catholic teachers and educators, so also did the Education Department of the National Catholic Welfare Conference become the voice of the American bishops on education. Both organizations were reflections of a national search for order on the part of the American Catholic community. Beyond this common goal, the similarity ends. Whereas the NCEA was established as a national forum for educational ideas, the NCWC's Department of Education was created to defend Catholic schools against increasing government involvement in the Catholic schools and to provide a unified voice on education for the hierarchy.[31]

Sensitive to the concerns of the conservative bishops, the directors of the new department emphasized the supportive role of their work. Their statement of purpose referred to the education department as a "clearinghouse of information," and "an advisory agency" in support of Catholic education at all levels. Every effort was made to make the new department as non-threatening as possible to a skeptical hierarchy.[32]

By 1930, most Catholic educators and bishops agreed that the superintendent movement, the NCEA, and the NCWC had positive effects on the quality of Catholic education. But educators—particularly those involved with NCWC's education department—had to defend themselves periodically against complaints that the NCWC was "a bureaucratic colossus grasping for a monopoly of ecclesiastical power."[33] To be sure, the NCWC found their own arguments against federal control of education coming back at them. "Catholic leaders in their choice or organizational strategy," notes historian Fayette Veverka, "embraced the social forces they so vigorously sought to restrain in the larger society. Power rather than principle was the real issue as Catholics, more pragmatic than ideological, sought to preserve and protect the interest of Catholic schools."[34]

## CONSOLIDATING CONTROL, 1915-1950

The thirty-five years from 1915 to 1950 were years of consolidation in Catholic education. After several decades of internecine warfare over the proper direction for parochial schooling and an exhaustive search for order that led to the establishment of diocesan school boards and professional standards for Catholic teachers, the American hierarchy sought to centralize and solidify their authority and control over parochial education.

This campaign to consolidate the administrative controls over parochial education was not a formal one, administered by any set of directives from the National Catholic Welfare Conference or the Curia. It was, rather, the result of the collective management styles of a new generation of bishops who were determined to run their dioceses with economy and efficiency. To do so required the centralization of authority over all diocesan social institutions including the schools. It was a trend that took place in almost every American diocese between 1920 and 1950.[35]

Centralization is evident to a significant extent in the rising popularity of the school superintendent. In the first two decades of the twentieth century, the Catholic hierarchy worked hard to establish diocesan school boards. But these bodies were too large and cumbersome to be effective. In an effort to improve the administration of the schools, many bishops appointed superintendents.

The men who led the major archdioceses during the middle years of the twentieth century were the most visible members of a new generation of American Catholic leaders. Gone were the energetic individuals of the nineteenth century; by 1921, all of the liberal Catholic bishops and their conservative antagonists were dead. The twenties marked the emergence of a new generation in Church leadership.[36]

A collective portrait of the men who headed the dozen largest dioceses in the United States in 1920 reveals many shared characteristics. Unlike the generation that had preceded them, these new bishops were American-born and a majority had been trained in Rome. Of Irish heritage for the most part, they served long tenures, averaging over 25 years of service as bishops. These men— particularly the five men who led the largest archdioceses—devoted themselves to raising the visibility of the Church in America. They hoped to bring greater prestige and self-esteem to the Church in general and parochial schools in particular.[37]

Edward R. Kantowicz has evaluated the leadership styles of these five cardinal archbishops and found five common elements: giantism, "going first class," business-like administration, Americanism, and political influence. Giant-ism was a reflection of Catholic insecurity. Whenever the bishops established new institutions or got involved in construction, they built on a massive scale. New seminaries and/or cathedrals were evident in all five dioceses. These men were also determined to go first class in everything they did—they loved pageant and ceremony, good food and stimulating conversation. Yet, these men were not dilettantes and they ran their archdioceses with management practices culled from American business. Both individually and collectively, these men never missed an opportunity to profess their unswerving love of America and American values. Finally, these men cultivated contacts with national political leaders—presidents, congressmen, and governors—as a means of protecting the interests of the Church. "Builders, administrators, politicos, anti-intellectuals, and chauvinistic patriots, notes Kantowicz, "their leadership was crude but effective. They put the Church on the map."[38]

Indeed, they also put Catholic education on the map. During their long tenures, they built an unprecedented number of parish schools, established dioc-esan teachers colleges, and exercised unprecedented control over every element of Catholic education in their dioceses. The legacies of Cardinals William Henry O'Connell of Boston and Dennis Dougherty of Philadelphia are illustrative of these consolidator bishops.

O'Connell was the dean of big city Catholic leaders during the early 1920s to his death in 1944. In fact, O'Connell represented the changing of the guard, the arrival of a new generation.[39] The hallmark of the O'Connell years was modern, efficient administrative procedures for the Boston archdiocese. "As arch-bishop," notes historian David J. O'Brien, "he set out to modernize diocesan administration, and he soon made his diocese a model for others in the United States. The major feature of his work was the centralization of control in the hands of the archbishop who operated through a diocesan curia which retained day-to-day supervision of the finances and operation of all diocesan institutions and imposed clear guidelines upon parish administration."[40]

Parochial education was one of the activities that were of continuing interest to O'Connell. "Parish schools were expanded and educational adminis-tration reorganized to provide for a regular system of curriculum, examinations, health services and inspections," notes O'Brien. "The expanded educational system required the services of an increased number of teachers, so during O'Connell's years as archbishop the number of religious in the diocese more than trebled."[41] The growth of the parish schools in Boston had a momentum all its own.

Cardinal Dennis Dougherty of Philadelphia was second to no one in his interest and concern for parochial education. Indeed, his efforts to pressure recalcitrant pastors into establishing parochial schools were legendary. One biographer noted that Dougherty's views on education were shaped by a bitter public school experience. "Although he was an excellent pupil," wrote Hugh Nolan, "he met with some bigotry because of his religion and Irish background. The experience might have contributed to his later determination as archbishop of Philadelphia to establish a parochial school in every parish that could possibly support one."[42]

There is no question that Dougherty's greatest achievement was in the area of education. In fact, it was in this field that he did receive some national attention and recognition. "Perhaps the greatest of Dougherty's domestic accomplishments was the establishment of the unique system of free Catholic high schools for all Catholic boys and girls in his archdiocese," notes Hugh Nolan. "With a view to perfecting the schools as well as promoting vocations, he assigned more than 100 diocesan priests to teach full time in the boys' high schools. To assure that these schools should remain free, he legislated 'It is strictly forbidden to exact a fee from the pupils or from the parents or guardians of the pupils for this purpose'; each pastor was required to pay the tuition of his students."[43] No other prelate before or since has ever tried such an ambitious plan. Dougherty's commitment to educate was without limits.

O'Connell, Dougherty and their fellow consolidator bishops supervised the modernization of Catholic education. Under bishops such as these, parochial schools became fully competitive with their public school, counterparts. By 1950, it was not surprising to find major metropolitan areas in which fifty percent or more of the school children were enrolled in Catholic parochial schools. It was the drive and determination of men such as O'Connell and Dougherty that made such an achievement possible.


## BLESSINGS AND BURDENS, 1950-1960

A new generation of "builder bishops" dominated the Church in the 1950s. Francis Spellman had succeeded Patrick Hayes in New York and Samuel Stritch had replaced George Mundelein in Chicago, both in 1939. Richard Cushing had succeeded William O'Connell in Boston in 1946; and John O'Hara had taken over in Philadelphia in 1951 at the death of Dennis Dougherty. All of these new bishops were determined to meet the demand for more schools. Yet, unlike their predecessors, these new builder bishops could not quite keep up the pace.[44]

Typical of these school problems were those faced by Spellman and Stritch. Spellman's numbers were impressive. During the 1950s, he built more than 200 new elementary schools and by 1960, there was one child in parochial school in New York for every two children in public schools. But Spellman was frustrated. "In spite of the great progress made in expanding the Catholic school system in New York," noted historian Florence Cohalen, "the majority [of Catholic children] was not in it."[45]

Stritch fared little better than his brother bishop in New York even though he was even more vociferous in his determination. At the 1954 NCEA meeting in Chicago, Stritch noted the problems that he and his colleagues faced in parochial education, but he also stressed his commitment to finding a place for every Catholic child who wanted a Catholic education.

But this determination brought Stritch nothing but trouble. In 1953, despite an investment of 12 million dollars for elementary schools alone, Stritch reported "we have not yet met the demands of our people for adequate school opportunities. Four years later, Stritch's Catholic school superintendent complained: "we need more classrooms, more teachers, and more money." By the time Stritch left Chicago in 1958, he had invested $85 million in 75 elementary schools.

It was not enough. "Despite an apparent prosperity," notes historian James Sanders, "the Chicago Catholic educational program at both the elementary and secondary levels had moved into deep trouble by the late 1950s. In a sense it suffered from the weight of its own past success." Like Spellman, Stritch was forced to face the reality of not being able to meet the demand. Yet, he remained a committed educator. "We must not only have schools," he noted in 1956, "but we must have excellent schools."[46]

Stritch's colleague in Philadelphia, John O'Hara, did not worry so much about excellence as he did about enrollment. O'Hara's determination to meet the demand for Catholic education approached fanaticism. "From the first to the last," notes historian James Connolly, "the Philadelphia Catholic story of the 1950s is the story of the Catholic schools."[47] In only eight years, O'Hara oversaw the construction of 133 new parochial school buildings with 1,206 classrooms and 20 new diocesan high schools with 213 classrooms. These facilities provided for the total increase in the Catholic school population of over 102,000 pupils.

O'Hara was a strict conservative in all educational matters. He wanted every Catholic child in a Catholic school and every Catholic classroom staffed by a Catholic nun or priest. Dismayed by the failure of the archdiocese to attract sufficient sisters to staff his new schools, O'Hara went so far as to assign diocesan priests to teach in the schools.

But even O'Hara was forced to employ increasing numbers of lay teachers. "The percentage of lay teachers is as heavy as we ever care to have it," wrote Superintendent Edward Reilly in 1960. "In most cases the best lay teachers do not approach the average Religious in performance. Consequently, we feel strongly that the more lay teachers we have, the less effective will be our schools."[48]

In fact, the need for teachers was the critical weakness in the parochial school system.[49] For more than a century, Catholic bishops and educators had relied on underpaid women religious to staff their classrooms. Many went so far as to claim that such women were both morally and educationally superior to their public school counterparts. But beginning in the early 1950s, many Catholic bishops and educators refused to face the fact that parochial education had become increasingly dependent on lay teachers.[50]

## Educational Revolution, 1960-1990

The thirty years from 1960 to 1990 marked a generation of crises within American Catholicism as a whole. There was a general decline in Catholic participation in Church activities of all kinds: weekly attendance at Mass declined, record numbers of women religious and priests petitioned for dispensations from their vows, the number of marriage annulments skyrocketed, the number of young men and women entering the religious life dropped precipitously. Most disturbing, however, was the growing disillusionment among Catholics with the teachings of the Church. When Pope Paul VI wrote against artificial birth control in *Humanae vitae*, the majority of the laity ignored or disregarded his teaching. In this climate of declining Catholic religiosity, parochial education did not fare well.

The arrival of a new decade encouraged Catholic leaders and others to look ahead.[51] Calls for reform came from several prominent educators, among them Albert Koob. In a book with the provocative title *S.O.S. for Catholic Schools*, Koob and his colleague Russell Shaw further developed their ideas on new objectives for the Catholic schools. Koob argued that the solution to the Catholic school crisis was not in closing current institutions, but rather in transforming them into "dynamic centers of Christian education with the aim of serving the total community."

Above all, Koob encouraged Catholics not to abandon hope. "With intelligence, imagination and courage," he concluded his book, "the problems of Catholic education can be solved. The present crisis can become an avenue of growth and progress. The opportunity is there and where there is opportunity, there is also duty."[52]

A somewhat critical perspective by Andrew M. Greeley balanced Koob's upbeat message. In a book written with William C. Brown, *Can Catholic Schools*

*Survive?*, Greeley argued that the basic problem faced by Catholic education was a crisis of confidence. "And a crisis of confidence it certainly is," he wrote, "for the basic problem facing Catholic schools in the United States is not a loss of external support, but internal collapse of morale. There is a loss of nerve, a loss of connection, a loss of faith, a loss of enthusiasm. This is the root of the problem of Catholic education."[53]

For Andrew Greeley, the cause of the decline in Catholic schools was weak episcopal leadership and his answer was to shift control of the schools to the laity. Greeley openly accused the hierarchy of withdrawing their support for Catholic schools—particularly in inner cities—at a time when parental interest in parochial education was on the rise. To Greeley's thinking, Catholic schools were committing suicide.[54]

For Francis Phelan, recriminations such as those put forth by Andrew Greeley, served no useful purpose. Indeed, Phelan argued, recriminations and finger pointing further divided those who supported parochial schools. Phelan noted that there were many causes for the decline of Catholic schooling, so many in fact, that they were difficult to delineate without adding to the confusion. Phelan's plan of action was to encourage Catholic parents and educators to sustain parochial schools that responded to the interests of local communities and neighborhoods.[55]

No organization felt the impact of the decline in Catholic schooling more than the NCEA. Not only was there a decline in the number of schools during the 1970s, there also was a decline in the NCEA membership. In 1967, for example, the NCEA elementary school membership stood at 9,275; ten years later, the number had dropped to 5,832. The answer of the NCEA was to become more responsive to its constituents, to systematically collect data and document trends in Catholic education, to encourage more research in the field, and to build upon the significant developments of Vatican II.

At the NCEA's seventy-fifth anniversary celebration in 1978, the NCEA president reflected on the previous decade of decline and the NCEA's new identity. John F. Meyers emphasized that developing new constituencies was the key to the future. He placed a particular importance on parental involvement. "That's what the NCEA is—the community of all those involved in Catholic education," he wrote, "As long as we can keep them working together and help them to be truly professional, I think we will do a great service to Catholic education."[56]

Meyers' confidence in the future survival of Catholic education—however broadly defined—was not shared in other quarters. To be sure, the rate of decline in the Catholic elementary school population was slowing, but the numbers continued to drop between 1974 and 1980. The continued decline was due in part to a smaller pool of Catholic school children, but that was small comfort. Parents and press alike continued to ask the same question in the late 1970s that they had asked a decade earlier. Could Catholic schools survive?[57]

But Catholic parents and educators had not given up hope. During the last half of the 1970s, it was increasingly common for these advocates to ask a different question—will state or federal aid be the salvation of parochial schools? Many of these educators thought so. During these years it was increasingly common to find pastors and parents awash in the sea of paperwork required of grant and public-aid applicants. These efforts were buoyed in part by the news that Senator Daniel P. Moynihan of New York would introduce a federal tax credit proposal to further ease the burden of parochial school parents. The Supreme Court also offered some encouraging news in June 1977 in reaffirming earlier rulings that the states could provide textbooks, slides, and other educational materials to parochial schools.[58] Perhaps there was a light at the end of the decade. Certainly, this was on the minds of Catholic educators as they looked to a new decade.[59]

But the 1980s were no different from the previous two decades – a mixed message from the Supreme Court on the question of school aid and a continuing decline in Catholic school enrollments. In a typically provocative essay published in *America* at the end of the decade, Father Andrew M. Greeley asked if Catholic schools were facing a "golden twilight." A widely published and respected sociologist, Greeley concurred with those commentators who pointed to demographics as a major cause of the decline. "The Catholic population," Greeley noted, "gradually moved away from the places where the existing schools are. Enrollment has declined because of the lower birthrates in the last two decades....Catholic schools seem to be entering a twilight — not facing immediate extinction, perhaps, but slipping slowly into darkness."[60]

Greeley's essay was tinged with sadness. The words he used were those of eulogy. Gone were the indignant phrases attacking the bishops and others who had abandoned parish schools, just a sense of loss. Greeley had little hope that his data or any other data would change the attitudes of bishops and pastors who could not "afford" Catholic schools or parents who were "too sophisticated" to send their children to parochial schools.[61]

## TOWARD A NEW CENTURY, 1990-2000

The 1990s were years of speculation on many aspects of American life and culture. Certainly the future of American Catholic parochial education was discussed generally and specifically in the thousands of parochial schools across the nation. Not surprisingly, after 30 years of sustaining Catholic schools through sheer tenacity, some Catholic educators were reluctant to predict a bright future for their schools.

And yet there was no indication that Catholic leaders had lost any of their commitment to Catholic education during that decade. Studies by John Convey and others suggested that more than 95 percent of the nation's bishops clearly perceived the value of Catholic schools as an essential part of the Church's educational ministry and perhaps one of the best means of evangelization. Although less supportive than the bishops, 84 percent of all parish pastors shared in this assessment of Catholic education. As Convey noted, this strong commitment did not decline at all between 1986 and 1996; in fact, the indication of commitment increased.[62]

What these bishops and pastors understood is the substantial value of the long-standing Catholic educational traditions of tenacity, adaptability and community. The appeal of these traditions was evident in the call for public school reform, education vouchers and charter schools during the middle years of the decade. Essays in the *Wall Street Journal*, the *New York Times*, *Time* Magazine, *Newsweek* and other national publications singled out Catholic education for particular praise.[63]

Presidential candidates, state and local politicians, and scores of commentators also weighed in with their own views. In 1996, for example, Bill Clinton argued for "charter schools" — public schools that would emulate Catholic schools in every way except catechesis and Bob Dole championed "education vouchers" to lighten the financial burden of parents who wanted to send their children to private or religious schools.[64] The recent support by President George W. Bush for education vouchers and faith-based social service organizations also is good news for hard pressed parents who would like their children to attend parochial schools.

So why do parish schools continue to struggle in the twenty-first century if they are doing such a good job? The answer is complex, tangled with changing social values, changes in family structure, changes in the form and content of public education, and the cost of private education relative to other living expenses.

But the most powerful reason that Catholic parents do not support parish schools in the manner of their parents and grandparents is that there is no pressure to do so. "There is nothing like the presence of an external enemy," noted William Byron in 1990, "to solidify a community in shared identity and mutual support. Catholics are more comfortable in the United States today. They are less rigid about their religious practice."[65] Their grandparents and parents saw parish schools as a form of protection and security for their children against a frequently hostile American society. In an increasingly pluralistic, ecumenical world, discrimination against Catholics has become a distant memory.

When Catholic leaders first established parish schools — especially in the century between 1830 and 1930 — their stated goal was to serve both their Faith and their nation.[66] By all accounts and measures, parish schools did an extraordinary job of meeting those stated goals. So is there a continuing need for parish schools? Catholic educational leaders responded that these schools should be supported precisely because they are a model alternative to public education. Where Catholic schools had once followed every innovation introduced in public education, the roles have been reversed. Catholic schools are now laboratories for the development of effective tools in reaching a broad cross section of children.

It is clear that the future of Catholic parochial education will be determined by a coalition of leaders — bishops, priests, educators and, most importantly, the parents of the children who are educated in these schools. And with this reflection comes a new vitality. Catholic educational leaders seem more willing to experiment with new ideas and respond to the diverse and changing needs of today's Catholic students. In short, Catholic schools have become leaner, more cost-effective institutions than their public counterparts. Out of adversity had come a new identity.

## ENDNOTES

1   The most recent history of American Catholic education is Timothy Walch, *Parish School: American Catholic Parochial Education from Colonial Times to the Present,* (New York, 1996).

2   Neil G. McCluskey, ed., *Catholic Education in America: A Documentary History* (New York, 1964), 47.

3   Patrick W. Carey, *People, Priests, and Prelates: Ecclesiastical Democracy and the Tensions of Trusteeism* (Notre Dame, 1986); Jay P. Dolan, *The American Catholic Experience* (Garden City, NY, 1985), 110-124; Timothy Walch, ed., *Early American Catholicism, 1634-1820: Selected Historical Essays,* (New York, 1988), 363-96.

4   William K. Dunn, *What Happened to Religious Education? The Decline of Religious Teaching in the Public Elementary School, 1776-1861* (Baltimore, 1958), 262-272; Neil G. McCluskey, ed., *Catholic Education in America: A Documentary History* (New York, 1964), 51-64; Vincent P. Lannie, *Public Money and Parochial Education: Bishop Hughes, Governor Seward and the New York School Controversy,* (Cleveland, 1968), 29-102.

5   Hugh J. Nolan, ed., *Pastoral Letters of the American Catholic Hierarchy, 1792-1970* (Huntington, Indiana, 1971), 17-126; McCluskey, *Catholic Education in America,* 51-64; Timothy Walch, *Diverse Origins of American Catholic Education: Chicago, Milwaukee and the Nation* (New York, 1988), 101-104; Robert F. Heuston, The *Catholic Press and Nativism, 1840-1860.* (New York, 1976).

6   McCluskey, *Catholic Education in America,* . 54-55; Nolan, *Pastoral Letters,* 25.

7   Nolan, *Pastoral Letters*, 17-126.
8   McCluskey, *Catholic Education in America*, p. 59; Nolan, *Pastoral Letters*, 90.
9   For background on Kenrick, see Hugh J. Nolan, *The Most Reverend Francis Patrick Kenrick, Third Bishop of Philadelphia, 1830-1851* (Washington, D.C., 1948); on Hughes, see Richard V. Shaw, *Dagger John: The Unquiet Life and Times of Archbishop John Hughes* (New York, 1977).
10  Vincent P. Lannie and Bernard Diethorn, "For the Honor and Glory of God: The Philadelphia Bible Riots of 1844," *History of Education Quarterly* 8 (Spring 1968): 44-72; Nolan, *Francis Patrick Kenrick*, 288-342.
11  John G. Hassard, *The Life of the Most Reverend John Hughes, D.D.* (New York, 1866), 389 reprinted in Timothy Walch, *Catholicism in America* (Melbourne, FL., 1989) 149.
12  Lawrence Kehoe, *The Complete Works of the Most Reverend John Hughes*, 2 vols., (New York, 1865) II:714-715.
13  Nolan, ed., *Pastoral Letters,* 137-139; McCluskey, *Catholic Education in America*, 78-81.
14  Nolan, *Pastoral Letters*, p. 138; McCluskey, *Catholic Education in America*, 81.
15  Dunn, *What Haened to Religious Education?* 273-275; Harold A. Buetow, *Of Singular Benefit: The Story of U.S. Catholic Education* (New York, 1970) 155-156.
16  James A. McMaster and later Bernard McQuaid led the conservative campaign for a total Church commitment to Catholic education. On McMaster, see Thomas T. McAvoy, "Public Schools Versus Catholic Schools and James McMaster," *Review of Politics* 28 (1968): 19-46; On McQuaid, see Norlene M. Kunkel, *Bishop Bernard J. McQuaid and Catholic Education* (New York 1988).
17  McAvoy, "Public Schools Versus Catholic Schools and James McMaster," 22-25; Thomas T. McAvoy, *A History of the Catholic Church in the United States* (Notre Dame, 1969), 229-230; Neil G. McCluskey, *Catholic Education Faces its Future* (Garden City, 1970) 67-77.
18  For a general history of education at the Third Plenary Council, see Philip Gleason, "Baltimore III and Education," *U.S. Catholic Historian* 4 (1985): 273-313; Francis P. Cassidy, "Catholic Education in the Third Plenary Council of Baltimore," *Catholic Historical Review* 34 (1948-49): 257-305, 414-436; and Bernard J. Meiring, *Educational Aspects of the Legislation of the Councils of Baltimore, 1829-1884* (New York, 1978).
19  McCluskey, *Catholic Education in America*, 93; Nolan, ed., *Pastoral Letters,* 115.
20  McCluskey, *Catholic Education in America*, 94.
21  William Scanlan, "The Development of the American Catholic Diocesan Board of Education, 1884-1966," unpub. Ed.D. dissertation, New York University, 1967.
22  James A. Burns, "Schools, In the United States," *Catholic Encyclopedia,* 16 vols., (New York, 1907-1912), 582.
23  Scanlon, "The Development of the American Catholic Diocesan Board of Education, 1884-1966," Figure 10.
24  Michael J. Relihan, "The Parish School System As the Lay Educator Sees It," *NCEA Bulletin* 25 (1928):480-492.
25  *Ibid.*, Figure 10.
26  Elizabeth McKeown, "The National Bishops Conference: An Analysis of Its Origins," *Catholic Historical Review* 66 (1968):565-583, and McKeown, *War and Welfare:*

*American Catholics and World War I* (New York, 1988). See also Donald C. Horrigan, *The Shaping of the NCEA* (Washington, D.C. 1978) and Edgar McCarren, "The Origins and Early Years of the National Catholic Educational Association, "(Ph.D. diss. The Catholic University of America), 1966.

27 Horrigan, *Shaping of the NCEA*, 3.

28 Horrigan, *Shaping of the NCEA*, 4.

29 *Ibid.*, 4-5.

30 Francis Howard, "Educational Association," *Catholic Encyclopedia*, 305.

31 Horrigan, *Shaping of the NCEA*, . 5-6.

32 James H. Ryan, *A Catechism of Catholic Education* (Washington, 1922), 17; Fayette Veverka, *For God and Country: Catholic Schooling in the 1920s* (New York, 1988), 96-99.

33 Michael Williams to John Burke (1922) cited in John B. Sheerin, *Never Look Back: The Career of John J. Burke* (New York, 1975):85-86; Veverka, *For God and Country*, 107.

34 Veverka, *For God and Country*, p. 108; see also Patricia Byrnes, "Saving Souls and Educating Americans, 1930-1945," in Jay P. Dolan, et al., *Transforming Parish Ministry* (New York, 1989), 115-116.

35 The best overall discussion of the new generation of leaders is Edward R. Kantowicz, "Cardinal Mundelein of Chicago and the Shaping of Twentieth Century American Catholicism," *Journal of American History* 68 (1981):52-68; on the NCWC, see Elizabeth McKeown, "The National Bishop's Conference; An Analysis of its Origins," *Catholic Historical Review* 66 (1968):565-583.

36 Kantowicz, "Shaping Twentieth Century Catholicism," 52-56; James Hennesey, *American Catholics* (New York, 1981), 234-254.

37 Kantowicz, "Introduction" in his *Corporation Sole: Cardinal Mundelein and Chicago Catholicism* (Notre Dame, 1983), 1-18; Kantowicz, "Cardinal Mundelein of Chicago: A Consolidating Bishop," in David J. Alvarez, ed., *An American Church* (Moraga, CA, 1978), 63-72.

38 Kantowicz, *Corporation Sole*, 5.

39 The best biography of O'Connell is James M. O'Toole, *Militant and Triumphant: William Henry O'Connell and the Catholic Church in Boston, 1859-1944* (Notre Dame, 1993). Also of great value is Paula M. Kane, *Separation and Subculture: Boston Catholicism, 1900-1920* (Chapel Hill, NC, 1993). The information about O'Connell's primary education can be found in his autobiography, *Recollections of Seventy Years* (Boston, 1934), 6-7, also noted in David J. O'Brien, "O'Connell, William Henry," in *Dictionary of American Biography,* Supplement 3 (New York, 1973), 568-570.

40 *Ibid.*, 568-569. See also James Gaffey, "The Changing of the Guard: The Rise of Cardinal O'Connell of Boston," *Catholic Historical Review* 70 (July 1973):225-244. See James M. O'Toole, *A Guide to the Archives of the Archdiocese of Boston* (New York, 1982), xvi-xvii, 8-9, 20-29.

41 O'Brien, "O'Connell," 569. Also see William H. O'Connell, *Sermons and Addresses*, 7 vols., (Boston, 1922-1938) 4:158 and Robert H. Lord, et al., *History of the Archdiocese of Boston, 1634-1943*, 3 vols., (New York, 1944) 3:525-526.

42 Hugh J. Nolan, "Dougherty, Dennis J.," *Dictionary of American Biography,* Supplement 5, (New York, 1977), 178.

43 *Ibid.*, 179; see also, Thomas J. Dougherty, *Philadelphia's Finest: A History of Education in the Catholic Archdiocese of Philadelphia, 1692-1970* (Philadelphia, 1970), 172-203.

[44] There are only a few studies of worth on these three dynamic figures. Of value are: Steven Avella, *The Confident Church: Catholic Leadership and Life in Chicago, 1940-1965* (Notre Dame, 1992), Thomas J. McAvoy, *Father O'Hara of Notre Dame: The Cardinal Archbishop of Notre Dame* (Notre Dame, 1967) and Robert I. Gannon, *The Cardinal Spellman Story* (Garden City, 1962). See also, Thomas E. Blantz, "Stritch, Samuel A.," *Dictionary of American Biography*, Supplement 6, (New York, 1980); Robert F. Trisco, "Meyer, Albert Gregory," *Dictionary of American Biography*, Supplement 7, (New York, 1981), and Gerald P. Fogarty, "Spellman, Francis Joseph," *Dictionary of American Biography*, Supplement 8, (New York, 1988).

[45] Florence D. Cohalen, *A Popular History of the Archdiocese of New York* (New York, 1983), 302.

[46] James W. Sanders, *The Education of an Urban Minority: Catholics in Chicago 1833-1965* (New York, 1977), . 202-203; "Current Comment," *America* (September 8, 1956): 514.

[47] James Connolly, ed., *History of the Archdiocese of Philadelphia* (Philadelphia, 1976), 457; Thomas Donaghy, *Philadelphia's Finest*, 235.

[48] Quoted in Donaghy, *Philadelphia's Finest*, 251.

[49] Joseph E. Cuneen, "Catholics and Education," *Commonweal* (August 7, 14, 1953); Urban Fleege, "Catholic Education Needs a 'New Look'" *America* (April 24, 1954): 96-101; Robert Hartnett, "On Asking the Right Question" *America* (April 24, 1954):102-103.

[50] Harold T. O'Donnell, "The Lay Teacher in Catholic Education," in F. Michael Perko, ed., *Enlightening the Next Generation: Catholics and Their Schools, 1830-1900* (New York, 1988); Annette Cronin, "Catholic Schools Need Lay Teachers," *America* (April 24, 1954); John J. Reilly, "Idea for More Teachers," *America* (April 24, 1954).

[51] Neil G. McCluskey, "Neil G. McCluskey on Catholic Schools," *America* (January 10, 1970):22-23; Michael O'Neill, "Giving Americans a Choice — Alternatives to Public Education," *America* (January 24, 1970); Albert C. Koob, "Where is the Catholic School Heading," *America* (September 19, 1970).

[52] C. Albert Koob and Russell Shaw, *S.O.S. for Catholic Schools* (New York, 1970), 132-150.

[53] William C. Brown and Andrew M. Greeley, *Can Catholic Schools Survive?* (New York, 1970), 22, 24.

[54] Andrew M. Greeley, "The Catholic Schools Are Committing Suicide," *New York Times Magazine* (October 21, 1973).

[55] S. Francis Overlan, "Why Are Parochial Schools Closing?" *America* (September 14, 1974):111-113.

[56] Quoted in Horrigan, *Shaping of the NCEA*, 28.

[57] For statistics on declining enrollments, see Andrew D. Thompson and Eugene F. Hemrick, *The Last Fifteen Years: A Statistical Survey of Catholic Elementary and Secondary Formal Education, 1965-1980* (Washington, 1982).

[58] *New York Times* (May 15, June 25, 1977).

[59] *New York Times* (March 25, June 6, September 30, 1978), (May 13, 1979), (April 21, October 9, October 12, October 21, November 16, December 27, 1980).

[60] Andrew M. Greeley, "Catholic Schools: A Golden Twilight?" *America* (February 11, 1989):106-108, 116-118.

[61] *Ibid.*, 118.

[62] John Convey, "Views of Bishops and Priests Concerning Catholic Schools: A Ten Year Perspective," in James Youniss, John Convey, and Jeffrey A. McLellan, eds., *The Catholic Character of Catholic Schools* (Notre Dame, IN, 2000): 14-37; Kathleen Carr, "Leadership Given to the Religious Mission of Catholic Schools," in Youniss, Convey, and McLellan, eds., *The Catholic Character of Catholic Schools*, 62-81.

[63] Among others, see the following articles: Timothy Walch, "Catholic Schools Are Worth Saving," *Cedar Rapids Gazette* (February 1, 1996); Sol Stern, "Why the Catholic School Model is Taboo," *Wall Street Journal* (July 17, 1996); Andrew Greeley, "Why Catholic Schools Work So Well," *Washington Post* (July 28, 1996); Denis P. Doyle and Bruce S. Cooper, Religious Schools Can Be a Solution," *Washington Post* (September 1, 1996); Margaret Carlson, "Hail, Mary and Regina," *Time* (September 23, 1996); Karen W. Arenson, "Parochial School Mystique," *New York Times* (September 22, 1996) and Kenneth L. Woodward, "Catechism Lessons," *Newsweek* (September 23, 1996).

[64] Blaine Harden, "Dole Supports Public Funds for Private Schools," *Washington Post* (July 19, 1996); David S. Broder, "Awaiting A School Choice Showdown," *Washington Post* (July 24, 1996); Mary B.W. Tabor, "Ohio Upholds Public Funding of Private and Religious Schools," *New York Times* (August 1, 1996); Joe Klein, "Parochial Concerns," *Newsweek* (September 2, 1996); Rene Sanchez, "Cleveland Charts New Educational Course," *Washington Post* (September 10, 1996); Mona Charon, "Catholic Schools Could Succeed at Challenge," *Iowa City Press Citizen* (September 11, 1996); Charles J. Sykes, "Why Educators Fear School Vouchers," *San Diego Union-Tribune* (September 12, 1996); Jacques Steinberg, "New York Chancellor Won't Aid Parochial School Plan," *New York Times* (September 12, 1996); Mirta Ojito, "Private Program for Troubled Students Echoes N.Y. Catholic School Plan," *New York Times* (September 12, 1996); and Richard Lacayo, "Parochial Politics," *Time* (September 12, 1996).

[65] William J. Byron, "Catholic Education in America," *Vital Speeches of the Day* 61 (June 1, 1990): 489; Timothy Meagher, "Ethnic, Catholic, White: Changes in the Identity of European American Catholics," in Youniss, Convey, and McLellan, eds., *The Catholic Character of Catholic Schools*, 190-218; Timothy Walch, "The Past Before Us: Three Traditions and the Recent History of Catholic Education" in Youniss, Convey, and McLellan, eds., *The Catholic Character of Catholic Schools*, 176-189.

[66] David J. O'Brien, "American Catholicism and Diaspora," *Cross Currents* 16 (Summer 1966): 308-309. See also Marvin Lazerson, "Understanding American Catholic Educational History, " *History of Education Quarterly* (Fall 1977):298-99.

## CHAPTER 6

# THE CALL FOR A LIVING, CONSCIOUS AND ACTIVE FAITH: NCEA ESTABLISHES THE DEPARTMENT OF RELIGIOUS EDUCATION

*Alfred McBride, O.Praem*

I n the years immediately following the conclusion of Vatican II, there was a shift in the teaching of religion. Teachers and authors of textbooks sought ways to apply the fresh insights of the Council to the Christian Formation of Students in parish-based religious education (CCD) and Catholic schools. Other changes were already in place before the Council. We will discuss these changes after noting the activity of the Superintendents regarding religious education. After that we will treat the development of NCEA's Department of Religious Education from 1972 to the present.

In March 1969, at a meeting of superintendents in Atlanta, the group stated, "We urge the formation of a department of religious education in every diocese which will provide staff and/or consultative resources to the office of the Superintendent of education."[1] Already a number of dioceses had appointed an associate superintendent for religious education. Some of them worked only with schools. Others served schools and parish-based programs.

In June 1969, NCEA convened a meeting of associate superintendents of religious education at the Cenacle Retreat House in Metarie, Louisiana. Hosted by Father Emile Lafranz and chaired by Msgr. John F. Meyers, the forty participants issued *"The Metarie Statement,"* a visionary document that presented a comprehensive plan for religious education that is substantially valid to the present day.[2]

Noting that the bishop is the first catechist of a diocese, the statement identified three needs:

a) The need to coordinate diocesan efforts in religious education with other educational efforts in the diocese, e.g .CCD, campus ministries and the apostolate of continuing education.

b) The need to foster professional organizations of religious educators within the diocese.

c) The need to recognize that effective catechesis demands that the adult population of a diocese be involved in the current developments in the field of religious education.

The authors of the statement addressed a controversy surrounding the major textbooks in use at the time. They believed that the attacks on the texts were unwarranted and caused a collapse of confidence that was injurious to the field. "We deplore the attacks against the orthodoxy of many modern textbooks. Specifically, we reject the attacks that have been made against the following materials."[3] They named four elementary series and six secondary ones.

As might be presumed, they commented on their expectations of a religion teacher. After citing a number of professional qualifications they noted: "It is the special responsibility of the religion teacher to initiate the students in the authentic Catholic teaching as made explicit by the Church's magisterium. In the light of the current rapid communication media, it is necessary to distinguish theological speculation from the formal teaching of the Church." [4]

The Metarie participants urged the formation of diocesan religious education offices across the board. Connected to this was the need to have direction from the NCEA. In the autumn of 1972, Msgr. John F. Meyers, executive director of the superintendent's department, selected Father Alfred McBride, O.Praem., to be the first executive director of the newly formed National Forum for Religious Educators. It would later be called the NCEA Department of Religious Education. The appointment was approved by the president, Father C. Albert Koob, O.Praem. It was meant to serve the needs of religious education for both parish-based programs and those of Catholic schools, as well as adult education programs.

## The Context

Before proceeding with an account of the activities of this new office, it is helpful to establish the background and context of catechetical development prior to the council. Following is a brief overview of catechesis from the Baltimore Catechism to Vatican II.

## The Baltimore Catechism

For millions of Catholics in the United States, the word catechism meant the Baltimore Catechism. It brought back memories of memorized questions and answers, the method used for centuries to impart a basic knowledge of the teachings of Jesus Christ as given to us by the Church. That method, popularized by Martin Luther, was adopted by both Protestants and Catholics (with some modifications) all the way up to the twentieth century. What, briefly, is the history of the Baltimore Catechism?

Numerous catechisms in the question-answer format were published after the promulgation of the Roman Catechism in 1566. Two of them specifically influenced the Baltimore Catechism. First was "The Sincere Christian," the catechism of George Hay of Edinburg, published in 1781.[5] Archbishop John Carroll abridged Hay's catechetical writings, many of whose texts appeared in the Baltimore Catechism. In Ireland, Archbishop James Butler of Cashel produced a catechism in 1775. The Synod of Maynooth revised it in 1875. Substantial portions of this edition appeared in the Baltimore Catechism.

At the Third Plenary Council of Baltimore in 1884, the bishops of the United States published a national catechism for our country. It was composed by Januarius De Consilio, a priest of Newark, New Jersey, and John Lancaster Spalding, Bishop of Peoria, Illinois.[6] Its 72 pages contained 421 questions and answers in 37 chapters. Its order was: creed, sacraments, prayer, commandments, and Last Things. Its publication coincided with the bishops urging every parish to have a Catholic school. Supporting this policy was the arrival in America of many new religious congregations devoted to the teaching ministry. A simpler form of this catechism was developed for younger children. In 1941 the bishops revised this catechism and reversed the sequence of topics to: creed, commandments, sacraments and prayer.

The Baltimore Catechism served the need for creedal unity for the millions of immigrant Catholics who crowded American cities and towns. Its impact was felt right up to the dawn of Vatican II.

What brought about the gradual development of other ways to teach religion to our students? We can assign the causes to the emergence of new teaching methods based on the psychological development of the students and the growth of biblical and liturgical studies.

## Psychological Development

Throughout the early twentieth century extensive research was done on how children learn and on their readiness for a given body of teaching. Scholars tracked their receptivity to knowledge at given stages and the development of their reasoning skills. As this research entered the catechetical mainstream, writers of textbooks and teachers of the materials adapted their approach to the readiness of the students. It was argued that the memorized question-and-answer method in a "one size fits all" was inadequate to meet the needs of the students to understand the material This method was too fixed on memory alone.

There should be a broader approach that addressed the intuitive, imaginative, and reasoning capacities of students. Teachers should go beyond "What does the Church teach?" to "What does the Church mean by her teaching and how does it apply to everyday life?" The method also emphasized using the human experiences of the students to help them understand the truths of divine revelation.

## *Growth Of Scriptural And Liturgical Studies*

The explosion of new interest in Scripture and the liturgy as sources of our spiritual growth affected the teaching of religion as teachers incorporated these studies   into catechetical lessons. In the 1950s, Jesuit Father Johannes Hofinger[7] proposed what he called the "Kerygmatic Method" (or, salvation history) catechesis. Kerygma implied a joyful proclamation of a message of the Good News of salvation. The Christian mystery should be presented as an event and not just an idea. Hofinger based his concept on the way the apostles and Fathers of the Church taught religion. They presented scripture as the record of God's mighty deeds of love for us and our call to respond to that graciousness with faith and love. This scripture-based catechesis was intimately connected to Word and Sacrament in the celebration of the liturgy. Behind it was this unifying principle: God the Father entered history with redeeming covenant acts of love for Israel. The prophets reinterpreted that love for successive generations and foresaw a Messiah.

This covenant and prophetic promise was perfectly realized in the Incarnation, life, death, and Resurrection of the Word made flesh, Jesus Christ. It continues in the Spirit-guided life of the Church and the sacraments. All through this process, God calls us to a living, active, and conscious faith response. What impact did this have on the content of catechesis? It caused the content to become biblical, historical, and interpersonal. Faith about God was expressed in more vivid, concrete, salvation-historical, and interpersonal language. Just like the Baltimore Catechism, it was based on God's revelation, but in a historical and personal way.

How did the kerygmatic approach work?  Unfortunately, the writers and teachers often did not know how to communicate a systematic and comprehensive knowledge and understanding of basic Catholic teachings in this new context of a biblical-liturgical catechesis.

Numerous reasons account for this: lack of scriptural knowledge, inability to translate basic teachings into a biblical-liturgical language, a tendency to substitute psychology for religion, etc. A common religious vocabulary was lost. The result has been well documented: widespread religious illiteracy. Baltimore Catechism alumni knew the basics of their religion, but may not have progressed in their understanding and witnessing of it as they matured. The newly catechized people were willing to understand and witness, but they needed something substantial to ponder. That is the reason why the pope and bishops have commissioned the new Catechism of the Catholic Church, a topic addressed later in this chapter.

## DEPARTMENT GROWTH AND ISSUES FACED

### National Leadership

The first step taken by the new religion department was the creation of a National Conference of Diocesan Directors of Religious Education (NCDRE). Not only did they gather together annually for mutual support and sharing of concerns, they also were a working group that produced a series of documents that served their field. Msgr. Meyers established the precedent of the "working" workshop for the annual meetings of NCDRE. In 1970 they published the *Criteria for the Evaluation of Religious Education Programs*.[8] The instrument was a self-survey of a given religion program carried out by the religion faculty in cooperation with the administration. Input from students, parents and clergy was desirable.

The guiding principles began with the basic one about God's revelation as manifested in liturgy, scripture and doctrine. We are to respond freely to this revelation with faith and through the community of faith, the Church. Another theme was the call to build a unified world that "cherishes the dignity of the human person." The document remains a useful tool, though most easily used in the school setting.

Another influential publication was the *Qualities and Competencies of the Religion Teacher*.[9] Under the able guidance of Sister Sarah Fassenmyer and Sister Genevieve Schillo of Catholic University's School of Education, the NCDRE began by identifying the kinds of competencies that make a good religion teacher. This would be a performance-based approach to catechesis that is useful in training teachers toward continual self-improvement.

It was also seen that the qualities of a teacher's life are even more important. These included faith, holiness, depth of commitment to Christ, the Gospel, the Church and the kingdom's goals of love, justice and mercy. The diocesan directors identified seventeen competencies for the religion teacher along with rating scales to assist the teacher's self evaluation. Examples of such competencies are: the competency to carry out a variety of goal-directed learning experiences, the competency to evaluate student learning and general progress in relation to program goals.

Other projects taken on by NCDRE were:

a) a commentary on the General Catechetical Directory[10]

b) the development of five models for "total religious education" – an effort to unite the energies of leadership of those in parish and school religion programs;

c) a study of evangelization and its connection to all catechesis

d) *I Believe in God*,[11] designed to help youth ministers carry out their important faith leadership for young Catholics.

The department was greatly enriched by the arrival of Sister Kathleen Marie Shields, C.S.J. Her many years in the St. Paul-Minneapolis archdiocesan religious education office served her well at the national level. She is a woman of prodigious energies, profound faith, and a remarkable ability to translate the policies and philosophy of what emerges at the national level and bring it all down to earth for teachers both in schools and parish programs. She has been engaged in the same ministry for the diocese of Honolulu for over twenty years.

## *Parish Directors*

Another development was the creation of the National Association of Parish Coordinators-Directors of Religious Education (NPCD). As parish-based catechetical programs grew, they were accompanied by the hiring of professional religious educators with degrees in religious education from various universities around the country. Normally referred to as DRE's, these leaders were organized into their own professional group for mutual support, self-improvement, and ongoing growth in their chosen field. Like the diocesan directors, they meet annually, produce newsletters, and exert leadership in the field. During Msgr. Kelly's tenure, Wayne Smith was the staff person who served for ten years.

As these national organizations within NCEA grew to serve religious education there evolved a parallel organization, The National Conference of Diocesan Directors of Religious Education (NCDD later changed their title to the National Conference of Catechetical Leadership (NCCL) Their principal focus has been on parish-based religious education. Because the department's organizations and theirs served a similar purpose and constituency, it was inevitable that rivalry and competition affected our relationships. The department's goals embraced both school and parish programs, while theirs was addressed mainly to parish programs. Happily, all the directors of the Department of Religious Education– Father Alfred McBride, Msgr. Francis Kelly, Michael Carotta, and Robert Colbert – were dedicated to fruitful dialogue with NCCL over the years. Serious efforts were mounted to merge the two organizations but were unable to reach a satisfactory outcome. One of the agenda items frequently raised was the contrast between a classroom, school model approach to religious education and a parish-based method which tended to rely strongly on many forms of participative learning, such as the experiences of the students and an emphasis on community building.

### *Reoi-Rekap*

Early on, Msgr. Jack Meyers and George Elford approached Father McBride with a proposal to develop a religion test for students in grades 8-9, whether in schools or parish programs. Such a test would evaluate the beliefs, attitudes, and practices of the students. It would give teachers a report on the religious literacy of their students as well as an appreciation of their attitudes to faith, morality and Church authority. It would also provide a report on the students' mass attendance, prayer habits, and commitment to charity and social justice. The test would be developed in cooperation with the Educational Testing Service that would yield the results and return them to the parishes and schools. No individual scores would be given to the students, but the teachers would receive the generalized results.

When this plan was publicized it met with considerable resistance. Typical of the complaints was the very idea that one's religion could be graded, that a low mark would be an affront to the faith of a test-taker. It was decided to convene a national meeting of a wide-ranging representation of religious education leaders to discuss the proposal. After much discussion, some of it predictably heated, the project was approved. The fears of parish-based leaders were calmed when it was seen that the results would not be a reproach to an errant teacher so much as a useful way to see how the faith life of students could be improved. Moreover, the students would not receive scores on their performance. The instrument would be named the Religious Education Outcomes Inventory (REOI).

The project was and is an outstanding success. In the very first year, more than 100,000 students took the test. Several years later a similar instrument (with comparable resistance) was developed for grades 11-12. It was called the Religious Education Inventory of Knowledge, Attitudes and Practices (REKAP).

### *ACRE*

Eventually a similar evaluation instrument was developed for grade 5. From that time the three levels (grade 5; grades 8-9; grades 11-12) were combined under one title: The NCEA Assessment of Catechesis/Religious Education (NCEA ACRE).

While there was an abundance of anecdotal satisfaction with these tests, there was a need to have a formal analysis. Obtaining a grant from the Knights of Columbus, Dr. Andrew Thompson undertook a study of the results of these tests and published his findings in his work, *That They May Know You.*[12] He provided a detailed analysis of the strengths and weaknesses of students' responses in the areas of their beliefs, attitudes, and practices.

His reports centered on ten key themes of catechesis: God, Jesus Christ, Church, Grace, Sacraments, Conscience and Moral Principles, Sexuality, Social Justice, Prayer, Spirituality, and Christian Eschatology. His findings suggested that more emphasis was needed on religious knowledge and a clear appreciation of Catholic identity. While there was a commendable commitment to charitable endeavors and the need for justice, there was not an equal devotion to the Church nor an understanding of what that means. Their understanding of traditional theological and religious language was poor. There was considerable room for growth in knowledge of scripture, ecclesiology and in a traditional Catholic vocabulary.

### *National Catechetical Directory*

In l975 the Catholic National Conference of Catholic Bishops (NCCB) created an office for the writing of a catechetical directory for the United States. Msgr. Wilfrid Paradis oversaw the process and was ably assisted by Sister Mariella Frye. The goal was to take the Vatican's *General Catechetical Directory* and adapt it to the American scene. Father McBride served on the oversight committee for the next five years up to the time of its publication under the title of *Sharing the Light of Faith.*[13]

This National Directory was focused on *how* religious education would be presented to all its constituencies, those in primary, junior high, senior-high, young adults, and adults in general whether they are in schools or parish programs. This was an ambitious project that surfaced some assumptions about teaching religion; they were hotly debated and eventually tabled. Among these was a view of divine revelation as "ongoing revelation," in the sense that the revelation in Jesus Christ was not definitive. Some tried the device of using a capital "R" for the traditional notion and a small "r" for ongoing revelation. This view was rejected.

Another major issue centered on the matter of "basic teachings." Noting the prevalence of religious illiteracy, it was argued that the directory should contain a list of basic teachings, something like the one that Archbishop John

Whelan (chairman of the committee) had composed. Again after turbulent opposition, it was agreed to include the list. Without doubt the five-year process, that included national consultations, produced a relatively useful document. It gave positive direction on the ways to present Catholic doctrines and morality to a variety of persons including adults, with a sensitivity to the disabled, with an ecumenical outlook, and with an appreciation of the many rites of the Eastern Churches in the United States.

Its success can be measured by the impact it had on the writing of textbooks, the policies of diocesan religious education offices and the frequency of quotes from it in magazines such as *Living Light, The Catechist* and the *Religion Teachers Journal*. Father Berard Marthaler's excellent commentary on the Directory was instrumental in making it respected, understood and accessible to a big audience.

## COMMUNITY OF FAITH

During the days of the early immigrant Church in the United States most urban Catholics lived in ethnic neighborhoods. So strong was the Catholic identity caused by Irish, Italian, French, Polish and similar enclaves that even the few non-Catholics in such areas identified themselves as being "in St. Patrick's or Transfiguration parishes." They could do this with the assurance that others knew exactly what part of the city they were talking about. In those times Catholic community was a given - strong, proud, emotional, definite. The community put flesh on the doctrines, collective moral principles and practices, and the life of faith. The individual families were the family of the Church.

After World War II the immigrant enclaves gradually broke up as prosperity caused upward mobility and the migration of millions of Catholics to suburbs where they now lived next door to Protestants, Jews, and people of other persuasions. Often they sent their children to public schools where the multiplicity of faiths and convictions replaced the parochial schools of the past. Mary Perkins Ryan raised a storm with her book, *"Are Parochial Schools The Answer?"*[14] Would not a warm participative liturgy and parish programs even be better than the old ways?

Her book tended to make some people forget that Catholic schools were effective centers of religious education. Despite a decline in the number of Catholic schools, the number eventually stabilized and recently new schools are opening. But it was true that American Catholics as a separate community of ethnic groups was disappearing. What would replace this Catholic separatism? Msgr. Russell Bleich of the Davenport, Iowa, diocese developed new models which he called Communities of Faith.[15] Some would apply to the Catholic school itself; others would be adapted to the parish in a new dimension. His principle was enlightening, "What was once assumed must now be created."

Another reason for consciously creating community was the emergence of permanent deacons and lay teachers and lay leaders in the life of a parish and of a school. The gradual disappearance of a tightly-knit community of women-religious running a school obviously signaled a need for a new way to express community in this situation. Vast numbers of laity filled teachings positions in the schools and leadership of parish religious education programs. A substantial number of women-religious still serve the needs of parishes and schools, but the landscape has changed.

Not only did the new suburban parishes, as well as the traditional ones, exist in pluralistic worlds, the very texture of rectory, parish and school now hosted an army of laity ready to fulfill their baptismal call in the life of the Church. Avery Dulles' *Models of the Church*,[16] provided the needed theological framework for what Msgr. Bleich initiated with his Community -of- Faith movement. It has ceased to be simply a movement and is now a normal feature of parishes and schools.

## IMPLEMENTING A PASTORAL

In 1972 NCCB published a pastoral, *To Teach as Jesus Did*,[17] in which they stated that the goals of religious education were: Message, Community, Service. Its publication gave birth to a remarkable and very successful cooperation between the NCEA Department of Religious Education and that of USCC. In our discussions with our counterparts in their office of religious education lip-service was often paid to the principle that USCC would set policy and NCEA would implement it.

Keeping that distinction was not always easy. But this pastoral made it possible on a grand scale.  In some cases a bishops' pastoral, despite its burning relevance, tended to stay on the shelf. We decided to form a traveling workshop to spread the good news about "To Teach as Jesus Did." Our team included Msgr. Meyers, George Elford, Dr. Mary Angela Harper, Sister Kathleen Marie Shields, and Father McBride. Collectively, we covered the relevance of the pastoral to catechesis, research on the effectiveness of religious education, the financing of parish programs, the role of boards, and how to apply it to elementary and secondary religious education.

Over a two-year period we brought the workshop to twenty-five dioceses representing all regions of the country. We pushed the pastoral into the blood-stream of the Church, with the result that virtually every diocese in the country eventually devoted their annual diocesan religious education convention to a discussion of the pastoral. This was a grace and it modeled a form of cooperation that led to other long-lasting ways to help the Church's mission of the Word.

## ADULT EDUCATION

As lifelong education and professional self-improvement became a commonplace in the culture, it became obvious that religious education should not stop with Confirmation. It ought to be an ongoing project for all Catholic adults. Growth in the understanding of the truths of faith should be considered an ideal counterpart to the deepening of faith itself. It was already clear that doctrine developed organically over the centuries. Should not each Catholic, throughout the adult years, also be developing his or her appreciation of Catholic doctrines as well?

The department participated in this desire to involve Catholic adults in continuing religious education. Detroit's Jane Wolford Hughes was for us an icon of the movement and provided the leadership for the cause. Connected to this was the increase of the family education project. Experiments were developed that involved the training of Catholic parents to be the religion teachers of their children.

Efforts on behalf of adult religious education continue to this day. Where this is most evident is in parish scripture-studies programs that remain popular and enriching. The impact of movements of spirituality such as charismatic renewal, Cursillo, "Christ Renews His Parish" and more recently, the Neocatechumenate illustrate forms of religious formation of adults. The Rite of the Christian Initiation of Adults (RCIA) is not only a matter of training adult candidates for full initiation into the Church, but it is also dependent upon the education of the adult trainers who imbibe the old lesson that a good way to learn something is to teach it.

## STAGES OF MORALITY AND FAITH

As developmental psychology penetrated popular consciousness, it began to affect religious education. National and diocesan conventions and institutes of religious education began offering lectures and workshops on stages of moral development and stages of faith development. Identifying steps in moral growth seemed helpful both in getting moral discourse back into religious education and allowing for a more precise understanding of how students make moral decisions. Similarly, a developmental approach to faith growth seemed to provide religious educators the insights they needed to chronicle the general steps of faith that students climb and to minister more fruitfully to them because of this.

But the problem with the moral development model was its subjectivity. It did not seem to allow for an objective moral order as part of the journey of the student. Some progress has been made in this area by more discriminating religious educators who bring both objective moral principles and laws and the subjective stages together. It is still not clear how successful this will be. Likewise, the faith-steps approach, at least as first presented, was too rigid and also had a subjective bias. Probably, if both models had simply presented these stages as metaphors of a fluid human situation and were more willing to include the objective aspects of morality and doctrine, their contributions could have been more helpful.

One last comment needs to be made. There was enthusiasm for the values-clarification method among religious educators for a brief time. Its "games" were clever, but its substance was lacking, again because of its sheer subjectivity. In a religious context, the stage theories not only lacked an objective bearing, but also sidestepped the work of prayer and grace and the fundamental reality of God's revelation and our faith response. This was a flawed methodology.

## METHODOLOGY

Msgr. Francis Kelly, the second executive director of the religion department, held a twelve-year tenure [1979-90] that was marked by attention to a proper methodology in religious education. He also placed a spotlight on the need for religious literacy among our people and nourished the growth of the parish DRE's.

Msgr. Kelly was drawn to examine the principles and practices of catechetical methodology after he studied the results of surveys of the religious knowledge of students as well as their understanding of the truths. In his book, *The Mystery We Proclaim* he writes: "The troubling part of the research is that the authors of *Faith Without Form* tell us there is 'nothing specifically Catholic or even Christian in the vague approach to faith reflected in the responses of many students. Their concept of God was vague, they reflected little knowledge of doctrine or history, and their ideas about morality and sin were very subjective and defined according to their own desires and conveniences. [18],

It must be acknowledged that recent decades have seen in some circles in the Church a certain tentativeness about offering the full content of the faith, a glamorization of an approach of questioning, doubt, and searching, as if these were values in themselves. The Letter to the Hebrews reminds us that 'faith is the assurance of things hoped for, the conviction of things not seen (Hebrews 11:1).[19]

Msgr. Kelly later outlined the principles of an acceptable methodology that allowed for a variety of methods; particularly those that insisted on being guided by the various catechetical documents of the pope and bishops; that found value in both inductive and deductive approaches; that retained a space for experiential learning within a context of a systematic and comprehensive presentation of the truths of faith; that made room for memorizing some of the formulas of faith; and that specified learning objectives that foster faith growth and conversion.

Finally, Msgr. Kelly offered five steps that would guide a catechist to have an ecclesial methodology. The first step is the "Preparation." The catechist needs to set up the conditions for the possibility of deepening God's revelation in the hearts of those being served. This requires techniques that will foster both interior and exterior silence so that the hearts of people will be open to the presence of the Holy Spirit.

The second step is "Proclamation." The catechist will deliver a faithful and effective announcement of the truths of faith as found in the Scriptures and in the Church's living tradition, enunciated by the popes and bishops – the Magisterium. The catechist must realize that these truths come from revelation and make sense under the guidance of the Holy Spirit.

This is followed by "Explanation." This explanation should be based on the Church's understanding of the truths of revelation. The catechist is advised to use a participative method to draw out the meaning of the truth for the hearts of the people. Through participation, the understanding of the Lord's teachings can be made relevant to people's life story and contemporary issues.

The fourth step is "Application." The outcome of catechesis should be a life of witness and service. Our people need to be able to be witnesses to the divine Person of Jesus as the world's only savior and to his way of life. Numerous examples of faith witness are found in the Acts of the Apostles and the writings of St. Paul. Practical services of love, justice and mercy are also a fruitful result of catechesis. Jesus taught the need to feed the hungry, clothe the naked, visit the sick and those in prison and other forms of service. Our roots for this can be found in scripture and the long history of ecclesial service.

The final step in this methodology is "Celebration." Catechesis begins with a faithful attentiveness to God's Word. It concludes with a joyful celebration of the Holy Eucharist in which is contained the entire treasure of the Church. The celebration of the Mass stands at the center of Catholic life. Our whole lives flow toward the altar and flow outward from it. This fifth step unifies the other four into the desired total response looked for in catechesis – cognitive, affective and behavioral. Christian prayer is also a thread that weaves the five stages into a tapestry of catechesis that provides the vision and tactics that a challenging catechesis seeks.

Among his numerous other accomplishments at NCEA, Msgr. Kelly worked with NCEA's Secondary Schools Department to offer summer workshops for high school religion teachers and campus ministers. He also promoted close cooperation with NCCL and fostered the growth of NPCD. In his tenure the department of religious education acquired a sound identity, a clear purpose and a solid structure that assured its promising future. Michael Carotta succeeded Msgr. Kelly and served the department for two years.

Robert Colbert became the next executive director and served the field for 11 years. During his very productive tenure he sponsored the following projects:

- Coordinated and helped develop NPCD's National Convocation (1993 in New Orleans) held in conjunction with the NCEA Convention.
- Launched and coordinated the sponsorship of Shepherding the Shepherds' Retreat for Parish DREs by dioceses across the United States.
- Introduced NCEA Catechetical Scholars Program that consists of two one-week sessions that provide professional development opportunities for veteran diocesan leaders and the opportunity to research a topic related to catechesis and leadership
- Managed major revision of NCEA's assessment tool ACRE; changed the name to NCEA ACRE (Assessment of Catechesis/ Religious Education), negotiated a partnership with the Center for Educational Testing and Evaluation at the University of Kansas that currently handles the scoring and reporting of the data.
- Partnered the development of the Spiritual Growth Leadership Institute at Boston College.
- Introduced annual Parish Catechist Congress (in Philadelphia in 1996) held during NCEA Convention and NPCD Convocation.
- Helped develop 13 texts related to catechesis and the ministry of the DRE.
- Represented the NCEA and NPCD on USCCB Committee on Catechesis.
- Increased department staff to 5 full time members

Robert Colbert's years at the department corresponded with the historic publication of the new *Catechism of the Catholic Church*.[20] It would gradually have a dramatic impact on religious education both in the area of the content of the textbooks and the orientation of teachers toward a more comprehensive and systematic appreciation of the teachings of Christ and the Church. As we conclude, it seems appropriate to offer a brief reflection on the new Catechism and its value for our religion department.

## THE NEW CATECHISM

On October 11, 1992, Pope John Paul II published his Apostolic Constitution, *Depositum Fidei*, introducing the *Catechism of the Catholic Church*. He chose a publication date that marked the thirtieth anniversary of the opening of Vatican II. In this document, he wrote, "I declare it (the Catechism) to be a sure norm for teaching the faith. . . . Therefore, I ask the Church's pastors and the Christian faithful to receive this Catechism in a spirit of communion and to use it assiduously in fulfilling their mission of proclaiming the faith and calling people to the Gospel life."[21] This exhortation reflects the epistle to Timothy which stresses the need to serve the deposit of faith with loving care. "O Timothy, guard what has been entrusted to you. . . . Guard this rich trust with the help of the Holy Spirit that dwells within us" (I Tm 6:20; II Tm 1:14).

Such also was the vision of Pope John XXIII when he asked the Fathers of Vatican II both to guard and to present better the heritages of our faith. Why? To make the Gospel more accessible to the Christian faithful and to all people of good will. Hence the council did not concentrate on condemning the errors of our time, but rather strove calmly to demonstrate the power and beauty of Christian doctrine.

This same positive spirit pervades the Catechism. It contains the inherent beauty and intrinsic attractiveness of the teachings of Christ that appeal to the mind and heart. Pope Paul VI said that the full presentation of these teachings must be at the heart of evangelization. "There is no true evangelization if the name, the teaching, the life, the promises, the kingdom and the mystery of Jesus of Nazareth, the Son of God are not proclaimed"[22]

The *Catechism of the Catholic Church* contains this hidden energy of the Good News and will be more effective when all of us absorb its spirit and content. Convinced people convince others. When we embark on a lifelong journey of faith conversion, our faith conviction will affect others. Converted teachers convert students by the grace of the Holy Spirit working both in the witnessing teacher and the listening student.

Our Holy Father goes on to say, "This *Catechism* is given that it may be a sure and authentic reference text for teaching Catholic doctrine and particularly for preparing local catechisms."[23] The positive tone of the *Catechism* illustrates its non-polemical character.

One of the practical outcomes of the *Catechism* should be a religious literacy which will enable Catholics to know, explain, apply, and defend their faith. Numerous studies have identified this need. Our Holy Father specifies this as a goal of the Catechism. "It is offered to all the faithful who wish to deepen their knowledge of the unfathomable riches of salvation. The *Catechism of the Catholic Church* is offered to every individual who asks us to give an account of the hope that is in us (I Pt 3:15) and who wants to know what the Catholic Church teaches."[24]

Finally, the *Catechism* is meant to stir up the faith of the reader. It calls the Catholic community to acquire a living, conscious and active faith in Jesus Christ. It would seem that it can become a charter for the future of religious education at NCEA. We are only at a beginning stage in appreciating what the Catechism can do for the health of the Church. The work of Bishops' Office for the Catechism, especially in assessing conformity of catechetical materials and textbooks to the Catechism is an important new step. The imminent publication of a *National Adult Catechism* is another significant development. For over thirty years the NCEA Department of Religious Education has been an effective leader in the field. The new *Catechism* will prove to be a dynamic tool for the growth period ahead.

## ENDNOTES

[1] Minutes of the annual meeting of the Department of Chief Administrators of Catholic Education, Atlanta Georgia, 1969 (NCEA Office files).

[2] NCEA statement produced during a meeting of associate superintendents in Metarie, Louisiana, June 1-3, 1969 (NCEA papers, Archive of the Catholic University of America, Washington, D.C.).

[3] *Ibid.*

[4] *Ibid.*

[5] Referenced in *The New Catholic Encyclopedia*, Vol. 3 pp. 230-231 (New York: McGraw-Hill, 1967).

[6] *Ibid.*

[7] Johannes Hofinger, S.J., *The Art of Teaching Christian Doctrine* (Notre Dame, IN: University of Notre Dame Press, 1957).

[8] National Catholic Educational Association, *Evaluative Criteria for Religious Education Programs* (Washington, D.C.: National Catholic Educational Association, 1975).

[9] Sarah Fassenmeyer and Genevieve Schillo, *Qualities and Competencies of the Religion Teacher* (Washington, D.C.: National Catholic Educational Association, 1973).

[10] Thomas F. Sullivan and John F. Meyers, *Focus on American Catechetics: A Commentary on the General Catechetical Directory* (Washington, D.C.: National Catholic Educational Association, 1972).

[11] NCDRE, *I Believe in God: Faith Packet for Youth Ministers and Adult Education* (Washington, D.C.: National Catholic Educational Association, 1973).

[12] Andrew Thompson, *That They May Know You* (Washington, D.C.: National Catholic Educational Association, 1982).

[13] United States Catholic Conference, Department of Education, *Sharing the Light of Faith* (Washington, D.C.: United States Catholic Conference, 1979).

[14] Mary Perkins Ryan, *Are Parochial Schools the Answer?* (New York: Holt, Rinehart, Winston, 1964)

[15] See John J. Augenstein, "CACE: 90 Year of Leadership, *Momentum* (February 1999)

[16] Avery Dulles, *Models of Church* (New York: Doubleday & Company, 1978).

[17] National Conference of Catholic Bishops, *To Teach As Jesus Did* (Washington, D.C.: United States Catholic Conference, 1972).

[18] Francis Kelly, The Mystery We Proclaim (Huntington, IN: Our Sunday Visitor Press, 1999).

[19] Kelly, 64.

[20] United States Catholic Conference, *Catechism of the Catholic Church* (Washington, D.C.: United States Catholic Conference, 1995).

[21] *Depositum Fidei*, Apostolic Constitution on the Publication of *the Catechism of the Catholic Church,* October 11, 1992.

[22] *Evangelii Nuntiandi*, (On Evangelization in the Modern World) #22.

[23] *Depositum Fidei.*

[24] *Ibid.*

# PART II
# CHURCH AND STATE

## CHAPTER 7

# CHURCH-STATE/CHURCH CULTURE: THE SURVIVAL OF CATHOLIC SCHOOLS

A s George W. Bush began his presidency, he met with religious leaders and created a stir when he was unknowingly caught by a microphone stating his support for school vouchers for parochial schools and for government support of faith-based welfare organizations. The controversy over school vouchers brings to mind past events in Catholic education's efforts either to preserve its right to exist within a pluralistic culture or to gain a share in public funding for what is a contribution to American life. Yet, the debate over whether proposals, such as Bush's, violate the First Amendment is a relatively recent issue in American history. In the nineteenth century, the majority of Americans presumed the public schools should inculcate Christian values, but this meant Protestantism. Only in the mid-twentieth century did the debate center on the First Amendment.

In 1789, when John Carroll and other ex-Jesuits founded the Georgetown academy, which developed into Georgetown University, he envisioned, not so much Catholic education in the contemporary sense, as education open to Catholics. While Georgetown was largely his creation, he also sat on the board of trustees of St. John's College in Annapolis and received an honorary degree from Washington College in Chestertown, Maryland. He also explained to an English ex-Jesuit friend that he did not plan to establish a school in Philadelphia because the College of Philadelphia, now reorganized as the University of Pennsylvania, was open to all denominations and had a Jesuit on its board.[1] Georgetown was intended primarily for Catholics, education for whom was prohibited in

Maryland during the colonial period, and for providing a future body of clergy, but, from the beginning, it enrolled a significant number of non-Catholic students. The broadside announcing its inception stated that it would "be open to Students of EVERY RELIGIOUS PROFESSION."[2]

But such openness would not survive long in other parts of the country. In Carroll's time, Catholics accounted for less than 2 percent of the population. From their original centers in Maryland and Pennsylvania, they were expanding to Boston and New York, not through natural increase, but through immigration. In reaction to immigration, some Protestants became nativists, opposed to both immigration and Catholicism. In the summer of 1834, nativists burned "Mount Benedict," the Ursuline convent in Charlestown, Massachusetts, which, in fact, educated many upper-class Protestant girls. In the trial that ensued, only one rioter was convicted, but was then pardoned. When the nuns tried to sue for damages, a minority of the legislative committee investigating their claims argued they had no right to sue, because "Catholics acknowledging . . . the supremacy of a foreign potentate or power, could not claim under our government the protection as citizens of the commonwealth . . . ." In the bishops' 1837 pastoral letter, written by Bishop John England of Charleston, they sharply distinguished between the "civil and political allegiance" that citizens owed to the states and the federal government and the "spiritual and ecclesiastical" loyalty that Catholics rendered to the pope. No state could intrude into the ecclesiastical realm and no religious authority, even the pope, had jurisdiction over the political.[3] For more than the next century, Catholics would have to make similar defenses of their citizenship. In the nineteenth century, however, the Catholic response was now to develop a sub-culture, a defensive posture that influenced education on every level.

In 1841, Bishop Benedict Fenwick, S.J., of Boston, a native of Maryland, founded the College of the Holy Cross in Worcester, Massachusetts. With his experience in the Ursuline Convent burning, he decided his new institution would be one "into which no Protestant shall every set foot." He now envisioned the "philosophy" training of a college not only as preparing students for future professions, but also as preserving their faith in a hostile culture.[4]

But the major effect of nativism on Catholic education would be on the elementary-school level. This was the first encounter of the Church, not with the Church-State question, but with the broader society. In New York City, the issue arose because the Public School Society, which had charge of the common funds for education, was dominated by Protestants intent on inculcating Protestant Christianity in the public schools. This meant reading the King James version of the Bible and using readers designed to praise the heroes of the Reformation and denigrate popery. In 1841, Bishop John Hughes of New York sought a share of the funds for his developing Catholic schools or at least to have Catholic teachers placed in the public schools in predominantly Catholic neighborhoods. He argued that, as citizens, Catholics were being deprived of their rights. In this, he had the support of Governor William Seward, but not of the Public School Society. Although Hughes' dispute led to the creation of the Board of Education for New York City, he now focused on expanding his own parochial school system.[5] What is important to note is that at this time Seward saw no problem with public funding of Catholic schools or with providing teachers of the same ethnic and religious background as their students.

Hughes' fight in New York influenced what Bishop Francis P. Kenrick did in Philadelphia. Early in 1843, Kenrick had obtained permission from the Philadelphia school board to allow children to read any version of the Bible approved by their parents and not be compelled to read the King James version. Anti-Catholic nativists construed this as an attempt to remove the Bible from the public schools altogether. Tension between nativists and Irish immigrants led to rioting during two periods in 1844, May 6-9 and July 5-7. Two Catholic churches were burned and several people were killed. After the first riots, Kenrick shut down his churches to allow a cooling-off period. A grand jury blamed the May rioting on Kenrick who, it stated, was trying to remove the Bible from public schools. Ironically, at this time, Kenrick was working on his own translation of the Bible that he hoped would make it more accessible to the American Catholic reading public than the then current Douay version. Incidentally, when the Philadelphia nativists threatened to take their violence to New York, they met a more formidable opponent. After being refused police protection for his churches, Hughes armed his parishioners, surrounded his churches, and threatened to make New York a "second Moscow," if so much as a match was struck to destroy his edifices.[6]

Ante-bellum nativism contributed to the establishment of a separate Catholic school system that spread throughout the country, particularly after the Civil War. This Catholic system may have had the effect of gradually removing religion from the public schools altogether. By 1890, Archbishop John Ireland of St. Paul defended Catholics against the charge that they opposed public schools. Although he praised the state schools, he lamented that they did not teach Christianity that was at the heart of western civilization.[7] With the ratification of the Fourteenth Amendment, moreover, the First Amendment was now applicable to the states. But Catholics in post-bellum America were definitely receiving mixed signals about the future of their educational endeavor. On the one hand, at least in regard to Indian schools, the United States was still a Christian, albeit a Protestant nation. This became clear in the allocation of Indian agencies among Christian denominations during the administration of Ulysses S.

Grant. In 1872, the government distributed seventy-three agencies among various denominations, although on the basis of their missionary work to date, Catholics expected to receive thirty-eight, but obtained only seven. As a result, in 1874, the national hierarchy formed the Bureau of Catholic Indian Missions to provide for the missions and to lobby in Washington.[8] The government, however, had little problem in promoting cooperation between Church and State for these Indian schools.

On the other hand, Grant displayed insensitivity, at best, toward Catholics—his vice president, Schuyler Colfax, had been a member of the Know Nothing Party in Indiana, the nativist political party in the 1850s.[9] In 1875, Grant addressed Union Army veterans in Des Moines that they should

> Encourage free schools and resolve that not one dollar appropriated for
> their support shall be appropriated for the support of any sectarian
> schools. . . . Leave the matter of religion to the family altar, the church,
> and the private school, supported entirely by private contributions.
> Keep the church and state forever separated.[10]

In December 1875, he also proposed a constitutional amendment requiring all states to establish public schools, "forbidding the teaching in said schools of religious, atheistic, or pagan tenets; and prohibiting the granting of any school funds, or school taxes, or any part thereof, either by the legislative, municipal, or other authority, for the benefit or in aid, directly or indirectly, of any religious sect or denomination . . . ."[11] Shortly later, James G. Blaine formally introduced such an amendment, which was passed by the house, but was not ratified by the states. The defeated amendment was a harbinger of the issues the Church would face seventy years later.

In the meantime, Catholics were striving to operate their own schools without state support. In his 1890 address, Archbishop Ireland sought to make common cause with Protestant denominations in promoting religious schools. He noted that already in Poughkeepsie, New York, the local parish sought to diminish the financial burden on its congregation by leasing its school to the public school board during class hours. Similar plans operated in Georgia, New Mexico, Pennsylvania, and Missouri.[12] In the Poughkeepsie arrangement that began in 1875, the school board paid the teachers' salaries and supervised the secular instruction. Outside of regular class hours, the school reverted to the parish which then conducted religious instructions. One Protestant minister visited the school and expressed the sole reservation that religious images were still on display. Although this school plan had the approval of Archbishop John McCloskey, shortly to become the nation's first cardinal, it was opposed by some

Catholic lay people. James McMaster, the irascible editor of the New York *Freeman's Journal*, had already conveyed to Roman officials his opinion of the low moral standards of public schools, even where there were Catholic teachers. The archbishops of the country, in the meantime, reported that the public schools were then non-sectarian and presented no danger to the faith, but McMaster rejected their opinion. Armed with information about Poughkeepsie, he persuaded officials of the Congregation of Propaganda Fide in Rome to turn the matter over to the Holy Office, which issued an instruction in 1875 noting the dangers of public schools and calling for the construction and improvement of Catholic ones. Only in 1876, however, did Propaganda publish this instruction, which, in 1884, became the basis for the decree of the Third Plenary Council in 1884 calling for every parish to build a school within two years after the end of the council, unless the local bishop made other arrangements.[13]

But the council's legislation was impossible to realize. In 1891, Archbishop Ireland made arrangements, similar to those in Poughkeepsie, for his schools in Faribault and Stillwater. His plan, however, soon created controversy. Such an arrangement necessitated that English be the language of instruction, an issue that alienated German-Americans who viewed their language as a means for retaining the faith. He had earlier praised public education, moreover, and this system, though not unprecedented, seemed to surrender to the state what the Church in Europe and particularly in Germany during the *Kulturkampf* had tried to preserve—the right of the Church to educate. A pamphlet war now ensued. Father Thomas Bouquillon, professor of moral theology at the Catholic University, published *Education: To Whom Does It Belong?* He argued that the individual, the family, the State and the Church all had the right to educate, but, if parents failed to provide for education of their children, the State had the right to intervene to provide compulsory education. In response, René Holaind, S.J., professor of moral theology at Woodstock College, produced *The Parent First*, in which he argued that, since the United States was not a Catholic State, it had no rights over education, which, in any case was merely useful and not necessary. Though Ireland's plan gained Roman toleration, it was soon rescinded by the respective school boards.[14] Ironically, forty years later German-Americans would adopt a similar plan in Mercer County, Ohio, a farming community in the western part of the state. The arrangement was never contested, even after later Supreme Court rulings, partly because Lutherans nearby were doing the same thing. In other words, well into the twentieth century, some communities provided State support for parochial schools.

The general attitude toward Catholic schools seemed to be: if Catholics want their own schools, leave them alone, as long as the schools promote American citizenship. But there was one exception. In 1922, under the influence of the Scottish Rite Masons, the Oregon legislature enacted a Compulsory School Law that stated: "Any parent, guardian or other person in the state of Oregon, having control or charge or custody of a child under the age of sixteen years and of the age of eight years or over at the commencement of a term of public school of the district in which said child resides, who shall fail or neglect or refuse to send such child to a public school for the period of time a public school shall be held during the current year in said district, shall be guilty of a misdemeanor and each day's failure to send such child to a public school shall constitute a separate offense."[15] The act was to go into effect on September 1, 1926. Its proponents argued that private schools were "unpatriotic." They adopted the slogan "One flag, one school, one language!" It became the principal issue in the gubernatorial campaign of 1922, when Walter Pierce, the Democratic candidate, won the election by courting Ku Klux Klan support for the law.[16]

While the campaign was underway, Edwin Vincent O'Hara, superintendent of schools for the Archdiocese of Portland mobilized opposition to the act. On July 4, 1922, he gave an address arguing for the position "that the child belongs to the family is a teaching of religion and common sense" and "that it belongs to the state is an aberration of state paternalism the proper name for which is Prussian!" He thus reminded his audience of the recently ended First World War and of the American Catholic contribution to winning it. But he went on to spell out what became the gist of the Catholic argument against the bill:

> We proclaim the following principles: that the family is more ancient and a more fundamental social institution than the state; that to parents belong primarily the right and the obligation of educating their own children; that only when parents fail to do their duty has the state the right to interfere; that these rights of parents are primitive and inalienable, and may not be violated by the state without injustice; that the rights of parents to educate their children and to choose the instructors for their own offspring is the most sacred of human rights, and the exercise by the state of its police power to drag children from the homes of parents who are capable of and willing to perform their full duty in the education of their children, would be an indelible stain on the fair name of a free country.[17]

O'Hara's argument was reminiscent of the pamphlet war that raged around Ireland's school plan thirty years earlier.

Archbishop Alexander Christie of Portland consulted the bishops of his province, and all agreed that O'Hara should take the matter to court. The National Catholic Welfare Conference, only recently preserved from a Roman condemnation, pledged $100,000, and the Knights of Columbus promised any support that was necessary. Christie chose as his attorneys Judge John P. Kavanaugh, Frank J. Lonerghan, Dan J. Malarkey, and Hall S. Lusk with O'Hara as consultant. Since a specific plaintiff was required, O'Hara selected the Sisters of the Holy Names, who taught in most of the parochial schools in Oregon and had also been incorporated in the state since 1881. To strengthen their case, the attorneys then had the Hill Military Academy, a non-sectarian private school, join in the suit. Before the district court, they argued that the law was unconstitutional because it deprived the sisters and the academy of property without due process, it deprived Catholic parents of the right to choose what type of education they desired in conscience for their children, and it inhibited the sisters from the free exercise of their religious opinions. On April 1, 1924, the court declared the Oregon Compulsory School Law unconstitutional.

The court declared that the right of private schools to teach elementary grades "must be regarded as natural and inherent." The state, it declared, had "exceeded the limitations of its power—its purpose being to take utterly away from complainants their constitutional rights and privilege to teach in the grammar grades, and has and will deprive them of their property without due process of law." The court went on to say that the act would well have been entitled "an act to prevent parochial and private schools from teaching the grammar grades." As precedent, it cited *Meyer vs. Nebraska* (1923) which had overturned a state law requiring that only English be taught—the issue came to the court after the state fined a tutor for teaching German in a Lutheran grade school. It also issued an temporary injunction against implementation of the act until the Supreme Court heard the case. If there was no appeal, the injunction would become permanent. Governor Pierce immediately appealed the decision to the Supreme Court.[18]

The *New York Times* editorialized that the Oregon act had no precedent in any other state, but:

> the nearest analogy to this policy . . . is to be found in Russia under the present regime, and in Turkey under a bill which proposed specifically to prohibit attendance upon other than schools conducted by the Government. The law partook also of the spirit and method of the Prussian educational system. . . . While appeal will be taken in all probability to the Supreme Court, the decision of the District Court seems so sound as to make unlikely any reversal.

The *Times* continued that: "the State may and does require of the private and parochial schools the teaching of the same subjects, the observance of like standards, the same preparation of teachers and the same period of attendance as in the public schools. But to go further and to force all children into the public school is practically to take from the parent all discretion as to the education of the child." Falling short of recommending aid for parochial and private schools, the newspaper argued that "the private school is often a most valuable public school. Moreover it frequently offers freedom for experiment and special training that cannot always be had in the public school. We need the one as the complement of the other." But aside from the civic contribution of private schools, the editorial concluded, the court's decision would "have its greatest value in protecting the parental right against a socialistic invasion."[19]

On March 17, 1925, the Supreme Court heard the case. On June 1, relying on its earlier Nebraska decision, it handed down a unanimous decision upholding the lower court's finding that the law was unconstitutional. Speaking for a unanimous court, Justice James C. McReynolds declared that the law would deprive the sisters of their right to property and to the income derived from it. He also stated that "rights guaranteed by the Constitution may not be abridged by legislation which has no reasonable relation to some purpose within the competency of the state. The fundamental theory of liberty upon which all governments in this Union repose excludes any general power of the state to standardize its children by forcing them to accept instruction from public teachers only." In a sentence, which would be adopted by Catholic defenders of parochial schools, the decision declared that "the child is not the mere creature of the state."[20]

The decision of the high court had far reaching implications, for acts similar to the one in Oregon were then pending in Michigan, Washington, and other states. The editors of *America*, the Jesuit weekly, linked the decision to the rights guaranteed by the Declaration of Independence that "do not exist by grant of the State," but "belong to man not because he is a citizen, but precisely because he is a human being, and they are rooted in the nature given him by an all-wise Creator." Had "the right of the father to control the education of his child . . . been denied by the Supreme Court, as it was denied by the Oregon school law, no right would have been held sacred by the political philosophy which looks to the civil power as the source and sanction of all rights and duties."[21]

Indirect aid to Catholic schools presented a more ambiguous situation. In 1930, the Supreme Court upheld a Louisiana statute that provided text books to all students, regardless of the school they attended. Chief Justice Hughes read the opinion in *Cochran v. Louisiana Board of Education* that "the taxing power of the state is exerted for a public purpose" and hence was not using public money for private institutions or for aid to Catholic schools.[22] Yet, other tensions remained that had been developing since the end of the nineteenth century. John Ireland had predicted that "secularists and unbelievers will demand their rights." While conceding them their rights, he declared, "let them not impose upon me and my fellow-Christians their religion, which is secularism."[23]   By the 1940s, Ireland's prediction was becoming a reality.  In the years after World War II, anti-Catholicism had again broken out.  Paul Blanshard and the organization, Prot-estants and Other Americans United for the Separation of Church and State (POAU), sought to show the incompatibility of Catholicism with American democracy.  But, the issue was basically one of secularism or freedom from religion.  As early as 1943, John Courtney Murray, S.J., the theologian at Woodstock College who pioneered the discussion of religious liberty, broached the question of the need to combat secularism through "intercredal cooperation." To do this he argued that it was not Catholic doctrine that there should be a union of Church and State wherever Catholics constituted a majority.  In his endeavor, he faced opposition both inside and outside the Church.[24]

At issue in regard to education was *Everson vs. Board of Education Ewing TP.*  A New Jersey statute allowed the reimbursement of parents for the cost of using public transportation buses to send their children to parochial schools.  The appellant, Everson, argued that this was tax support of parochial education—the statute made no reference to private schools that were run for profit.  The lower New Jersey court declared the statute unconstitutional, but the Court of Errors and Appeals of the State of New Jersey upheld it.  The case was then appealed to the Supreme Court, which heard it on November 20, 1946.  While awaiting the court's response, Murray penned an article for *America*.  His rhetoric was sometimes harsh as he attacked "secularist educators and clerical Protestantism" for "bringing their influence to bear to write into public policy the exclusion of parochial school children from all public aid, Federal or State."  By "clerical Protestantism," he meant primarily the editors of *The Christian Century* who had editorialized against a similar bill then pending in Wisconsin.  The bill, they declared, was "the camel's nose under the tent" or "the thin edge of the wedge" that would "split American democracy wide open."  Murray accused "clerical Protestantism" of waging its campaign, not "under the devise of 'religious liberty' or 'freedom of conscience,'" but under the "banner" of "'separation of Church and State' that negative, ill-defined, basically un-American formula, with all its overtones of religious prejudice."  *The Christian Century,* for its part, saw a conspiracy on the part of "the Roman Catholic Church," which had "never accepted the American principle of separation of Church and State and its corollary principle of religious liberty."[25]

Murray chastised the journal for its misinterpretations of papal teaching on Church-State relations, a point on which he was then in dispute with his Catholic theological opponents.  He then addressed Thomas Jefferson's metaphor of the "wall of separation between Church and State," then emerging as the paradigm for Church-State relations.  Unhappy as he was with the metaphor, he argued that it did "convey a truth. There is a constitutional 'wall' between state authority and religious conscience. There is also a wall between state authority and the parental conscience; it was constitutionally affirmed in the famous Oregon School case." He also quoted *Chance vs. Mississippi,* in which the Supreme Court of Mississippi had approved providing free text books to non-profit private school students on the grounds that "useful citizenship is a product and servant of both the Church and the State, and the citizen's freedom must include the right to acknowledge the rights and benefits of each, and to import into each the ideals and the training of the other. . . . It is the control of one over the other than our Constitution forbids." Murray warned that transforming the "wall of separation" into an "iron curtain" would "deny all community of interest between Church and State.[26]

Murray argued for some State aid to parochial schools on the premise that "the general welfare of the United States" depended on "the co-existence and free functioning of two types of schools —the non-profit, tax exempt, church-related school (the original unit of American education) and the public school (the later growth)." When "all education" became "a state monopoly," he warned, "or tends to become such (i.e., when non-profit church-related schools become the object of explicit or implicit governmental discouragement, and discrimina-tory legislation fosters the belief that the single American school is the public school), at that moment American democracy will be dead or dying." He also asserted that the State was the "*parens patriae,*" and was "primarily 'parent' of children, not of schools." From this derived the "child-benefit theory," which Protestant opponents had seen as part of a Catholic plot to undermine American laws. To deprive children in parochial schools of a share in State support meant for Murray that the State became the "*parens patriae*" only to the children in public schools. Opponents of aid to parochial schools, he asserted, argued that Catholics were exercising a "free" and merely "private" choice in sending their children to their schools, but ignored the fact that "the present parochial school fulfills an essentially public function—that of preparing an educated citizenry."[27] Reminis-cent of Ireland's predictions and of some of the arguments in the Oregon case, Murray warned his readers that a false understanding of the separation of Church and State "deflects all governmental aid singly and solely towards the subsidization of secularism, and the one national 'religion' and culture, whose agent of propa-gation is the secularized public school." It was a development that European Catholics in the nineteenth and twentieth centuries had resisted and that "many thinking Protestants" viewed "with alarm."[28]

*America* published Murray's article on February 15, 1947, five days after the Supreme Court issued its 5-4 decision in favor of the New Jersey statute. The majority consisted of Chief Justice Fred M. Vinson and Justices Hugo L. Black,

Stanley F. Reed, William O. Douglas, and Frank Murphy. Both the majority and minority appealed to Jefferson and James Madison. Balancing the two sections of the First Amendment between establishing religion and prohibiting its free exercise, the decision, read by Black, drew the analogy between the state providing police and fire protection with funding transportation for parochial school children. Cutting off such services, the court reasoned, would make it more difficult for church schools to operate, "but such is obviously not the purpose of the First Amendment. That Amendment requires the state to be a neutral in its relations with groups of religious believers and non-believers; it does not require the state to be their adversary. State power is no more to be used so as to handicap religions, than it is to favor them." Since the parochial schools met "New Jersey's requirements" to provide secular education, the State neither financially contributed to the schools nor supported them, but did nothing "more than provide a general program to help parents get their children, regardless of their religion, safely and expeditiously to and from accredited schools." The court concluded that "the First Amendment has erected a wall between church and state. That wall must be kept high and impregnable. We could not approve the slightest breach. New Jersey has not breached it here."[29]

Although Chief Justice Morrison R. Waite had used the Jeffersonian metaphor of "a wall between church and state" in *Reynolds v. U.S.* (1879), it did not play a major role in his decision. Now it became the preferred lens through which to view the First Amendment. But the court in 1947 was closely divided. The language of the dissenters closely approximated an understanding of the First Amendment about which Murray warned. In a dissenting opinion, joined by Justice Felix Frankfurter, Justice Robert H. Jackson claimed that at the heart of his objection was the inclusion only of parochial schools, but not other private ones, in the New Jersey provision.[30] As he developed his argument, however, he clearly opposed any aid to parochial schools. He cited canon law to back up his assertion that the church schools in question "are parochial only in name-they, in fact, represent a worldwide and age-old policy of the Roman Catholic Church." He considered it no "exaggeration to say that the whole historic conflict in temporal policy between the Catholic Church and non-Catholics comes to a focus in their respective school policies. . . . It [the Church] does not leave the individual to pick up religion by chance. It relies on early and indelible indoctrination in the faith and order of the Church by the word and example of persons consecrated to the task." In contrast, he thought "Our public school, if not a product of Protestantism, at least is more consistent with it than with the Catholic culture and scheme of values for "it is organized on the premise that secular education can be isolated from all religious teaching so that the school can inculcate all needed temporal knowledge and also maintain a strict and lofty neutrality as to religion. The assumption is that after the individual has been instructed in worldly wisdom he will be better fitted to choose his religion."[31]

Jackson considered the parochial school to be such a "vital . . . part of the Roman Catholic Church" that "to render tax aid to its Church school is indistinguishable to me from rendering the same aid to the Church itself." He further denied the court's analogy between providing police and fire protection for Catholic institutions and compensating for transportation, for such protection safeguarded the lives of people, not of Catholics as such.[32] Hence, he denied the premise of Murray's argument that the State should be concerned with students, not schools, and that Catholic students as future citizens fell under the protection of the State as "*parens patriae*".

Justice Wiley B. Rutledge viewed the support of bus fares for parochial school children as but a first step toward total support. He felt sympathy for "the burden which our constitutional separation puts on parents who desire religious instruction mixed with secular for their children," but "if those feelings should prevail, there would be an end to our historic constitutional policy and command." He denied that the Catholic child was subject to any "discrimination," for he or his parents decided to forego the right to attend a public school. The "atmosphere" of the public schools, he continued, "is wholly secular," a "constitutional necessity, because we have staked the very existence of our country on the faith that complete separation between the state and religion is best for the state and best for religion."[33] In short, for Rutledge, secularism was to be the national religion, as Murray had feared.

With the court so narrowly divided and both sides arguing from Jefferson and Madison, it was only a matter of time before the court would swing in the other direction. In the meantime, another case was making its way to the Supreme Court. In 1940, the school board of Champaign County, Illinois, had made an agreement with the Champaign Council on Religious Education, a voluntary association of concerned parents, to provide Catholic, Jewish, and Protestant instruction once a week in the public schools during the regular school day. While the teachers, including several Protestants, four Catholic priests, and one rabbi, were employed by the council, they were approved and supervised by the superintendent of schools. Parents who wished their children to attend these classes had to sign a card granting permission. Students who did not participate were to leave their classrooms for secular instruction elsewhere in the school. Mrs. Vashti McCollum, an atheist, objected that this arrangement caused embarrassment to her son who did not attend the religious classes. The Illinois courts had upheld the policy, so Mrs. McCollum was now appealing.

The issue reached beyond aid to parochial schools and was of concern to Catholics and Protestants as well. In April, 1947, Charles P. Taft, president of the Federal Council of Churches, wrote Archbishop John T. McNicholas, O.P., of Cincinnati, chairman of the administrative board of the National Catholic Welfare Conference about appointing a committee to meet with Protestant and Jewish leaders about religion in public education. Although McNicholas was benevolently disposed toward the project, he had to refuse because the Vatican forbade such formal cooperation with non-Catholic groups, for fear of promoting religious indifference.[34] But some Protestant spokesmen were not as sympathetic with Catholic concerns for education, and some Catholic leaders may well have fanned the flames they sought to quench.

In June, 1947, Cardinal Francis Spellman, Archbishop of New York, addressed Fordham University's commencement audience. He compared the outbreak of anti-Catholicism in the wake of *Everson* to the bigotry of the 1928 Al Smith campaign for president. Secular newspapers, he claimed, "denounced the decision as . . . an egregious blunder which will lead to union of church and state, an attack upon our cherished free American public schools, the opening wedge in breaking down the wall between church and state." The Protestant press, he argued, was more hostile still, and here he cited *The Christian Century*, which had stated that "no pulpit can be silent on this issue." He then quoted headlines reporting attacks on the Church from Methodist, Baptist and Presbyterian leaders. Recalling Catholic patriotism in all the nation's wars, he lamented that "once again a crusade is being preached against the Catholic Church in the United States." This time, however, the attack was not on "Catholicism as such" or its dogmas and practices or its clergy, but on "the Catholic Church as a social institution, as a cultural force in the United States." Quoting Jackson's opinion that the public school was more compatible with Protestantism than Catholicism, the cardinal declared that this approach "assumed that all American people must agree to the dogma that in the sight of God all churches are of equal value." Whoever did not accept that position was branded "a heretic from the democratic faith. And the best that may be said for the dissenter is that he should not be persecuted, but definitely he is a sore spot on the body politic, to be barely tolerated because the Constitution says he must."[35]

Spellman's argument may have seemed extreme, but at least one letter to the *Times* bore out his charges. Stanley I. Stuber, director of public relations for the Northern Baptist Convention, Clyde R. Miller, a professor at Columbia Teachers College, and Guy Emery Shipler, editor of *The Churchman,* took the cardinal to task. They asserted that "what animates the anxiety of millions of American citizens with respect to the Roman Catholic Church is to be found not in the activities of the Catholic Church 'as a social institution, as a cultural force,' but rather in the political activities of the members of the Catholic hierarchy who, as representatives of a foreign power, the Vatican State, have been carrying on unceasing propaganda and utilizing continuous and insistent pressure on press and radio and state and federal officials to break down our United States constitutional guarantee of separation of church and state." To support their argument, they had only to cite the Vatican opposition to the separation of church and state. Their argument, nevertheless, was premised on what Spellman had rejected, i.e. that one religion was as good as another and all should be strictly spiritual with no temporal expression.[36]

*The Christian Century*, in the meantime, weighed in with an editorial entitled "The Cardinal Looks for Trouble." There was no "attack," said the journal, but there was "the beginning of a spirited defense against certain aggressive policies by which Roman Catholics are trying to get for their church certain special advantages from the Government. In that defense, *The Christian Century* is glad to play its part."[37]

This public sparring over aid to parochial schools as a Church-State issue occurred as the *McCollum* case was coming before the Supreme Court. Although the controversy over *Everson*, helped shape the debate, the Champaign arrangement presented difficulties for Catholic leaders as well, for it gave the superintendent of the public schools the right to approve the qualifications of the priests teaching the classes. Murray again addressed the issue in two articles in *America*. Charles Clayton Morrison, the retiring editor of *The Christian Century*, wrote that he had continued to sound the alarm by using the "metaphor of the 'camel's nose,' . . . [and] the image of the 'thin edge of the wedge' being driven by the Roman Catholic hierarchy into the 'wall of separation.'" These "metaphors" were an "appeal to fear. It was a question, not so much of invoking constitutional arguments on particular issues, as of evoking the spectral phantom of the Catholic Church dominant in America, notably in education." Reflecting Spellman's charges, Murray argued that the "appeal to fear" had been so successful that "in many quarters anti-Catholic feeling is at a new high." But now "some more sober-minded and far-seeing Protestants" had begun "to wonder if perhaps fear and suspicion of Catholics have not clouded the real issues, created an atmosphere in which their discussion is almost futile, and even prepared the way for newly victorious advances of secularism in American life." Even *The Christian Century*, he noted, recognized the need "to keep reaction to Catholic aggressiveness from being on the Ku Klux Klan and nativist level."[38]

In his second article, by which time, as will be seen, the court had ruled on the *McCollum* case, he argued that "the special problem of the relations between government—Federal and State—and education conducted under religious auspices, which was originally left to the area of legislative policy, still remains in that area. The 'establishment' clause never was, and is not now, relevant to its considerations." The Fourteenth Amendment guaranteed the traditional "privileges and immunities of citizens of the United States" and one of these, he asserted "has been their privilege to manage their own educational system, and their immunity from Federal control . . .The only relevant Federal constitutional issue in the case rises from the 'free exercise' clause, not from the 'establishment' clause." Murray believed Morrison "in principle, . . . agrees with the Scottish Rite Masons and the secularist professional educators who would love to see written into the Federal constitutional law the extraordinary dictum of Mr. Justice Rutledge in the *Everson* case, that a 'wholly secular atmosphere' in our public schools is 'a constitutional necessity.'"[39]

Murray was concerned that Morrison's "alliance with his Masonic and secularist-educators friends" had as a goal "a monolithic, completely secularized, government-controlled 'American' educational system." The issue of the separation of Church and State, he argued, was simply a device "to fracture the constitutional principle of the freedom of the American people to legislate on the relations between government and education . . .." Not without cause, he feared that the movement to reverse *Everson* and *Chance* by denying aid to parochial schools could culminate in a reversal of *Pierce* and a denial of the right of those schools to exist, as the Masonic journal, the *New Age* was already proposing.[40]

Murray also challenged Justice Jackson's "assumption that a church-affiliated school has the same relation to government as the church to which it is affiliated," because the "government has no jurisdiction over the church; but it has jurisdiction over the school" and accepted "attendance at . . . [church-affiliated] schools as compliance with compulsory-education laws." "All schools rendering a public service are equal before the law," he asserted, "regardless of their religious or non-religious character," just as "all citizens are equal before the law." But his contention went deeper. Whereas Morrison had claimed that any government aid to church schools created an invidious "interlocking relationship" of church and state, Murray countered that "obviously, in the field of education both State and Church function; each has an interest in the child and a certain jurisdiction over the child—in the one case as a citizen, in the other as a child of God." In exercising its concern for "the child's education as a citizen," the state's "functions remain separate from those of the Church." To forbid the "simultaneous functioning in a field of common interest," Murray concluded, was to "forbid the child to be simultaneously a citizen and a child of God."[41]

Murray had made a persuasive case, but it had no influence on court decisions. By the time he published his second article, the court had decided the *McCollum* case by vote of 8 to 1, with Justice Reed dissenting. The decision stated that "the First Amendment had erected a wall between Church and State which must be kept high and impregnable," but in the Champaign arrangement, "not only are the state's tax supported public school buildings used for the dissemination of religious doctrines. The State also affords sectarian groups an invaluable aid in that it helps to provide pupils for their religious classes through use of the state's compulsory public school machinery. This is not separation of Church and State."[42]

While the court had reached a nearly unanimous decision, some of the concurring opinions contained important insights. The court had remanded to the Illinois courts Mrs. McCollum's further objections to such practices in the schools as the use of the Bible and memorization of psalms. Justice Jackson countered that "If we are to eliminate everything that is objectionable to any of these warring sects or inconsistent with any of their doctrines, we will leave public education in shreds. Nothing but educational confusion and a discrediting of the public school system can result from subjecting it to constant law suits."[43] To illustrate how "by 1875 the separation of public education from Church entanglements . . . was firmly established in the consciousness of the nation," Justice Frankfurter quoted the "famous remarks" of Ulysses S. Grant to Union Army veterans but, ironically, had to cite those remarks from the *Catholic World*.[44]

Justice Reed, the sole dissenter, provided his own interpretation of Jefferson's "wall of separation." He quoted from a report of Jefferson as rector of the University of Virginia, which received the approval of the Board of Visitors, who included Madison, and was later incorporated into the university regulations. Jefferson had written:

> Should the religious sects of this State, or any of them, according to the invitation held out to them, establish within, or adjacent to, the precincts of the University, schools for instruction in the religion of their sect, the students of the University will be free, and expected to attend religious worship at the establishment of their respective sects, in the morning, and in time to meet their school in the University at its stated hour.

Reed concluded that "Thus, the 'wall of separation between church and State' that Mr. Jefferson built at the University which he founded did not exclude religious education from that school. . . . A rule of law should not be drawn from a figure of speech."[45] Reed also cited the examples of the United States Military Academy and Naval Academy, where attendance at church services was still compulsory.

*America* praised Reed's opinion and added that "by its decision the Supreme Court takes the unprecedented action of forbidding local communities, even with the approval of the highest authority in the State, from legislating with regard to the relations between government and religion and religious education."

"Judicial action," it went on, "has been substituted for the political process. The secularization of the public school, already too much advanced through the political process, is now declared to be a constitutional necessity, a dictate of the First Amendment itself." It concluded that "the treat of civic and educational confusion which this decision, in Mr. Justice Jackson's opinion, so seriously involves, should in the future arouse all religious groups to an active consciousness of our common interest in pursuing the welfare of our country."[46]

Catholics were not alone in seeing the dangers brought about by the court's decision. On June 17, 1948, several Protestant leaders issued a statement protesting the decision. Included among the signers were John Colman Bennett, Robert L. Calhoun, Harry Emerson Fosdick, H. Richard Niebuhr and Reinhold Niebuhr. The court's interpretation of the First Amendment, they said, created "a situation in which forms of cooperation between Church and State that have been taken for granted by the American people will be endangered" and "will greatly accelerate the trend toward the secularization of our culture." Like Murray and Justice Reed, they stated that Jefferson's "wall of separation" was a "misleading metaphor" and called upon "our great religious communities . . . to explore the possibilities of working together" in order to maintain "the religious foundations of our national life."[47] Due to Vatican prohibition of formal Catholic cooperation with other religious groups, no Catholics could sign the statement, but the bishops did quote the statement in their pastoral letter of November 1948, entitled "The Christian in Action." Attacking secularism, they used many of the arguments Justice Reed evoked against the court's interpretation of the "wall of separation," particularly Jefferson's own policy for the University of Virginia. They further pledged their readiness "to cooperate in fairness and charity with all who believe in God and are devoted to freedom under God to avert the impending danger of a judicial 'establishment of secularism' that would ban God from public life."[48]

Left unanswered by *McCollum* was the question of "released time," the provision for students to be released from public schools during class hours to attend religious instruction elsewhere. Residents of New York City challenged a city education law providing for this system, but the New York Court of Appeals upheld it. When the case went before the Supreme Court in January 1952, the appellees were represented, among others, by the solicitor general and attorney general of New York and an attorney for the Greater New York Coordinating Committee on Released Time for Jews, Protestants and Roman Catholics. In addition, the attorneys general of eight states filed *amicus curiae* briefs. On April 28, 1952, Justice Douglas read the decision for the majority of six upholding the law. While upholding an "absolute" separation of Church and State, the court also stated: "The First Amendment, however, does not say that in every and all respects there shall be a separation of Church and State. Rather, it studiously defines the manner, the specific ways, in which there shall be no concert or union or dependency one on the other. That is the common sense of the matter. Otherwise the state and religion would be aliens to each other - hostile, suspicious, and even unfriendly."[49] In language that was even more provocative, the court declared: "We are a religious people whose institutions presuppose a Supreme Being. We guarantee the freedom to worship as one chooses." To argue against any state cooperation with religious authorities to allow religious instruction, it said, "would be to find in the Constitution a requirement that the government show a callous indifference to religious groups. That would be preferring those who believe in no religion over those who do believe."[50] Unlike the *McCollum* case where public school classrooms were used for religious instruction, in the New York case, "the public schools do no more than accommodate their schedules to a program of outside religious instruction." The court concluded that "We cannot read into the Bill of Rights such a philosophy of hostility to religion."[51] Dissenting from the opinion were Justices Black, Frankfurter, and Jackson, who, each in his own way, argued that New York case fell under *McCollum*.

The language of *Zorach* seemed to slow the course toward secularism, future decisions would rule out Bible reading or recitation of prayers composed by school boards. As early as 1952, a case came before the court seeking to overturn a New Jersey law allowing the daily reading, without comment, of several verses of the Old Testament before classes began in public schools. The court, however, skirted the issue by declaring that one appellant lacked legal standing and the other, a female student, had graduated before the case came before the court.[52] Clearly the way was already paved for the cases in the 1960s.

In the meantime, the burden of operating Catholic schools worsened with the influx of Federal money into the states' public school system in the 1950s. The controversy over any aid to parochial schools intensified. When John F. Kennedy declared his candidacy for president, POAU asked each candidate where he stood on diplomatic relations with the Vatican and on aid to parochial schools. In an interview with *Look* in 1959, Kennedy said that, in regard to aid to parochial schools, as a citizen, he was bound to uphold the Constitution as interpreted by the Supreme Court.[53] In his 1960 speech to the Houston Ministerial Association, he took the same position. But he added that, if ever there was a conflict between his "conscience," not the Church, and his office, he would resign. This seemed to imply that religion was strictly private—the secularism that Murray opposed.[54]

In the almost two hundred years surveyed in this chapter, the Church's educational work first faced opposition from a hostile Protestant majority who regarded Catholic loyalty to the pope as un-American. From the late nineteenth century to the middle of the twentieth, the Church's creation of its own educational system to preserve the faith of its members may have actually contributed to the removal of religion from the public schools, to the inculcation of secularism that was hostile to religion. Whether the opposition was Protestantism or secularism, however, the Catholic argument showed surprising consistency. John Hughes, John Ireland, and John Courtney Murray all argued for the rights of Catholics as citizens who had those rights independent of the State. Ireland and Murray, in particular, warned Protestants that the opposition to Catholicism was really opposition to religion. Despite their arguments that Catholics as citizens had the right to determine the nature of their children's education and that parochial schools fulfilled a secular purpose, the tide had turned toward Justice Rutledge's assertion that the "wholly secular" atmosphere of the public schools was a "constitutional necessity" and Catholics could not claim any "discrimination" when they freely chose not to use those schools.

## ENDNOTES

1   Robert Emmett Curran, *The Bicentennial History of Georgetown University* (Washington, DC: Georgetown University Press, 1993), 11-13.

2   Ibid., 26.

3   Hugh J. Nolan, (ed.), *Pastoral Letters of the United States Catholic Bishops* (4 vols.; Washington: NCCB/USCC, 1984), I, 90.

4   Benedict Fenwick to George Fenwick, Boston, Nov. 27, 1838, quoted in Anthony J. Kuzniewski, S.J., *Thy Honored Name: A History of the College of the Holy Cross, 1843-1994* (Washington: The Catholic University of America Press, 1999), 22.

5   James Hennesey, S.J., *American Catholics: A History of the Roman Catholic Community in the United States* (New York: Oxford University Press, 1981), 107-109. The most thorough study of this episode is Richard Shaw, *Dagger John: The Unquiet Life and Times of Archbishop John Hughes of New York* (New York: Paulist Press, 1977, 139-175.

6   Shaw, 195-202.

7   John Ireland, *The Church and Modern Society* (2 vols.; St. Paul, MN: The Pioneer Press, 1905), I, 220-224.

8   Francis Paul Prucha, *Christian Reformers and the Indians, 1865-1900* (Norman, OK: University of Oklahoma Press, 1986), 52-57.

9   On Colfax as an active member of the Know Nothings, see Willard H. Smith, *Schuyler Colfax; the Changing Fortunes of a Political Idol* (Indianapolis, Indiana Historical Bureau, 1952), 54-60, 298-300.

10  The President's Speech at Des Moines," *Catholic World*, 22 (1876), 434-35.

11  Given in Steven M. Avella and Elizabeth McKeown (eds.), *Public Voices: Catholics in the American Context* (Maryknoll, NY: Orbis Books, 1999), 73-74.

12  Ireland, 230.

[13] I treat this at greater length in *The Vatican and the American Hierarchy from 1870 to 1965* (Stuttgart: Anton Hiersemann Verlag, 1982; Wilmington, DE: Michael Glazier, 1985), 13-14, 34.

[14] Ibid., 69-80.

[15] Section 5259, Oregon Laws, cited in *Pierce v. Society of Sisters*, 26 U.S. 510 (1925), note.

[16] Timothy Michael Dolan, *"Some Seed fell on Good Ground: The Life of Edwin V. O'Hara* (Washington: The Catholic University of America Press, 1992), 42-43.

[17] Quoted *ibid.*, 44.

[18] *New York Times*, Apr. 1, 1924, I, 1:2 and 3:2.

[19] *Ibid.*, Apr. 2, 1924, 18:3.

[20] *Pierce v. Society of Sisters*, 268 U.S. 510 (1925), 534.

[21] *America*, 33 (June 13, 1925), 208.

[22] *Cochran v. Louisiana State Board of Education*, 281 U.S. 370 (1930), 375.

[23] Ireland, 225.

[24] Fogarty, *Vatican*, 347-354.

[25] John Courtney Murray, S.J., "Separation of Church and State: true and false concepts," *America*, 76 (Feb. 15, 1947), 541.

[26] *Ibid.*, 542.

[27] *Ibid.*, 544.

[28] *Ibid.*, 545.

[29] *Everson v. Board of Education of Ewing TP*, 330 U.S., 1 (1947), 17-18.

[30] *Ibid.*, 20.

[31] *Ibid.*, at 23-24 (Jackson, J., dissenting).

[32] *Ibid.*, 24-25.

[33] *Ibid*, at 58-59 (Rutledge, J., dissenting). Portions of the decision and of the dissenting positions are given in the *New York Times*, Feb. 11, 1947, 1.

[34] See Fogarty, *Vatican*, 356-357.

[35] *The New York Times*, June 12, 1947, 1, 22.

[36] *Ibid.*, June 14, 1947, 14.

[37] *Ibid.*, June 20, 1947, 15.

[38] John Courtney Murray, S.J., "Dr. Morrison and the First Amendment: I," *America*, 78 (March 6, 1948), 627-628.

[39] John Courtney Murray, S.J., "Dr. Morrison and the First Amendment: II," *America*, 78 (March 20, 1948), 684.

[40] *Ibid.*, 685.

[41] *Ibid.*, 685-686.

[42] *McCollum v. Board of Education*, 333 U.S. (1948), 212.

[43] *Ibid.*, 235.

[44] *Ibid.*, at 218 (Jackson, J. concurring).

[45] *Ibid.*, at 246-247 (Reed, J., dissenting).

[46] *America*, 78 (March 20, 1948), 673.

[47] Archives of Woodstock College, Georgetown University, Murray Papers, attachment to Carroll to Murray, Washington, Dec. 27, 1957.

[48] Hugh J. Nolan (ed.), *Pastoral Letters of the United States Catholic Bishops* (Washington: United States Catholic Conference, 1984), II, 87-89.

[49] Zorach et al. v. Clausen et al., 343 U.S., 212.

[50] *Ibid.*, 313-314.

[51] *Ibid.*, 315.

[52] *Doremus v. Board of Education*, 342 U.S. 429 (1952).

[53] Fogarty, *Vatican*, 383-384.

[54] Contrary to popular opinion, Murray played at most a minor role in preparing the speech that was only read to him over the phone; see Donald E. Pelotte, S.S.S., *John Courtney Murray: Theologian in Conflict* (New York: Paulist Press, 1975), 76.

## CHAPTER 8

# RECENT HISTORY OF CATHOLIC SCHOOLS AND PUBLIC FUNDING, 1960 TO PRESENT

❦

*Lawrence McAndrews*

At the beginning of a wave of immigration which brought over a million Catholics in each of the decades between 1880 and 1920, the United States Catholic bishops at the Third Plenary Council in Baltimore in 1884 ordered a parochial school built for every parish. Yet the National Catholic War Council (later National Catholic Welfare Conference), founded by the American bishops in 1917, opposed federal aid to nonpublic education as an invitation to control of parochial school curriculum and administration by a "Protestant" government.

The National Catholic Welfare Conference won its first major victory in 1925 when the Supreme Court, in *Pierce v. Society of Sisters*, ruled unanimously against an Oregon law prohibiting attendance at nonpublic schools during school hours. By the end of World War II, political and economic progress as well as the enactment of the G.I. Bill had brought Catholics into the American main-stream, causing a reversal of the NCWC's opposition to federal aid to education in 1944. Three years later, in *Everson v. Board of Education*, the Supreme Court offered the bishops a powerful rationale for their new position: that public aid to nonpublic schools does not violate the First Amendment's separation of church and state if the tax monies benefit the children rather than the schools. This "child benefit theory," the Court ruled, justified a New Jersey statute permitting the state to reimburse nonpublic school parents for their children's transportation to and from school.[1]

The next year, in *Illinois ex rel McCollum v. Board of Education*, the court ruled unconstitutional a Champaign, Illinois, released-time religious education program in the public schools, sponsored by a council of Catholic, Jewish, and Protestant groups. Justice Hugo Black argued in his majority opinion that the use of tax-supported property and the release of students from their mandatory attendance in secular classes violated the First Amendment's separation of church and state as well as the Fourteenth Amendment's equal protection under the law. In 1952, however, the court upheld a New York plan which allowed public schools to release pupils during the school day to receive instruction at religious centers. Justice William Douglas, in the majority opinion in *Zorach v. Clauson*, distinguished between the on-campus Champaign and off-campus New York programs. Over the dissent of Justice Black and two others, Douglas explained that unlike *McCollum*, the Zorach case involved neither the use of tax-supported property nor the release of students from public school classes.[2]

The National Defense Education Act of 1958, which aided nonpublic as well as public schools, was the first significant legislative victory for the NCWC. Spurred by the Soviet launch of the Sputnik space satellite the previous year, this Cold War measure allocated "categorical" federal aid for loans to college students; research and development at colleges and universities; mathematics, science, and modern foreign language instruction in elementary and secondary schools; and guidance, counseling, and testing in elementary and secondary schools. Efforts to expand upon this achievement in the next four decades, however, would achieve mixed results. Changes at the White House, in Congress, and on the Supreme Court would help insure that the more popular public aid to Catholic schools became, the more elusive it remained.[3]

## THE KENNEDY ADMINISTRATION

One month into his administration in February 1961, the first Catholic president, John F. Kennedy, announced that his three-year proposal for federal support of elementary and secondary school construction and teachers' salaries would exclude nonpublic schools. "In accordance with the clear prohibition of the Constitution, no elementary or secondary school funds are allocated for constructing church schools or paying church schools' salaries," said the new President, "and thus nonpublic school children are rightfully not counted in determining funds each state will receive for its public schools." Calling Kennedy's proclamation "the first official Presidential statement excluding parochial schools since President [Ulysses] Grant urged that no public funds be given to any sectarian-controlled school," George Reed of the NCWC Education Department vowed to fight the White House.[4]

To avoid a collision with the hierarchy of his Church, Kennedy agreed to an expansion of Title III of the National Defense Education Act to include nonpublic school loans for the construction of science, mathematics, foreign language, physical fitness, and lunch facilities. The NCWC and the Kennedy Administration devised a plan by which the Senate would pass the revised NDEA separate from the public-school bill and send it to the House, where its consideration would precede that of the public-school bill. The expanded NDEA never reached the Senate floor, however, and on June 11, Democratic Speaker of the House Sam Rayburn of Texas announced that consideration of the public school bill would precede deliberation on the NDEA in the House Rules Committee. On July 18 Catholic Democrat James Delaney of New York cast the deciding Rules Committee vote against the "discriminatory" public school-only bill, H.R. 7300, and on October 3 Kennedy signed a two-year extension of an unamended National Defense Education Act.[5]

## THE JOHNSON ADMINISTRATION

In mid-November 1963, with the Second Vatican Council meeting in Rome, and with forty-nine percent of the American people backing public aid to Catholic schools, Indiana Democrat John Brademas of the House Education and Labor Committee initiated a series of secret discussions among Commissioner of Education Francis Keppel, National Education Association President Robert Wyatt, and NCWC representatives William Consedine and Monsignor Francis Hurley. A month later, the three sides privately agreed in principle to a plan basing nonpublic and public school aid on a poverty formula. In May 1964, however, the House Education and Labor Committee specifically provided that no funds in President Lyndon Johnson's anti-poverty bill be diverted to any general aid to education program. Consedine responded, "In advance of the Committee's action the *Wall Street Journal* unfortunately but accurately reported such a change would be a 'Catholic victory.'" Instead, the "victory" would have to wait.[6]

The long-delayed breakthrough for proponents of Catholic school aid came in Johnson's January 22, 1965, education message, in which the President abandoned his predecessor's insistence on "general" aid for public school construction and teachers' salaries for a program of "categorical assistance" for "disadvantaged" nonpublic as well as public school students under the *Everson* "child-benefit" rationale. "The gain to the public schools from general aid," " Keppel said of Johnson's decision, was less important than "the spirit of interfaith cooperation in other parts of the society, particularly with regard to civil rights."

Realizing that Johnson's landslide election in November 1964 and the greatest legislative majority since World War II made its enactment a virtual certainty, NCWC Director of Education Frederick Hochwalt gave the diluted bill his "reserved approval." NEA Executive Secretary William Carr concluded, "It was categorical aid or nothing, so we took the categorical aid."[7]

On April 9, 1965, President Lyndon Johnson signed the Elementary and Secondary Education Act. Title I of the Act allocated $1.06 billion to be distributed by state education officials to assist local school district projects directed at "educationally deprived children." The funds were not to finance either construction or teachers' salaries, but could pay for "shared-time" programs by which nonpublic school pupils attend classes at public schools. Title II provided $100 million for the purchase of textbooks and other materials and the expansion of school libraries for nonpublic and public school children, through public agencies. Title III earmarked $100 million for "supplemental services and centers" open to nonpublic as well as public school children. Title IV allocated $100 million to modernize and coordinate federal education research, and Title V assigned $100 million to improve state education agencies.[8]

Several obstacles nonetheless discouraged nonpublic school aid after the passage of the ESEA. First, the National Education Association, representing most public school teachers and administrators, announced its opposition to additional categorical aid within the ESEA. Second, the Supreme Court, in *Flast v. Cohen* in June 1968, supported the right of taxpayers to sue and test the constitutionality of the ESEA's provisions for textbooks, "supplemental services and centers," and "shared time" programs for nonpublic as well as public school children. Third, Catholic lobbyists struggled to maintain their enthusiasm in the face of such resistance. Johnson Administration Congressional liaison Harold "Barefoot" Sanders concluded that on Capitol Hill, the "church groups were ... rather ineffective." In the fourth consecutive year of declining enrollments and the third successive year of underutilization of federal funds by Catholic schools, Cardinal Joseph Ritter of St. Louis lamented, "If we were confronted with the question of whether we should start parochial schools today, I am sure they wouldn't be started."[9]

Not all the news was bad for nonpublic school interests, however. USCC Director of Education Monsignor James Donahue told the Senate Education Subcommittee in August 1967 that the ESEA had already served over 1.2 million nonpublic school students. Commissioner of Education Harold Howe, addressing the 1968 convention of the National Catholic Educational Association, applauded Catholic schools' commitment to the urban poor. The Supreme Court, in *Board of Education v. Allen* in June 1968, upheld a New York law providing secular textbooks to nonpublic school children.[10]

## THE NIXON ADMINISTRATION

In his Special Message to the Congress on Education Reform on March 3, 1969, President Richard Nixon formally announced the creation of the Commission on School Finance to "help states and communities to analyze the fiscal plight of their public and nonpublic schools." Within a month, Nixon had added a Panel on Nonpublic Education, chaired by Clarence Walton, President of The Catholic University of America. While the commissions deliberated, the Office of Economic Opportunity acted, unveiling a plan to test tuition vouchers for parents of nonpublic school students in selected communities. At a November 1970 meeting at the Office of Education, USCC expressed "friendly interest" in the study, while leaders of the American Federation of Teachers and NEA registered their strong opposition to the proposal's purported affront to public education. By the end of the year, Nixon had approved the experiment, to be conducted by Christopher Jencks of the Center for the Study of Public Policy.[11]

Just as the campaign for nonpublic school aid was gathering momentum, it suffered a serious setback. On June 28, 1971, in the *Lemon v. Kurtzman* and *Early v. Dicenso* decisions, the Supreme Court ruled that Pennsylvania and Rhode Island laws permitting aid for nonpublic school teachers' salaries were unconstitutional. In a unanimous opinion in the *Lemon* case (only Justice Byron White dissented in *Dicenso*), Chief Justice Warren Burger rejected the separation of "secular" and "sectarian" aspects of parochial school education so that teachers of the former could constitutionally receive funds. The court thus added a third criterion to the 1963 *Schempp* formula for interpreting the First Amendment: not only whether legislation "is a mask to advance religion" or if its primary effect is to help or harm religion, but whether it constitutes an "excessive entanglement" with religion. On the same day, in the *Tilton v. Richardson* case, the court, by a 5-4 margin, upheld the Higher Education Facilities Act of 1963, which authorized federal monies for construction at religious as well as secular colleges. In its majority opinion, the Court argued that "since religious indoctrination is not a substantial activity or purpose of these church-related colleges and universities, there is less likelihood than in primary and secondary education that religion will permeate ... secular education."[12]

As had happened so often before, the Supreme Court forced the nonpublic school interests to reassess their positions. "The Court, while refusing to go so far as to say that all direct aid to sectarian educational institutions is forbidden," wrote USCC General Counsel William Consedine in July 1971, "has serious doubts as to whether it is prepared to sustain any substantial amount of direct assistance." USCC Legislative Liaison James Robinson added that the Court's actions had rendered general federal aid to nonpublic schools "politically impractical." The President's Panel on Nonpublic Education concluded: "The Court's decisions appear to rule out the concept that secular and religious teaching in church-related schools can be distinguished and separated for purposes of providing support. Also ruled out would be any form of aid to church-related schools that would require a continuing process of distinguishing between secular and religious functions...." Although the Supreme Court had precluded direct federal aid to nonpublic schools, these analyses agreed, it had not prohibited all forms of assistance. "The school aid decisions are disappointing and disturbing," wrote Considine, "But they should not be the occasion for despair. The history of constitutional law in the last twenty-five years is full of twists and turns." The newest twist, the USCC and the president's panel concurred, should be tuition tax credits, a form of indirect federal aid which could pass the three-pronged *Lemon* test. Such a provision for nonpublic school expenses on a parent's federal income tax return, proponents believed, would favor lower-income taxpayers; enlist the support of various Protestant, Jewish, and independent schools; invite bipartisan backing in Congress; and win the endorsement of the president.[13]

In March 1972, Nixon approved the final reports of the Commission on School Finance and the President's Panel on Nonpublic Education. Among the former group's recommendations were "the provision of child benefit services and considerations of additional forms of assistance to nonpublic schools." The major recommendation of the latter group was "a federal income tax credit for tuition, limited to a fixed percentage of tuition paid for nonpublic schools only, with both a maximum credit for children and a phase-out of higher income taxpayers." In April Nixon told the NCEA convention, "I am committed to these propositions: [that] America needs her nonpublic schools; that these nonpublic schools need help; that therefore we must and will find ways to provide that help."[14]

Hearings on the tuition tax credit bill, H.S. 16141, began before the House Ways and Means Committee in August 1972. Health, Education, and Welfare Secretary Eliot Richardson, Treasury Secretary George Shultz, and Budget Director Caspar Weinberger strongly endorsed the legislation, and Committee Chairman Wilbur Mills, Democrat of Arkansas, expressed his hope that the bill would reach the House floor before the end of the session. The American Federation of Teachers and the NEA led the opposition to the measure. AFT Director of Nonpublic School Teachers John Murray considered tuition tax credits "unconstitutional," while NEA President Catherine Barrett worried that "all taxpayers with no school-age children, or those who send their children to public schools, will be taxed to make up the difference of the loss to the Treasury." The committee reported H.S. 16141 on October 2 by an 18-6 vote. But the press of other legislation and the final month of election-year campaigning assured that tuition tax credits went no further in the Nixon Administration.[15]

# *NCEA Presidents*

During its 100 years, NCEA has been led by Secretary Generals, Executive Secretaries and Presidents appointed by the Board of Directors.

*Most. Rev. Francis W. Howard*
*(1904-1929)*

*Rev. Msgr. George Johnson*
*(1929-1944)*

*Rev. Msgr. Frederick Hochwalt*
*(1944-1966)*

*Rev. C. Albert Koob*
*(1966-1974)*

# *The Faces of Catholic Education—*

# A PICTORIAL HISTORY

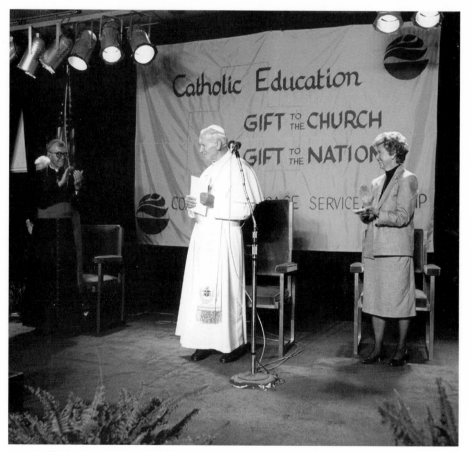

Sr. Catherine McNamee, NCEA President, and Archbishop John Roach, Chair
of the NCEA Board, welcomed Pope John Paul II at the
NCEA Convention in New Orleans, 1987

*Rev. Msgr. John Meyers*
*(1974-1986)*

*Sr. Catherine T. McNamee, CSJ*
*(1986-1996)*

*Leonard F. DeFiore*
*(1996-2001)*

*Michael J. Guerra*
*(2001-)*

# *Past and Present*
# *Board of Directors of NCEA*

*1950*

Bishop Denis J. O'Connell,
First Chair of the Board

Bishop Gregory J. Aymond,
Current Chair

*2003*

*Not pictured: Elayne Bennett, Andrea Roane, Janet Murray, Sr. Glenn Anne McPhee*

# *Annual Bishops' Reception*

Each year since 1988 NCEA has celebrated the contributions of U.S. bishops to Catholic education during a reception held in conjunction with the fall meeting of the United States Conference of Catholic Bishops in Washington, D.C.

*Cardinal Bernardin and Robert Kealey*

*Cardinal Keeler with Michael and Mary Ellen Guerra*

*Sr. Glenn Anne McPhee (USCCB Secretary of Education), Msgr. John Jordan (NCEA), Archbishop William Levada (San Francisco)*

*Robert Colbert and Fr. Francis Kelly with a Department of Religious Education display*

*Beverly Carroll, Bishop Joseph Howze and Sr. Mary Frances Taymans, SND*

# *Annual NCEA Convention and Exposition*

Are you going to NCEA? —The annual convention has become synonymous with the Association

*Sr. Ann Dominic Roach, Boston Superintendent and Sr. Catherine McNamee with Massachusetts Senate President William Bulger, Minute Men and others at the opening ceremony of the annual convention in Boston, 1991*

*Msgr. John Meyers and Fr. Alfred McBride greet Mother Teresa who was a keynote speaker in Chicago, 1976*

*New Jersey School children participate in the opening liturgy, Atlantic City, 2002*

*Nancy Brewer, long-time convention director retired in 1999 after 46 years of service to NCEA*

*Local marquee welcoming NCEA, 1976*

*The first NCEA convention, St. Louis, 1904*

*The ever-popular candy samples have been a staple of the conventions*

*Exhibition Hall, 1950*

*Exhibition Hall, 2000*

# The National Congress on Catholic Schools for the Twenty-first Century

The National Congress on Catholic Schools for the Twenty-first Century met in Washington, D.C. in November 1991 to strategize about future directions for Catholic schools and inaugurated the annual NCEA Seton Award gala.

*Congress Planning Committee: Michael Guerra, Sr. Mary Anne Governal, Sr. Mary Ann Eckhoff, Robert Kealey, Stephen O'Brien*

*Conference participants at work*

*Catholic school children encouraged the participants*

*Panelists Regina Haney and Governor Pete Dupont (Delaware)*

# *Annual NCEA Seton Awards*

The NCEA Seton Awards recognize individuals who have made a significant contribution to Catholic education and America's children. Awardees are presented with the Seton Medal and a scholarship is given in the name of the recipient to a Seton Scholar, a Catholic school student from the awardee's home area.

*Elizabeth Ann Seton Medal*

*Among the first Seton Awardees at the National Congress were Lynne Cheney and Scholar Carolyn Greiber pictured with Andrea Roane, Sr. Catherine McNamee and Bishop Thomas Kelly*

*2000 Seton Awardees and Seton Scholars*

*Gala banquet, Washington, D.C., 1998*

# *Catholic Schools Week Events on Capitol Hill*

Washington, D.C. area students visit Congressional offices to lobby on behalf of Catholic schools during National Appreciation Day For Catholic Schools each year. The event is the centerpiece of Catholic Schools Week, jointly sponsored by NCEA and USCCB.

*Vice President Dan Quayle with students, teachers and NCEA members*

*Congressman Dale Kildee with students and their teacher*

*Students pose for the annual picture on the Capitol steps*

*Students from his state of Virginia present Senator George Allen with a Catholic school button*

# *National Events in Support of Parental Choice in Education*

The Partners for Justice Symposium in 1999 gathered parents, educators and policy-makers to strategize about school choice initiatives.

*NCEA President Leonard DeFiore presented the NCEA Children's Choice Award to Senators Joseph Lieberman and George Voinovich in recognition of their support for school choice*

*School choice supporters rally before the U.S. Supreme Court during oral arguments in the Cleveland voucher case (2002)*

# U.S. Presidents and NCEA Leaders

*Msgr. Hochwalt attended President Truman's signing of the Higher Education Act*

*Father Koob, NCEA Board members and representatives of the U.S. Conference of Catholic Bishops meet with President Nixon*

*Msgr. John Meyers and President Reagan at the NCEA Convention in Chicago*

*Sr. Catherine McNamee and Catholic school superintendents met with President Bush following the National Congress on Catholic Schools*

*Michael Guerra and President Clinton*

# Contributions of Religious Congregations

Sister Damian Aycock (center) of the Ursuline Congregation, the first women religious to begin Catholic schools in the United States, represents all religious congregations as the first NCEA Seton Award was presented in recognition of the role of religious orders in the growth and development of Catholic education

Sister Mary Emil Penet, IHM, a prime mover in the Sister Formation Movement, established by NCEA in 1954, that revolutionized the academic preparation of women religious engaged in teaching

Brother Theodore Drahmann, FSC, one of the giants in Catholic education — educator, administrator, mentor, author and friend

# International Presence of NCEA

NCEA has been an active member of the InterAmerican Catholic Education Association (CIEC) as well as the Catholic International Education Office (OIEC).

*Father Koob at the CIEC meeting in Bogota, Columbia, circa 1960*

*Michael Guerra addressing the OIEC Congress in Brasilia, 2002*

*2002 NCEA delegation to the OIEC World Congress: Robert Kealey, Michael Guerra, Catherine Kealey, Sr. Mary Tracy, Sr. Rosemary Hocevar, Sr. Dale McDonald, Carol Stabile, Claire Helm*

# Activities of the NCEA Departments

*Students and faculty at Mt. St. Mary's Seminary, Emmitsburg, Maryland—a founding member of NCEA's Seminary Department (1904)*

*Msgr. Robert Wister, (second from left) Executive Director, with members of the Seminary Department—Rev. John Strynkowski, Archbishop John May, Rev. Vincent Cushing and Fred Hofheinz of the Lilly Endowment (1992)*

*Fr. Neil D'Amour, CACE Department (standing, second from left) and Sr. Mary Richardine Quirk, Elementary Department (seated, second from right)at a 1960s meeting with the National Catholic Welfare Council and Catholic Home and School Association*

*Frank Savage and Dan Curtin, former and present CACE Executive Directors with Sr. Rosemary Collins, School Superintendent, Savannah and Archbishop Kevin Boland—celebrate liturgy during the CACE convention*

*Sr. Dominica Rocchio at the microphone during a Secondary Department symposium*

*College presidents gather at the ACCU annual meeting at St. Thomas University, 1995*

*NCEA Religious Education Department's ACRE revision committee: John Poggio and Douglas Glasnapp (University of Kansas), Diana Dudoit Raiche (NCEA), Joseph Pedulla (Boston Collage)*

*Father Francis Kelly, Executive Director and committee members at a NPCD meeting, 1980s*

*Distinguished Elementary School Principals pose with Robert Kealey, Executive Director, after receiving their awards at the NCEA convention*

*Regina Haney with members of the St. Vincent de Paul School receiving an Outstanding Board award*

*Art DeCabooter, chair of NABCCCE, conducting a workshop for members*

# NCEA National Headquarters in Washington, D.C.

*Massachusetts Avenue, 1951*

*Original NCEA logo*

*Dupont Circle, 1969*

*Traditional NCEA logo adopted in 1969*

*Georgetown, 1982 - present*

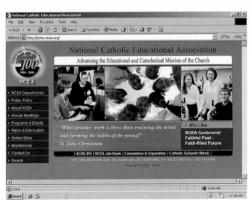

*Cyberspace, 1997*

*NCEA centennial logo*

## The Ford Administration

Among the elementary and secondary education programs which President Gerald Ford inherited from Nixon on August 9, 1974, were the OEO (later National Institute of Education) voucher experiments. Executive Secretary to the Department of Health, Education, and Welfare David Lissy reported "considerable pressure" from representatives of East Hartford, Connecticut, for White House funding of its voucher project. Roger Semerad of the White House staff acknowledged "continued pressure" from New Hampshire State Board of Education Chairman William Bittenbender to increase the federal budget for that state's voucher experiment. "The administration's commitment to the project in New Hampshire," Semerad added, " is well-known."[16]

That commitment was also in jeopardy. The AFT and NEA continued to oppose vouchers as threats to public education. Congress continued to reduce the budget of the NIE, which housed the voucher projects. And the courts continued to interpret narrowly the First Amendment prohibition on the federal "establishment of religion." On May 19, 1975, in *Meek v. Pittenger*, the Supreme Court overturned a Pennsylvania law permitting publicly funded auxiliary services (for disabled, disadvantaged, or exceptionally talented students) administered with publicly owned instructional equipment and materials by public school personnel at nonpublic schools.[17]

Education Commissioner Terrel Bell wrote in July 1975, "It is my understanding that the constitutionality of the solutions [to declining nonpublic school enrollments], if anything, has been more restricted by *Meek v. Pittenger*." Two weeks later, White House aide Arthur Quern advised the president, "Almost any new form of aid which might be considered [tax credits, tuition reimbursement, vouchers] would only survive a constitutional challenge if they were available to both public and private school students. Making them available to both is fiscally impossible." Quern thus recommended that "the president not give any expanded aid to nonpublic education since almost any course would be unconstitutional or too expensive."[18]

Two months after taking office, Ford had announced, "I'm thinking a [tuition] tax credit proposal is a good proposal... There is no reason why there should be a monopoly on education just on the public side... And I would hope that we could find some constitutional way in which to help private schools." His administration then began its search, only to have Bell and Quern find tuition tax credits, like vouchers, to be unconstitutional. Another year of inaction on tuition tax credits indicated that the president did, too.[19]

## THE CARTER ADMINISTRATION

Because the right to a religious education for low-income and middle-income American children "lies at the core of America's diversity and strength," presidential candidate Jimmy Carter, after considerable vacillation, pronounced himself in October 1976 "firmly committed to conducting a systematic and continuing search for constitutionally acceptable methods of providing aid to parents whose children attend nonsegregated private schools." At the time, eighty-five percent of nonpublic elementary and secondary schools were religiously affiliated, and seventy-five percent of these religious schools were Catholic.[20]

Within eight months, however, the Supreme Court had dampened such enthusiasm. In June 1977, in its sixth nonpublic school aid decision in seven years, the Court ruled in *Wolman v. Walter* that Ohio could provide parochial schools with speech, hearing, and psychological tests; remedial training and counseling outside the school; and standardized examinations. But the state could not loan instructional materials or finance field trips. While the former types of assistance "will not create an impermissible risk of the fostering of ideological views," wrote Justice Harry Blackmun for the majority, the latter forms of aid blurred the distinctions between "secular" and "sectarian" education.[21]

The latest setback from the High Court was not enough to deter nonpublic school aid's Congressional advocates, however. Democratic Senator Daniel Patrick Moynihan of New York and Republican Senator Robert Packwood of Oregon devised a bill that provided a tuition tax credit of up to $500 for parents in nonpublic schools and colleges. Congressional opponents cited the measure's $4.7 billion price tag in an era of inflation; claimed that two-thirds of the credit would reach the wealthiest fifteen percent of parents; predicted that nonpublic schools would nullify the credit by raising tuition; and, in the wake of the *Wolman* decision, challenged its constitutionality. The Carter administration agreed that it was "very expensive" and "probably unconstitutional." On October 19, the first anniversary of Carter's pledge to their organization, the Chief Administrators of the National Catholic Educational Associational nonetheless passed a resolution at their annual meeting urging the president to enact nonpublic school tuition tax credits. In November the USCC's Administrative Board directed the bishops to resurrect their campaign for tuition credits.[22]

Carter's alternative to college credits and his opposition to elementary and secondary school credits could not prevent the Senate Finance Committee from reporting out by a 14-1 margin on February 23 a consolidation of Delaware Republican William Roth's $250 college tuition plan and the Moynihan-Packwood $500 primary-secondary school proposal. The "modest efforts" of Carter's ESEA expansion, Budget Director James McIntyre and Domestic Policy Advisor Stuart

Eizenstat informed the president the next day, had not stalled the "momentum building behind the Moynihan-Packwood tuition credit."[23]

Three months later, Elizabeth Abramowitz, education specialist on the Administration's Domestic Policy Staff, denied that Carter had abandoned his campaign promise. "We are fulfilling president Carter's pledge to aid private schools," she wrote Rev. John Meyers, President of the NCEA, "by creating an Office of Nonpublic Schools within the Office of Education, by requiring states to guarantee equitable participation in various Federal programs, and by including nonpublic school representatives on all advisory committees in the Education Division of the Department of Health, Education, and Welfare." She estimated that the Carter Administration would add 100 million federal dollars for nonpublic elementary and secondary school students for Fiscal Year 1980.[24]

But neither the president's stick nor his advisor's carrot deterred the proponents of tuition tax credits. After a Harris poll showed two-thirds of Americans in favor of nonpublic elementary and secondary school tuition tax credits, the issue came to a vote on the House floor. On June 1, a 209-194 vote restored elementary and secondary schools to the college tuition tax credit bill reported by the Ways and Means Committee. Proclaiming "freedom of choice" in education, 107 Democrats joined 102 Republicans in the majority. The House then passed, 237-158, a bill providing tuition tax credits at all levels of education. The $1.2 billion House measure, sponsored by Democrat Charles Vanik of Ohio, included a $50 elementary and secondary school tuition credit for 1978, up to $100 for 1979 and 1980. The credit would extend solely to nonpublic schools, and about fifty percent of the recipients would be families with incomes over $20,000. The $5.2 billion Moynihan-Packwood bill included a $500 elementary and secondary school tuition credit beginning in 1980. It would extend to nonpublic as well as public schools which charged tuition, and about forty percent of the beneficiaries would be families with incomes over $20,000.[25]

By August 2, however, the pendulum had swung against the legislation in the Senate. Cardinal John Krol, Archbishop of Philadelphia, emerged from a meeting with Republican Senator Richard Schweiker of Pennsylvania with a count of forty-six supporters, forty-eight opponents, and six undecided. Moynihan responded by circulating copies of the 1972 and 1976 Democratic party platforms to all Congressional Democrats, including 1972 Presidential candidates Senator Hubert Humphrey of Minnesota and Senator George McGovern of South Dakota, to remind them of their party's past support for nonpublic school tuition tax credits. On August 3, the Senate Finance Committee halved the cost of the Moynihan-Packwood credit. Four days later, Carter met with Senator Kaneaster Hodges of Arkansas to plot the administration's strategy. On August 15 the Senate voted 65-26 in favor of college tuition credits, but 57-41 against elementary and secondary school credits. Twenty-eight Senators supported the former but opposed the latter. Two days after the votes, Carter spoke more vigorously than ever against tuition credits: "I do not favor the tuition tax credit approach to college students, and I even more strongly oppose on constitutional grounds government financing of the elementary and secondary schools which are privately operated."[26]

Carter reiterated his "strong opposition to any tuition tax credits" at his September 26 breakfast meeting with the Congressional leadership. On September 28, after the House conferees voted 4-3 to drop elementary and secondary school credits from the House bill (with Catholic Democrats Vanik, Daniel Rostenkowski of Illinois, and James Burke of Massachusetts in the minority), the House-Senate Conference Committee reported a college tuition tax credit bill. Secretary of Health, Education, and Welfare Joseph Califano would recall Carter's relief that "he would not have to veto a bill with widespread Catholic support." In November President Carter declared victory, signing the package of college grants and loans (but not tuition tax credits) known as the Middle Income Student Assistance Act.[27]

Four months later the bishops approved a two-to-four-year campaign for tuition tax credits, and Moynihan and Packwood reintroduced their legislation. But on May 25, 1979, in *Beggans v. Public Funds for Public Schools*, the Third Circuit Court found a New Jersey nonpublic school tuition tax credit plan unconstitutional. "Even if parents of dependents in nonpublic schools do have greater expenses than those supporting dependents in public schools," the court decided, the state "may not equalize the burden by granting a benefit to taxpayers with dependents in private or parochial schools." The Supreme Court, despite the clamor by tuition credit partisans, let the decision stand.[28]

## THE REAGAN ADMINISTRATION

Two weeks after the election of tuition tax credit supporter Ronald Reagan, Rev. Thomas Gallagher of the Education Department of the United States Catholic Conference pronounced himself "quite optimistic" about the prospects for such legislation. In its December 13 issue, the Jesuit periodical *America* editorialized, "Never before has the political environment been better for the passage of a tuition tax credit." On February 24, 1981, asserting that "there has never been a better political climate for the passage of a tuition tax credit bill," Moynihan, Packwood, and Roth re-introduced 1978's failed initiative. Packwood predicted that the bill would be part of a Reagan administration tax reduction measure in the first session of the Ninety-Seventh Congress. The USCC's Director of Educational Assistance, Edward Anthony, counted 144 representatives and thirty-five senators who had voted for tuition tax credits. A month later the opposition American Federation of Teachers found forty-seven senators in support of, or leaning toward, tuition tax credits.[29]

In an October 13 statement to the Chief Administrators of Catholic Education, Reagan reiterated his dedication to tuition tax credits. He added, however, that "due to the difficult budget pressures we will face in the months to come, and given our determination to address immediate and severe problems facing the nation's economy, my commitment to work with Congress to construct a tuition tax credit bill will necessarily require that we initiate our efforts later in the Ninety-Seventh Congress."[30]

"Later" came in Reagan's January 25, 1983, State of the Union address, in which he called for "passage of tuition tax credits for parents who want to send their children to private or religiously affiliated schools." In his budget message on January 31, Reagan boasted of having reduced federal education spending by one billion dollars from 1981 to 1982, and pledged to "stabilize" such expenditures at $13.1 billion, including the addition of tuition tax credits. Then on February 16, after meeting with Cabinet members, Congresspersons, and interest-group representatives, Reagan submitted another tuition tax credit bill to Congress. Under the measure, tax credits would cover up to fifty percent of tuition, and would come in three phases: $100 in 1983, $200 in 1984, and $300 in 1985, for parents with incomes under $40,000. Parents earning more than $40,000 would receive smaller credits. The loss to the treasury would be $200 million in 1984 and $800 million by fiscal 1986.[31]

The Senate Finance Committee reported the Reagan bill, S.528, on May 24, with Democrats Moynihan, Russell Long of Louisiana, and Bill Bradley of New Jersey joining Republicans Packwood, Roth, Robert Dole of Kansas, John Danforth of Missouri, William Armstrong of Colorado, David Durenberger of Minnesota, Steve Symms of Idaho, and Charles Grassley of Iowa in the majority. On June 29 in *Mueller v. Allen*, the Supreme Court upheld a Minnesota statute permitting a state income tax deduction for education expenses. The Reagan proposal differed from the Minnesota statute, however, by offering credits rather than deductions, covering tuition but not textbooks or transportation, and targeting parents of nonpublic but not public schoolchildren.[32]

On July 22 Reagan's Deputy Assistant Director for Legal Policy William Barr nonetheless told the Administration's Coalition for Tuition Tax Credits that the Reagan bill "is constitutional, and that no changes should be made on that [legal] basis." The new administration strategy was to attach the tuition tax credit bill to popular railroad retirement benefits legislation, forcing the House to act on the entire measure. Barr did allow, however, that "if it becomes feasible," the administration would "give in" to adding public school parents to the bill.[33]

The process never went that far. The railroad bill passed both houses of

Congress in time for the August recess, but without the tuition tax credit amendment. On November 16, Dole offered S.528 as a rider to the legislation, and, after an hour of debate, the Senate voted 59-38 to table the amendment. Thirty-five Democrats and twenty-four Republicans were in the majority, with nine Democrats and twenty-nine Republicans in the minority. Ten Catholic Senators from both parties voted to table S.528.[34]

The news continued to be bad for advocates of public aid to Catholic schools. By 1984, forty percent of Catholic high schools and twenty-seven percent of Catholic grade schools had closed in the previous two decades. In 1985, in a pair of 5-4 decisions in *Aguilar v. Felton* and *Grand Rapids v. Ball*, the Supreme Court prohibited public school teachers from entering parochial schools to teach remedial classes funded under Title I of the ESEA. Writing for the majority, Justice William Brennan maintained that such accommodations by the New York City and Grand Rapids, Michigan, public school systems, even in classrooms in which religious symbols were absent, "were in effect [to] subsidize the religious functions of the parochial schools by taking over a substantial portion of their responsibility for teaching secular subjects." As a result of the decision, parochial school students would have to visit public schools after school hours or off-site vans during school hours for Title I instruction. "The Court, with remarkable ease," lamented Richard Duffy, the USCC's Director of Federal Aid, "has nullified legislative judgments aiming to assist the education of school children in Grand Rapids and New York City."[35]

## THE BUSH ADMINISTRATION

Presidential candidate George Bush, like Ronald Reagan, promised in 1988 to support federal tuition tax credits or vouchers for parents of nonpublic school children. The erosion of Bush's position came, however, even before he had taken the oath of office. A White House Workshop on Choice in Education held ten days before the end of the Reagan presidency narrowed the definition of "choice" to public schools. Neither President Reagan nor President-elect Bush addressed the gathering. Secretary of Education Lauro Cavazos replaced a speech advocating nonpublic school vouchers, which had been written for him by Assistant Secretary of Education Patricia Hines, with one opposing such aid.[36]

On April 18, 1991, when Bush introduced America 2000, his proposal for national educational standards, he redefined "choice" to include nonpublic schools. "We can encourage educational excellence by encouraging parental choice," said the President. "It's time parents were free to choose the schools that their children attend. This approach will create the competitive climate that simulates excellence in our private and parochial schools as well."[37]

Bush's return to his campaign stance on school choice offered considerable cause for optimism. "[There is] the general expectation that the Administration will get much of the program enacted, a rare prospect for the Administration's domestic proposals," wrote the *New York Times* Adam Clymer of America 2000 in April 1991. Six months later, after aggressive intervention by Chief of Staff John Sununu and Pennsylvania Republican Representative William Goodling, the House Education and Labor Committee passed a compromise version of the Bush plan, H.R. 3320, leaving public and nonpublic school choice at the discretion of local school districts and in conformity with state constitutions. "Any bill that includes a choice element in it and at least does not prohibit the participation of private schools is all to the good," applauded NCEA President Sr. Catherine McNamee. "We have a fundamental difference in strategy. We would argue for taking a strong position [against nonpublic school choice] and falling back, " lamented NEA legislative Director Michael Edwards. Education Subcommittee Chairman Dale Kildee acknowledged the administration lobbying effort: "I think the factor that has changed is the strength the White House has been able to exert." Edward Kealy, director of federal programs for the National School Boards Association, viewed the vote as the culmination of "ten years of advocacy by the Bush and Reagan administrations."[38]

The victory would be short-lived, however. The Senate Labor and Human Resources Committee reported S. 2, sponsored by Massachusetts Democrat Edward Kennedy and limiting choice to public schools. After neither H.R 3320 nor S. 2 came to a floor vote in 1991, the Chairman of the House Education and Labor Committee, Michigan Democrat William Ford, opened the 1992 session by proposing H.R. 4323, a public-school-only choice proposal backed by the NEA and AFT. Committee Democrats explained that they had supported the previous compromise only for fear of greater concessions to nonpublic schools, and before the Senate adoption of its public-school-only bill. After a party-line vote released the bill from committee, the House passed it, 279-124, on August 12. In the Senate, Kennedy resurrected S.2, which won in committee and on the floor. A 36-57 vote on January 23 rejected an amendment, sponsored by Utah Republican Orrin Hatch and supported by the White House, which would have established six demonstration projects in which federal monies would finance nonpublic school choice.[39]

## THE CLINTON ADMINISTRATION

During the 1992 Presidential campaign, Democratic Governor Bill Clinton of Arkansas contended that nonpublic school "choice" would simply transfer badly needed federal funds from public schools to nonpublic schools and would violate the First Amendment's separation of church and state. Six months into the new administration, however, the Supreme Court ruled unanimously in *Jones v. Clear Creek Independent School District* that public school systems which open their doors to after-school community organizations must admit religious groups as well, effectively overturning a New York state law that banned the use of public school property for any religious purpose. In the court's majority opinion, signed by six justices, Byron White wrote that the refusal by the Center Moriches, Long Island school district to admit religious groups to its high school did not violate the three-pronged test established by the court in the *Lemon* decision of 1971: that the aid to a religious institution "has a secular purpose, does not advance or inhibit religion as its principal effect, and does not foster an excessive entanglement with religion." The court stopped short, however, of overturning *Lemon*, which Antonin Scalia, in a separate opinion joined by Clarence Thomas, likened to a "ghoul in a late-night horror movie," and which Anthony Kennedy criticized more temperately in his separate opinion.[40]

Later in the same term, the court ruled 5-4 in *Zobrest v. Catalina School District* that a sign-language interpreter paid by the Tucson, Arizona, school district may accompany a deaf child into a Catholic high school. Citing the "child-benefit" precedent established in the 1947 *Everson* case, Chief Justice William Rehnquist argued for the majority, "If the Establishment Clause [of the First Amendment] did bar religious groups from receiving general government benefits, then a church could not be protected by the police and fire departments, or have its public sidewalk kept in repair."[41]

The momentum for nonpublic school choice would not last, however. In November 1993, California voters overwhelmingly rejected a nonpublic school voucher initiative despite the support of the state's Republican governor, Pete Wilson. In June 1994, in *Board of Education v. Grumet,* the Supreme Court ruled against the state of New York in abolishing the separate Kiryas Joel school district as a violation of the Establishment Clause of the First Amendment. The majority opinion, authored by Justice David Souter, argued that the law creating the special district had transcended the constitutional guarantee that religious communities can "pursue their own interests free from governmental interference." Justice Scalia's dissenting opinion lamented that the decision "takes to new extremes a recent tendency in the opinions of this court to turn the Establishment Clause into a repealer of our nation's tradition of religious toleration." In the same year, the Supreme Court of the Commonwealth of Puerto Rico struck down a plan by which low-income parents of nonpublic school students would receive from the island's department of education a $1500 voucher for reimbursement of educational costs. While a private school deserves police and fire protection, the court ruled, the Puerto Rican constitution's prohibition of public funds to support nonpublic schools applied to "public services or assistance that support its educational mission." The year ended with the 103rd Congress having defeated nonpublic school vouchers, when amendments to Clinton's "Goals 2000: Educate America Act" failed by a 300-130 House vote in 1993 and a 52-41 Senate vote in 1994. Bishop Robert Banks of Green Bay, Wisconsin, chairman of the USCC Education Committee, said of nonpublic school choice, "The message was it was not to be discussed."[42]

The Republican ascendancy on Capitol Hill offered nonpublic school advocates new hope for federal school choice legislation. But a 7-7 vote in 1995 killed an amendment to the Department of Education appropriations bill, proposed by House Republican Frank Riggs in the Early Childhood, Youth, and Family and Educational Opportunities Committee, which would have transferred $30 million of Elementary and Secondary Education Act Title I money to a three-year school choice demonstration project for low-income parents. In 1996 two Senate floor votes, 54-44 and 52-42, sank an aid package for the District of Columbia which would have allowed the city council to vote for nonpublic school vouchers.[43]

A third study of the Milwaukee voucher program the following year, however, favorably compared "choice" to "non-choice" students, and "choice" students after several years in the program to the same students when they entered. The Supreme Court's 5-4 decision in *Agostini v. Felton* in 1997 effectively overturned its 1985 *Aguilar v. Felton* verdict by permitting "the on-site delivery of [ESEA] Title I services for students enrolled in religiously affiliated schools." Citing the *Zobrest* decision, Justice Sandra O'Connor's majority opinion asserted that "we have abandoned the presumption in *Meek* and *Ball* that the placement of public employees on parochial school grounds inevitably results in ... state-sponsored indoctrination or ... a symbolic union between government and religion." Echoing his three immediate predecessors, Secretary of Education Richard Riley hailed the decision as "a positive step forward for American education."[44]

The fortunes of nonpublic school advocates continued their ebb and flow during the following three years. In September 1997, the first study of the Cleveland voucher program showed improvement by those participants tested after their first year. In December 1997, however, a second study of the program tested the "choice" students and found them no better off than their peers outside the program. In May 1998, the District of Columbia voucher plan finally passed both houses of Congress, only to have the president finally act on his threat to veto it. In June 1998, the Wisconsin State Supreme Court ruled that the expansion of Milwaukee's nonpublic school choice to religious schools passed the *Lemon* test: "because it has a secular purpose, it will not have the primary effect of advancing religion, and it will not lead to excessive entanglement between the

State and participating sectarian schools." But Wisconsin Republican governor and voucher advocate Tommy Thompson opposed extending it to other parts of the state because "it's going to take some time to evaluate." For the first time, the 1998 Gallup Poll found a majority of Americans in favor of nonpublic school choice. In June 2000, by a 6-3 margin in *Mitchell v. Helms*, the Supreme Court upheld the Chapter 2 federal program supplying computers and other "instructional equipment" to parochial schools because, in Justice Clarence Thomas's majority opinion, it "neither results in religious indoctrination by the government nor defines its recipients by reference to religion."[45]

Yet from 1991 to 1998, voters rejected nonpublic school vouchers in four states. In August 1999, on the eve of the first week of school, Judge Solomon Oliver of the Federal District Court in Cleveland allowed that city's voucher students to attend classes, but only for a semester, after which he ruled the program unconstitutional under the First Amendment. However, under various appeals, the program continued operating as it was litigated through state and federal courts, culminating in a U.S. Supreme Court validation of the voucher program in *Zelman v. Simmons-Harris* in 2002. In March 2000, Judge Ralph Smith of the Circuit Court of Florida ruled the voucher program there in violation of the state constitution's provision for "free public schools," but it continues in operation pending appeal in federal court. In June, by a 6-3 margin in *Santa Fe Independent School District v. Doe*, the Supreme Court struck down student-led organized prayer before football games as, in Justice John Paul Stevens' majority opinion, potentially a "personally offensive religious ritual" endorsed by Sante Fe high schools.[46]

As the twenty-first century began, 18 states permitted public loans of textbooks, 26 states allowed public transportation, and 28 states authorized public auxiliary services to nonpublic schools. But 35 state constitutions prohibited some form of public aid to nonpublic schools. And over four decades after the enactment of the National Defense Education Act, there remained no large-scale federal aid to Catholic schools.[47]

**ENDNOTES**

[1]     Lawrence McAndrews, *Broken Ground: John F. Kennedy and the Politics of Education* (New York: Garland Publishing, 1991), 27.

[2]     Timothy Boggs, "An Analysis of the Opinions in the United States Supreme Court Decisions on Religion and Education from 1948 through 1972," (Ed. diss., University of Colorado), 1973, 43, 80.

3  McAndrews, 9-10.
4  Ibid, 64, 69.
5  Ibid, 75, 80, 94.
6  Ibid, 134, 135, 162, 163.
7  Ibid, 177, 166, 172.
8  Ibid0, 219.
9  McAndrews, 173; Lawrence McAndrews, "Unanswered Prayers: Church, State, and School in the Nixon Era," *U.S. Catholic Historian*, (Fall 1995): 84; "NEA Support for Federal Aid," *School and Society*, 12 October 1968, 328; Interview of Harold Sanders by Joe Frantz, 24 March 1969, Tape 2, Lyndon B. Johnson Presidential Library, Austin, TX, 37; "Trouble in the Classroom," *Time*, (2 June 1967): 56.
10  "Statement of Very Rev. Msgr. James C. Donahue, Ph.D., Director, Department of Education, U.S. Catholic Conference, Before the Subcommittee on Education, Committee on Labor and Public Welfare, U.S. Senate," 10 August 1967, United States Catholic Conference Papers, Archives of The Catholic University of America (after ACUA): 1; The diocesan school superintendents would reject a plan proposed by Msgr. Donahue to make such a commitment the schools' top priority, in Gerald Fogerty, "Catholic Schools: Their Past and Future," *America*, (28 September 1968): 254; "NEA Support for Federal Aid," (12 October 1968): 328.
11  Letter from Richard Nixon to Bishop Joseph Bernardin, 3 March 1970, Box 36, Folder: USCC: (ACUA) Folder: Church: Church and State: Federal Aid to Education 1970, January-June, USCCP (ACUA) "The Jencks Tuition Voucher Plan," *America*, (20 June 1970): 644-645; Memorandum from James Robinson to Bishop Joseph Bernardin, (11 February 1971): Box 36, Folder: USCC (ACUA) Church: Church and State: Federal Aid to Education 1971 January-April, USCCP: 1-2; Carl Megel, "Voucher Plan Opposition Growing," 4 November 1970, American Federation of Teachers Office of the President, Box 32, Folder: 32-22, Legislative Department, Volume 2, 1969-70, American Federation of Teachers Papers, Reuther Library, Detroit, MI; Memorandum from John Ehrlichman to George Schultz and Casper Weinberger, 19 December 1970, White House Central Files, Subject File, Confidential, Box 11, Folder: [CF] FA 3 Federal Aid, Education (1969-70), Richard M. Nixon Presidential Papers, National Archives, College Park, MD.
12  Leo Pfeffer, "The Parochiaid Decision," *Today's Education/NEA Journal*, (September 1971): 64; Daniel Moskowitz, "Public Funds and Private Schools," *PTA Magazine* 68 (May 1974): 19; David Kucharsky, "Parochiaid Disallowed," *Christianity Today*, (16 July 1971): 34.
13  William Consedine, "The School Aid Decision: Preliminary Analysis," 6 July 1971, Box 57, Folder: USCC: Departmental Committees: Education, USCCP (ACUA) 3; Memorandum from James Robinson to Bishop Joseph Bernardin, 15 July 1971, Box 36, Folder: USCC(ACUA) Church: Church and State: Federal Aid to Education 1971, July-December, USCCP, 1; "A Summary Report of the Steering Committee Authorized at the Washington Conference on Nonpublic Schools," 8 July 1971, Box 57, USCC: Departmental Committees: Education, 1971, USCCP, 1-3; Letter from Bishop Joseph Bernardin and Bishop William McManus to Joseph Cardinal Dearden, 26 August 1971, Box 36, Folder: USCC: Church: Church and State, 1971, July-December, USCCP (ACUA) 7.
14  Memorandum from Lew Engman to the President, 6 March 1972, President's Office

Files, Box 88, Folder: Memoranda for the President, 12/17/71-2/20/72, RMNPP, 1-2; Memorandum from Lew Engman to George Schultz, Peter Flanigan, and Kenneth Cole, 29 March 1972, White House Central Files, Subject File, Conference Files, 1969-74, Box 11, Folder: [CF] FA 3 Federal Aid — Education [1965-70], RMNPP; "Nixon: Verbal Fence-Mending," *National Review*, (26 April 1972): 442.

15  Stanley MacFarland, "Public Aid to Nonpublic Education: An Overview of Federal Activities, " 13 February 1973, American Federation of Teachers Office of the President, Box 1, Folder: 1-9, Nonpublic School Tax Credit, 1972-73 [3 of 3], AFTP, 3; "Statement by Mr. John J. Murray, Director, Department of Nonpublic School Teachers, AFL-CIO, on H.R. 16141 Before the Committee on Ways and Means, United States House of Representatives, Ninety-Second Congress, Second Session," 6 September 1973 (Washington, D.C.: United States Government Printing Office, 1972): 4; Memorandum from Robert Lynch to Most Rev. Archbishops and Bishops, et. al., 3 October 1972, Box 36, Folder: USCC, ACUA, Church: Church and State: Federal Aid to Education 1972, USCCP(ACUA): "Intensive Effort Essential," CREDIT Newsletter, 2 October 1972, Box 36, Folder: USCC: Church: Church and State: Federal Aid to Education, 1972, USCCP, ACUA.

16  Memorandum from David Lissy to Roger Semerad, 29 October 1974, White House Central Files, Subject File, Education, Box 6, Folder: FA 3 Education 8/9/74-8/26/74, Gerald R. Ford Presidential Library, Ann Arbor, MI, 1-2; Memorandum from Roger Semerad to Jerry Jones, 26 February 1975, White House Central Files, Subject File, Education, Box 6, Folder: ED 2/1/75-4/10/75, GRFPL, 1-2.

17  "Report of the Committee on Education," 15 August 1975, ED 89-67, Box 10, Folder: 7/30 Agenda Committee on Education, 12/14-15/69, USCCP, 2; Lissy to Semerad, 2; Memorandum from Arthur Quern to James Cannon through James Cavanaugh, 6 August 1975, White House Special Files, David Lissy Files, Box 10, Folder: Nonpublic Schools [2], GRFPL, 1.

18  Memorandum from H. Reed Saunders to Terrel Bell, 14 July 1975, David Lissy Files, Box 10, Folder: Nonpublic Schools [2], GRFPL, p. 1; Memorandum from Arthur Quern to James Cannon through James Cavanaugh, 30 July 1975, White House Special Files, David Lissy Files, Box 10, Folder: Nonpublic Schools [2], GRFPL, 2.

19  Gerald Ford, "The President's New Conference of October 9, 1974," *Public Papers of the Presidents of the United States: Gerald R. Ford*, 1974 (Washington, D.C.: United States Government Printing Office, 1975), 251-252.

20  "Saving Diversity by Distinctions," *America*, (5 February 1977): 93; "The Commitment to Nonpublic Schools," *America*, 9 April 1977, 311; Mary Hanna, *The American Catholic People* (Cambridge, MA: Harvard University Press, 1979), 128.

21  "A Parochial Decision," *Newsweek*, (4 July 1977): 50.

22  "School Tax Credits?" *Newsweek*, (26 December 1977): 76; "Private Schools," 12 December 1977, Staff Files, Domestic Policy Staff: Eizenstat, Box 195, Folder: Education—ESEA [CF, OA, 22] Jimmy Carter Presidential Library, Atlanta, GA, 4; Letter from Msgr. Francis Barrett to Jimmy Carter, 11 November 1977, White House Central Files, Subject File, Education, Box ED-3, Folder: ED 7/1/77-12/31/77, JCPL.

23  "Shanker Raps Senate Panel on Tuition Tax Credits," 24 February 1978, White House Central Files, Subject File, Box FA 12, Folder: FA 3 1/1/78-7/31/78, JCPL, 30; Memorandum from James McIntyre and Stuart Eizenstat to the President, 24 February 1978, White House Central Files, Subject File—Education, Box FA 10,

24  Folder: FA 3 1/1/78-2/28/78, JCPL, 10.

Letter from Elizabeth Abramowitz to Rev. John Meyers, 5 May 1978; White House
Central Files, Subject File, Education, Box ED-3, Folder: ED 1/1/78-9/30/78, JCPL.
25  "Proposal for Tuition Tax Credit Campaign," 13 February 1979, Box 37, Folder:
USCC: Church: Church and State: Federal Aid to Education: Tuition Tax Credits
1979, USCCP,ACUA: 3; Marjorie Hunter, "House Approves Credit for Tuition by
a 237-158 Vote," *New York Times*, 2 June 1978, sec. A,. 1, and sec. B, 17; "Meeting
with Senator Daniel P. Moynihan," 6 June 1978, Presidential Diary Collection, Box
PD-32, Folder: 6/7/78 Backup Material, JCPL, 3.
26  "Telephone Call from [John Cardinal] Krol" and handwritten notes, 2 August 1978,
Box 37, Folder: USCC: Church: Church and State: Federal Aid to Education: Tax
Credits, 1973-78, USCCP; "Meeting with Senator Kaneaster Hodges," 7 August
1978, White House Central Files, Subject File, Education, Box ED-2, Folder: ED
8/1/78-12/31/78, JCPL; Memorandum from Thomas Kelly to Most Rev. Archbish-
ops, 18 August 1978, Box 37, Folder: USCC: Church: Church and State: Federal
Aid to Education: Tax Credits, 1973-78, USCCP (ACUA) "Presidential News
Conference," 17 August 1978, "Weekly Compilation of Presidential Documents,"
Box 37, Folder: USCC: Church: Church and State: Federal Aid to Education: Tax
Credits, 1973-78, USCCP, ACUA, 1444.
27  "Congressional Leadership Breakfast," 25 September 1978, Presidential Diary, Box
PD 39, Folder: 9/26/78 Backup Material, JCPL, p. 3; Joseph Califano, *Governing
America* (New York: Simon and Schuster, 1981), 301; "Proposal for Tuition Tax
Credit Campaign," 13-15 February 1979, USCCP (ACUA) 5.
28  Memorandum from John Harmon to Griffin Bell, 30 March 1980, Shirley Hufstedler
Collection, Box 7, Folder: Tuition Tax Credit [1], JCPL, 2-3; "Confidential Minutes
of Discussion on Advisory Committee on Public Policy and Catholic Schools," 11
September 1979, Box 37, Folder: USCC: Church: Church and State: Federal Aid
to Education: Tuition Tax Credits, 1979, USCCP, ACUA, 2.
29  Memorandum from Rev. Thomas Gallagher to Catholic School Superintendents, 19
November 1980, Box 70, Folder: USCC: Departmental Committees: Education: Tax
Credits, USCCP, 1; "Tuition Tax Credits: Now or Never," *America*, (13 December
1980): 380-381; "Packwood Introduces Tuition Tax Credits," 24 February 1981,
Box 70, Folder: U.S. Departmental Committees: Education Tax Credits, 1981
January-June, USCCP, ACUA: "Coalition Status: Senators' Positions on Tuition Tax
Credits," AFT Office of the President, Box 10, Folder: 10-15, Tuition Tax Credits,
1981 [1 of 3], AFTP; Stephanie Overman, "Political Climate Ripe for Tax Credits,
USCC Team Says," 23 February 1981, Box 70, Folder: USCC Departmental Committees: Education: Tax Credits, 1981 January-June, USCCP, ACUA.
30  Thomas Edsall, "Reagan Win May Be Far Reaching," *Washington Post*, 13 August
1981, sec. A, 2; telegram from President Ronald Reagan to the Chief Administrators
of Catholic Education, 16 October 1981, Box 70, Folder: USCC: Departmental
Committees: Education Tax Credits, 1981 September-December, USCCP, ACUA,
1-2.
31  "Minutes, Committee on Public Policy and Catholic Schools," 19 January 1983, Box
ED 89-59, Folder: Public Policy, 9/8/83, USCCP, 1; Ronald Reagan, "Address Before
a Joint Session of the Congress on the State of the Union," 25 July 1983, *Public Papers
of the Presidents of the United States: Ronald Reagan*, Book I, 1983 (Washington, D.C.:

U.S. Government Printing Office, 1984), 106; Ronald Reagan, "Message to the Congress Transmitting the Fiscal Year 1984 Budget," 31 January 1983, *Public Papers of the Presidents of the United States: Ronald Reagan*, Book I, 1983, 145; Memorandum from Judy Barnacke to Tuition Tax Credit Petition Drive Coordinators, et. al., 18 March 1983, AFT Office of the President, Box 64, Folder 64-16, AFTP, p. 1; Juan Williams, "White House Pushes for Tuition Tax Credit," *Washington Post*, 5 March 1983, sec. A, 5.

[32] Thomas Brandt, "White House Uses Rider to Save Tuition Credit," *Washington Times*, 3 June 1983, sec. A, 3; Edwin Dorn and Mary Frances Berry, "Tax Credits for Tuition Address the Wrong Issue," *Los Angeles Times*, 13 July 1983, in *Congressional Record*, 28 July 1983, E82.

[33] Memorandum for J. Stephen O'Brien to the Executive Staff, 25 July 1983, Box ED89-59, Folder: *Mueller v. Allen*, 1983, USCCP, ACUA.

[34] Memorandum from Frank Monahan to Msgr. Daniel Hoye, 21 November 1983, Box 70, Folder: USCC: Department Committees: Education: Tax Credits, 1983 November-December, USCCP, ACUA.

[35] Jay Dolan, *The American Catholic Experience* (New York: Doubleday, 1985), 442; Linda Greenhouse, "High Court Bars Public School Teachers from Parochial Classrooms," *New York Times*, 2 July 1985, sec. A, 14; Edward Fiske, "Ruling Means City Must Work Out How to Get Help to Parochial Pupils," *New York Times*, (2 July 1985): sec. A, 14.

[36] Edward Fiske, "Lessons," *New York Times*, (11 January 1985): sec. B, 14.

[37] "Remarks by the President at Presentation of National Education Strategy," 18 April 1991, Bush Presidential Records, Office of Policy Development, Charles E. M. Kolb Subject File, Box 12, Folder: Johannes Kuttner, America 2000 [OA/ID 06978] [1 of 2], George Bush Presidential Library, College Station, TX, 3.

[38] Adam Clymer, "For the Education Plan, A Rare Rosy Forecast," *New York Times*, 17 April 1991, sec. A, 19; Julie Miller, "House Panel's Vote Marks Sea Change on the Choice Issue," *Education Week*, (6 November 1991): 137.

[39] "Scorned School Bill Dies in Senate," *Congressional Quarterly Almanac*, 1992 (Washington, D.C.: Congressional Quarterly, 1993), 455-461.

[40] William Clinton, "Remarks to the AFL-CIO Convention in San Francisco, California," 4 October 1993, *Public Papers of the Presidents of the United States: William J. Clinton*, Book II, 1993 (Washington, D.C.: United States Government Printing Service, 1994), 1672; Linda Greenhouse, "Justices Allow Religious Groups After Hours Use of Public Schools," *New York Times*, (8 June 1993): sec. A, 1, 23.

[41] Linda Greenhouse, "Court Says Government May Pay for Interpreter in Religious School," *New York Times*, (19 June 1993): sec. A, 1, 8.

[42] Voters in California Reject Proposal on School Vouchers," *New York Times*, (3 November 1993): sec. A, 24; "Linda Greenhouse, "High Court Bars School District Created to Benefit Hasidic Jews," *New York Times*, (28 June 1994): sec. D, 21. Within days of this decision, however, the New York legislature passed new legislation drafted by Democratic Governor Mario Cuomo which the state supreme court upheld the following year as "religiously neutral, accommodating the Hasidic residents of the village of Kiryas Joel without singling them for favorable treatment," in Joseph Berger, "Court Affirms Public School for Hasidim," *New York Times*, (9 March 1995): sec. D., 21; Frank Kemerer and Kimi King, "Are School Vouchers Constitutional?" *Phi Delta Kappan*, (December 1995): 309-310; "House Passes

High School Job-Training Bill," *Congressional Quarterly Almanac*, 103rd Congress, First Session, 1994 (Washington, D.C.: Congressional Quarterly, 1995): 398; Thomas Content, "School Choice is Alive," *Green Bay Press-Gazette*, (12 November 1994): sec. 1, 1.

43 "Labor-HHS Bill in Limbo at Year's End," *Congressional Quarterly Almanac*, 104th Congress, First Session 1995 (Washington, D.C.: Congressional Quarterly, 1996): 11-57; John Leo, "Choice Words from Teacher Unions," *U.S. News and World Report*, (11 March 1996): 17.

44 "Study Finds Pupils are Helped by Program," *Milwaukee Journal-Sentinel*, (16 October 1997): sec. A, 16; Charles Russo, Allan Osborne, Gerald Cattaro, and Philip D. Mattia, "*Agostini v. Felton* and the Delivery of Title I Services to Catholic Schools," *Catholic Education*, (March 1998): 263; Linda Greenhouse, "Court Eases Curb on Aid for Church-Run Schools," *New York Times*, (24 June 1997): sec. B, 9; "Excerpts from Ruling Allowing Aid to Church Schools for Remedial Classes," *New York Times*, (24 June 1997): sec. B., 9.

45 Tamar Lewin, "School Voucher Study Finds Satisfaction," *Milwaukee Journal-Sentinel*, (18 September 1997): sec. A, 12; "Public vs. Private," *U.S. News and World Report*, (23 November 1998): 5; George Will, "In 1998, It's Liberals Who Block Schoolhouse Door," *Milwaukee Journal-Sentinel*, (30 November 1998): sec. A, 8; Robert Coles, "Wisconsin's Historic Decision," *America*, (29 August-5 September 1998): 5; Scott Hildebrand, "Private-School Choice Unlikely to be Expanded," *Green Bay Press-Gazette*, sec. A, 2; Tamara Henry, "Majority Backs Public Money for Private Schools," *USA Today*, (26 August 1998): sec. D, 1; Linda Greenhouse, "Justices Approve U.S. Financing of Religious Schools' Equipment," *New York Times*, (29 June 2000): sec. A, 21.

46 "Vouchers," National Education Association Center for the Advancement of Public Education [cited 15 April 1998], http://www.nea.org/index.html/, INTERNET; Pam Belluck, "Federal Judge Revises Order, Allowing Vouchers for Now," *New York Times*, 27 August 1999, sec. A, 1; "Excerpts from Supreme Court Opinions on Prayer," *New York Times*, (20 June 2000): sec. A, 22.

47 "Public Assistance to Private Schools and Private School Children," Department of Education, United States Catholic Conference [cited 12 June 2000], http://www.nccbuscc.org/education/parentassn/publicasst.html/, INTERNET.

# PART III
# CHARISM AND ETHOS

## CHAPTER 9

# FOR AND FROM
# FAITH FOR THE COMMON GOOD:
# THE CHARISM OF CATHOLIC EDUCATION

>⌒⌒⌒

*Thomas H. Groome*

D uring a public radio conversation around school vouchers, or what I prefer to call "parental school choice," I found myself defending the faith-based education that takes place in Catholic schools because an opponent cited it as inimical to the common good. His point was a simple one: the primary function of Catholic schools is to catechize in a sectarian kind of way and so should never receive support from the public budget. I insisted that he was caricaturing the purposes of Catholic schools and misunderstanding their faith-based education; in fact, they educate *for* and *from* a faith perspective that serves mightily the common good. His come back was to ask rhetorically, "but surely every Catholic school is motivated by Catholic faith." How could I not say "yes," but then be heard to concede the argument.

Besides more time to think, what I needed was a longer essay to lay out the subtlety of faith-based Catholic education. For indeed it has always been motivated by Catholic Christian faith, and intended to promote such faith in the lives of its students. And yet, that very same faith prompts it to educate in a holistic kind of way that—when at its best—eschews sectarianism or placing Christians "over against" the world. Catholicism and thus Catholic education has a genius for integrating faith and culture, Gospel and life, and of caring for all without distinction—being "catholic"—so that it eminently serves the common good. Parenthetically, this fits it entirely for public support.

179

Here, away from the firing line, I elaborate that the very charism of Catholic education is to educate both Christian disciples and good citizens. In fact, our foreparents would never have made such a distinction—Christian faith and life in the world were to be totally integrated. However, to encourage a conversation between Catholic educators and efforts to reform American public education (Part III of my essay), I've found it helpful to distinguish—without separating—that Catholic education educates *for* faith and *from* a faith perspective. By this I mean that it intends to catechize in Catholic Christianity—*for* faith—but its broader intent is to give a good education. Indeed, it does the latter *from* a faith perspective, in other words, motivated and permeated by faith-based commitments and values. However, this Catholic faith itself demands good citizenship and service to the common good. Further, educating from such a faith perspective lends the spiritual foundations needed for life-giving pedagogy. So, my basic thesis is that Catholic education serves the common good precisely by how it educates *for* and *from* a faith perspective. This is well substantiated by the story of Catholic education.

## Part I: Educating Disciples and Citizens— For the Common Good

### *From The Beginning*

The Hebrew scriptures make clear that the teacher was a revered figure, performing a social service that bridged the functions of priest and prophet—the worship of God and the well-being of society. Yes, they were to educate *for* faith, so their work was considered tantamount to prayer, as giving praise to God. But such faith required faithfulness to the covenant, that they live together in community as a people of God should live. The covenant demanded that the Hebrews "choose life" for themselves and others, (Deuteronomy 30:19), that they live with the peace and justice—the shalom—that God intends for all people. In other words, their educating *for* faith served the common good as well.

As the canonical corpus of Jewish sacred writings emerged during the Second Temple period (circa 400 b.c.e.), Jews became "people of the book" and thus even more intent on formal study. Here began their renowned commitment to education—a rich legacy to the present day. The synagogue became a school as much as a place of worship, dedicated to systematic study of the sacred texts. Again, the prime intent was to educate *for* faith. However, because the focus was on texts and their interpretation, it became all the more imperative to teach reading, writing, and rhetoric besides. So, educating *for* faith encouraged a total education, serving well the common good. The first Christians would come to a similar perspective.

The four Gospels most frequently describe Jesus' public ministry as "teaching." People often called him "teacher" and he seemed to welcome this address. They recognized him as "teaching with authority" (Matthew 7:29) and eventually came to see him as incarnating "the wisdom of God" (1 Cor.1:24). It is very evident that Jesus intended to educate *for* faith; his whole ministry reflected the invitation "have faith in God" (Mk: 11:22), and faith in himself as "the way, the truth, and the life" (John 14:6). The knowledge he intended was that people "might come to know . . . the only true God, and the one [God] sent, Jesus Christ" (John 17:4).

It is equally clear that such faith required living as a person of God according to Jesus' own way of life—as disciples. And the guiding vision for faith as Jesus modeled and preached it, was the reign of God. This was a deeply spiritual symbol for Jesus, inviting disciples to let God reign in their hearts. However, it was a profoundly social symbol as well, demanding that people do God's will of peace and justice, love and compassion, freedom and fullness of life for all "on earth as it is done in heaven." His whole life-purpose was "for the life of the world" (John 6:51), that people "might have life, and have it to the full" (John 10: 10). At least as Catholic tradition has interpreted it, faith after the way of Jesus can never be a "private" or purely personal affair; it always demands living for God's reign in the world—for the common good.

The Gospels are clear that Jesus intended disciples to continue his teaching ministry. In fact, he began to share this work with them during his lifetime (see Luke 10:1-20, etc), and promised that whoever teaches with integrity the ways of the covenant "will be called greatest in the kingdom of heaven" (Matthew 5:19). Then, the Risen Christ assembled the disciples on a hillside in Galilee and gave all present the great teaching commission: "Go, therefore, and make disciples of all nations . . . teaching them to observe all that I have commanded you." The teaching, then, would be of a "way of life" after *the way* of Jesus—for the life of the world.

As Jewish faith had prompted a commitment to holistic education, so Christian faith and the memory of Jesus began to do likewise. Further, those first disciples began to realize that the "salvation" effected by God in Jesus was also holistic, something for the whole person—not simply for souls in a narrow sense—to bring about God's reign in society, and indeed throughout all creation (see Romans 8). The saving work of Jesus should be continued in the public as well as the personal realm. Thus, to teach Jesus and the faith that Jesus taught would require Christians to teach *for* faith and *from* a faith perspective for the common good of all.

### Early Church as Educator

The early Church sensed that its overarching mission was to continue God's work of salvation in Jesus—helping to bring about the reign of God. And they recognized that education would be an integral aspect of this saving work. In all the listings of ministries in the first Christian communities, the *didaskaloi*—teachers—are always included and well placed; Paul has them third after apostles and prophets (see 1 Corinthians 12: 28). It is interesting to note that the *Didache*, among the earliest documents concerning the educational mission of the Church, lists teachers ahead of bishops and implies that they are entitled to preside at Eucharist.[1]

It appears that the first Christian schools—in the formal sense—began in great cities like Alexandria and Antioch, toward the end of the second century. Their leaders, people like Clement (150-215), head of the school in Alexandria and his successor Origen (185-254), began to realize that the catechetical ministry of the Church—teaching the Gospel—should be set within a holistic education. To bring about God's reign in Jesus, the Church should teach the "four Rs" as well as the four Gospels.

Those early Christians came to realize, too, that secular learning was also of God, that it could support their evangelizing interests by providing what Origen called "stirrups to reach the sky"—the spiritual wisdom of Christian faith. In a similar vein, Augustine proposed that "catholic" means to be open to truth, wherever it can be found. And he insisted that reason and revelation need each other, thus encouraging open inquiry—so essential to any education worthy of the name. The foundations were being laid for a Catholic education that would indeed be grounded in and intend to promote faith but would do so in ways that serve the common good.

Before long, those early pioneers began to forge what scholars have called a "Christian paideia," uniting Gospel and culture into a Christian humanism to educate disciples in faith *and* have a life-giving influence on society. Their concern was not simply to catechize Christians but to educate—albeit from a faith perspective—in ways that promoted the welfare of the public realm. As Clement had urged, they saw good education as "a work of salvation," integral to Jesus' saving mission in the world.

There were dissenting voices to the Church's open-minded and holistic education. Why should it take on general education? Enough to teach the Gospel! Tertullian, for example, insisted that "Jerusalem has no need of Athens"; he meant to separate faith from culture, the Church from holistic education. Tertullian would have the Church simply teach *for* faith—and no more. Happily, wiser voices prevailed, launching Catholic education that would teach whatever needed to be taught, and *from* a faith perspective. The seeds sown in those early years would bear much fruit, and especially for the common good of society. Indeed, for many ensuing centuries, the Church would be "the educator" of the Western world—educating both *for* and *from* faith.

## *Monastic and Cathedral Schools*

As Augustine lay on his deathbed (430), the Vandals were already at the gates of Hippo. Thereafter, uncultured tribes—unflatteringly nicknamed "barbarians"—swept over the empire and the rich tradition of Greek and Roman scholarship was severely threatened. But the vestiges of education and enlightenment were kept alive and then revived by the Church. In fact, the common good of Western society came to hinge on its educating.

The Celtic monasteries remained beacons of learning during those "dark ages." Irish monasticism had a particular commitment to scholarship, and especially to copying manuscripts in order to preserve the classic texts of Western culture. The great monasteries of Clonard, Durrow, and Clonmacnoise were like modern day universities with as many as 3000 students, and the Abbey of Kildare under St. Brigid (d. 523) was a center of learning, culture, and peace-making. St. Columba (c.521-97), educated at Clonard, founded the great monastic center of learning at Iona that became a seed-bed for the revival of education throughout Europe. Now, as the Church set out to convert the "barbarians," it realized that it must also educate them. To do less would fall short of God's work of salvation.

From their founding in the sixth century, monasteries following the Rule of St. Benedict were committed to education. The most famous Benedictine schools emerged at Monte Cassino in Italy, Tours in France, Jarrow in England, Fulda in Germany, and there were many lesser known ones. Likewise some leading schools grew up around great cathedrals like Canterbury, Seville, Liege, Utrecht, Cologne, Paris, and Orleans. At first, the monasteries and cathedral schools were only for the education of future monks and priests. Enter the emperor Charlemagne.

Charlemagne (c.742-814) became King of the Franks in 771. For the next 28 years he pacified and extended the Empire to include most of Western Europe, with its center in Aachen, where he was crowned Holy Roman Emperor in 800. But Charlemagne recognized that military might alone could not pacify his huge empire. Gradually he came to see the clue to social stability and the common good as education, and the most likely educator to be the Church. So, in 787, Charlemagne decreed that all monasteries and cathedrals must open their schools to every boy in the empire who desired an education. Sadly, it didn't occur to Charlemagne that girls should also be educated, but at least he had sown the seed of "universal education."

The Carolingian schools favored a socratic method to teach the seven liberal arts as revived by Charlemagne's own mentor, Alcuin, at the Palace School. The liberal arts were divided into the trivium, a study of classic texts through grammar, rhetoric, and dialectic, and then the more advanced quadrivium of music, arithmetic, geometry, and astronomy. While these "arts" were considered a preparation to study sacred scripture and the patristic legacy, they also made for a well-educated person. Thus began Catholicism's great tradition of "liberal" education, so named because it was to liberate people from ignorance toward a better life. Through the monastic and cathedral schools of the Carolingian renaissance, the Church had become the educator of the Western world. It was now fully engaged in educating *for* faith and doing general education *from* a faith perspective to serve the common good of all.

Around 1150, the first of the great universities emerged at Salerno and Bologna, dedicated to the study of medicine and law respectively. The University of Paris followed shortly thereafter, and then Oxford, Cambridge, Padua, Pisa, Salamanca, Lisbon, and many others that continue to this day. The founding of the universities was a watershed in the history of Western education.

Though the emperor or local ruler often gave the universities official recognition and guaranteed safe passage to their teachers and students, the whole university movement was extensively the work of the Church. Most had a rector or chancellor who was ecclesially appointed; their power to grant degrees was by papal charter; the professors were clerics, especially Dominicans, Franciscans, and Augustinians, and likewise many of the students; and Catholicism lent the common faith and language that enabled faculty and students from diverse cultures to work together.

Scholastic theology took its place at the very heart of the university as the "queen" of the sciences, and provided the "sacred canopy" for all study and education. This bonding of faith and culture to educate for the common good was by now a one-thousand-year tradition of the Church. Yet, Thomas Aquinas (1225-74) lent renewed rationale for the partnership between Christian faith and good education: "just as grace does not destroy nature but perfects it, so sacred doctrine presupposes, uses, and perfects natural knowledge."[2] With this synthesis, the Church was set to educate in faith for the common good for another 1000 years.

## THE ALLIANCE WELL TESTED

The Church's schools and universities of the late Middle Ages gave rise to the great cultural revival called the Renaissance. Among other things, the Renaissance returned to the classical learning of Greece and Rome, and championed a humanism centered on the dignity and value of the person. Indeed there were other factors—the growth of urban society, invention of the printing press, the crusades, discovery of "the new world"—yet it was Catholic education that spawned the Renaissance. But this was an uneasy alliance. For the Renaissance encouraged freedom of inquiry, unfettered by creeds of faith or by Church directives. Could the Church embrace such a movement and still educate both *for* faith and *from* a faith perspective?

Though threatened at first and ever remaining cautious, the Church's own long tradition of uniting faith and culture enabled it to embrace the Renaissance spirit in its educational ministry. An eminent instance of this new paideia was the *Ratio Studiorum* of St. Ignatius of Loyola; it was suffused with Renaissance humanism and commitment to open inquiry. The alliance between revelation and reason, faith and culture, church and education had been well tested but could continue, educating *for* faith and *from* faith for the common good.

The Protestant Reformation evinced a deep ambivalence about the Church sponsoring general education. The reformers certainly encouraged personal interpretation of scripture and thus lent a major impetus to universal literacy. Yet, their cry of "scripture alone" as the guide of faith encouraged mistrust of what Luther called "the whore, reason." In a sense, they revived the old Tertullian sentiment, "Jerusalem has no need of Athens." Further, the reformers emphasized the sinfulness of human culture and social structures. Martin Luther (1483-1546) made a total separation between the Kingdom of God and the "Kingdom of man"—the public realm—with the latter being inherently corrupt. That Christians should help to realize the values of God's reign within "the earthly city" was rejected as futile by the reformers. Concomitantly, they downplayed the "good works" aspect of Christian faith, with the latter amounting to total trust in God's grace and mercy. Again, this did not encourage Christian agency in the world. With such a separating of faith from culture, of God's reign from human history, why bother with general education; enough to teach "the Gospel."

Luther was anxious to wrest control of general education from the Church of Rome and loudly condemned the cathedral and monastery schools as "tools of the devil." Yet, he also knew the imperative of good education—albeit, not the work of the Church. His solution was to insist that the state take on the function of general education, taking it out of the hands of the Church. In 1524 Luther wrote his famous educational manifesto urging the German civil rulers to establish government-sponsored and publicly-funded schools for the welfare of both state and church. They did, and thus launched the national school system throughout Europe. Luther and the German princes had initiated what we now call "public" education.

This development presented a new question: should the Church continue to do general education? Should it now defer to the state to sponsor schools for the common good, and limit itself to catechesis—educating *for* faith? Its long tradition prompted Catholicism to continue to do general education *from* a faith perspective as integral to its "work of salvation." However, the structural arrangements now varied. Many of the Catholic countries entrusted and funded the Church to sponsor their "public" education. In other countries, Catholic schools continued to flourish, but funded independently by the Church or by student tuition. The most eminent instance, of course, is the American Catholic school system.

Prior to the Reformation, the Dominicans, Franciscans, and Augustinians had papal approval to be involved in general education as a function of their ministry. Likewise, Geert De Groote (1340-84) had founded the Brothers of the Common Life in 1376, likely the first order of vowed religious brothers dedicated to educating the common people. In the post-Reformation period, the Church approved a great number of new teaching orders of men and women, beginning with the Ursulines founded in 1535 by St. Angela de Merici (1475-1540), and the Jesuits of St. Ignatius of Loyola (1491 - 1556) who received papal approval in 1540. These orders saw educating *from* a faith perspective for the common good as integral to their religious charism; they would be the valiant mainstay of Catholic education into the present.

The Council of Trent (1545-63), in fact, discouraged women's religious orders from participating in general education. The Church was still getting used to the idea that women should be educated, but found it too much of a reach that they should be educators as well. However, the faith and persistence of many courageous women, who often knowingly functioned contrary to the expressed directives of the Church, prevailed over papal chauvinism and led gradually to approval. Those great women knew instinctively that to educate both *for* and *from* faith required the full participation of women as teachers and students; nothing less would serve the common good.

Some of the notable women's orders dedicated to teaching that emerged in this era were: the Congregation of Notre Dame cofounded in 1598 by Blessed Alix le Clerc; the Visitation sisters cofounded in 1610 by St. Jane Francis de Chantal (1572-1641); the Institute of the Blessed Virgin Mary founded circa 1615 by Mary Ward (1585-1645); the Daughters of Charity, cofounded circa 1633 by Louise de Marillac and Vincent de Paul (1591-1660); the Sisters of St. Joseph founded in 1650 by John Peter Medaille. And many new teaching orders of religious men emerged like the Oratorians (1575), the Vincentians (1625), the Sulpicians (1641), and the Brothers of the Christian Schools founded by John Baptist de la Salle in 1684.

Through these and subsequent myriad religious orders, the Catholic Church continued to be a major sponsor of education down to the present. With the revival of the missionary movement in the nineteenth century, Catholic religious orders brought their commitment to education throughout the world. They had a particular and life-giving impact on the developing nations; not since the early days of the Church was it so evident that education is "a work of salvation." Their pedagogy, and especially that of the women's orders, was an enlightened one that anticipated or reflected the humanizing pedagogies of great educational reformers like John Comenius (1592-1670), Johann Pestalozzi (1746 - 1827), and Friedrich Froebel (1782-1852).

The Enlightenment movement that emerged during the eighteenth and nineteenth centuries championed a deeper and more critical rationalism than any renaissance before it. This marked the dawn of what has come to be known as "modernity." Ironically, the Enlightenment had a kind of blind faith in the power of critical reason, and was prejudiced against "common sense" and the authority of tradition. The battle cry, in the dictum of Emmanuel Kant (1724-1804), was "dare to think" and he meant for and by yourself, apart from all "authority" and especially free of the Church's magisterial role. The Enlightenment's skepticism challenged the whole fabric of traditional Catholicism and especially its conviction that education *from* a faith perspective could serve the common good.

As with its predecessor, the Renaissance, the Church was defensive at first and has ever remained a bit cautious toward the Enlightenment. Yet it came to recognize that its own tradition of wedding faith and culture, revelation and reason, enabled it to appropriate the assets of the Enlightenment, while remaining convinced that education from a faith perspective could well serve the common good. At Vatican I (1869-70), even while somewhat on the ropes, Catholicism reiterated its age old conviction that "Faith and reason ... are .. mutually advantageous ... right reason demonstrates the foundations of faith ... and faith ... sets reason free."[3]

Thereafter, much of the scriptural, historical, theological, and pastoral scholarship that encouraged the "aggiornamento" (renewal) of the Second Vatican Council (1962-1965) came to appropriate the critical methods and canons of modernity. Yet, Vatican II reiterated Catholicism's ancient partnership with education, insisting that because of "the mandate she has received from her divine Founder to proclaim the mystery of salvation to all," the Church always has a "role to play in the progress of education" and in honoring every person's "inalienable right to an education."[4] Catholic education had survived the critiques and challenges of modernity, and continued to educate *for* faith and *from* a faith perspective to serve the common good.

## PART II: AMERICAN CATHOLIC SCHOOLS AND THE COMMON GOOD

Throughout history, there is likely no more compelling instance of Catholic education for discipleship and citizenship than the school system created by the U.S. Catholic community. Its whole impetus was both to "conserve the faith" and, at the same time, to integrate the hordes of Catholic immigrants into this great "American experiment." As Anthony Bryk and colleagues have amply verified, American Catholic education has been and continues to be a powerful influence for the common good.[5] And its story goes back to the very first Catholic settlers in this "new world."

Outside of the original colonies and ranging from the sixteenth to nineteenth centuries, Spanish missionaries created a system of mission centers whose purpose included the education of the native peoples. Beginning in 1606, Spanish Franciscans opened a formal school in St. Augustine, Florida, with the stated purpose "to teach children Christian doctrine, reading, and writing." Children needed to be educated in faith and for life.

Likewise, the first French missionaries and explorers who came into the Great Lakes region and Mississippi Basin from Montreal and Quebec, understood their mission work to include education. The first French-sponsored Catholic formal school for boys was opened by Franciscans in New Orleans in 1718, and the Ursulines opened a school there for girls in 1727. For both, the intent was to catechize and to improve the lot of their students—educating *for* and *from* faith for the common good.

In the thirteen original colonies, the English settlers vigorously opposed education by or for Catholics, at first only a small minority of indentured laborers and servants. In 1642 the Massachusetts Bay Colony enacted a law that required a school in every settlement; the stated intent was to offset the influence of "Ye Olde Deluder Satan" by teaching children how to read the Bible. Thereafter and throughout the colonial period of a century and a half, each colony had what claimed to be a common school system; it was, however, controlled by the Protestant churches and clergy. A Protestant ethos and an overt anti-Catholic bias permeated the whole curriculum, (check out, for example, the McGuffey readers). Even into the late 1700s, the few Catholic schools run by Jesuits, Franciscans, and Ursuline sisters received no public support and experienced much opposition, while Protestant denominational schools had full freedom and public funding.

Independence (1776), and the Bill of Rights (1791) with its guarantee of religious liberty, coupled with a major influx of Catholic immigrants from Europe (Catholic population rose from circa 25,000 in 1776 to 6 million by 1850), brought new opportunity and need for Catholic education. Catholics in the colonies began to challenge the Protestant control and curriculum of the schools that posed a threat to the faith of their children; as such, the common schools were not serving the common good.

At first, many Catholic bishops favored a truly "public" school system, free of undue Protestant influence. This was also the intent of such educational reformers as Horace Mann (1796-1859)—a nonsectarian school system supported by the public purse. However, this proposal met with stiff opposition from the establishment which insisted, in effect, that the common schools proselytize children into a Protestant ethos. In response, and spearheaded by such bishops as John Hughes (1797-1864) of New York, Catholics began to establish their own schools and petitioned the states for the same public funding as enjoyed by other denominational schools and academies. They felt they deserved such funding precisely because they were serving the common good, preparing good citizens as well as Christian disciples.

The somewhat predictable outcome, however, was that one state after another prohibited state funds to all denominational schools. This refusal of public funds, coupled with organized anti-Catholic sentiment in "nativist" groups like the Know-Nothings, was the catalyst for U.S. Catholics to establish their own independent school system. They would continue to educate *for* and *from* a faith perspective for the common good, albeit without support from the common purse.

The vast system of American Catholic education was made possible by the generosity of parents and parishioners, and especially by the religious orders of women and men who emerged to staff the schools for minimum living allowance. Between 1840 and 1900 more than 60 European religious orders of women and men came to teach in the United States. The emergence of the first American sisterhoods also gave major impetus to the parochial school system. The Sisters of Charity of St. Joseph were founded by St. Elizabeth Ann Seton (1774-1821) circa 1809; the Dominican sisters of St. Catherine were founded in Kentucky in 1822; the Oblate Sisters of Providence were founded in Baltimore in 1829, the first congregation of African-American sisters in the United States; the Servants of the Immaculate Heart of Mary were founded in 1845 at Monroe, Michigan.

The Catholic bishops of the United States, assembled at the First Plenary Council of Baltimore in 1852, urged that every parish build a parochial school, a plea reiterated by the Second Plenary Council of 1866. But the Third Plenary Council of 1884 (of "Baltimore Catechism" fame) was even more emphatic, decreeing that "near each church, where it does not exist, a parochial school is to be erected within two years. All Catholic parents are bound to send their children to the parochial school."

Though this mandate of Baltimore III was only very partially realized because of financial and other constraints, it lent new impetus to the founding of parochial schools. By 1900 there were as many as 3,500 Catholic elementary schools in the country (about 45% of the 8,000 parishes). By 1920 this number had doubled to 6,551 schools with 41,581 teachers and 1,759,673 pupils. Catholic elementary school enrollment doubled twice again until it reached an all time high in the mid-1960s with four and a half million children enrolled. Similarly, the secondary schools grew from about 100 in 1900 to 1552 by 1920, to 2119 in 1940, and 2392 in 1960 with an enrollment of almost a million students.

In 1789 the great John Carroll (1735-1815), Archbishop of Baltimore, founded the first Catholic institution of higher education at Georgetown, confined to the Jesuits. During the nineteenth century, religious orders opened some 200 Catholic colleges for men in the U.S. Among the early ones that have survived and grown into renowned colleges and universities were: St. Louis University (1832), Fordham (1841), Notre Dame (1842), Villanova (1848), Holy Cross (1852), Santa Clara (1855), Manhattan (1863), Seton Hall (1856), and Boston College (1863). Colleges for women were slower to emerge, but among the first were St. Mary's, Indiana (1895), Notre Dame, Maryland (1896), the College of New Rochelle (1897), and Trinity College, Washington, D.C. (1897). By 1964 there were 120 Catholic colleges for women. Most of both the men's and women's colleges have since become coeducational.

Enrollment in American Catholic schools reached a high of five and a half million students in the mid-1960s and then declined, due, at least in part, to the decrease in vowed religious to staff the schools, thus requiring higher tuition. In 1965, 85% of faculty and staff were religious and 15% laity; thirty years later those figures were directly reversed—85% laity and 15% vowed religious. However, by the early 90s, the decline seemed to bottom out and now there are signs of resurgence with new schools opening, and some closed ones reopening.

U.S. Catholic schools amount to the largest independent school system in the history of the world. It has had its phenomenal growth while receiving next to nothing by way of public funding—from federal, state, or city government. Yet, these Catholic schools have been extraordinary in their success at turning out fine American citizens. One need only look to the myriad of Catholic school graduates who, past and present, have given leadership in every aspect of American public life, and to the less known but countless number of ordinary good citizens who went through Catholic schools. With some irony, Bryk et al make the point that the very school system founded and funded to serve the common good often does so poorly. Meanwhile, the Catholic school system, refused funding on the grounds that it would be inimical to the common good, serves it with great distinction.

## Part III: Catholic And Public Education: A Partnership?

I wish to propose a conversation—two-way—between American Catholic education and American public education. Indeed, the current educational crisis in our country would advise a dialogue between the public and all independent systems—for example the large network of Lutheran schools—but, as throughout, my focus is on Catholic schools. And while I imagine this as a wide-ranging and enduring dialogue, encouraging a vital partnership and deeper cooperation between the two systems, here I make only a very modest beginning. But think about it! Surely from its two-thousand-year story, Catholic education has wisdom to contribute to the current public discourse about the reform of public schools. By the same token, Catholic education has shown itself capable of adapting to changing times, and of learning how best to respond to the needs of its context. I believe American Catholic schools could learn from the public system how to make adjustments that would enhance their contribution to the common good—while remaining faithful to their defining charism to educate *for* and *from* faith.

There is a deep crisis in American public education; the worrisome statistics are widely known and need not be rehearsed here. Undoubtedly, some American education is the best in the world. But too much of it is also among the worst in the world – at least in the democratic world—and it is worst of all where we need it to be best of all, namely, in our poor rural neighborhoods and inner cities. By contrast, Catholic schools read like a success story, with far better scores on just about every measure, and typically at half the cost. But rather than being self-congratulatory or smug, American Catholics must be deeply concerned about the national school crisis.

To begin with, 80% of American Catholic school-age students are in public schools. But even if every Catholic child was in a Catholic school, we should still be concerned about the public school system because we are good citizens who care about the common good of our country. The Catholic sense of the  common good is that everyone in a society should enjoy its essential benefits—like a good education—while the disadvantages experienced by some are to the detriment of everyone.

Typically, Catholic education is seen as an alternative to public education. Indeed, this is a practical view in many inner cities and valid for parents everywhere who want a faith-based education for their children, with the spiritual and moral formation that such an education makes explicit in its curriculum. Now we need to move beyond the mindset of "alternative" and imagine Catholic education as a partner with public education, working together for the common good. In this partnership, let me suggest that *public education can learn from Catholic education its dire need for a spiritual foundation*, and, conversely, *Catholic education can learn from public education to avoid sectarianism and every semblance of proselytizing,* while continuing to educate *for* and *from* a faith perspective.


## PUBLIC EDUCATION IN NEED OF SPIRITUAL FOUNDATIONS

Let me say boldly that the success of American Catholic schools suggests to the public system that it, too, needs a spiritual foundation for how and why it educates. Rather than avoiding such a foundation as inimical to its purpose, it needs as much to educate well for the common good of all. In fact, resistance to a spiritual vision is the current Achilles' heel of American public education. Here the reader must suspend the standard reaction "but the Constitution forbids it"— spirituality infringing on the public sector—and be open to imagine new possibilities. The people who designed our currency did!

The fact is that we have a Constitution—and other nation-defining documents like the Declaration of Independence and the Pledge of Allegiance— that are grounded in great spiritual values. Their architects could never have proposed nor convinced the fledgling America to become *one nation under God*, that *all people are created equal* or insist upon *liberty and justice for all* on purely philosophical grounds. Might it be possible that such a Constitution *requires* rather than forbids education with a spiritual vision. And might it be possible that our standard mind-set—a "wall" of separation—is nothing more than blind acceptance of the Enlightenment bias against religion, even extending this preju-dice to spiritual values.

When at its best, all education has a spiritual vision in that it reaches into "the deep heart's core" (William Butler Yeats) and changes people in life-giving ways. Good education invites students to reach beyond present knowledge and wisdom into limitless horizons, to move out of themselves into life-giving rela-tionships, to grow into their own unbounded potential and responsibilities, to care for others and the common good as well as for themselves, to ever find "the more" in the midst of the ordinary of life, to learn how to learn for lifelong learning. In other words, *good education fosters the human capacity and desire for the Transcendent.*

It was this recognition that prompted the great philosopher, Alfred North Whitehead (1861-1947), to insist: "We can be content with no less than the old summary of educational ideal which has been current at any time from the dawn of our civilization. The essence of all education is that it be religious."[6] Reading Whitehead in context makes clear that by religious he means what we would now call "spiritual." In sum, he proposes education that engages and nurtures the complete possibilities of the person—the soul.

Whitehead was only representing the better understanding of education that has endured throughout the history of Western civilization. Beginning some 2500 years ago, Plato described the function of the teacher as "to turn the soul" of the student toward "the true, the good, and the beautiful." Picking up on Plato's spiritual understanding of education, Augustine, writing some thousand years later, said that the teacher's function is to engage "the teacher within" each student, and he meant the divine capacity at the core of people. A similar note of engaging the soul resounds in all the great philosophers of education— Comenius, Rousseau, Herbart, Montessori, and so on.

In our own day, Parker Palmer urges attention to "the inner landscape of a teacher's life" and likewise to the students' inner lives as key to quality education.[7] Though Palmer uses spiritual language sparingly, he clearly advises teachers to work out of their own souls and to engage the depths of their students. And his work is enjoying a wonderful reception among public school teachers, indicating their readiness to reclaim spiritual moorings. Without as much, I believe, all efforts to reform American public education will fall far short. Current proposals address only symptoms—e.g. how to raise math scores—and presume upon the favorite elixir, more money, especially for educational technology. The federal government is currently spending up to $100 billion to put a computer in every public school classroom.

There is some evidence that increased funding well spent—e.g., to hire more teachers and create smaller classes—can have positive results, but beyond this, the gross correlation between school spending and student performance is not impressive. Per-pupil expenditure in public schools increased by 22% in the 70s and by 48% in the 80s but SAT scores declined almost 100 points. And a study by the Rand Corporation found that personal computers are only "marginal contributors" to student learning.

Indeed, federal and state governments ought to supplement the local school budget as needed to insure that every child has fair access to a quality education, regardless of the property-tax base where she or he lives. Likewise, teachers deserve a reasonable workload, and salaries commensurate to their profession and the crucial social service they render. Sadly, compared to teachers in other Western democracies and, indeed, to professions in our own society, American educators are grossly underpaid. Graduates of Boston College who become teachers can expect a starting salary of $20,000 a year less than graduates entering other fields (in the "30s" compared to the "50s"), and Boston teachers are relatively well-paid. But neither money nor technology are panaceas for our public schools.

The wisdom that two thousand years of Catholic education would offer to American public schools is that they reclaim their spiritual foundations and *renew a humanizing and holistic vision for American education*. I say "renew" because America's founding mothers and fathers had such a vision for the nation, and thus for its schools. Education is *humanizing* as it empowers students to become fully alive human beings, people who care for both their own and the common good, who relish the gift that is life and accept its challenges, who exercise their rights and honor their responsibilities, who champion justice and compassion toward all, who are confident in their own identity but open to other cultures, traditions, and perspectives, who know and appreciate the knowledge of the sciences, the wisdom of the humanities, the aesthetic of the arts.

*Holistic* education engages students' heads, hearts, and hands—the whole person—teaching them to think critically and creatively for themselves, forming them in universal values and virtues, educating them in the arts and crafts they need for life, and to be artisans of life for all. Such a "philosophy" for our schools would be in marked contrast to the ethos of easy liberalism and crass pragmatism that currently holds sway.

Now here is the crux of the issue; a humanizing and holistic vision needs more than a philosophical grounding; its roots must be spiritual in order to bear such fruit. But talk of the spiritual triggers the American paranoia about separation of Church and State. This is an unfortunate overreaction; I'm convinced that American education can draw upon spiritual resources without proselytizing on behalf of a particular religion, without violating the Constitution or its First Amendment. That Amendment—"Congress shall make no law respecting an establishment of religion nor prohibiting the free exercise thereof"—was intended to protect religions from undue government interference, not to exclude all spiritual values from the public realm.

Though Madison argued wisely for a "thin line," let us agree to leave "the wall" of separation in place; indeed, in some ways it has served us well. But surely the ban on an established religion should not exclude common spiritual values from our school system. There is a world of difference between proselytizing on behalf of a particular religion and allowing a spiritual vision to permeate the nation's approach to education.

Presuming that we should ban spiritual resources from how and why we educate, meanwhile Americans seem thoroughly complacent about the impoverished philosophy that presently permeates our schools. This I would characterize as a crass pragmatism concerned only with "the cash value" (William James), and an easy liberalism that avoids deep human values lest they be "imposed" on students. We naively presume that such philosophy is neutral. But it is as value-laden as any spirituality, imparting an impoverished self-understanding and outlook on life, with little commitment to serve the common good.

The very notion of a value-free education or educator is a contradiction in terms—an oxymoron. The most we can do is choose from where we will draw the defining values that shape our schooling. As noted, the U.S. Constitution and the Declaration of Independence—indeed this whole "American experiment"—reflects deep spiritual values, and requires as much of education that would serve the nation.

There are core spiritual values around which many of the great world religions and spiritualities can reach consensus—more than for any particular philosophy. For American educators to allow such spiritual convictions to permeate their teaching and the ethos of our schools would be transforming. These include:

- *Human beings have equal dignity, rights and responsibilities.* This would encourage a liberating and integrated education for all instead of a functional and fragmented one.

- *Life in the world is a gift charged with purpose and meaning.* This could encourage students to find hope and joy in living in contrast to nihilism and escapism—drugs, alcohol, etc.

- Our *human identity is essentially communal; we need and must care for each other.* This could prepare accountable community members, educate for the common good of society and offset the reigning individualism.

- *Living life well requires wisdom that encourages responsibility.* This could lend a noble purpose to all study, with every discipline reaching beyond knowledge to foster an ethic for life.

- All the great spiritualities teach *justice for all and compassion for the needy.* This suggests education in critical consciousness, in commitment to social transformation and service to those most in need.

- At their best, most spiritualities are *universal in outlook, emphasizing the bondedness of all people.* This could educate for open-hearts and open-minds, to appreciate—more than tolerate—diversity, and to cherish truth wherever it can be found.

- All spiritualities are convinced that *the human vocation is to live in "right relationship" with God*—however named—*with oneself, others, and creation.* An education for right relationship would literally transform American society.

Such spiritual values—and my list is far from exhaustive—now seem far distant from the reality of American public schools, but we must ask why and then why not? It certainly does seem as if a spiritual foundation is the key asset of Catholic schools—with far less well funding that public schools, yet outperforming the latter on every score. By way of a spirituality expressed in core values and ethos, I'm convinced that there is very little "going on" in Catholic schools that could not also be present in public ones.

## Catholic Education, Free of Sectarianism and Proselytizing, Educator to the Nation

From the American public school system, Catholic schools might learn to appreciate and build upon the distinction I have made throughout this essay between education *for* faith, and education *from* a faith perspective. The success of public schools in learning to avoid religious proselytizing—remember early failures in this regard—now confronts Catholic schools to recognize that educating *for* faith and *from* a faith perspective need not be collapsed into each other. While Catholic schools will always offer education *for* Catholic faith to Catholic students, it could offer a good education *from* a faith perspective to "anyone who applies"—without the slightest hint of proselytizing. As such, it could become an educator to the nation, not simply to the American Catholic community. For its two thousand year history, Catholic education has educated both *for* and *from* faith. But it was its appreciation for both that gave the system of Catholic education its original green light and subsequent *raison d'être*. For the Church discerned that its educational mission—integral to its work of salvation—entailed both catechesis *for* faith and providing a holistic education. The latter is indeed done *from* a faith perspective, and yet it is done, too, for its own sake—not simply to "convert" people to Catholicism.

I first encountered a Catholic-school system making this distinction in practice during a visit to Pakistan. The first Catholic school in Pakistan was founded in 1856 by the Sisters of Jesus and Mary, a French order, and the system burgeoned thereafter. It now numbers about 550 schools of various kinds, many of which are huge institutions, providing schooling from kindergarten to college. St. Joseph's, Karachi, for example, is more than 100 years old and has over 3,000 students. Clearly a jewel in the crown, yet it is only one example of what is widely considered the best educational system in Pakistan.

Many Catholic schools were nationalized in 1972 and are now fully funded by the Pakistani government. All are predominantly Muslim in faculty and enrollment; most have less than 5 percent Christian students. In deference to their communities, these schools display none of the symbols of Catholic Christianity; they scrupulously avoid proselytizing Muslim children to Christian faith, and, in fact, require them to take a religion curriculum in Islam. Muslim parents vie to enroll their children in Catholic schools knowing that they will receive an excellent education *and* formal instruction in their own faith tradition.

I became intrigued by the fact that, though scrupulously avoiding proselytizing to Christianity, and providing religious education in Islam, these schools are readily recognized within Pakistani culture as very different from traditional Muslim schools and distinctly Catholic in their "philosophy"—read spirituality. This is evident in their whole curriculum—what, how, and why they teach. So, they reflect deep commitment to the value and dignity of the person—boys and girls; they encourage a positive outlook on life, pushing back against the fatalism of the surrounding culture; they nurture a sense of community and of responsibility to others; they foster a strong commitment to justice, peace and reconciliation; they encourage critical thinking and appreciation for the spiritual wisdom of other traditions.[8]    Here is a Catholic school system that scrupulously avoids proselytizing to Catholic Christianity.

The word "catholic" comes from the Greek *katha holos*. Though it is usually taken to mean "universal," this was more Aristotle's use of the term. Etymologically, it literally means "including everyone"; or, as James Joyce put it well in *Finnegan's Wake*, "catholic means here comes everybody." It is a blessed day, then, that sees so many children from other or no religious tradition registering in American Catholic schools. Already it is common to find Catholic schools in our inner cities with up to 90% enrollment from other traditions. It looks as if we are moving closer to being a truly "catholic" system. The faith prerequisite for attending a Catholic school should be about the same as that required for eating Quaker Oats for breakfast; it's my favorite and I'm not a Quaker.

Catholic schools will always intend to educate its Catholic students in their faith and form them in Catholic Christian identity. However, like their sister schools in Pakistan, and reflecting the age-old distinction between educating *for* and *from* faith, they can and must avoid every semblance of proselytizing to Catholicism. They can do so while remaining thoroughly Catholic in their foundational values and ethos. And while many graduates will choose to go home to God by paths other than Catholic Christianity, the quality education they receive in Catholic schools will be truly a "work of salvation"—and an eminent service to the common good as well.

Taking it that the ethos and spirit of a school can be thoroughly Catholic, and provide a good education without catechizing its non-Catholic students, let us reflect briefly on an appropriate religion curriculum. At first blush, the religion curriculum seems like a bit of a challenge, but I prefer to see it more as an opportunity for some creativity. Let me reiterate, every Catholic school should offer a religion curriculum that teaches fully and faithfully the "whole story" of Catholic Christian faith, with Catholic students expected to participate. But beyond teaching what is distinctly Catholic, a "mixed" school can readily have a generic Christian curriculum—with lots of scripture, Christian moral formation, and nurture in good Christian values—that would be appropriate for students of any mainline Christian denomination.

By the middle grades, the curriculum could also introduce children to the great world religions. And where numbers warrant, there could be offerings in what is specific to other Christian traditions or in other religions—like the

Catholic schools of Pakistan. American Catholic colleges have been doing as much for years. With a bit of imagination, and without at all watering down a thorough religious education in Catholic faith, we could craft an ecumenically sensitive religion curriculum for our grade and high schools as well. At worst, non-Catholic parents could opt to have their children do "study hall" instead of participating in the schools' religion curriculum.

Catholic schools, educating *for* and *from* faith, have always served the common good of their society. They are also capable of simply educating *from* a faith perspective and rendering an excellent education, devoid of every semblance of proselytizing. In fact, their faith base—their spirituality—helps to insure the quality of the education they can render to all.

Contrary to my fellow-guest on that radio talk-show, American Catholic schools deserve to be fully funded by the government—as in all the other Western democracies—and precisely because it will be money very well spent. They will educate, as they have always done, for the common good. Alongside of and in partnership with public schools—and with other independent systems—Catholic schools can become educators to the nation.

## ENDNOTES

1   See, "The Didache" in *Ancient Christian Writers*, Vol. 6, (Westminster, MD: Newman Press, 1948), esp. Chapters 14 and 15.

2   Thomas Aquinas, *Summa Theologica*, (Westminster, MD: Christian Classics, 1981), Ia, I, 8 ad 2.

3   Vatican I, "Constitution on Faith," in *The Church Teaches*, (Rockford, IL: Tan Books, 1973), 34.

4   "Declaration on Christian Education," in Walter Abbott, ed., *Documents of Vatican II* (New York: America Press, 1966), 638-39.

5   See Anthony Bryk, Valerie Lee, and Peter Holland, *Catholic Schools and the Common Good* (Cambridge: Harvard U. Press, 1993).

6   Alfred North Whitehead, *The Aims of Education and Other Essays*, (New York: The Free Press, 1929), 14.

7   See Parker Palmer, *The Courage to Teach*, (San Francisco: Jossey Bass, 1998).

8   For an in-depth development of the core spiritual values of Catholic education, see my *Educating for Life: A Spiritual Vision for Every Teacher and Parent*, (New York: Crossroad, 2001). This book was inspired by my visit to Pakistan.

## CHAPTER 10

# MORE DEMOCRACY, MORE RELIGION
## BALTIMORE'S SCHOOLS, RELIGIOUS PLURALISM, AND THE SECOND WORLD WAR

### *Maria Mazzenga*

"**W**E'RE AT YOUR SERVICE, UNCLE SAM!"
About a month after the United States entered the Second World War in December 1941 *The Young Catholic Messenger,* a weekly magazine that could be found on the shelves of Catholic school libraries throughout the country, published an article titled "United We Stand." The article pledged Catholics' support for the nation during the war and outlined some of the ways young Catholics could "do their part for victory." Catholic youth "are making crusades of prayer, sacrifice, Masses and Communions for victory and peace and for our soldiers and the leaders of the country. 'Count on us Uncle Sam!' They are saying."[1] This braiding of Catholicism and Americanism occurred again and again in homefront Catholic educational circles. World War Two-era Catholic Americanism differed from earlier versions in that it was no longer a response to accusations by Protestants that Catholics weren't fit for American institutions because of their membership in a hierarchical church headed by the pope. Homefront Catholic educators no longer felt compelled to express their Americanness in defensive tones.

The reasons for the emergence of a newly confident Catholic Americanism lay in developments outside as well as inside the Catholic educational community. Catholics were particularly encouraged by the fact that American public school educators had become more welcoming toward members of non-Protestant religious groups than ever before in the early 1940s, as numerous articles from the wartime publication *Education for Victory* suggest. A 1942 issue of *Education for Victory* featured excerpts from an address delivered by the President of the National Conference of Christians and Jews, Everett Clinchy, to members of the Institute on Education and the War. Clinchy suggested creating new courses on intercultural relations emphasizing that the "worshipers at many altars in this country agree that Protestants, Catholics, Jews are separate and yet united, like the hands, feet, eyes, and ears of one single body."[2] As public school educators expressed more inclusive attitudes toward Catholics during the war, then, Catholic educators exhibited more confidence in their Americanness.

This chapter elaborates on such developments in examining religion, nationalism, and Baltimore, Maryland's public and Catholic educational institutions during the Second World War. A number of strains of thought came together to transform dramatically both the public and the Catholic schools of Baltimore during these turbulent years. First, the terrible shadow cast by totalitarian regimes overseas and the necessity of involving every community of the city in the homefront effort altered educators' attitudes toward education. As news of Hitler's nationalist determination, the rapidity with which Mussolini's Italy succumbed to Fascist extremism, and the intensity of the Japanese commitment to their nation hit the city, Baltimoreans grew prouder of American democratic institutions, and ashamed by the increasingly obvious ways these institutions contradicted their democratic ideals. Thus a combination of sincere recognition of discriminatory behavior toward minorities and the necessity of involving all Baltimoreans in homefront service generated a new consciousness that found bold expression in all of the city's schools. Broad expressions of democratic inclusiveness were accompanied by a renewed emphasis on religious participation across denominations. The increase in religious activity occurred for more individual and community-based reasons than the renewed emphasis on secular democratic American ideals, but the two developments fused, as this chapter will show, with religious and political expression often making a joint appearance. Thus a new generation of Catholic and public school youth would learn to view their national and religious sympathies as interwoven and complementary. More democratic expression, one might say, generated more religious expression.

This phenomenon of complementary political and religious ideals reflected the rise of what I will call "triple-melting-pot Americanism." This is a form of national expression that placed Catholics and Jews on par with Protestants as chief American religions for the first time in United States history. The notion of a Protestant, Catholic, and Jewish "triple melting pot" first appeared in a 1944 study by Ruby Jo Reeves Kennedy.[3] While Kennedy's study focused on intermarriage trends in New Haven, Connecticut, Will Herberg would later turn her thesis that Protestants, Catholics, and Jews had become equal partners in an

American triple melting pot into an influential book published in 1955, *Protes-tant-Catholic-Jew, An Essay in American Religious Sociology*. Herberg saw the emergence of a triple melting pot as representative of the inclusion of Catholics and Jews in American life. While Herberg's thesis has a number of problems, particularly with respect to his analysis of American Catholics, his expansion of Kennedy's triple-melting-pot idea to describe a renewed emphasis on organized religion across America is useful. [4]    Here, I draw upon the idea of triple-melting-pot Americanism to make two central points related to education in homefront Baltimore. First, this chapter describes the increase in religious tolerance within Baltimore's public schools. Second, it explains the increase in American patrio-tism within the Catholic schools.

## THE PRESENCE OF THE PAST: BALTIMORE'S SCHOOLS IN 1940

The Catholic schools of Baltimore had reproduced many of the educa-tional practices of the city's public schools by 1940, for better and for worse. Baltimore's network of Catholic institutions drew in a great variety of youth of varied economic and racial backgrounds, even as it followed local patterns of racial and economic exclusion. Such circumstances originate with the founding of the diocese in 1789. Despite Baltimore's Catholic origins, Catholics were not a welcome religious minority in early America, and to construct communal insti-tutions that contradicted the Protestant majority's social practices would have drawn hostility from American Protestants. Catholics who wanted to find a home in the United States therefore felt compelled to follow many of the local insti-tutional practices of the Protestant majority. With the aim of building a strong United States Catholic Church, religious authorities from the eighteenth through the twentieth centuries inclusively used their schools to offer Catholics of every background a safe haven in which to maintain and cultivate their religious faith, one in which the discriminatory practices of the majority would nonetheless find expression. Through a historical process of negotiation, a uniquely American Catholic educational system had emerged in Baltimore by the 1940s. [5]

Baltimore's Catholic and public educational institutions, responsible for educating nearly 150,000 youth of all backgrounds in the 1940s, reflected the contradictions present in schools across America. The nation's reputation as the land of opportunity notwithstanding, Baltimore's African Americans, like those in other cities, were relegated to inferior schools in both the Catholic and secular communities. [6]   On the other hand, Baltimore, like other American cities of the 1940s, had a substantial population of European-American youth who benefited enormously from the city's schools. For European immigrants and their children, the city's public and Catholic schools had been wondrously inclusive institutions.

Individuals with surnames like Krolczyk, Strumsky, Mulligan, Ciepiela, and Mason all roamed the halls of the highly-respected public Polytechnic High School for boys in 1943.[7] The Catholic all-female Seton High School boasted that "Fifty-nine parishes [of sixty-one] in Baltimore and vicinity were represented" in the graduating class of 1941.[8]

Similarly, public and Catholic schools both eased and reproduced economic inequalities present in the city as a whole. Seton High School drew students from a variety of economic backgrounds, and parish schools offered children throughout the city a low-cost, high-quality Catholic education. Polytechnic was well known for its custom of offering young men of all economic backgrounds a first-rate education. At the same time administrators from both parochial and public schools felt helpless to prevent working-class students in both communities from dropping out of school after the eighth grade to contribute to meager family incomes. As in other cities, moreover, where young Baltimoreans attended school affected the quality of education received, with youth attending schools in poor communities receiving instruction in more crowded classrooms and with older textbooks. Public schools in poor black communities were almost universally "reconditioned units previously used by white children," according to one 1939 study, and were almost always inferior to schools in more economically stable white communities.[9] Economic inequalities were also present in the Catholic schools. Eleanor Apicella, for example, traveled a mile or so from her working-class Little Italy neighborhood in the 1930s to attend the Notre Dame Institute, a Catholic school in which middle-to-upper class German- and Irish-American girls predominated in the 1930s and 40s. "I felt very comfortable in Little Italy until I went to high school" at Notre Dame, she recalls, "girls from all over the city and suburbs [were there]... a lot of suburbia. They made us feel inferior when we told them we were from Little Italy because Little Italy in those days was *the* slums... I had never been aware of that until I went there." On the one hand, then, Apicella managed to secure a secondary education in the city's most highly respected Catholic school while on the other, she felt uncomfortable among most of her peers.[10]

More industrialized than much of the early- twentieth-century south, yet "Southern" in its racial practices and social traditions, Baltimore and its schools reflected the cultures of both the northern and southern United States. Throughout the first half of the twentieth century Baltimore attracted a large number of both African Americans and European immigrants—in the 1940s the population of African Americans stood around 20%, the number of European immigrants comprised about 7% of the city population. Thus Baltimore was a segregated city that also drew a large population of immigrants hoping to find work in its strong industrial sector. The city's schools remained legally segregated until the

1950s. In 1939, 31,050 pupils attended the city's black public schools, with 84,129 youth attending white schools. Some of the city's parishes housed both blacks and whites, but churches and parish schools were as firmly segregated as non-Catholic institutions. In 1944 there were 25,893 Catholic youth in parish schools divided along racial lines, with 25,206 whites and 687 blacks in such schools.[11] The combination of migrants from the American South and from Europe nonetheless made for an ethnically dynamic school population. Of 61 city parishes, for example, nine were national, and four were African American. All of the national and African-American parishes had schools, and each had youth clubs and events that encouraged youth to maintain and cultivate ethnic traditions. While segregation and ethnic discrimination clearly existed in the city's Catholic schools, then, children were nonetheless imparted with an ethnic Catholic consciousness, one that would gain a new respect during the war.[12]

Progressive educational trends often reached Baltimore before finding their way into cities further south, and both Catholic and public schools were influenced by American Progressive educational ideals. With its network of institutions of higher education, Baltimore's schools would be exposed to a variety of educational trends pioneered by Progressive reformers. While these would find their most direct expression in the public schools, Progressive reforms such as scientific management, an emphasis on centralization, and attention to education for democracy also found their way into Baltimore's Catholic schools during the early twentieth century. Along with the public schools, the Catholic schools became increasingly professionalized and standardized by the 1940s. Baltimore's Archbishop Michael Curley, moreover, advocated such standardization in the Catholic schools, believing it would improve education for students of all backgrounds. By the 1940s, the city's schools were a collage of ethnic and socioeconomic groups, unified by standardized practices and an increasingly professional set of administrators and teaching staff. As we will see, the nation's entry into the war generated an appreciation for the diversity of Baltimore's school population, even as school administrators advocated unity and standardized educational practices.

### *"Dangerous Theories": War in Europe and Catholic Education in the United States*

"Christian doctrine and Christian morality are under attack from all quarters," Pope Pius XI declared in a 1938 letter to members of the United States hierarchy. "Dangerous theories which a few years ago were but whispered in conventicles of discontent," he elaborated, "are today preached from the housetops and are even finding their way into action." The woeful result: "private immorality and public subversion have in many places raised the banner of revolt against the Cross of Christ."[13]

From his post in Europe, Pius XI had publicly condemned Fascism in 1931, and both Communism and Nazism in 1937. This Pope was no great fan of the American way of life either, as his 1931 encyclical, *Quadragesimo anno,* a reiteration of the critique of laissez-faire capitalism first issued by Leo XIII in 1891, proves. Nonetheless, Pius XI felt compelled to turn to the United States hierarchy in his mission to preserve the Christian principles toward which many of his European contemporaries seemed so indifferent. The 1938 letter contained a special request to the American bishops convening at The Catholic University of America that year. The pope urged them to develop "a constructive program of social action, fitted in its details to local needs, which will command the admiration and acceptance of all right-thinking men."[14]

In one sense, Pius XI's decision to aim his request at the hierarchy of the United States was a shrewd one. His writings suggest that he recognized that much in American life contradicted Catholic moral teaching, but he also knew that "private immorality" was something American Catholics felt specially equipped to address. With Europe succumbing to war, perhaps the United States would be more receptive to the Church's moral teachings. Despite the Great Depression American Catholics were an ambitious lot in the 1930s and 40s—perhaps they could infuse their democratic political system with Christian compassion and moral rectitude in ways contrary to the powerful totalitarian regimes of Europe. On the other hand, the United States citizenry, historically Christian and theo-retically in favor of religious pluralism, had in fact proven themselves capable of horrific acts toward religious minorities, Catholics included, at many points in the past. The Catholics of America might be asked to preserve the moral doctrines of the Church, but they would have to use caution in presenting a Catholic vision to their nation.

The bishops took up the pope's letter as an opportunity to prove to the world that the Catholic Church's moral principles could indeed find refuge in the United States. They believed that religious tolerance, and tolerance toward humans of all cultural backgrounds, could be sown through well-constructed educational programs. "To carry out the injunction of the Holy Father, it is necessary that our people, from childhood to mature age, be ever better instructed in the true nature of Christian democracy." The bishops of the United States reasoned that a "precise definition must be given to [Catholics] both of democracy in the light of Catholic truth and tradition and of the rights and duties of citizens in a representative republic such as our own." The bishops promptly established the Commission on American Citizenship to carry out their mandate. The commission's first assignment: "compile at once a comprehensive series of graded texts for all educational levels." These texts, the bishops anticipated, "will build an enlightened, conscientious American citizenship."[15] The educational materials, the bishops explained to the commission, must ensure that youth "be held to the conviction that love of country is a virtue and that disloyalty is a sin."[16] Loyalty to the nation was as important as devotion to Catholic ideals. The textbooks created by the commission mark a new conviction among American Catholic educators that American and Catholic ideals could more than simply coexist: they complemented each other. As we will see, the materials produced by the Commission on American Citizenship would meet a population more than ready to champion a World War Two era Catholic American patriotism. But first, a brief look at how the wartime emphasis on democratic ideals inspired religious tolerance in American public education.

## *"Dangerous Theories": War in Europe and Public Education in the United States*

Public school educators in the United States were as alarmed as the pope with the rise of fascism and ethnic prejudice in Europe. They too believed that the educational system was the ideal channel through which the "dangerous theories" of racial and religious exclusion spreading throughout the world could be countered. American public school educators did not, of course, have a leader in Europe, and their response to the spread of exclusionary theories would vary in a number of ways from the Catholic Church's. Being secular institutions, the public schools could not overtly make use of a particular set of religious beliefs to counter prejudice, as the Catholic Church could. Instead, American public school educators would make use of secular democratic ideals to promote tolerance and religious pluralism.

The Bureau for Intercultural Education was to the public schools what the Commission on American Citizenship was to the Catholic schools. The bureau was an offshoot of the Service Bureau for Intercultural Education, an organization founded in 1934 by Rachel Davis DuBois, a Quaker pacifist who sought to end military conflict by promoting tolerance between cultural groups. During the war years, the reorganized Bureau for Intercultural Education would focus on "unity and understanding among all cultural groups," a message, historian Stuart Svonkin notes, "specifically tailored to fit wartime demands for social cohesion."[17] Jewish-American agencies, acutely sensitive to prejudice because of the violent anti-Semitism spreading throughout Europe, contributed large subsidies to the reconstituted bureau. This Jewish influence was significant, as where the organization under DuBois emphasized the cultural distinctiveness of particular ethnic and racial groups, Jews sought also to emphasize unity and understanding. The wartime emphasis on social cohesion generated an educational program in which the similarities among particular groups in addition to their differences would form the core themes. "Also significant was the fact that Jews," as Svonkin notes, "had been troubled by the earlier characterization of them as an *ethnic* group, and would thus promote creation of materials that addressed Jews as a *religious* group among other religious groups."[18]  Practically speaking, the Bureau's purpose was to promote intercultural understanding on a local level, in elementary schools and high schools in addition to colleges.  Public school teachers in Pennsylvania, New York, Michigan, and Indiana, all received assistance on teaching intercultural relations from the bureau.  The organization also distributed intercultural curricular materials to schools throughout the United States, and would assist Baltimore educators in preparing its own adaptation of the program, "Better Intercultural Relations," a publication disseminated in the city's public schools.  As we will see, both the bureau and Baltimore's version of its program would heavily emphasize the significance of religious tolerance in American democratic institutions.


## "EDDIE PATTERSON'S FRIENDS"

When the United States was pulled into the Second World War by the bombing of Pearl Harbor in 1941, the Catholics of Baltimore abandoned their isolationism and wholeheartedly dedicated themselves to national victory.  A huge upswing in church attendance and religious classes accompanied celebrations of Americanism within almost every city parish during the war.  Catholics' prewar certainty that their religious example presented a model of morality and character for all Americans to follow imperceptibly gave way to Catholic proclamations that their United States was the best country in the world.  Catholics had never doubted their Americanness, but prewar expressions of Catholic Americanness were nearly always infused with defenses that one could be both Catholic and American.  During World War II so many Catholics became involved in defending the nation overseas and on the homefront, that this defensive posture quickly disappeared.  If Catholics, after all, were sacrificing their lives and dedicating themselves to wartime service for the nation alongside Protestants, did they really need to defend their patriotism?  In 1940 the Baltimore Catholic Church possessed close to 195,000 members in 61 city parishes.  These parishes had been more insulated in earlier days, safe havens for Catholic worship in a city that had historically suffered bouts of anti-Catholic prejudice.[19]  Institutionally diffused throughout the city from its earliest days, the Church helped defuse anti-Catholic sentiment there, serving to "contain" Catholics within parishes, perhaps rendering them less threatening to nativists.  World War II marked the beginning of the end of parish insularity, with Catholics posing less and less of a threat to nativists as they threw themselves into the national effort to win the war.  All local Catholic institutions mobilized toward winning the war as American involvement in the

world conflict deepened, but few would exhibit the ensuing fusion of Catholicism
and Americanism as articulately and passionately as the city's Catholic schools.
The dedication of Catholic administrators, teachers, and students to the nation
during the war inevitably caused a rush of things secular into their schools.

How was a "Catholic Americanism" spun in Baltimore's Catholic schools
during the war years? First of all, practices cloaked in red, white, and blue—ration
book distribution, war bond sales, scrap collection—rapidly found their way into
everyday Catholic school life. Neighborhood Civilian Defense training took place
in school classrooms and auditoriums. Catholic school children zealously raised
funds for war bonds. Air raid drills during school hours kept Catholic students
poised for an Axis attack on the city, a real possibility early in the war. Students
collected recyclable material like paper, metal, and grease under the direction of
teachers. One member of the Sisters of Mercy, the second largest teaching order
in the city, modified her junior high school geography classes to track the
movements of American troops around the globe. Her students "adopted"
soldiers with whom they corresponded and sent "care packages." Such activities
gained poignancy as draft-age relatives of teachers and students alike went off to
war themselves, some never to return home. With two young brothers killed
overseas and students suffering similar losses of friends and relatives, one city
Catholic school teacher held solemnly observed classroom "services" with her
students regularly between 1942 and 1945. One member of the School Sisters
of Notre Dame (SSND), an order that staffed 26 Baltimore schools during the
war, noted that so many of her students possessed soldier-relatives that American
patriotism came readily. In addition to daily prayer for soldier relatives and
friends, her students conducted a letter-writing campaign called "adopt-a-soldier."
On a lighter note, Sister Emeline Evler's, SSND's five-year-olds were so committed to planting their own Victory Garden that "some of my kids, one day, hid"
beneath an underpass and took "turns pulling out the spring onions" that had
sprouted in a nearby canning factory garden. She overlooked the transgression
and planted the purloined items in a classroom garden. "A few weeks later sisters
would come in and say 'what smells so bad?' and we would laugh." In short, as
one teacher put it, in the city's Catholic schools' "patriotism was very high."[20]

American patriotism transformed the Catholic school curriculum itself,
as the materials produced by the Commission on American Citizenship amply
illustrate. By 1943 the Commission constructed a range of texts, pamphlets, and
periodicals promoting a uniquely Catholic-American inclusiveness, many of which
found their way into Baltimore schools during the war. *These Are Our People,* a
text of the "Faith and Freedom" series published by the commission in 1943 under
Baltimore Archbishop Curley's imprimatur and used in the city's Catholic schools,
offers an example of the inclusive direction the Catholic-American patriotism of

the war years could go. *These Are Our People* expressed an appreciation for the nation's commitment to political freedom, as the following lines from the poem "Ellis Island" indicate:

> The children come from many lands
> Beyond the wide, gray sea
> From old lands where they lived in fear
> And longed for liberty...
> O brave new land, be true to them,
> Give them your strength, your power,
> And keep alive the flame of faith
> Within their darkened hour.

The civic faith promoted in "Ellis Island" was a leaf in an American Catholic diptych, paired in the *These Are Our People* text with "Our God and Our Country," an explicit delineation of the religious foundation of the American nation:

> Long ago, God, our Father, created the rich gifts that make our country great...
> God, our Father, made a plan for us in our country. The people who fought to keep our country blessed followed God's plan. We too must know and follow God's holy plan....
> We must obey the laws of home, school, Church, and State.
> We must love all people because they are children of God. We, the children of America, must help to carry on God's plan for our great and blessed country. [21]

"Ellis Island" and "Our God and Country" bear the influence of a Catholicism reflecting the different ethnic and religious groups involved in *These Are Our People's* creation and the national wartime national emphasis on religious and cultural pluralism. Members of the commission included officers of the American Lithuanian Roman Catholic Federation, Ancient Order of Hibernians, Daughters of Isabella, Knights of Columbus, Polish Association of America, the Tuskegee Institute, and National Negro Congress. Commission materials were also sent to 100 Protestant clergymen and 25 prominent Rabbis for approval.[22] Taken together, "Ellis Island" and "Our God and Our Country" thus present a vision of national citizenship to which no triple-melting-pot American would object. Coupled with the explicit religious instruction inculcated through the catechism, every Catholic school student would make the God of "Our God and Country" the same God that made Ellis Island's promise possible. Commission members went out of their way to ensure that this deity was not objectionable to Protestants or Jews.

Another story from *These Are Our People*, "Eddie Patterson's Friends," constructs a radically inclusive American micro-society steeped in Christian moralism. The story revolves around the exemplary practices of a young white boy (Catholic, of course), Eddie Patterson, who "listened more often than he spoke; but gave everyone who spoke to him a wide smile. He never shouted with joy at anyone's coming, but he gave every child who came an honest gladness of welcome..." Eddie, the boys of the neighborhood agreed, was "a good scout." Moreover, "The smiling Yim Kee, whose father ran the Chinese laundry," liked to watch Eddie for hours, always "smiling," though strangely, Yim "said nothing" when in Eddie's company. "Frank Bell, the boy whose father had been taken away by the police" also admired Eddie. Rounding out Eddie's gang of outcast friends was "eager little Silas Jefferson, whose father worked as a porter on a train." Less controversial, but as deserving of Catholic tolerance as sons of criminals, Chinese, and African-Americans, were the great variety of European Americans and non-Catholics living in Eddie's multiethnic town:

> Boys and girls of the neighborhood came [to visit Eddie], Waylands and Kirchners, Laflins and Kellys, Bellaks and Ferraros and Bakers. Children came from the other side of St. Martin's parish. Children came from the public schools, and children who seemed to have no known school at all, children of many races and creeds.[23]

The nameless factory town in which the Patterson family lived epitomized socio-economic ideals espoused in *Rerum novarum* and *Quadragesimo anno*, and reflected the inclusion of labor leaders William I. Green, Sidney Hillman, and John L. Lewis, and even General Motors executive John J. Raskob, on the Commission for American Citizenship. Mr. Patterson, as the story explained,

> Worked in the car shops, the only big industry of the town. The car factory covered acres and acres of ground. In the long, low buildings men and women worked to make railway cars and what went into them. They made wheels and axles and rollers. They made car bodies. Then made seats and tables and chairs and beds for the cars. They covered seats with heavy cloth. They painted wood and steel.... Their work made travel comfortable for many people.[24]

All of these respectable factory laborers lived in the same town as the Patterson family. Eddie's sister Mary earned "plenty of money" in one of the offices at the car factory, which she duly contributed to the family economy. Eddie, his parents, and his seven brothers and sisters "lived in a house that did not look big but which somehow seemed to have room for them all." Eddie's older brother Daniel even joked that their house had "rubber walls."[25]

This apparently economically stable, racially and religiously inclusive community had its problems, of course. But the story's use of American-style social problems and issues strengthened the narrative rather than weakening the message, making it especially relevant to young readers. The plot of "Eddie Patterson's Friends" revolves around a scheme masterminded by the misguided and socially insecure Patterson sisters to exclude their brother's unpopular friends from a birthday party planned by Eddie's mother. Katie alleges that Eddie "finds the queerest people" and befriends them. "It hurts me when all the other girls in the block laugh at Eddie's crowd," cries Katie to sister Mary, "they'll laugh if we let Eddie ask anyone he wants to the party." "Let them laugh," the mature Mary responds in inclusive Catholic fashion. But Katie convinces her other sister Lucy that boys like Yim Kee, Frank Bell, and Silas Jefferson should not attend the party, and that guests should be limited to "the neighbors' children, some of the boys and girls in Eddie's room at school, and the younger brothers and sisters of our friends."[26] Apparently, none of the nearby children possessed the objectionable traits of Silas Jefferson, Yim Kee, or Frank Bell. An unexpected measles outbreak thwarts the scheme at the last minute, however, and Eddie's Catholic-American inclusiveness wins the day, with all outcasts ultimately in attendance. The final scene of "Eddie Patterson's Friends" expresses the Commission's ideal vision of Catholic citizenship succinctly. "Eddie," agreed everyone at the party, "is the best citizen of us all...

> At the moment the good citizen was staring, a little wildly, at the flowers and the candles, at the scraps of cake, at the melting ice cream, at the few candies left on the table. Around him shone happy faces, white and yellow and black.[27]

Through such stories, *These Are Our People* both acknowledged the legitimacy and reality of social, cultural, and racial differences and proposed ways of transcending them when they threatened to rupture into intolerance.

*These Are Our People* not only accomplishes its goal of offering youth of the United States a *Catholic* vision of citizenship, it offers an *American Catholic* vision reflective of the rising cultural and religious pluralist spirit of the war years. It makes an effort to appreciate the real religious, racial, and cultural diversity of 1930s and 40s Catholic America. The glossary of the book, for example, promotes tolerance in exposing young readers to a variety of non-Anglo names, translating those names into the English language: "Juan. The Spanish Name for John." "Jan. The Polish name for John." and "Lucia. The Italian name for Lucy."[28]

*These Are Our People's* vision of an egalitarian Catholic America presented Baltimore youth with a truly radical vision of society indeed. Despite their economic and ethnic inclusiveness, class disparities organized along ethnic and racial lines were prevalent in the Catholic schools of 1940s Baltimore. The Catholic secondary schools, in particular, both reflected and promoted these class/ethnic disparities.[29] The Irish resided at the top of the educational hierarchy, not far ahead of the Germans, mostly English-speaking in the 1940s Church. The list of 140 graduates of the 1941 class at the prestigious Notre Dame Institute in Baltimore is predominantly German and Irish in name. Only five Polish and five Italian names appeared on the graduation roster, with achievement medals going to Alice Mildred Kearney, Kathleen Engers, Mary Agnes Weller, Regina Zander, Grace Madden, Evelyn Jacobs, and Margaret Mary Doyle that year. Madeleine Schmaus received a full tuition scholarship to Mount Saint Agnes Junior College. No achievement awards or scholarships went to young women with Italian or Polish names. African-American women, moreover, from "no known school at all" from the white perspective, were permitted to attend only St. Frances Academy run by the oblate Sisters of Providence, the first community of African-American women religious founded in Baltimore in 1899. As Guinevere Spurlock notes, St. Frances was the only Catholic high school in Maryland open to African-American Catholics. None of the parish schools for African-American Catholics went beyond the eighth grade. Spurlock notes that the demand for Catholic education reached a high point in the 1940s, remaining high into the 1950s. The absence of secondary Catholic schools for African-American women, then, cannot be attributed to lack of interest.[30] At the white diocesan Seton High School, a much larger and more inclusive all-female school where nearly all of the city's parishes were represented by the graduates of 1941, this ethnic hierarchy nonetheless also prevailed. The graduates were overwhelmingly German and Irish in name. Junior high school prize winners at St. Martin's and St. Rose of Lima parish schools, both set in inner-city ethnic Baltimore, were also almost wholly Irish and German in name in 1941. African-American Catholics attended parish schools that generally educated male and female students to the eighth grade. African-American Catholic boys could secure Catholic education to the eighth grade, but not beyond, as white ethnics could, as no Catholic high schools for African-American boys existed in the city.[31] Such circumstances reflect what historian Paula Fass calls an "elongated pyramid" in the social structure of the Catholic high school system. "At the top were those who attended elite, and almost exclusively college-oriented, private schools. Below them were the students in diocesan and parish high schools" and "at the bottom, pushed out of the Catholic track entirely, were the majority of Catholic students who for one reason or another chose to attend public schools or could not get into or remain at the Catholic schools."[32]

This pattern of class and ethnic assimilation is in evidence in the testimony of the students who found themselves in the minority at the elite Catholic schools. Third-generation Italian-American Julia Poggi attended the Notre Dame Institute in the 1920s. Having some knowledge of dialect Italian, she enrolled in a standard Italian class at the school with two other girls, "myself, another Italian girl and one socialite [non-Italian American], whose pronunciation was horrible." The "socialite, she never mixed with the two 'peons.' We were not her class." Poggi criticized this class discrimination, but also absorbed it. She claims to have avoided cultivating friendships with Little Italy neighbors "we had one or two girls that we... we sort of selected our company... they were northerners" (of northern Italian descent and middle class, like Julia herself).[33] These class/ethnic conditions persisted through the 1930s, as Eleanor Apicella's testimony suggests. In the late 1930s Eleanor Apicella and about five or ten other girls from Little Italy "really didn't mix in too much with the other girls because we felt we weren't equal to them, [we thought,] they're better than we are." Apicella similarly absorbed the class prejudices of her Notre Dame Institute peers. Like Poggi, Apicella later behaved much like those who had once made her feel so ashamed, moving out of Little Italy and keeping her former residence in the Italian neighborhood secret for years.[34]

Ed Kane, who attended all-male Mt. St. Joseph's High School in the early 1940s, thought students from the institute were "goody-goody." They sang a song about institute girls: "We don't smoke and we don't chew, and we don't go out with boys that do; Our class won the bible!" The diocesan Seton High School students, however, were different, "less upper class." Nonetheless, Kane and his friends at Mount St. Joseph's had their own strict dress code distinguishing the fashionable from the square: "black and white saddle shoes, knit tie, gray flannel slacks." The shoes had to be "Hess', the slacks, from Hamburgers."[35]

Kane was a young user of the educational materials produced by the Commission on American Citizenship, which reminded students that all Catholics were equal. At his school the materials were required reading and he and his classmates were quizzed on its messages. While it is difficult to know the exact impact of the materials on the thinking of homefront Catholic youth like Kane, the fact that he read and enjoyed the stories of the commission's publications suggests that some of its messages must have sunk in. Kane was a fan of the Committee's *Young Catholic Messenger*, a magazine available to him and other students at Mt. St. Joseph's school library containing news of the war, Catholic adventure stories, as well as the appeals for tolerance in the series' textbooks. He found the stories in the magazine "interesting" and recalled as an adult reading stories about animals and the New York World's Fair in particular.[36] Such publications helped young Catholics understand their role as Americans in the war. One issue informed its adolescent readers that "To Catholics, patriotism is a solemn religious duty.... Remember that your duty to your country comes next to your duty to God. Pray and do penance for victory and a speedy and just peace."[37]

Through such publications young Catholics learned to associate religious faith with American nationalism, seeing in the United States an increasingly tolerant context in which religious ideals were permitted to flourish unimpeded. The commission materials clearly presented young readers with an idealistic vision of life in America, contradicted in many ways by the experiences of local Catholic youth in cities like Baltimore. At the same time, these educational materials helped young Catholics envision a *Catholic* version of America's demo-cratic ideals. Their articulation of a Catholic Americanism, moreover, fit com-fortably with a similar brand of local Baltimore expression. Over and over again, teachers' addresses and students' speeches celebrated a Baltimorean Catholic American patriotism during the war years. Student Joseph Clark spoke on "The Americanism of the Catholic School" at a 1941 Catholic school graduation ceremony. At St. Martin's Junior High School, pupils performed a play called "The First American Flag" that year. God and nation were increasingly conflated, with the godly Catholic school education touted as an antidote to secular society's rampant materialism. The Catholic schools, one Baltimore *Catholic Review* piece editorialized, performed a particularly crucial function in "our hour of national danger" because they "have never been poisoned by the materialistic theories, the malign influence of which has at length been revealed in its logical worldwide consequences." The religious and moral ideals promoted in the Catholic schools were specially suited to the "defense of America." Catholic parents knew that "in offering their children the advantages of Catholic education they are not only safeguarding their precious religious heritage but contributing as well to the perpetuation of fundamental Americanism."[38]

## BALTIMOREANS ALL

If American patriotism infused Catholic school life, religious tolerance became a hallmark of the homefront public schools. This rise in religious tolerance was limited primarily to a new Protestant tolerance of Catholics and Jews, but it marked a break from a past of deep local religious intolerance on the part of the Protestant majority toward members of such groups. Accordingly, Marie Chittick, a ninth-grade English teacher at Patterson Park High School in Baltimore, wondered in 1943 how educators throughout the city could "encourage tolerant attitudes for all the races, creeds, and varied nationalities that comprise the United States, and endeavor to eradicate deep-seated prejudices so destructive of national unity?" Chittick advocated distributing lists of distinguished individuals of different religious and ethnic backgrounds, as she did in her special *Americans All* unit that year.[39] Chittick's concerns with anti-religious prejudice were also evident on the state level. With a new focus on character building, doubtless a result of a belief that contemporary totalitarian leaders and their followers lacked character and morality, state administrators advocated that public schools cooperate with local churches in youth training programs, as such institutions were fine examples of "character-building agencies."[40]

Public school teachers throughout the city accordingly began experimenting with ways of promoting tolerance toward those of all creeds, arriving at some innovative solutions. One Baltimorean wrote a play called "This Freedom," presented in 1942 by the students of Hamilton Junior High School. "This Freedom" recounted the history of American freedom giving special attention to the role of ancient Hebrews attempting to escape bondage in Egypt, and medieval Catholics who revolted against greedy feudal lords in Europe. In this drama, Catholics and Jews were as instrumental in forging American democracy as the freedom-loving colonists who revolted against England in the eighteenth century.[41]

Music, like drama, played a part in encouraging religious tolerance in the public schools. Ernest G. Hesser, the Director of Music Education for the Baltimore Public Schools, compiled a "Musical Program in Wartime" and distributed it to city schools. Every music session should "begin with the singing of our National Anthem" directed Hesser, but, he added

> let us not forget the value of music in our churches. America is fighting
> to preserve spiritual values for us and our children. Even as the war
> is forcing us back to the true conception of the home, so likewise it
> is awakening us to a deeper appreciation of the church, the bulwark
> of spiritual values. We need, as never before, the 'faith of our fathers,
> known of old,' their patriotic fervor and willingness to sacrifice, and
> their assurance that right makes might.[42]

Hesser's wartime song list included "Faith of Our Fathers," "Brother James's Air," "The Lord's Prayer," a Slavic hymn, and the Hebrew "Song of Hope"..... a catalog that would please all triple-melting-pot Americans.[43]

Betsy Ross Public School #68 in Baltimore hosted two plays during the war years that illustrate the emphasis on religious tolerance and triple-melting-pot Americanism in its most local form. "Democracy and Her Helpers" offered a visual representation of Franklin Roosevelt's Four Freedoms: Freedom from Want, Freedom from Fear, Freedom of Religion (a slight modification of the original Freedom of Worship phrase), and Freedom of Speech. Following this depiction of the wartime pillars of democracy, the students focused more tightly on the religious aspect with their play, "Freedom of Religion." This play featured six children, and three religious denominations. A girl outfitted for a Catholic first communion represented Catholics, a boy dressed as a rabbi represented Jews, and a boy dressed as a Pilgrim represented Protestants.[44] Here, the Catholic and Jew are asserted as equals of the Protestant Pilgrim in the American religious experience.

Suggesting the power of religion in the wartime nation, the "Freedom of Religion" play actually sought to use religious tolerance to promote racial inclusion, including a boy in blackface in its cast for no obvious religious reason. The seemingly odd inclusion of a boy in blackface reflects a new faith in religious pluralism to promote color tolerance, the obvious racist implications of not actually including an African-American child (Betsy Ross School was segregated) in the drama aside. The Betsy Ross public school "Freedom of Religion" play, like the Catholic schools' *These Are Our People* sought to gather peoples excluded on non-religious grounds into the wartime nation. In Catholic and public schools alike, religious tolerance became a mighty strain of the American national idea. This morally-charged American nationalism imparted Baltimoreans with a mandate to include the excluded—a mandate almost powerful enough to destroy segregation in the city's school system, though not quite. Jim Crow's downfall would take another decade, but the religious tolerance of the war years formed a significant step in the right direction.

The publication of *Better Intercultural Relations* in 1947 by the Baltimore Department of Education marked the zenith of war-influenced expression of triple-melting-pot Americanism in the Baltimore public school system. This publication, the first of a projected series aimed at curing racial and religious prejudice, was a local version of the works funded by the Bureau for Intercultural Relations based in New York. On religion, the booklet asserted that by "helping pupils to understand religious customs, and ritual, and their basic significance," the materials would help students "substitute respect for others' religion in place of prejudice." Its publishers hoped that such lessons would be "interwoven with the whole fabric of the curriculum."[45]

Though many believed the United States "could never be strong because it represented so many diverse groups," the authors of *Better Intercultural Relations* told its readers, Americans "proved to the world that people of many backgrounds and faiths would unite for a common ideal." The booklet went on to describe where young Marylanders fit into this diverse America. The first Maryland settlers were "people of all faiths." They had been "about equally divided between those of Roman Catholic and Protestant beliefs. There was at least one person of Jewish faith" aboard.[46] Such attention to Protestants, Catholics and Jews was a product of the triple-melting-pot Americanism of the World War II years.

## CONCLUSION

In 1943 one Maryland public school administrator who had just finished enumerating ways of linking the schools with local churches to promote "character building" among students cautioned "it must be remembered that the schools are for the children of all people and that nothing bordering on sectarianism should be permitted."[47] This warning is filled with irony: the public schools had been dominated by a Protestant religious ethos for decades, much to the chagrin of Catholics and Jews alike. By the closing months of the war, however, Protestant domination of the culture of public education had started to disintegrate, as the wartime emphasis on religious tolerance caused educators and students alike to recognize that the schools had indeed been infusing public school education with Protestant belief for decades. Realizing that the United States was much more than a Protestant nation, yet one that publicly respected religious pluralism presented a number of thorny problems that remain unresolved today. It was one thing to allow a child to wear a Catholic communion dress in a school play depicting religious freedom, quite another for that student to expect a teacher to alter a lesson she might find objectionable based on her Catholic beliefs. Similarly, how far might a Catholic school teacher allow American patriotism to permeate the Catholic classroom? The case of Sister Emeline Evler's five-year-old pupils stealing vegetable sprouts from a local Victory Garden, as innocent as it seems, offers a clear example of the problem. Because Americans were in the midst of a worldwide war, one in which the democratic way of life seemed under siege by totalitarian ideologies, such transgressions seemed minor and insignificant and were therefore overlooked. Certainly the teacher would have seemed peevish if she had told the children to return the sprouts to the place they had found them because keeping them would have amounted to a violation the Catholic belief that stealing was wrong. Such was the case with religious faith and American democratic ideals during the war. While Americans fought an anti-democratic enemy, limited expression of religious beliefs in the public schools seemed to accentuate the virtue of the nation's democratic institutions. For Catholic Americans, religious and political beliefs had become so intertwined that keeping national patriotism out of the Catholic schools would have seemed un-Catholic. When the national imperative came to an end, however, the issue of how much religion to allow into the public schools and how much secularism to allow into the Catholic schools would become a more urgent one.

# ENDNOTES

[1] "United We Stand," *The Young Catholic Messenger*, January 9, 1942, Commission on American Citizenship Materials, Archives of The Catholic University of America Archives, Catholic University, Washington, D.C. (hereafter ACUA).

[2] "The American Dream," excerpt from address delivered by Everett Clinchy, *Education for Victory*, September 15, 1942 (Washington, D.C.: United States Office of Education), 5. Other articles on religious tolerance and education during the war in *Education for Victory* include: "Proclamation, American Education Week, November 8-14" November 2, 1942, 6; "Activities of School Children Related to the War Effort" and "Educational Policy Concerning Young Children and the War," April 15, 1942, 5-9.

[3] Ruby Jo Reeves Kennedy "Single or Triple Melting Pot? Intermarriage Trends in New Haven, 1870-1940," *American Journal of Sociology* (January 1944).

[4] Herberg asserted that the "newcomer is expected to change many things about him as he becomes American—nationality, language, culture. One thing he is not expected to change—and that is his religion." While Herberg's *Protestant-Catholic-Jew*, in fact, shows that the *character* of religious attachment *did* change across generations to adapt to American secularism, with religious groups indeed abandoning particular religious practices that did not fit into modern American mass culture, his assertion of the primacy of religious attachment as a facet of American identity in general is nonetheless useful for understanding Jews' and Catholics' emphasis on their religious identity during the war. Will Herberg, *Protestant-Catholic-Jew, An Essay in American Religious Sociology* (New York: Doubleday and Co.,1955), 35; Kennedy "Single or Triple Melting Pot?"; Philip Gleason offers an excellent critique of Herberg's book in his essay "Hansen, Herberg, and American Religion" in *Speaking of Diversity, Language and Ethnicity in Twentieth Century America* (Baltimore: Johns Hopkins University Press, 1992), 231-250.

[5] On the formation of Catholic institutions in Baltimore see Maria Mazzenga, "Inclusion, Exclusion, and the National Experience: European- and African-American Youth in World War Two Baltimore" (Ph.D. diss., The Catholic University of America, 1999), chapter 1.

[6] Earl R. Moses, "Indices of Inequalities in a Dual System of Education," *Journal of Negro Education* X:2 (April. 1941) 239-244; *Annual Report of the Board of School Commissioners of Baltimore City to the Mayor and City Council 1945*, 132, box 89, ms. 2010, War Records Collection, Maryland Historical Society, Baltimore, Maryland (hereafter, WRC-MHS).

[7] Polytechnic High School Yearbook, *Poly Cracker* (Baltimore: 1943).

[8] *Catholic Review* (Baltimore): Seton High School graduates, June 13, 1941; "St. Rose of Lima Has a Record Class", June 20, 1941, 3; "60 At St. Martin's Finish Grade School", June 20, 1941, 3.

[9] Earl R. Moses, "Indices of Inequalities in a Dual System of Education," *Journal of Negro Education* X:2 (April. 1941): 239-244.

[10] Eleanor Apicella interviewed by Doris Stern, October 31, 1979, tape, Baltimore Neighborhood Heritage Project Oral History # 203, Maryland Historical Society, Baltimore Maryland.

[11] Moses, "Indices of Inequalities in a Dual System of Education," 239-244; *Official Catholic Directory, 1944* (New York: P.J. Kennedy & Sons, 1944);

[12] "Baltimore City Catholic Parishes, 1944," chart compiled from Notitiae Summaries, 1944, Archdioceses of Baltimore and Washington, Archives of the Archdiocese of Baltimore, Baltimore, Maryland.

[13] Sister M. Annunciata, O.P. "The Commission on American Citizenship," *Catholic University Bulletin* Oct. 1965, 7, Commission on American Citizenship Materials, ACUA.

[14] Ibid.

[15] Ibid.

[16] Ibid.

[17] Stuart Svonkin, *Jews Against Prejudice; American Jews and the Fight for Civil Liberties* (New York: Columbia University Press, 1997), 64.

[18] Ibid, 64.

[19] On anti-Catholicism in Baltimore, see Maria Mazzenga, "Inclusion, Exclusion, and the National Experience," chapter 1.

[20] Sister Emeline Evler interviewed by Maria Mazzenga, January 31, 1995; "Sisters of Mercy and World War Two Survey", conducted by Maria Mazzenga and Sister Helen Sigrist, O.S.M, 1995; [Anonymous] SSND Sister interviewed by Maria Mazzenga, January 31,1995. Ed Kane interviewed by Maria Mazzenga, January 15, 1995.

[21] Sr. M. Thomas Aquinas, O.P. and Mary Synon, *These Are Our People* ("Faith and Freedom Series") (Washington, DC: The Catholic University Press, distributed by Ginn and Company, Boston, 1943), 11-13, 411-13, Commission on American Citizenship Materials, ACUA. The "Faith and Freedom" Series became extremely popular: from an output of 10,000 books in the first years of publication, Faith and Freedom sales increased to approximately 3,600,000 basal and supplementary books in the fiscal year 1963-64; Sister M. Annunciata, O.P. "The Commission on American Citizenship," *Catholic University Bulletin* Oct. 1965, 8, ACUA. That the readers were used in 1940s Baltimore, see "Sisters of Mercy and World War II Survey," conducted in 1995.

[22] *Commission on American Citizenship, First Annual Report*, July1, 1939 - June 30, 1940 (Washington, D.C.: The Catholic University of America Press, 1940), 13, 30, Commission on American Citizenship Materials, ACUA.

[23] "Eddie Pattersons Friends", *These Are Our People*, 46.

[24] Ibid., 46-47.

[25] Ibid.

[26] Ibid., 44-56.

[27] Ibid., 55.

[28] *These Are Our People*, 11-13, 411-13.

29  For more on these inequalities in Catholic educational institutions generally, see Paula S. Fass, *Outside In; Minorities and the Transformation of American Education* (New York: Oxford University Press, 1989), "Imitation and Autonomy: Catholic Education in the Twentieth Century", 189-228, 203.

30  "Notre Dame Institute Has 140 Graduates", *Catholic Review*, June 20, 1941, 3; Guinevere C. Spurlock, *A History of St. Frances Academy* (M.A. Thesis, Morgan State College, May, 1974), 33, Josephite Fathers Archives, Baltimore, Maryland (hereafter, JAB).

31  *Catholic Review*: "Seton High School graduates, June 13, 1941;" "St. Rose of Lima Has a Record Class", June 20, 1941, 3; "60 At St. Martin's Finish Grade School", June 20, 1941, 3.

32  Fass, "Imitation and Autonomy", 202-203.

33  Julia Poggi interviewed by Jean Scarpaci, October 12, 1979, transcript, 35-36, 38-39, Baltimore Neighborhood Heritage Project Oral History #162, University of Baltimore Archives, Baltimore, Maryland.

34  Apicella interview.

35  Kane interview.

36  Kane interview; *Young Catholic Messenger* January 9, 1942, January 23, 1942, passim. ACUA.

37  Ibid.

38  *Catholic Review*: "St. Martin's Has 38 Graduates", June 20, 1941; "Why Have Catholics Continued to Build Religious Schools?" August 29, 1941.

39  Marie Chittick, "The Open Gate," *Baltimore Bulletin of Education* XXI:1 (September-December 1943), 19-21, box 89, ms. 2010, WRC-MHS.

40  "Report of the Committee on Administrative Policies for Cooperation With Other Agencies," 3, State Dept. of Education of Maryland, ms. 2010, boxes 82-83, WRC-MHS.

41  "This Freedom," by Harold Manakee, performed by the students of Hamilton Junior High School, 1942, box 89, ms. 2010, WRC-MHS.

42  Ernest G. Hesser, "Baltimore Department of Education Musical Program in Wartime," 2, box 89, ms. 2010, WRC-MHS.

43  Hesser, "Musical Program in Wartime."

44  Ella Beall, "Teaching Democracy and War," *Baltimore Bulletin of Education* (Sept.-Dec., 1943), 22-25, box 89, ms 2010, WRC-MHS.

45  "Foreword," *Better Intercultural Relations* (Baltimore: Baltimore Public Schools, 1947), misc. 40-14, JAB.

46  *Better Intercultural Relations*, 19.

47  "Report of the Committee on Administrative Policies for Cooperation With Other Agencies," 3.

## CHAPTER 11

# BEYOND THE REFLECTION OF PATENT LEATHER SHOES: THE CATHOLIC ETHOS OF GRADES K-12 IN THE TWENTIETH CENTURY

### Angelyn Dries, OSF

I n the continuing dialogue on "What is 'Catholic' about Catholic education," a look at the worldview or ethos found in kindergarten through high school for much of the twentieth century might provide some insight.[1]  Occasionally one learns one's characteristics through someone else "outside" telling us who we are.  We enter the conversation through the eyes of a Black Baptist woman, Laverra Allen, who, in the late 1950s and 1960s attended St. Francis School, a Catholic parish grade and high school for Blacks, in Natchez, Mississippi.

> ...we [Baptists] went through twelve grades, and the kids didn't bother us. It wasn't anything you thought about or anything, you know. Now that I think about it, I could ask a whole lot more questions, you know, but you went through the ritual of sayin' the Rosaries and studyin' the catechism and learnin', you know, just as if you were [a Catholic], and the only transition I found about it, is that I can remember when I was in seventh grade wanting to be a Catholic. And Mama would say that "that's no reason to be a Catholic, sweetheart, you know, and I was already, I had been baptized a Baptist and stuff, and she say, "Change your faith, if it's somethin' that you really have to do," she say, "but not because of your friends." She say, "God is going to be the same regardless to what you are as far as denomination," and that word

"denomination" stuck with me so long, I have not forgotten it.…
[Mama said,] You're not going to serve Him any better bein' a Catholic
than you would a Baptist unless'n you feel that there is a difference,"
she say, "and there's no difference. The culture might be something
that you would have to adjust to…" You know, it was, like, whatever
we did, she was involved in, and, so, it was, like, "We don't eat meat
on Fridays, Mama," and, you know, the thing with us is that a pork
chop dinner with sweet potatoes and homemade biscuits was the meal,
and Mama would save it 'til Sunday.

[To this day,] I still am at Mass on Ash Wednesday. Lent Season, you
know, I'm fasting, you know, and I find it more not custom, because
it's somethin' that I learned and like and I want to do. I had a couple
of friends, past Lent, and, [they said,] "You wash your face? You got
ashes on your face, you know. What's that dirt?" and I say, "That's
because I went to Mass this mornin' and it's Ash Wednesday," and they
went, like, "Hmmm. Okay. …it just amazes me that people don't
know the custom, so, therefore, they look at you and wonder why,
knowin' that I'm a Baptist…so, one of my girlfriends said to me, she
say, "You still do the rituals, huh?" And I say, "Yeh," because they mean
somethin."[2]

Laverra Allen, as a Black Baptist, clearly felt the impact of a Catholic
education and "culture," as her mother called it. Allen's case enables us to see
that the worldview of Catholic education in mid-twentieth century was larger,
more complex and varied than the stereotypic images portrayed in the last four
decades in the media, even though there are people who resonate with some of
the scenes and situations in productions like, "The Bells of St. Mary's."[3] What
preceded Laverra Allen's mid-twentieth century experience? Were there significant changes in the Catholic ethos after she graduated? Was her experience
typical? Given the varieties and location of Catholic schools over the century—
convent schools, free schools, academies, parochial schools, technical high schools,
frontier, rural, and urban—it is difficult to identify every pattern in the Catholic
ethos.[4] But this chapter will describe and define those "Catholic" in spirit,
sentiment and assumptions that prevailed for teachers and students from kindergarten through high school by using the general concerns of the National Catholic
Educational Association and mission-education programs as barometers to measure a Catholic ethos. Among the various mission programs that entered the lives
of school-age children, I will focus on some representative examples, the Holy
Childhood Association and the Catholic Students Mission Crusade. First, how-

ever, I will say a word about the overall "feel" of Catholic education nationally before we examine how that worldview was reflected in classrooms.

From the start, parochial education and the National Catholic Educational Association consciously defined themselves in constant interaction with American and international social and economic forces: anti-Catholicism, immigration, secularism, socialism, the Great Depression, totalitarianism, atheistic communism, state certification, standardization, racial tensions, and unionization. Internally, perhaps the best way to describe the Catholic atmosphere in the years 1900 through the 1970s is to use a more current term, "holistic." As understood here, holistic describes an engagement of the imagination, mind, will, and senses in an interactive manner, both for individuals and the community. This value was central both to the philosophy of Catholic education and to its practice. By the time parochial schools were starting to be centralized in the 1930s, Dr. Edward Jordan, head of The Catholic University of America's Department of Education,[5] summarized a theoretical framework in his 1931 presentation at the National Catholic Educational Association conference. Catholic education, Jordan noted, "studies human life in all its aspects, physical, psychological, social, civic, vocational, cultural, moral, and religious. It sees man as a whole and seeing him thus finds no difficulty in establishing a hierarchy of values in the things that are of concern to man."[6] Against a philosophical background of neo-Thomism, Catholic education presumed universally valid values which were adaptable to circumstances of place and time. A positive conception of the individual viewed persons as redeemed, responsible for their actions, involved in the love and service of their neighbor, and destined for eternal life. Healthy living was encouraged because of the "substantial union of the soul and body."[7] An entire range of personal, social, devotional, liturgical, intellectual, and material elements comprised the "Catholic" atmosphere at least during the first seventy years of parochial kindergarten through high school education in the twentieth century.

The 1901 *Catholic School Journal*, which had mailed its first issue in 1897, in the decade following the 1884 Third Plenary Council of Baltimore, illustrates the early understanding of such a broad-based education. The magazine contained articles on cleanliness, health and good eating habits, plans and blueprints for a school building, hints for teaching phonics, spelling words for each grade, and information helpful to teaching history, geography, catechetics, and special education. In the same issue, educators found diagrams to weave paper Easter baskets, learned stage directions for flag drills, and were instructed in the study of the New Testament under the aegis of The Catholic University's Rector, Thomas J. Conaty. Teachers read about educational trends both in the United States and in Europe. Thirty years later, a National Catholic Educational Association member argued from the same holistic perspective in his exhortation to include the study of scripture in grade and high school. Religion, he claimed, was comprehensive and, he continued, all of life—thinking, doing, living—was seen in scripture.[8]

The holistic nature of Catholic education suggested in the *Catholic School Journal* was carried out in the classroom itself. Hundreds of practices could be noted over the next decades. School prayer was devotional: recitation of the *Angelus* at noon, prayers at the start and end of the day, May crowning and classroom Marian shrines;[9] and liturgical: daily or weekly Mass school days; trips to the church for Stations of the Cross on Fridays in Lent; daily or weekly Masses, either with the class or the entire school; First Friday Masses, with the communicants, in observance of the fasting regulations, needing to pack a breakfast to eat later in the classroom; "dressing up" to play different parts of the Mass; choir practice; training of Mass servers; commemoration of saints' days; school dismissal in honor of the pastor's nameday; and in rural areas, processions around the fields on the spring rogation days. The introduction of civics in the 1950s and "Americanizing" activities, standing beside their desks to recite the "Pledge of Allegiance," or in good weather having the whole school assemble around the flag pole to raise the American flag helped fit Catholics as citizens of the United States and appeared to "neutralize" the foreignness of the many immigrants who filled the parochial classrooms. The school environment provided a rich imaginative quality for children, ranging from "acting" the Mass, participation in tableaux from the life of Jesus or the saints, or "dressing up" like priests and sisters for vocation days. Children participated in several forms of imitative behavior to model a way of life and to associate the children with other heroic men and women, whether living or in the communion of the saints.

Some of these practices reflected the work of the Commission on American Citizenship launched by the NCEA in response to Pope Pius XI's 1929 Apostolic Letter on education[10] and as a way to implement the U.S. Catholic Bishops' program for social action. The commission's work resulted in a statement of Catholic education principles, curricula and textbooks, including the *Faith and Freedom* readers, which often conveyed a religious or moral message. Dioceses could tailor the work of the commission to their specific needs and situations. The framework for the principles was enunciated in the three-volume, *Guiding Growth in Christian Social Living*, published in 1944. The purpose of the curriculum, schematized by grade level, was to "re-emphasize the teachings of Christ in their application to the problems of contemporary American life."[11]

At mid-century, William E. McManus, Superintendent of Chicago's Catholic schools, the largest Catholic School system in the country, evaluated the role of Catholic elementary education over the preceding half century. The same overarching values suggested in the 1901 *Catholic School Journal,* in Jordan's philosophic foundations enunciated in 1931, and in the 1940s *Guiding Growth* curriculum, were placed before the educators who came to the 1958 NCEA convention as seven duties: the communication of God's revealed truth, participation in liturgical and sacramental life; encouragement of the practice of virtue through personal example; the development of Christian attitudes toward social issues; the promotion of vocations to religious life; the development of responsibility toward the parish; and advancement of the Church's missionary activity around the world.[12]   On the latter point, McManus went so far as to say that the Catholic school is "a missionary enterprise, an outgoing institution, an open-door activity and the essential mission is to go forth and teach as Christ has commanded His Church."[13]   Mississippian Laverra Allen, whose story we heard at the start of this chapter, certainly felt this impact, not so much from explicit preaching, as from a kind of osmosis of "sacramental" and "ritual" life, which permeated the entire Catholic grade-and high-school environment.

To what extent did mission programs exemplify and contribute toward a holistic approach in Catholic education?  As parish schools began to centralize, especially in the large cities, any program or curriculum chosen for adoption had a greater chance of standardizing the education of students.  While centralization was helpful to the promotion of mission awareness in parochial systems,  mission programs were also assisted by individuals who were connected personally or organizationally with missions, either in the United States or overseas.   For example,  the Sisters of Charity, Mount St. Vincent on Hudson, New York, missionaries to the Bahamas in the late 1890s, found they were working with "the Colored People" more than they were with the colonials.  The sisters' publication to support the mission work, *Children of Providence*, featured articles on prominent contemporary and historical Black Catholics, as well as essays which portrayed the intellectual and spiritual leadership of women through the ages.   In the 1890s, two of the alumnae of the sisters' school in New York accompanied the sisters to the Bahamas to open the mission and one woman remained to teach with the sisters for several years.  *Children of Providence* was a bridge connecting the sisters, the young ladies of the mission, and the New York students.

## MISSION PROGRAMS, 1900-1970

The missionary consciousness in very young Catholics had been whetted at least as early as the beginning of the twentieth century through diocesan participation in the Pontifical Association of the Holy Childhood.  The idea behind the association was to invite children to pray for the evangelization of children around the world and to contribute a penny or two a month toward that purpose.[14]  The money was used to establish orphanages and asylums for abandoned babies, many of whom were girls.  Subscriptions to *Annals of the Holy Childhood* provided monthly mission stories for teachers to tell their students.[15]  After the 1920s, the newsletter added pictures and a more "modern" format.  Children were to say a "Hail Mary" daily and recite the prayer, "Holy Virgin Mary, pray for us and the poor pagan children."  Members received a medal and a membership card.  Parents were urged to enroll their babies as an act of thanksgiving for baptism.  Money was raised through the pennies children gave and through the sale of rosary booklets, almanacs, calendars, Easter and Christmas cards, donated jewelry, cancelled stamps, and tinfoil.  By 1922, about one third of school-aged children belonged to the Association.  Enrollment in 1940 reached one million and by 1960 the *Catholic Almanac* noted two million members in the Association.

Between 1892 and 1922 almost $1,500,000 had been raised by children and diocesan directors.  Not content to let cold figures be the last word, the national director painted a picture of the impact of the children's pennies:

> What [do these figures] mean?  Well, get a large sheet of white paper; draw on it an outline of Asia, Africa, South America and Oceania.  Mark on this map with a cross the two hundred and eighty-eight missions (not including our Indians) that were helped last year by the Holy Childhood.  Crimson these crosses with a drop of red ink, and to your surprise you will find that your alms and prayers have helped to spread the merits of the Precious Blood over practically the whole pagan world, thereby bringing it nearer and making it dearer to the Creator who loves all creatures with a father's heart.[16]

After the children gathered five dollars, they were allowed to choose a name for a child "ransomed" in another country.  Children participated, albeit vicariously, in the baptism and in the alleviation of other children's economic needs brought on by social and political inequities.  The philosophy of the association was further expressed through special parish processions and liturgies in awareness of children around the world.

In 1988, the original aims of the association were reiterated in their newsletter in language which had dropped the use of the term, "pagan babies," but which still emphasized children's role in the evangelization process: an acknowledgement of the sacredness of childhood, children's growth in faith through helping others, children as apostles for other children, and an emphasis that children view themselves as part of a church universal.[17]

Junior and senior high school students had further opportunities for mission awareness and knowledge through membership in the Catholic Students Mission Crusade (CSMC), an organization which penetrated Catholic schools more deeply than the Holy Childhood Association. Two Society of the Divine Word seminarians, Clifford King and Robert B. Clark, were cognizant of the immensely popular Student Volunteer Movement, which recruited college-age Protestant students for missions overseas. Convinced that the zeal of Catholic Americans could be roused as it had been for Protestants, the two seminarians, with the advice of Bruno Hagspiel, SVD, inaugurated a similar organization for college and seminary students, the Catholic Students Mission Crusade (CSMC). Within two years, the membership was opened to grade and high schoolers. The crusade's purpose was, first, to organize all Catholic students in the country as a "band of home apostles," who throughout their lives, would study mission issues and promote mission among "all classes of Catholics." Secondly the organization intended to create a "band of field apostles" to go forth as missionaries, either as laity, clergy, or religious.[18] From a membership of 10,000 grade, high school, college and seminary students in 1920, the organization grew to 800,000 members in 1941 and was listed in 1960 as having one million constituents in 3,100 educational institutes across the country.

A national board organized the biannual conferences and the staff at the CSMC office at the "Crusade Castle" in Cincinnati, Ohio, dispatched the day-to-day work of the organization. Among the notable early national youth leaders of the Crusade were Maryknoller John Considine, who later founded the Fides News Service at the Propaganda Fide Office in Rome and became the prominent Director of the Latin American Bureau in Washington, DC in the 1960s. Frank A. Thill, the first national CSMC leader, became Bishop of Concordia, Kansas in 1938 and continued his interest in mission throughout his life. For fifty years, J. Paul Spaeth was the Director of Unit Activities, and, along with his wife, Louise, continued writing and working in mission-related areas.

*The Shield,* the CSMC's quarterly publication (1921-1971), kept local units informed of activities, issues, and materials to be used for mission education and formation. The program of the Mission Crusade included education on mission topics, training for sacrifice, prayer, and personal service, promotion of mission vocations, and the advancement of the missions through various electronic and print media.

Publications from the Mission Crusade included mission statistics, dramas, debate topics, discussion club courses, information about the geography, history, and culture of mission lands, printed posters of mission subjects, illustrated mission lectures, and suggested writing assignments which employed mission themes in English, geography, history, and religion classes. Classrooms, where most of the local unit work took place, also contained mission maps, prayer cards, certificates, and biographies of mission "heroes" and "heroines." Local CSMC study clubs used several significant books compiled by CSMC units or by the national office. In 1948 Josephite Father John T. Gillard wrote, *The Negro Americans: A Mission Investigation.* In the 1950s *Fundamentals of Missiology* and *Perspectives in Religion and Culture* introduced high school and college students to the basics of mission theory and practice and provided a look at anthropological foundations for mission. Study-club books in the 1960s focused on economic, cultural, political and religious developments in Asia and Africa.[19]

The holistic nature of mission was sometimes directed through other agencies, as well, many of them having been influenced by persons who had belonged to CSMC in their youth. In 1943, John Considine jotted in his diary that he had met in Cincinnati with the NCEA Mission Education Committee. In his notation for the day of the meeting, Considine wrote,

> We took the doctrinal teachings on missions, then figured the attitudes and habits we wished to establish; finally, the instrumentalities, which was practically an acceptance of the program I proposed. Teacher's Manual and school mission text and mission supplement for religion class, with units for social studies class named for "immediate consideration." The series of geography books was fixed as the idea for attainment through awakening attention among Catholic publishers.[20]

Considine's work and that of the CSMC were part of what became the mission component of the pervasive curriculum established by NCEA in its 1944 *Guiding Growth in Christian Social Living.*[21] In addition to the knowledge gained about missions, a mission program, as noted in this curriculum, "provides its members with opportunities for creative self-expression, broadens their social consciousness, offers instructive as well as pleasurable activity, and acquaints them with ordinary parliamentary procedure and democratic practice."[22]

Student leaders and moderators, usually numbering around 3000, attended the CSMC biannual conferences. Missionaries gave talks about their experience with other religions and cultures, participants met students from other countries, and Crusade pageantry and processions captured the imagination of the participants. In the 1948 mission congress held at the University of Notre Dame, for example, more than 50 exhibits portrayed mission life on all the continents. The crusaders viewed articles, utensils, statues and objects from people around the world. Life-size African huts and other regional reproductions introduced students to world religions and social cultures where missionaries served. Participants interacted with exiled Chinese Thomas Cardinal Tien, CSMC co-founder Clifford King, who had escaped from the Japanese in China and in the Philippines, and leaders of mission congregations and national mission agencies.

## MISSION EDUCATION AND ITS DEMONSTRATION OF A CATHOLIC ETHOS

The CSMC focused the considerable energies of youth and affected the curriculum, club activities, and vocational choices.[23] Students from kindergarten through high school learned that mission was at the heart of what it meant to be Catholic. Student connections to particular missionaries or mission areas of the world concretized mission theology. Readings, study clubs and attendance at biannual meetings promoted an ongoing relationship between leading missiologists, missionaries and students. Through various mission activities Catholic youth developed sensitivities toward global realities and the social dimensions of Catholicism, participated at least minimally in evangelization, and practiced the values of sacrifice, empathy, and generosity. As was true for several other organizations of the period, the dominant theological underpinning and image for the "mission apostolate" was the Mystical Body of Christ. Familiarity with the motif and leadership skills of CSMC often ushered some members into local branches of the Young Christian Students or, later as adults, into the Christian Family Movement.

Mission programs above all stimulated the imagination and affectivity of the grade and high school students. Great "martyr" models called for imitative behavior, at least in the desire to "give one's all" in the service of God and neighbor. The mind was fed with knowledge of specific mission situations and, at least, a glancing awareness of the large and sometimes frightening world of communism and other "isms" beyond the classroom. At the heart of the mission program were the values of the goodness of the human person redeemed by Jesus Christ, membership in a community of faith, and responsibility for society. The socialization process included not only one's classmates but the global community, as well.

## MISSION PROGRAM SHIFTS
## IN RELATION TO CULTURAL AND SOCIAL CHANGES

The Catholic Students Mission Crusade, which had figured so predominantly in grade and high schools, came to what appeared an abrupt end in 1970. After fifty years as a national organization, five hundred delegates at the convention voted to turn over mission work to local agencies. In 1971 the *Catholic Almanac* no longer listed the organization. The demise of the national office corresponded with a number of significant shifts in the American Catholic experience, which, in turn, impacted the Catholic-school culture. The shift reflects transformations in mission theology and practice but more broadly indicates other critical ecclesial, social, cultural and economic changes in American life.

First, a look at changes in mission understandings. Running parallel with mission programs, the "crusade" element of CSMC was steeped in symbolism which was expressed in elaborate ceremonies, ranking orders of paladin, and other accouterments of medieval pageantry.[24] Cultural imitations of medieval practices linked Catholics' allegiance to the papacy and to America. Apologetic themes were loosely related to the crusades to evoke a spirit of sacrifice and rested on the scholastic use of reason "to convert from error to truth."[25] Young Catholics could take the offensive when Catholics were attacked around the world, especially in countries affected by Communism. By 1970, the crusading mentality lost its force in the wake of the momentous changes expressed at Vatican II, in the Church's relationship to the world, and in the decrees on missionary activity and the Church's relationship to other world religions.

Mission theology enunciated in the Vatican II missionary document, *Ad gentes divinitus* (7 December 1965), "that the Church by its very nature is missionary,"[26] a position also taken by the CSMC. However, for much of pre-Vatican II mission theology, the understanding of the universal call to mission rested more on geography—certain countries were "pagan" and others were not—than on an identification of mission with baptism. Both theologies, though, presupposed that Catholics shared a common humanity with all persons around the world. After 1969, fewer women and men entered mission communities and some missionaries, caught in the turmoil of intense political and social upheaval in their mission locations and sometimes in their religious congregations, left their congregations. By the mid-1970s, many mission magazines were published in a reduced format or ceased publication. Notable among these was *Worldmission*, published by the national office of The Society for the Propagation of the Faith. Schools no longer had the comprehensiveness of the CSMC programs for their curricula, libraries, and activities. The focus of Catholic education had turned elsewhere.

## 1950S AND 1960S: FROM STABILITY TO MOBILITY

Other factors which affected the Catholic ethos in schools just after mid-century were social, economic and cultural. The growth of the population after World War II expanded the numbers of students in the Catholic schools. More teachers were needed for classrooms which bulged with fifty and sixty students in one room. While religious orders had been the mainstay of the faculty, new members were often sent to teach a few months after they entered religious life, with little training as educators.

Catholics had moved up the economic ladder and were able to move to new homes outside of the urban areas where they had grown up. Starting in the 1950s, suburbanization led to the formation of new communities of people who did not share the same neighborhood or ethnic background and who were starting over as "intentional" communities in new parishes. The Catholic grade and high school were no longer the formative social community in the parish they had been. Public dissent and national media concentration on the issues of racial protest and the dissent on the war in Vietnam in the 1960s and 1970s reflected a climate of experimentation. The Catholic subculture was affected by anti-authoritarian streaks and social movements, such as that of a Saul Alinsky-style of community organizing, that asked local church membership to forge bonds among oppressed groups to effect systemic change. Teenagers were emerging as a "mass" with their own culture, as was evidenced in the popularity of music stars like Elvis Presley and the Beatles.

## 1970s: From Security to Questions

The answer to the 1970s question, "Should Catholic schools continue?" was by no means certain. Studies in the late 1960s through the 1980s by James Coleman and Andrew Greeley focused on the value of Catholic grade and high school education which were controversial. Other sociologists indicated that Catholic schools were thought to be elitist and a haven for those, both Catholic and Protestant, fleeing desegregation of public schools and that Catholic children were expressing prejudicial racial attitudes and demonstrated a minimal social consciousness.[27] Catholics questioned the role of the parochial school system in reducing racial tensions in the school and society. By 1967, over 450 Catholic schools had closed, many of them in the heart of urban areas. In an effort to deal with declining enrollments in central city schools, a few cities, such as Cleveland and Milwaukee, developed "urban community schools." Other cities attempted to work regionally to improve educational programs. Reform was called for in teacher preparation and in ways to teach students to think critically and scientifically. Within the post-Vatican II parishes of the late 1960s and 1970s, congregations were experimenting with liturgical renewal, with the formation of parish councils, and with education boards, thus focusing their energies upon their internal and structural life. With a new emphasis on an adult-centered parish and adult education, parochial schools received less revenue and suffered from lower enrollments from the parish and fewer children attending parochial schools.

## The Catholic Ethos in the 1970s and 1980s

One may observe the effect of these cultural and ecclesial changes in both the theory and practice. Fundamentally, the formal scholastic philosophy which had supported most types of K-12 Catholic education between 1920 and 1970 became inverted. Rather than thinking in terms of first principles applicable to particular situations, experience and diversity were emphasized without regard necessarily for general principles. High-school curricula developed courses on "Search for Self." Even a proposed multi-ethnic curriculum in 1973 suggested self awareness and self growth as a goal in its curriculum.[28] The Catholic schools seem to have been appropriating the traditional Protestant values of individualism and freedom. Much of the 1970s was spent with experimentation in the mechanics of classroom structure: the "open" classroom, large and small group instruction, team teaching, "modular scheduling." In still another direction, "values clarification" became an important methodological presupposition for teachers.[29] The holistic nature of Catholic education expressed through much of the twentieth century up to 1970 was not as clearly and obviously present because the particulars of its formation as "over and against" the values of Protestant America, seemed no longer to be necessary factors in American Catholic life. The nineteenth-century ethos of parochial education as the bulwark of Catholic identity in a Protestant culture no longer held true. Catholics had risen socially, politically, and economically and now saw themselves as part of American life. The small experiments in mission fund raising they made as children seem to have launched them successfully as adults into the market economy.

By 1970 a search began for a new philosophy of Catholic Education and experts looked to the documents of Vatican II and to the American Bishops' 1973 document, "To Teach as Jesus Did," sources which emphasized a lifespan vision of faith community formation. Philosophically, the education watchwords of the 1970s were "message, community, and service," and in 1980, one author had modified this to "community, service, and doctrine."[30] Efforts were made to create a school community characterized by "freedom and love." In 1985, Catholic educators were to be "integrators of life and culture," and leaders in a "community of learners and believers."[31]

Children now were more likely to have a lay person in roles of teacher and principal. The number of sisters and brothers who taught in grade and high schools began to dwindle, not only because of departures from religious life, but because more and more sisters were moving from children's education to parish ministry, adult formation and social work. Sisters themselves had drawn attention to the need for better preparation for all their ministries. Sister Bertrande Meyers' 1941 dissertation on the education of sisters and a 1947 paper delivered on the topic by Sister Madaeleva Wolf, C.S.C., at a meeting of the NCEA subcommittee led to the significant Sister Formation Conferences (1954-1972), whose intent was to develop an integrated, holistic and professional approach to sisters' education and religious development.[32]

The liturgical side of Catholic education turned from devotional practices and emphasized children and teens planning a "special" liturgy or paraliturgy/bible service. On Good Friday, high schoolers, along with adults in the parish, took part in a "Way of the Cross," through areas of the city affected by poverty and crime. Children went to Mass with their classmates less regularly. The "prayer corner" in the classroom more typically contained a bible, rather than a statue. Sacramental preparation involved children's parents. New theological vocabulary, such as "evangelization," seemed alien to many teachers, but in reality the faculty at Laverra Allen's Mississippi school were "evangelizing" for decades before the word entered the professional religious-education texts.

## RESURGENCE OF MISSION EMPHASIS

In 1984 "Mission" was the topic of the NCEA annual conference and six years later, the theme was, "Global Education: Transforming our World." The diversity and pluralism of American society were reflected in the composition of Catholic schools. No longer were port cities like New York and Los Angeles the only cities with multiple ethnic groups in need of education. Hispanic, Vietnamese, Hmong, and recent immigrants from Central and South America were more frequently found in Catholic grade and high schools all around the country. Diversity and pluralism became key issues upon which to frame an effective education.[33]

While the 1986 bishops' pastoral letter on mission, "To the Ends of the Earth," did not become the touchstone for examining the foundation of Catholic education, as did the Vatican II documents and "To Teach as Jesus Did" in the 1970s, it might be suggested that a more integrated mission program can be one of the factors in a Catholic education that would involve the imagination, the emotions, the senses, the mind, and the will. One encouraging example of this is the Columban Fathers' program for grade and high school, "Come and See!" The program is co-curricular and has been correlated with the *Catechism of the Catholic Church*. The high school program, *"Barrios,"* is available in Spanish and in English.[34]

Today, children in grade and high school save their dimes and quarters in "'rice bowls," again looking outward in service and concern toward others. Many grade and high schoolers serve meals in programs for the cities' poorest persons. Students participate in Habitat for Humanity and some venture into unfamiliar geographic areas to aid people in need. To prepare for the sacrament of Confirmation, young Catholics engage in programs of service and experience the opportunity to reflect on the significance of social justice issues involved. High school students write letters to their Congressional representatives to draw attention to injustices. With new American martyrs, especially in Central and Latin America from the 1960s on, new missionary biographies today urge Catholic boys and girls, as well as the Protestant classmates, to think beyond their own needs and wants. Returned missionaries still visit classrooms to share their experience of life in other social and religious cultures. Community formation of students occurs through stable "home-room" groupings over the four years of high school education, through conflict resolution training, and through participation in *"cursillo"* type weekends, such as "Teens Encounter Christ."

Catholic education today is more internally self-conscious about its "Catholic" identity. In some circles, an identification of "Catholic" solely with doctrine and a certain type of authority does a disservice to the general trend of the Catholic heritage of parochial schools and their ethos in the twentieth century. The holistic nature of Catholic education needs to be retained and mission theology needs once more to pervade Catholic education. We are at an important juncture for Catholic educators to advance the formation of the whole person, the mind, the heart, the will, the senses, the imagination.[35] Then, like Laverra Allen, our Black Baptist Mississippian, when asked why they do something, students can respond, "Because it means something."

ENDNOTES

1   See, for example, the discussion of Catholic identity for schools in the 1980s in Michael Pennock, "The Heart of Catholic Schools," *Momentum* 11 (May 1980):24-27; Edwin J. McDermott, *Distinctive Qualities of the Catholic School* (Washington, DC: National Catholic Educational Association, 1985); and the entire issue of *Chicago Studies* 28.3(November 1989).

2   Typescript of Laverra Allen interview conducted by Timothy Murphy, 1994, pp. 4-5. Natchez Project. Glenmary Research Center, Nashville, Tennessee.

3   See Mary Ann Janosik, "Black Patent Leather Shoes Really Do Reflect us: Community, Catholic Education and Traditional Values in Two Generations of Hollywood Film," *U.S. Catholic Historian* 13.4 (Fall 1995):97-116.

4   On the varieties of Catholic education from its inception in this country, see, Timothy Walch, *The Diverse Origins of American Catholic Education: Chicago, Milwaukee, the Nation* (New York: Garland, 1988), and Timothy Walch, *Parish School: American Catholic Parochial Education from Colonial Times to the Present* (New York: Crossroad, 1996). For the spectrum of these types and locations of schools in nineteenth century Detroit area, see JoEllen McNergney Vinyard, *For Faith and*

*Fortune: the Education of Catholic Immigrants in Detroit, 1805-1925* (Champagne: University of Illinois Press, 1998). On the history of parochial education, see Timothy Walch, *Parish School: American Parochial Education from Colonial Times to the Present* (New York: Crossroad Publishing Company, 1996). For an overview of the national debate on parochial education in the nineteenth century, see Philip Gleason, *Keeping the Faith. American Catholicism Past and Present* (Notre Dame, IN: University of Notre Dame Press, 1987).

5  On the centralization of schools, see Timothy Walch, "Big City Schools," *U. S. Catholic Historian* 13.4(Fall 1995):1-18.

6  Edward B. Jordan, "The Philosophy of Catholic Education," *The National Catholic Education Association Bulletin* XXVIII.1(November 1931):53-56, here 61.

7  IBID, 62.

8  John M. Wolfe, "The Place of the Sacred Scriptures in the Process of Catholic Education," *The National Catholic Education Association Bulletin* XXVIII.1(November 1931):478-488. Another example of holistic education can be seen in Sisters M. Fidelis and M. Charitas, SSND's "A Character Calendar," which was featured for over a year in the *Catholic School Journal* in the early 1930s. Each month the sisters presented several saints of that month with a brief statement about the saint's life, a quotation from the Mass of the day, a suggestion from *The Imitation of Christ*, a statement of an ideal, a practical suggestion for the day, and a slogan. See, for example, *CSJ* 30(November 1930):425.

9  On the role of devotions for school children, see A. A. Lings, "Devotions in the Parish School," *Catholic School Journal* 35(April 1935):72-73.

10  The 1929 papal letter directed that the "Christian spirit" permeate every aspect of Catholic education.

11  Sister Mary Joan, OP and Sister Mary Nona, OP, *Guiding Growth in Christian Social Living* (Washington, DC: The Catholic University of America Press, 1944-46), 3 volumes, here vol. 2, v.

12  William E. McManus, "An Evaluation of Catholic Elementary Education in the USA," *The National Catholic Education Association Bulletin* LV.1(August 1958):224-235, here 227. In 1953, Catholic University historian, Henry J. Browne's analysis of the first half of the twentieth century's Catholic schools included: preserve schools from Protestant attacks; better standards of teaching developed because of state teacher requirements; sisters were asked to do too many tasks, including that of janitorial services; centralization of the school system under a diocesan head, rather than a pastor; dissatisfaction with the catechism and teaching of religion until the late 1930s; the development of the *Guiding Growth in Christian Social Living* curriculum. Henry J. Browne, "The American Parish School in the Last Half Century, " *NCEA Bulletin* 50.1(August 1953):323-334.

13  Ibid, 226.

14  William F. Stadelman, CSSP, *The Association of the Holy Childhood. History of the American Branch* (Pittsburgh, PA: The Colonial Press, [1922]). After its initial foundation in France in 1843 with a branch in New Orleans and Baltimore by 1846, the Holy Childhood Association was reactivated in 1897 by Spiritan Father John B. Williams. He introduced the organization across the United States through extensive travel and had much success, especially in German-speaking parishes.

15  Between the late 1920s and the 1950s, a few national mission magazines produced

"junior" versions for grade and high school students. The publication from the national Holy Childhood Association in the 1980s and early 1990s was "It's Our World," published three times a year.

16   Ibid, 20.

17   "Pontifical Mission Aid Societies Newsletter," Number 2(January 1988), 3. Claremont, California.

18   For a short history of the Catholic Students Mission Crusade, see Angelyn Dries, OSF, *The Missionary Movement in American Catholic History* (Maryknoll, NY: Orbis Books, 1998): 86-92.

19   The overarching ability of mission education to penetrate grade and high school curriculum and the mindset for young Catholics can be seen in the outline presented in a 1941 issue of *Catholic Action*, the monthly National Catholic Welfare Conference publication: Sr. Rosaria, PBVM, "A Student Plan for Catholic Action" (Document 58), in Joseph P. Chinnici and Angelyn Dries, *Prayer and Practice in the American Catholic Community* (New York: Orbis Books, 2000), 166-170.

20   Considine Diaries: 5(3)I:1942-1944 United States, p. 41. Maryknoll Mission Archives, Maryknoll, New York.

21   Sister Mary Charlotte, RSM, "The Mission Program," in Sister Mary Joan [Smith , OP and Sister Mary Nona, OP, *Guided Growth in Christian Social Living*, vol.2, 369-374. The same article appeared in the other two volumes. Sister Charlotte was one of the writers of the *Faith and Freedom* readers.

22   Sister Mary Charlotte, "The Mission Program," in Sister Mary Joan and Sister Mary Nona, OP, *Guiding Growth in Christian Social Living*, v. 2, 369.

23   Jeanne Marie Lyons, *Means of Fostering the Missionary Vocation in the Catholic Primary and Secondary Schools* (Washington, DC: The Catholic University of America Press, 1941).

24   On the use of medieval motifs in the United States, see, Philip Gleason, 11-34.

25   IBID, 27.

26   "*Ad gentus divinitus*," ("Decree on the Church's Missionary Activity," 7 December 1965) #2, in Austin Flannery, OP, ed., *Vatican Council II, The Conciliar and Post Conciliar Documents* (Northport, NY: Costello Publishing Company, 1992), vol. 1, 814.

27   In addition to the large sociological studies on Catholic education, see James C. Donohue, "Catholic Education in Contemporary American Society," *National Catholic Educational Association Bulletin* 64.1 (August 1967):13-17 on the point of racism and prejudicial attitudes.

28   Genevieve Schillo and Mary Sarah Fasenmyer, *Many Peoples—Shared Dreams: A Curriculum Guide for Multi-ethnic Studies* (Washington, DC: Chief Administrators of Catholic Education, National Catholic Educational Association, 1973).

29   The trend in the direction of values clarification and the use of the word "value" can be seen in Carleen Reck, SSND, *Toward a Catholic Value-Oriented Curriculum* (Washington, DC: National Catholic Educational Association, 1980). The NCEA had noted in 1973 that clarification of a value system was an "essential component in the maturation of young people." Schillo and Fasenmyer, 1.

30   Michael Pennock, "The Heart of Catholic Schools," *Momentum* 11(May 1980):24-27. For an overview of the post Vatican II foundations for Catholic education, see Louise Mayock and Allan Glatthorn, "NCEA and the Development of the Post-

31   conciliar Catholic School," *Momentum* 11(December 1980):7-9, 46-47.

32   Edwin J. McDermott, 21ff.

33   Marjorie Noteman Beane, *From Framework to Freedom: A History of the Sister Formation Conference* (Lanham, MD: University Press of America, 1993). While "integrity," a key word based on the unifying principles in scholastic philosophy, was the starting presupposition in the Sister Formation Movement, the leaders eventually abandoned the premise.

34   While ethnic diversity existed prior to the 1960s in the Catholic school system, and the topic was not brought up formally for consideration by the NCEA in their national conference in 1950.

35   In the 1999 academic year alone, 6,967 teachers in 547 Catholic schools grades K-8 used the program with 128,680 students. 207 high schools have used, "As Water in the Desert," a video program which correlates baptism with mission. Additionally, 174 parishes used the mission materials with 21,817 persons, in addition to the schools which have purchased materials in other years and who continue to use them. 64 schools have used the program for anywhere from ten to eighteen years. The Maryknoll Society also provides mission and justice and peace video materials and posters for grade and high school, though the packets are less developed for teachers than are the Columban materials.

  Andrew Greeley uses the findings of social science to explain the holistic nature of Catholicism in general and especially highlights the role of imagination. His analysis cites several studies of Catholic education. See Andrew Greeley, *The Catholic Imagination* (Berkeley, CA: University of California Press, 2000).

# PART IV
# RACE AND ETHNICITY

## CHAPTER 12

# ETHNICITY AND PARISH SCHOOLS: AFRICAN AMERICANS

~~~~~~

## *Cecilia A. Moore*

" Sanctity" was a hit in Harlem, rivaling the coolest jazz performances and attracting record-breaking crowds. The actresses and actors were local talent, not unusual for a community that was home to Langston Hughes, Zora Neale Hurston, and Richard Wright. What was special about these thespians was that they attended Resurrection School, one of several Catholic parochial schools in Harlem. "Sanctity" rendered the life of St. Elizabeth of Hungary and was written in the genre of the medieval miracle play, complete with a musical score, by Violet Clifton. To stage the play, Resurrection students and their teachers, Sisters of St. Francis of Baltimore, drew upon the artistic, musical and intellectual resources of Harlem as well as greater Manhattan. They used the Department of Medieval Art and Architecture at the New York Public Library as their workshop. Here they found inspiration for costume and scenery designs from French and German sources and learned the intricacies of theatre movement. Resurrection boys and girls transformed simple cambric fabric and gold paint into medieval brocade costumes with their mothers' help. Resurrection mothers went "to school at night to cut, and fit, and sew in order that children, not theirs alone, mind you, but the children of the parish, might know beauty for a few brief hours." [1]   Other members of the community helped build the student-designed set that included plans for "a Gothic window, cathedral door, and medieval tapestry" and a cyclorama. In constructing the cyclorama, they used the directions of a professional draper from a local Jewish theatre company, who was reportedly "most generous with his time and advice." [2]

Since Resurrection-School students studied church music, particularly Gregorian chant, they were prepared to learn the music for "Sanctity," which included a thirteenth-century Crusader's song. To master this song they welcomed the expertise of the faculty of the Federal Music School in Harlem, which was part of Works Progress Administration of the New Deal. The faculty arranged the orchestration for the play as "only a master hand could have done what these Negro musicians did for the play. Thoroughly trained in the best music schools of the country, Columbia, Chicago, Juilliard, these men gave generously of their time and talents in order that a group might interpret the life of a medieval saint."[3]  And the Negro Theatre in Harlem donated the services of its "production man" to help the students interpret "the story of a thirteenth-century woman whose one burning desire was that people should 'see God' and in consequence his lighting accented every nuance of the author's message." [4] To this the students added their own interpretation of the play. They suggested changes they thought would make obscurities in "Sanctity" understandable to everyone in the audience. The students " *had* caught the meaning—absolutely, and they wanted the audience to catch it."[5]

Sister M. Rosa reported on the success of "Sanctity" in the August 1938 issue of *Catholic World*. "Saints versus Swing in Harlem," appeared in the "Ball and Cross" section of *Catholic World*. An orb topped with a cross was an ancient Christian symbol that represented the victory of Christianity over the world, but *Catholic World* used the "Ball and Cross" section to report on Catholicity's engagement with the world. For Catholic readers of "Saints versus Swing in Harlem," Catholic education in Harlem qualified as an excellent example of Catholicism's engagement with the world. Sister M. Rosa invited readers to admire the great things that were happening in Harlem's parochial schools. African-American children and their parents, teachers and community united to present a gift to Harlem from the treasures of the Roman Catholic tradition— a medieval miracle play. In this story readers saw cooperation and faith, two hallmarks of Catholic education, in action. It took the whole "village" of Manhattan to put on "Sanctity." According to Sister M. Rosa, their efforts produced much desired results. The students had an excellent learning experience and the play's success showed that Harlemites were not "completely wedded to swing music and movies."[6]  She explained "swing there is in Harlem—plenty of it—but side by side with swing we have the music of the saints——delicate, elusive, but vital, compelling—deep calling to the deep nature of the Negro."[7]

Catholicism was the culture in which these students were being educated and that they were presenting to Harlem. However, these same students also learned and lived the rich and resilient culture of Harlem. To Harlem, African Americans brought a culture which valued education, espoused a sound work ethic, treasured family ties, affirmed the importance of enjoying life, and reverenced religious faith. African Americans established houses of worship all over Harlem that filled Sunday mornings with sweet hymns and loud prayers of thanksgiving as well as jazz and blues clubs that filled Harlem nights with joyous, moving and at times ribald music, song, and dance. Many Catholics reading Sr. M. Rosa's article may not have seen the affinities or the common characteristics of these two cultures. In fact the title of the article even suggests a conflict between the two, "Saints versus Swing." In a traditional competition there are two parties and each tries to emerge victorious over the other; there is a victor and there is a loser. But, the competition between saints and swing in Harlem seemed to be driven by cooperation and enlightenment rather than by victory or loss. While Resurrection students and their teachers regarded the play as a way to present a story of holiness to Harlem, their ability to stage "Sanctity" depended on Harlem and the world outside the doors of their parochial school. In Resurrection School, African-Americans represented by Harlem, and Catholicism, represented by the school, were in harmonious balance with one another as the saints and swing lived "side by side." But, the history of the relationship between Catholic education and African Americans has not always been so mutually benevolent.

## NINETEEN CENTURY ORIGINS

Harriet Thompson sent a letter to Pope Pius IX in 1853. Representing herself and twenty-six other African-American Catholics, she informed him of the conditions under which African-American Catholics worked to keep their faith alive with little support from priests and bishops in the United States. Of particular concern to her was the denial of parochial school education to African-American Catholic youth in New York City. Mrs. Thompson told the pope that Archbishop John Hughes refused to admit black children to New York City's parochial schools. The archbishop's policy meant black children had no other choice but to attend the public schools which were dominated by Protestant culture. She claimed that in these schools children learned "that the Blessed Eucharist is nothing but a wafer, that the priest drinks the wine himself and gives the bread to us, and that the Divine institution of confession is only to make money and that the Roman pontiff is Anti-Christ."[8] These things greatly troubled Thompson and other African-American Catholics. Thompson shared the belief of her fellow Catholics of the day that faith and education were of a piece and that the Catholic Church was both a spiritual and educational institution. Her belief in the teaching role of the Church and her concern for the minds and souls of black-Catholic children emboldened her to reveal Catholic neglect of African Americans to the pope.

Harriet Thompson and the group of African-American Catholics that she represented were not alone in expressing concern for Catholic education for African-American children in the nineteenth century. Outside of New York there were several efforts to provide Catholic education for African Americans. The first African-American religious order, the Oblate Sisters of Providence organized in Baltimore in 1828 to preserve and promote the Catholic faith of African-American children and adults through education. The Oblates began a girl's academy and also taught free blacks in the city of Baltimore with the sanctioning of the Archdiocese of Baltimore. Eventually the Oblate Sisters of Providence would extend their educational mission beyond their private academy to parochial schools in the Archdioceses of Baltimore, New Orleans, and St. Louis and in the Dioceses of Richmond, Charleston and Leavenworth.[9] Bishop John England of Charleston, South Carolina, sponsored a short-lived school for African Americans in the basement of a church until local protest and acts of violence against the school forced its closing. In addition the Oblate Sisters of Providence, several other orders of women religious like the Sisters of the Holy Family, the Ursulines, and the Sisters of Charity also taught African Americans with varying degrees of success before the Civil War.[10]

Renewed efforts to make Catholic education more accessible to African Americans came with the end of the Civil War, which changed the social and political status of the majority of African Americans. For example, in the Archdiocese of Cincinnati immediately after the Civil War, there were efforts to establish a separate parochial school for African Americans, despite the fact that Cincinnati had a very small African-American population and very few African-American Catholics. Father Francis Xavier Weninger, S.J., was the founder of the St. Ann's church and school in Cincinnati.[11] Archbishop Martin J. Spalding of Baltimore regarded the recently freed African Americans to represent "'a golden opportunity for reaping a harvest of souls, which if neglected may not return.'"[12] In order to reap this "harvest," Spalding advocated the establishment of Catholic schools and churches for African Americans, more African-American religious communities for women, and African-American priests.[13] The schools, sisters, and priests would serve the missionary efforts of the United States Catholic Church as it worked to convert African Americans to Catholicism and to preserve the faith of those blacks who were already Catholic. The American bishops rejected Spalding's comprehensive plan and did not implement his proposal in any meaningful way. As a consequence of this neglect, Catholic education for African Americans did not receive much attention and well into the twentieth century African Americans experienced difficulty being admitted to Catholic schools, especially parochial schools.

In the tradition of Harriet Thompson, African-American lay Catholics continued to advocate for the right to Catholic education for African Americans after the Civil War. Black Catholic parents both wanted their children to be educated in the faith and to meet the obligation the United States bishops placed on all Catholic parents to send their children to parochial schools in the decisions of the Third Plenary Council of Baltimore in 1884. They advocated for the right to Catholic education through the Colored Catholic Congresses of latter nineteenth century. These lay Catholics believed education was necessary to complete the social, political, and intellectual emancipation of African Americans and to draw African Americans to the Catholic faith. At the first Colored Catholic Congress, convoked in Washington, D.C., in 1889, African Americans asserted their commitment to the Catholic education saying:

> The education of a people being the great and fundamental means of elevating it to higher planes to which all Christian civilization tends, we pledge ourselves to aid in establishing, wherever we are able to be found Catholic schools, embracing the primary and higher branches of knowledge, as in them alone can we expect to reach the large masses of Colored children now growing up without a semblance of Christian education.[14]

Congress delegates envisioned Catholic industrial schools where African-American youth would develop skilled hands, keen minds, and faithful hearts dedicated to the Catholic Church.[15] In addition, the delegates wanted African-American children to be admitted to all Catholic schools and institution of higher education. At every Congress, Catholic education for African-American youth figured prominently on the agenda. The delegates wanted Catholic education for their own children, but they also wanted the Church in the United States to recognize Catholic schools as a powerful means of education and emancipation. Thus they said, "we are anxious to witness the extension of our beloved religion among those of our brethren who as yet are not blessed with the true faith" and they believed this extension could best be achieved through Catholic schools.[16] Though the Colored Catholic Congresses ended in 1895, African-American Catholic advocacy for a greater Catholic investment in their educational needs continued. The Sisters of the Blessed Sacrament working with the Josephites, Holy Ghost Fathers, Sisters of the Holy Family and other religious orders responded to this call.

## THE BLESSED SACRAMENT SISTERS

In 1885, Francis Anthony Drexel, a prominent Philadelphia banker, left his fortune of fourteen million dollars to his three daughters, Katherine, Louise, and Elizabeth. The sisters decided to use their wealth to support Catholic missionary work among African and Native Americans. The Drexel sisters' zeal led them to support a constellation of evangelical works in these communities with an emphasis on education. In 1891, Katherine Drexel founded the Sisters of the Blessed Sacrament for Indians and Colored People to serve these communities, primarily as elementary, secondary, and college teachers.

With the assistance of the Blessed Sacrament Sisters, the Drexels established schools in the South, Southwest, Northeast, and Midwest, provided funding to already existing Catholic schools and sent sisters to teach throughout the United States at Catholic parochial and private schools.[17] The Blessed Sacrament Sisters' crowning achievement was Xavier University of Louisiana, which began operating as the only African-American Catholic college 1925. But before entering the field of higher education they dedicated themselves to private and parochial school elementary and secondary teaching.

St. Emma's Industrial Institute and St. Frances De Sales High School, both in Rock Castle, Virginia, about sixty miles from Richmond, were among the first and most successful of the schools. St. Emma's opened in 1895. Named in memory of the Drexel sisters' mother, St. Emma's was a military school for African-American boys. At St. Emma's students gained proficiency in a trade. The school's goal was to provide education in trades and in agriculture in a beautiful environment so that young men could learn to love the good and beautiful. They could then go out into the world with skills necessary to make decent lives for themselves.[18] The school building, which was once a plantation manor house, was indeed beautiful and the young men who attended St. Emma's received a first-rate industrial education that included courses in carpentry, farming, and shoemaking. Over time the emphasis shifted from industrial education to a stronger academic program. Though Blessed Sacrament Sisters did not teach at St. Emma's, the school was definitely connected to their work and their philosophy of Catholic education for African-Americans was quite apparent.[19]

Not long after St. Emma's was established, Mother Katherine Drexel bought the Mount Pleasant Plantation, which was on a hill facing the James River; it was not far from St. Emma's. Here she founded St. Frances de Sales High School, named in memory of the Drexel sisters' father. According to one biographer, Katherine Drexel thought it important for girls to have the opportunity to live with the sisters during their high school years so they could learn the Catholic way of living and the Catholic outlook so that Catholic culture could "permeate their whole being."[20] Mother Katherine also intended St. Frances de Sales to be a normal school so that upon graduation the young women could go out and teach in Southern schools for African-Americans. St. Frances de Sales was ready in 1899. Just before it was set to open, someone set the school's barn on fire.[21]   Apparently such acts were not unusual in the Drexels' experience of establishing Catholic schools.  Often, "Mother Katherine would initiate building projects and erect institutions with evidence of ill will from surrounding communities."[22]  This did not stop them.  During the first years of St. Frances de Sales, the focus was on industrial and normal school education, but eventually it became a fully accredited high school and attracting students, Catholic and non-Catholic, from all over the United States. In the early days, students did not pay tuition at either school, only after a period of time did they begin to add fees to the structure of education at St. Emma's and St. Frances de Sales.[23]

By the turn of the century, Blessed Sacrament Sisters could be found teaching in parochial schools in New Orleans, Biloxi, St. Louis, Nashville, Atlanta, Macon, and Savannah, Georgia, Montgomery, Harlem, Chicago, Columbus, Cincinnati, and Philadelphia.[24]  At most of the southern parochial schools they teamed up with Josephite or Holy Ghost Fathers who established many mission churches for African Americans in the early twentieth century.  Almost all of the missions had schools attached to them that accepted Catholic and non-Catholic children, with the majority of children being non-Catholic.  Often enrollment exceeded three-hundred or more and many youth and their parents converted to Catholicism as a result of the introduction to Catholicism they received in the parish schools.

The Blessed Sacrament Sisters taught at several schools in and around New Orleans, which had one of the largest populations of African-American Catholics in the United States.  The parochial elementary schools such as Blessed Sacrament, St. Peter Claver, Holy Ghost, and Corpus Christi served as launching pads for many black children to Xavier Prepatory School, which was a private school conducted by the Blessed Sacrament Sisters and Xavier University, also conducted by the Blessed Sacrament Sisters.  They established extracurricular activities for the parochial schools of New Orleans, which they ran out of Xavier University.  The activities included music, art, speech, and athletic clubs.  Each year the clubs showcased their talents at the Annual Spring Festival at Xavier University.

The Blessed Sacrament Sisters had two goals in mind with the extracurricular activities.  One was to give African-American students experience with college students and college life to instill in them the value of higher studies.  The second goal was to get Xavier students involved with the parochial schools of New Orleans.  The sisters explained "indirectly, leadership and good citizenship are fostered and in the Xavier graduate is inculcated the idea of community helpfulness and responsibility."[25]

Elementary schools tended to develop into high schools so that children could complete their education in a Catholic context.  Blessed Sacrament Sisters also moved into areas where Catholic presence was sparse. When a 1922 survey revealed that few rural southern black children had access to Catholic education, Katherine Drexel designed a plan to meet their needs. She decided to build small frame schools near rural parishes with the intention of having graduates of Xavier University teach at the schools. She initiated the plan in the Diocese of Lafayette, Louisiana, with the help of Bishop Jules B. Jeanmard. In all, Mother Katherine built twenty-two schools at the average cost of $3,000.00 per school. By the 1940s, these schools served over 2,500 children.[26] Sisters of the Holy Ghost, Sisters of the Holy Family, and Xavier graduates staffed the schools. In addition, by 1940 the sisters financed teacher salaries and the construction of about fifteen other Catholic schools for African Americans at the cost of about $24,000. The sisters envisioned a time when they would not have the funds to continue support for Catholic education for African Americans. In their fiftieth anniversary souvenir book they wrote, "it is a heavy drain on our ever-shrinking resources and inevitably there will come a time when the Sisters of the Blessed Sacrament will be unable to finance this marvelous work for the church and for the souls of these poor Colored children."[27]

## NATIONAL MOVEMENTS

In the 1910s the Committee for the Advancement of Colored Catholics launched efforts to open the doors of all Catholic schools to African Americans. The committee (later known as the Federated Colored Catholics) enjoyed the eloquent leadership of Dr. Thomas Wyatt Turner.[28] As a professor of biology at Howard University and Hampton Institute, Dr. Turner understood the value of a good education and as a Catholic he also valued the importance of religious education. Dr. Turner believed that withholding Catholic education from African Americans was tantamount to withholding the sacraments. Like the sacraments, education was a means of grace for all members of the Church. But, it was difficult to meet such obligations when in most areas of the United States Catholics practiced de facto segregation in parishes and schools. African-American Catholics faced a quandary. They were obliged by the United States bishops to send their children to schools that for most part would not accept them. Turner argued, "where so grave an obligation exists there must be an equally potent right to means necessary to its fulfillment."[29] Turner and the Federated Colored Catholics' work helped pave the way for the integration of Catholic schools that would begin in earnest in the late 1940s.

In 1937, the Catholic Interracial Council (CIC), which grew out of the Federated Colored Catholics, adopted the "Resolutions on Catholic Elementary Education," which called for "everything possible to be done to open wide the doors of every Catholic institution of learning, particularly elementary schools, to every Catholic child of whatsoever race or condition of life."[30] The CIC pledged to bring these resolutions to the attention of every diocesan superintendent of parochial schools in the United States. In support of these resolutions the CIC cited Jesus' welcome of all people unto himself, the Christian principle that love transcended race and class, Pope Pius XI's encyclical on Catholic education, the United States bishops' mandate that Catholic parents send their children to Catholic schools, and the rights of African-American Catholics to have a Catholic education as reasons for supporting these resolutions. They contended, "Catholic colored children have a God-given right to a Catholic education as a heritage that is inalienably theirs to fit them for the working out of their salvation as members of the true Church of Jesus Christ and to enable them to win admission into the Kingdom of Heaven."[31]

Members of the National Catholic Educational Association also began to advocate for greater inclusion of African Americans in Catholic education as well. In her address to the Middle Atlantic States Regional Unit of the NCEA at Bishop McDonnell Memorial High School in Brooklyn, New York, in 1946, Sister Cecelia Marie, O.P., asked Catholic educators to make an honest assessment of the practice of racial discrimination in Catholic education. She pointed out that it had been eighty-three years since the President Lincoln's Gettysburg Address in which he affirmed the American commitment to the principle that all persons were created equal. Sister Cecelia Marie reflected,

> Americans in general believe that all men are created equal; they also believe in freedom of speech and of religion; and they believe that America is the cradle of freedom, the land of opportunity and the home of democracy. In principle, most Americans, in the North at least, concede that Negroes have the same right to freedom and justice as all other citizens, but, in practice, the Negroes have not shared many of these rights. This contradiction between our profession and our actions constitutes the Negro problem.[32]

Catholic education participated in this contradiction too; and racial discrimination in Catholic schools violated justice and betrayed charity, the essence of Christian ethics.[33] Sister Cecelia Marie thought Catholic teachers could turn around this violation and betrayal by cooperating with the Catholic interracial movement that was working to fully integrate Catholic schools and to make Catholics more aware of the Catholic teaching on racial justice and equality.[34] She also considered prayer as a fundamental role in bringing about racial justice in Catholic schools. She said, "we should also have special devotions on feasts of saints most notable for their zeal for social justice, like the saintly and loveable Negro, Blessed Martin de Porres, through whose intercessions cures and favors are daily received."[35]  Sister Cecelia Marie insisted that Catholic educators had a moral responsibility to understand Catholic teaching on equal rights and equal dignity of all races, and to teach this to their students, and that such teaching be a part of "our Catholic text-books."

In an open letter to Catholic elementary teachers, Father Daniel O'Callaghan, S.J., urged his "co-workers in Christ" to "give the best answer to our very widespread, un-Christian, and un-American problem, the race question."[36]  O'Callaghan asserted that racial prejudice took hold in most people before they reached their teenage years.  Therefore, it was the responsibility of elementary school teachers to teach children about racial justice and equality.  He urged them to do this saying, "you alone can teach American children to see all men with the eyes of the Child Jesus, so that later they will see all men with the eyes of the Man Jesus."[37]  And, like Sister Cecelia Marie, O'Callaghan believed prayer would help bring about racial justice and equality.  He encouraged teachers to introduce their students to Blessed Martin de Porres and to pray daily for all members of the human family.

By the late 1940s, there was some progress made in the education of African Americans.  Many Catholic separate parochial and private schools for African Americans were well established and some Catholic parochial and private schools were becoming racially integrated, a process that required teachers to become more aware of special needs of black and white children in learning to be together in school.  How to make such transitions effective was the subject of "Color and the Mystical Body of Christ," by Sister Dorothy of Providence, F.C.S.P.  The theology of the Mystical Body of Christ taught that each person was due respect and had dignity because they each had a special role to play in the life and work of Christ and the Church in the world.  Sister Dorothy believed the theology of the Mystical Body of Christ issued a special challenge to all teachers and the way for them to "give themselves and their pupils a positive motive for noble living."[38]

Any serious reflection and application of the theology of the Mystical Body of Christ called into question American race relations and the practice of racial discrimination in the United States.  Sister Dorothy contended that the teacher who did not use the Mystical Body of Christ theology to teach children about the injustice of racial discrimination ignored a "gold mine of opportunity along with the confidence of his pupils."[39]

In her experience of teaching black and white children, Sister Dorothy identified few differences between them.  Both white and black children wished to have fun, to be popular, and to have things.  These desires made them human, and "natural sons and daughters of Adam and Eve and actual or prospective brothers of Christ."[40] Sister Dorothy believed all teachers needed to realize this and to make every effort to make these children happy. She said, "if God has entrusted some colored pupils to them, theirs is the power and the privilege of making concrete the oneness of all men in Christ."

In teaching African-American children in predominately white Catholic schools, Sister Dorothy recognized a need to help them to develop positive self-images and a sense of self-esteem. She believed nothing helped a child to build esteem more than the teacher showing the rest of the students that she had confidence in the student. For this reason, she urged teachers to take every opportunity to recognize the accomplishments and interests of African-American children publicly. She explained, "when given the opportunity, colored boys and girls often show a spontaneity and an originality that wins laurels for their school. Faith is alive in a predominately "white" school where the pupils choose as their Sodality president a boy or girl of unquestioned ability and outstanding virtue even if he or she is colored."[41] The Mystical Body of Christ was most alive in a school where African-American boys and girls were aside white boys and girls in the honor society, piano recital, oratorical society, and when black girls made it onto the May court along with white girls.

Sister Dorothy was conscious of the isolation and loneliness that many black children faced in predominately white Catholic schools. Recognizing the loneliness and exclusion of black children in the particularly social moments of the school day, like lunch and recess, was something to which teachers need to be especially sensitive. She advised, "recess time is a heartache for the colored child who stands alone watching the games. The child whom the teacher singles out for attention is soon the choice of the children. If he is not at once the captain of the team, he has at least the chance to play on it."[42] Teachers had the power to determine what the quality of the child's experience in the Catholic school.

The quality of a child's experience was dependent on whether or not he or she felt accepted and valued by his or her peers. For this reason Sr. Dorothy charged Catholic teachers with the responsibility to make sure that African-American students had friends, especially as they entered their high school years when it was most important to have "companionship." Teachers had the responsibility of directing friendships. She explained, "directing friendships requires a psychological insight born of grace and study, an bought by prayer and selflessness."[43] She promoted the value of interracial friendships and the teacher's ability to establish such relationships as a testament to the teacher's own "Christlike qualities." And, interracial friendships nurtured in school were essential to the future of the Mystical Body of Christ. If children learned to value each other without regard to color then they would make a world that was different and more in keeping with Jesus' teachings when they were adults. According to Sister Dorothy, interracial friendships were most important for white children because they gave them opportunities to learn that they had not cornered the market on social graces. She explained, "white boys and girls have no monopoly on Emily Post's arts. The experienced knowledge of this fact along with sincere religious teaching usually breaks prejudice."[43]

Finally Catholic teachers also had the obligation to be aware of how African Americans were treated in the United States. They needed to be conscious of the daily indignities black children learned to live with and how learning to live with these indignities affected their attitudes and personalities. Sister Dorothy believe that this was the area in which Catholic teachers needed to develop the most to make Catholic education most useful and fruitful for African-American children. She contended "that few have attained this mastery is evident in the many embarrassments that the colored boys and girls must learn to overlook. Teachers can do much to lessen their hurts if, again, they are selfless and understanding. In buses, on the streets, in stores, and even in church, colored people are made to feel their "color."[44] She felt certain that teachers who heeded this advice would make a truly positive difference in the lives of African-American children.

Sister Dorothy's advice became more and more germane as Catholic dioceses throughout the United States began to officially desegregate their Catholic schools and deal with the reality of what having a truly Catholic school meant. Some dioceses made the transition smoothly and other experienced more difficulties. One of the first dioceses to formally announce that its schools would admit children and youth without respect to race was the Archdiocese of St. Louis in 1947. In response to the overcrowded conditions of the African-American Catholic high school, St. Joseph's, in St. Louis, Archbishop Joseph E. Ritter decided that African-American students could attend the other schools in the archdiocese in the districts in which they lived.[45] This decision made ostensibly for practical reasons opened the door for the integration of the Catholic elementary schools that were crowded as well. Ultimately, Archbishop Ritter asserted a policy of integration of all Catholic schools. When a few parents protested this "Negro encroachment," Ritter stood his ground.

Those supportive of desegregation saw many positive outcomes for St. Louis blacks and whites as well. Ella Madden Lancaster wrote, "the white Catholic is learning the meaning of the doctrine of the Mystical Body. He is beginning to realize that racism is heresy and he is trying to rid himself of it."[46] The admiration of white non-Catholics for the Church's work to end segregation and the new esteem of black non-Catholics for their black Catholic friends were also advantages. The Catholic Church seemed less like a "white man's church" with the integration of Catholic schools.[47]    And, the greatest advantage was the broadening of educational opportunities for African-American students in St. Louis.

When Cardinal Hayes High School opened in New York in 1941 it was considered a "modern marvel" complete with a Grand Concourse that seemed to some like a "futuristic dream transported from the World's Fair."[48]    Cardinal Hayes had a complete library, auditorium, gymnasium, cafeteria, well-equipped chemistry, biology, physics, music and commerce rooms, and a Romanesque chapel at the heart of the school.    Young men from parishes in New York City as well as Westchester County attended Cardinal Hayes where they received "the best of the civilization of today and of the wisdom the Church can offer."[49] Cardinal Hayes' teachers included diocesan priests, Marists, and Xaverian and Irish Christian Brothers; and the student body was fully integrated.

Cardinal Hayes High School was regarded as a great example of the Mystical Body of Christ at work.    African-American and white boys studied, played, ate and socialized together at the school without distinction of color. When asked about how the school accomplished such an accepting climate for black and white students, one teacher remarked, "a boy is a boy to me.  One fellow may have large ears, another blue eyes, another dark skin.  Those accidentals don't have anything to do with the *boy* fundamentally.  I know the fellow by name."[50] But teachers also realized that the racial harmony the boys experienced at Cardinal Hayes would not be reflected in the society they would enter after high school. To help their students deal with the transition the teachers put their faith in the preparation they were giving these young men.  A monsignor at the school explained, "besides filling them with knowledge, we try to make gentlemen of them, and give them the assurance and self-confidence based on a true Christian humility."[51]

The formation of well-educated, self-confident Christian gentlemen was also the goal of the Josephite Fathers when they established St. Augustine's High School in New Orleans in 1949. This school was different from Cardinal Hayes in most respects.  It had no gymnasium, athletic field, or auditorium, a sparse library and a biology lab without running water.  Despite these privations, St. Augustine's athletic teams attained champion status, its thespians were well touted in New Orleans and most importantly of all, St. Augustine's students gained admission into prestigious colleges throughout the United States. [52] When *Time* reported on St. Augustine's High School in 1965, it had 750 students and 31 teachers, over half of whom were African-American laymen. Even though the civil rights movement was at its height and many Northern and Midwestern Catholic schools, like those in St. Louis and New York, had been integrated for quite some time, there were only African-American students at St. Augustine's High School.

The faculty looked forward to the day when white students would attend St. Augustine's but integration was not their first priority. According to Josephite Father Eugene P. McManus, "we are trying to get first class-citizenship in graduate schools and colleges. We want in."[53]

To this purpose, St. Augustine's students had to pass an entrance examination and to follow a strict academic curriculum and that required at least three hours of homework each evening. They also wrote weekly 300-word essays to develop their composition skills. All students also participated in a summer paperback reading program. Eighth graders were required to read at least twenty-five books a summer. Students also majored in subjects in high schools and various majors had intensive summer-study programs attached to them. St. Augustine's teachers believed all of this was necessary to prepare their students for college. One teacher explained, "unless our product is a quality one, we betray the hopes of a people filled with hope."[54] St. Augustine's students, faculty, and parents were committed to a better future for these young men and by extension to the community from which they came. Failure was not an option and as a consequence most St. Augustine students attended college, had a remarkable low dropout rate, and became teachers, doctors, lawyers, and business professionals.[55] Like Resurrection School, St. Augustine's was a Catholic school respectful of the culture of the students but also determined to invest in the students the best of the Catholic tradition that a Catholic school could deliver. St. Augustine's High School continues to this day.

## CONCLUSION

For most of the nineteenth-century ambivalence and hostility characterized the attitude of white Catholics towards the idea that Catholic schools should play a role in the lives of African-American children, Catholic and non-Catholic. After the Civil War, the hostility towards making Catholic education available to blacks lessened as Catholic leaders began to see Catholic education as a means of evangelization. But, rather than accept African-American children into already existing parish schools, a separate system of parochial schools and private schools was created for them as parishes and mission churches were established for blacks. By the late 1940s a Catholic initiative was led by African-American and white Catholics, to open all Catholic schools, especially the parish schools, to African-American children. Now, as the twenty-first century commences, the Catholic schools play a vital role in the lives of thousands of African-Americans, the majority of whom are not Catholics. Dioceses throughout the United States realize the importance of these schools and are working out how to keep parish schools alive as many urban schools are facing extinction. But if the tenacious spirit shown by over two-hundred years of black and white champions of African-American Catholic education is an indicator, the future of Catholic schools and African-Americans making a positive difference are definitely assured.

## ENDNOTES

1 Sr. M. Rosa "Saints Versus Swing in Harlem," *The Catholic World*, (August 1938): 603.

2 Ibid.

3 Ibid.

4 Ibid.

5 Ibid., 604.

6 Ibid.

7 Ibid.

8 Cyprian Davis, *The History of Black Catholics in the United States,* (New York: Crossroad, 1990), 95.

9 Joseph B. Code, "A Colored Catholic Educator before the Civil War" *The Catholic World* (January 1938) and Mary Seemater "Overcoming Obstacles: Serving Black Catholics in St. Louis, 1873-1993," *Gateway Heritage*, (Spring 2000).

10 James Hennessey, *American Catholics: A History of the Roman Catholic Community in the United States* (New York: Oxford University Press, 1981), 107.

11 Joseph H. Lackner, S.M. "St. Ann's Colored Church and School, Cincinnati, the Indian and Negro Collection for the United States, and Reverend Francis Xavier Weninger, S.J." *U.S. Catholic Historian*, (Spring and Summer 1988): 145.

12 Stephen Ochs, *Desegregating the Altar: The Josephites and the Struggle for Black Priests* (Baton Rouge: Louisiana State University Press, 1990), 39.

13 Ibid, 9.

14 *Three Catholic Afro-American Congresses* (New York: Arno Press, 1978), 68-69.

15 Ibid., 26.

16 Cyprian Davis, "The Holy See and American Black Catholics: A Forgotten Chapter in the History of the American Church," *U.S. Catholic Historian*, (Spring 1989): 166.

17 Davis, *The History of Black Catholics*, 136.

18 Duffy, *Katherine Drexel: A Biography*, 78.

19 Christian Brothers, Benedictine Brothers of St. Vincent Abbey, Latrobe, Pennsylvania, Holy Ghost Fathers, and laymen taught at St. Emma's.

20 Duffy, Katherine Drexel, A Biography, 199.

21 Ibid., 206.

22 Ibid.

23 Ibid., 207.

24 1891-1941 *Souvenir Volume of the Golden Jubilee of the Sisters of the Blessed Sacrament for Indians and Colored People.*

25 Ibid., 78.

26 Ibid., 81.

27 Ibid.

28 Davis, *The History of Black Catholics*, 202.

29 Thomas Wyatt Turner to the Hierarchy of the United States, 20 October 1931, NCWC: Social Action: Race Relations, Coll. 10, Box 7, Folder 2, Archives of the Catholic University of America.

30 "Resolutions on Catholic Elementary Education," *Interracial Review*, January and December 1937, 156.

31 Ibid.

32 Sister Cecelia Marie, O.P. "The Negro Problem," *The Catholic Mind*, June 1946, 337.

33 Ibid.

34 Ibid., 338.

35 Ibid.

36 Daniel O'Callaghan, S.J. "An Open Letter to Catholic Elementary Teachers," *The Catholic School Journal*, (March 1947): 85.

37 Ibid.

38 Sr. Dorothy of Providence, F.C.S.P., "Color and the Mystical Body of Christ," *The Catholic School Journal*, (March 1947), 83.

39 Ibid.

40 Ibid.

41 Ibid., 84.

42 Ibid.

43 Ibid.

44 Ibid.

45 Ella Madden Lancaster, "Catholic Education in St. Louis Today," *Interracial Review*, (July 1948): 106.

46 Ibid., 107.

47 Ibid.

48 Gertrude Haas, "At Cardinal Hayes High School," *Interracial Review*, (April 1945): 57.

49 Ibid.

50 Ibid.

51 Ibid., 58.

52 "St Augustine's High: Separate and Superior," *The Catholic Digest*, (June 1965): 97.

53 Ibid.

54 Ibid., 98.

55 Antoine M. Garibaldi, "Growing Up Black and Catholic in Louisiana: Personal Reflections on Catholic Education," *Growing Up African American in Catholic Schools*. (New York: Teachers College Press, 1996), 132.

## CHAPTER 13

# HISTORY AND INCULTURATION: THE LATINO EXPERIENCE OF CATHOLIC EDUCATION

*Anthony M. Stevens-Arroyo and Segundo Pantoja*

T he first Catholic grammar school in what is now United States territory was established in San Juan, Puerto Rico, in 1582. Other schools founded later in the nascent cities of Saint Augustine, Florida; San Antonio, Texas; Santa Fe, New Mexico, and the Franciscan missions of California under the impetus of Spanish colonizers offered education in secular subjects for Catholic children. Therefore, it may be said that the American church embraced its educational mission as early as the sixteenth century.[1]

These earliest Catholic schools in the Latino homelands, however, were doomed to eventual eclipse by a series of historical events. Social and political circumstances dictated that the Hispanic communities who were the first to enjoy the opportunities of a Catholic education would lose those privileges. As we cross over into the twenty-first century, the restoration of a parochial-school education for the myriad communities of persons of Latin-American origin in the United States remains a work in progress. This chapter will discuss the history of Catholic-school education for Latinos (also frequently described as "Hispanics"). But just as the distinction of being the first of America's Catholics to enjoy parochial school education was no guarantee that those schools would survive or flourish, so the enrollment of significant numbers of Latinos in Catholic schools is in itself no assurance that these schools serve their students as complements to evangelization and a full Catholic commitment.[2]

There is a growing consensus that what makes an education "Catholic" is inculturation — the process by which Gospel values are explained in a given cultural context so as to preserve effectively the essence of Jesus' message.[3] As contrasted with catechism lessons or one-dimensional instruction that rely on learning by rote, the integrative development of a Catholic way of thinking about all knowledge is the kind of education for which we all strive. Inculturation is not a Church version of a "touchy-feely" political correctness about diversity but an obligation to promote the Gospel without admixtures of racial and ethnic prejudices. For Catholics, inculturation produces believers who incarnate the Church's mission and creatively fashion new meanings for ancient truths. Their education empowers them to live the Gospel in the contemporary world. Any assessment of this important function of the Church in the United States regarding Latinos reveals the need for improvement. We will begin with a review of the historical reasons that the first American Catholics, the Latinos/Hispanics, have not benefited from the institutions of the Catholic schools as they might. Next, we will focus on the results of studies on Latinos in the Catholic schools of New York City.[4] Our interest, however, is on the various ways that inculturation affects opinions and convictions about Catholic schools, including responses from Latino/Hispanic Protestants who also seek a religious education for their children. We conclude with some suggestions for the future based on appraisal of what has been done to include Hispanics in Catholic education and what remains as an agenda for all of us.

## Historical Background

The starting point for assessment of the Latino experience of Catholic education is the historical moment of conquest of the Latino homelands by invading U.S. troops.[5] Unlike European immigrants, the first Latinos did not come to the United States: the United States came to them. In the 1820s, Florida was annexed after what historians have called "James Madison's Phony War."[6] In the 1830s, Texas revolted against Mexican rule in a war that brought together two peoples as patriots. But the Texas Republic undid those bonds before becoming a state of the Union. The entire Southwest, much of the Rocky Mountains, and California were annexed after the Mexican-American War that ripped two-thirds of Mexican lands from the mother country.[7] Fifty years later in 1898, Puerto Rico was annexed[8] in a war so characterized by injustice that Mark Twain wrote: "...the Stars and Stripes should be replaced with the Skull and Crossbones." These ugly chapters of Manifest Destiny and American Imperialism greatly affected the resident Catholic population of these homelands in ways whose effects are still being felt.

The triumphal arrogance and imperialist prejudices of many Protestants contaminated the public school system that encouraged among many in the United States to judge Latino Catholic culture and society as inferior.[9] Mexican-Americans in Texas and California lost title to their farms before the greed of Euro-American land speculators, creating poverty that was often defined by color lines. As Sarah Deutsch has pointed out, only six percent of land-grant cases were decided in favor of Mexican Americans by courts established in 1891 to protect their rights. Sadly, in many of the six percent of victorious cases, the lawyers wound up taking parts of the Latino farms as payment for legal fees, so that virtually all the land was taken by the invaders.[10] In Puerto Rico, it took only seventeen years for six sugar corporations to gobble up eighty percent of the island's agricultural fields.[11] As Rodolfo Acuña has bitterly described, the impunity of such maneuvers everywhere destroyed the social infrastructure of Latino societies— Mexican and Puerto Rican — and stigmatized Latino leaders, the community role models and the hopes of Latino children.[12]

The (mostly) English-speaking bishops of the United States, who were entrusted with jurisdiction over the conquered Latino homelands, were influenced by the negative image of Latinos and their religion in the popular culture of the United States. No doubt the bishops were alarmed at the concerted efforts of Protestant denominations to remove vestiges of "papism and superstition" from the new lands. Perhaps they considered the existing policies of Catholic accommodation to a Protestant majority as the only safe course for the native Latino Church now that it was under the flag of the United States. But in any case, there was no evidence of "re-vidication" by the United States Catholic Church of indigenous Catholicism and Latino culture.[13] Unlike Ireland and Poland, where Catholicism was firmly welded to the national identity and resisted the imposition of the invaders' religion and politics, the Iberian Catholic heritage of Latinos was denigrated as an impediment to full participation in the American Church. Nor was there episcopal support for Latin American causes such as the abolition of slavery and Cuban independence fostered by the saintly Cuban priest and patriot, Félix Varela, who was vicar general for the Diocese of New York until his death in 1853.[14] In sum, the American Catholic Church fell silent before the imperialist effort of the U.S. conquerors to make inferior all things native. It may have been a pious colonialism, but it was colonialism nonetheless.[15]

For those interested in the details, there are important works that focused upon Latinos and the Church.[16] The three-volume history published by the University of Notre Dame in 1994 provides a useful compendium.[17] We would not deny that there were points of light attempting to pierce the darkness of the Latino condition. Nor would it be fair to speak of the U.S. bishops in 1848 and again in 1898 as totally insensitive to inculturation as a powerful United States absorbed conquered Latino homelands.[18] Most importantly, the clergy and Catholic leaders at the parish level brought a high level of commitment to the Gospel that managed to overcome a clearly defined pastoral practice. But in the nineteenth century a prelate might rule his diocese much like a feudal lord so that the voices of local clergy or religious women or pious laypersons might never reach the ears of a prelate. As a result, the insensitivity to Latinos from, the Church can be found as part of a general pattern in many dioceses.[19]

The example of Archbishop Jean Baptiste Lamy in New Mexico serves to illustrate how this surrender of so much power to the ordinary greatly prejudiced the process of inculturation to Latino values. The favorable portrait of Lamy rendered by Willa Cather in *Death Comes to the Archbishop* (1927) needs to be tempered with more recent scholarship about Padre José Martínez and about the many native priests who escaped from the bitter confrontation of Bishop Lamy and the "Cura de Taos".[20] There was a vibrant and effective clerical leadership made up of New Mexican priests when Lamy took possession of his see. The French prelate trained in European seminaries where forms of Jansenism were daily fare, disdained the vitality of the existing popular religiosity and the communitarian flavor of New Mexico's ecclesiastical institutions. Lamy prohibited the folk celebrations that traditionally accompanied the Christmas midnight mass (*misa de gallo*), repressed the pious organizations such as the *Penitentes* and other lay-run *cofradías* that supplied catechism, paid burial fees and functioned as home loan associations. Lamy replaced native New Mexican pastors with foreign missionaries and worst of all, imposed a scale of fees for church services upon a populace that was not rich enough to use such forms of financing the Church. When Padre Martínez organized a resistance to such measures, the Archbishop dismissed both the objections and the objectors. Eventually, Martínez was excommunicated and with the stigma attached to him and to his causes, native vocations to the priesthood were set back for nearly a century in New Mexico.

Deprived of input from local leaders, the Church of New Mexico turned its back on three-hundred years of local Catholicism. New churches with French-style architecture were built, American-style Catholic schools were established, missionaries from European religious orders were imported, and the English language was privileged on the premise that the centuries-old already existing Catholicism was not acceptable.[21] A *protegé* of Archbishop Lamy, Placide Chapelle, was Archbishop of New Orleans when the Peace Treaty of Paris was negotiated, ceding Puerto Rico to U.S. control after the Spanish-American War. Chosen because of his experiences in Santa Fe, Chappelle sent one of his own, James Blenck, as the new bishop of San Juan, Puerto Rico. [22] Not surprisingly, Blenck ordered the Puerto Ricans to cease celebrating the *misa de gallo* and started on a road of Americanization that resembled the route of Lamy.

The Americanization of Latino Catholicism often began with the closing of existing seminaries or their total reorganization. The general effect was to undercut the creation of a native Latino clergy. By inviting religious orders from the U.S. and from Europe to help the American bishops, the native clergy already ordained at the time of the annexation was marginalized. Moreover, the invitation to the religious orders contained the plea to bring evangelization and missionary effort. Perhaps the anomaly of treating the oldest Catholic churches in America as "mission lands," can be explained by the popular presumption of the time that the Spanish or Latin American Catholic way was the wrong way of practicing the faith. The imported clergy in the Latino homelands frequently replicated many of the institutions of East Coast Catholicism: political alliances were formed with political parties, along with an entrepreneurship in real estate as a means of financing church ventures, what Notre Dame historian Jay Dolan called the "brick-and-mortar" priests.[23] In such circumstances, inculturation usually did not take place and the institutions for preserving traditional forms of Catholicism —popular religious practices and associations such as the cofradías — were under a virtual death sentence. There can be small wonder that the Protestant churches were able to make converts among Latinos, especially because they allowed native preachers and invited Latinos to be missionaries.[24]

In the light of these nineteenth century practices that went against inculturation of Latino values into Catholicism, it is fair to say that parochial school education was weighed down with a very heavy burden.[25] As the nineteenth century turned into the twentieth century, most Latinos in the United States lived in rural areas, whether in Southwest Texas, New Mexico, California or Puerto Rico, where Catholic schools were seldom found. Latinos living in city barrios, such as in La Placita neighborhood of Los Angeles may have been able to enroll in Catholic schools, but they often faced the specter of Americanization there.[26] The Spanish language national parishes which stood as bulwarks against Americanization usually lacked the resources for a parochial school. Although individual teachers may have striven for inculturation from a common sense appreciation of how best to educate Latinos, they were regulated by a denigration of Latino Catholicism from within much of official church leadership.

## Viva Cristo Rey

The beginnings of the Mexican Revolution (1910) intensified the stigmatization of the Mexican as one inclined to violence and incapable of democracy. Ironically, the first quarter of the twentieth century witnessed the emergence of a new attitude towards Mexican-American Catholicism, stimulated in part by the influx of Mexican Catholics fleeing the *Cristero* Wars after the Mexican Revolution, especially in parts of Texas and California.[27]   The conflicts in Mexico were provoked by a central government eager to impose radical secular values on a largely agrarian populace.   There was a concerted effort to destroy religion, especially Catholicism, by seizing church property and denying the clergy the right to evangelize. Mexican presidents attempted to equate the Mexican identity with this secularism.  In reaction, the *Cristeros* promoted a Mexican identity in which Catholicism was an essential ingredient.[28]   In defense of their Catholic identity, the *Cristeros* discredited the rulers in Mexico City by proclaiming Christ as King.  One of the *Cristero* martyrs, St. Miguel Pro, died with the words, "*Viva Cristo Rey!*" on his lips.  Fleeing persecution, *Cristeros* often became exiles in the United States.  Using church bulletins or founding Spanish-language magazines and newspapers, these leaders articulated a Mexican identity that was also Catholic.  Just as the Easter Rebellion of 1916 mobilized Irish-American Catholics around a cause that transcended politics, the *Cristero* War in Mexico altered the Catholicism of Mexican Americans in the United States.

The message of this emerging Mexican-American Catholicism should not be dismissed as ultra-conservatism.  While the *Cristeros* did not hide their disdain for the secularism of the Revolution, which they linked with the libertine immorality of Mexico's new elite, they were inclined to foster the teachings of the social encyclicals of Leo XIII.  They promoted not a restoration of Mexico's *ancién régime,* but a renewal of society in the mode of Catholic Action with social justice goals centered on the needs of labor.  In Puerto Rico during the 1930s, a similar cultural defense of Catholicism as the basis for national identity was promoted by the Nationalist leader, Pedro Albizu Campos.[29]

These affirmations were coupled with a growing sensitivity of missionaries and some visionary U.S. prelates, like Archbishops Cantwell in Los Angeles and Lucey in San Antonio,[30] who recast pastoral efforts to use Latino identity and long-standing Catholic customs as building blocks for the Church.  A generation of educated Latino Catholic laypersons, such as the Texas historian Carlos Eduardo Castañeda, enriched an understanding of Latino Catholicism.[31] The focus of Church ministry shifted from destroying the existing religiosity as a barrier to faith commitment towards incorporating these cultural foundations in a vigorous expression of Catholicism.  Some of these positive elements endured the harshness of the Depression and the overt racism that deported many persons who were deemed undesirable Mexicans, including as many as 60 percent who were U.S. citizens.  In Puerto Rico, some efforts to address social injustice were interpreted as sedition against U.S. rule of the island and met with acts of government retaliation.

The generation of Hispanic Catholics formed by the desperate 1930s and the war years emerged in 1946 ready for a fresh beginning in society and in the

Church.[32]    There were Catholic clerical leaders ready to recruit this post-war generation as allies in establishing programs of Catholic education for Latinos. Their contributions did not have an immediate impact on parochial schools, but they did create a new climate for recognizing the Latino presence within Catholicism in the United States.

## The Internal Migrations

Mexican Americans had always been a part of the gangs of railroad workers that laid track throughout the 19th century West. With the economic collapse during the Depression of the 1930s, desperate young men from New Mexico and Southwest Texas followed those railroad tracks into the urban centers like Chicago, Topeka, Toledo, and Denver. Puerto Ricans began a similar urban migration, especially those who had been drafted into the U.S. Armed Forces because of the 1917 legislation that made them citizens — without the vote, but eligible for the draft.[33]    With the end of World War II in 1945, however, what had been a trickle of migrants to the city became a flood.

The prosperity of the 1950s gradually emptied the city neighborhoods of Italians, Irish, Polish and other ethnics as the children of former immigrants moved to the burgeoning suburbs. This exodus to middle-class life left vacant the manufacturing jobs that had sustained city neighborhoods made up of Euro-American Catholics. Thus began the post-war migrations of Latinos: Mexican Americans went mostly to California and the Midwest; Puerto Ricans to New York, New England and the Midwest. It is important to note that these were migrations of citizens, born in the United States — some going back nine generations.[34] Although the Latinos may have seemed like foreigners who were seeking the same immigrant dream as the Irish, Italians and Poles, they were a new kind of migrant: the conquered peoples of America.[35]

The large archdioceses in cities like Chicago and New York were able to direct significant resources towards outreach programs for the Spanish-speaking. The progressive 1950s Catholicism measured itself by the passion of a commitment to Latinos and what was called, "the Inner City."[36] While there were bumps on this journey to social justice, the leadership within Catholicism adopted policies that gave Latinos a place within the urban church. Although it may be criticized today as too reliant on the model of the Euro-American immigration that anticipated a loss of culture and language once English was learned,[37] the Catholic Church in the 1950s recognized the challenge of the "Hispanic Presence." One of the keys to success proved to be the Cursillo, a movement imported from Spain which gave great impetus to the development of Latino leadership within the Church.[38]

The largely Mexican-American and Puerto-Rican awareness in the U.S. Church was altered by the Cuban Revolution of 1959 which brought hundreds of thousands of Cubans to the United States, mostly to South Florida.[39] Unlike the Latinos in terms of social class, education and politics, the Cuban immigration merits a study of its own.[40] There are some indications that the experiences of the Spanish-speaking apostolates to Mexican Americans and Puerto Ricans benefited the Cuban Americans who arrived in the United States after 1960. They encountered a Church already sensitized to the need for inculturation and a rapid mobilization of resources to address the material needs of the newly arriving Spanish-speakers. When coupled with the educational and social advantages that many Cubans brought in their flight from Communism, the Catholic apostolate to the Cubans became highly successful. There was a notable increase of Mass attendance among the Cuban Americans that made them more likely to practice their Catholicism in the United States than they had been while on the island.[41]

In 1964, President Lyndon B. Johnson launched the War on Poverty, which brought a massive influx of federal funds into the urban barrios. One of the key notions of this initiative was the requirement that neighborhood agencies had to be directed by members of the same "minority group" that was targeted to receive the benefits. Latinos and Latinas had many new opportunities for community involvement and employment in the civil service sector.[42] In 1965, while many neighborhood agencies were being established, the Civil Rights Act was passed and there was a drastic change in the immigration laws that allowed many more immigrants to enter the United States from Latin America. Suddenly, immigrants from Latin America multiplied the Latino urban population, made up almost entirely of native-born citizens who spoke Spanish. Thus, in addition to the increase of urban Latinos *via* internal migration from rural areas of Puerto Rico, Texas and New Mexico, there was a huge increase of immigration from Latin America. In the tenor of the times, the more the number of Latin American immigrants, the more needed were services from Latinos capable of assuming professional positions in the anti-poverty agencies. A symbiotic relationship was created between the Latinos already U.S. citizens and the immigrants from Latin America: the political clout of the former was increased by the influx of the latter.[43] The more that schools and agencies attended to the needs of the immigrants because of culturally sensitive service delivery, the more the people from Latin America were encouraged to come to the United States.[44] In this climate, the most politically active and upwardly mobile of Latinos realized that instead of assimilating as "Americans" and forgetting their Spanish, they should hold onto culture and language because their chances for employment were thus improved. This trend was reinforced with the Bilingual Education Act of 1967 that funded Spanish as a language of instruction within the public schools.

## The Latino Religious Resurgence

These important social and economic changes laid the foundation for a mobilization of Latinos across the United States that shared many parallels with the Civil Rights Movement led by the Rev. Dr. Martin Luther King Jr. The hero of the Latino militancy was César Chávez, who organized a national boycott of grapes in support of the strike by Mexican-American Farm Workers.[45] But whereas King was Protestant, Chávez was Catholic, and in a history not without contradictions, Latinos were mobilized by the militancy of Chávez, a Catholic *cursillista,* the way Black churches were mobilized by Baptist minister King.[46] The spiritual message of the Latino militants is seen in the poem, *I Am Joaquín.*[47]

The Catholic Church had undergone its own brand of radical reform with the Second Vatican Council.[48] Perhaps the most important decision affecting Latinos was the qualification of Spanish as "the language of the people" in the implementation of the conciliar decrees regarding the celebration of the liturgy. By accepting Spanish and other languages on an equal footing with English for worship within the United States, the bishops effectively made the Catholic Church a bilingual church. The council fathers restored the parity that had been lost to pious colonialism in the nineteenth century. The larger challenge, however, was for Latino Catholics to build the infrastructure of parish organizations, diocesan agencies, pastoral centers and the like to make the language decree effective in all aspects of Catholic life in the United States. This effort has been baptized as "the Latino Religious Resurgence" and has been evaluated from a socio-historical perspective.[49] The resurgence adapted the militancy of Chicano and Puerto Rican activist movements during the 1960s to needs within the church.[50] Thus, for instance, in the area of leadership, the resurgence developed an argument that reflected the secular norm that agencies serving Latinos should have Latinos as head administrators. Organizations such as *PADRES* and *Las Hermana*s articulated a vision of a Catholicism in which there would be Latino bishops in heavily Latino dioceses.[51] Parish pastors and school principals would be named according to a similar logic.

While many of the voices of Latino priests and Latina religious women were angry with the Church, they nonetheless loved the Church enough to fight for places within Catholic leadership. In this struggle, there was the affirmation of a unique Latino Catholic identity that benefited from a theological pedigree elaborated by an emerging local theology for Latinos. The convergence of militancy, commitment to the Church and a praxis based on theology is reflected in the first three Hispanic Pastoral Encounters held in 1972, 1977 and 1985. These encounters followed a careful plan that allowed for the ordinaries of each diocese to name official delegates, most of whom were chosen in democratic fashion from among the leaders of the Cursillo Movement, the permanent diaconate, pastoral formation, youth ministry and the like. Catholic educators were also included as official delegates. Over the course of several days, the participants met in workshops and developed documents carrying analysis of current issues and making policy recommendations. In the manner of a congress, the entire body voted on each report, which was then prepared by a team of theologians, pastoralists and canon lawyers for submission to the National Conference of Catholic Bishops (NCCB). In all three instances, the NCCB made a formal reply accepting certain norms, qualifying others and indicating a preferred mode of implementation. These encounters represented an extraordinary occasion for a form of democratic decision-making within the Church that awarded proportionate recognition to the episcopacy, clergy and laity as collaborating sectors of the Latino Catholic community.[52]

The encounters made recommendations on Catholic school education, although it was not the only focus for education. The policy documents encouraged a strategy to include retreats, movements, and religious instruction because these reach more Latino youth than the parochial schools. This may be called "moral education"[53] and it conveyed the message of inculturation. Thus, for instance, the militant Puerto Rican organization, the Young Lords, were very secular in New York City; but in Philadelphia, they were very close to the Catholic Church, largely because their emphasis upon Puerto Rican culture had been welcomed by Father Thomas Craven, the local priest.[54] The Church has found moral education to be a broader task than that of maintaining Catholic schools. Through retreats, youth movements such as the *Jornada,* and Young Catholic Workers, as well as parish-based religious education, the Church has provided specialized programs for Latinos and Latinas. Because many of these programs have a built-in practical application to life's special crises, they have been extremely effective in forming Catholic leaders among Latino youth.[55] However, rather than consider such approaches to be in opposition to Catholic schools, it has been suggested that such moral education supplement the formal instruction provided in classrooms.[56] In fact, without such a convergence of formal and moral education, we might face the problem of Catholic school graduates denouncing their educational experiences as efforts to strip them of their Latino identity. Two contemporary autobiographical works, *Family Installments* by Edwin Rivera and *Hunger of Memory* by Richard Rodriguez form part of a genre in which Catholic school graduates reminisce about their education in mostly negative terms.[57] Fortunately, there are more sympathetic accounts about Catholic school education.[58]

## THE RESPONSE OF THE NCEA TO THE HISPANIC PRESENCE

The poor record of public education with Latinos and Latinas even after a decade of bilingual education, made it increasingly clear that there was an important role for Catholic schools in the preparation of Latino Catholic leaders. During the last quarter of the twentieth century, there have been notable efforts within Catholic education to focus upon the special needs of Latino children. This attention accelerated with the encounters and in 1984, the NCEA published "Integral Education: A Response to the Hispanic Presence" which reflected a careful attention to the encounter documents and the many positive experiences within post-conciliar Latino Catholicism. The report wove together sociological data with the theological idea of inculturation while recognizing the cogency of the encounter documents on the importance of Catholic education opening itself to the growing numbers of Latinos and Latinas. The publication came as the fruit of a series of hearings held by the NCEA in New York, Miami, Chicago, and San Antonio and in Southern California for the church in San Diego and Los Angeles. With an introduction by Bishop Plácido Rodríguez, it reviewed the encounter resolutions (Chapter 3), recapitulated the excellence of Catholic education for Latinos in comparison with the record of public schools (Chapter 4) and proposed several models that might systematize bilingual/bicultural education within the curriculum of Catholic schools.

While "Integral Education" represented an idealistic blueprint for a parochial school system still reeling from multiple school closings and the loss of religious women as the backbone of Catholic education, there was a stiff dose of realism in the report. Fifteen years later, we now need to review how and/or if these recommendations have been implemented in each Catholic school, especially in light of the demographic explosion that has made Latinos/Hispanics the largest of "minorities" in the United States.

## LATINOS LAG ON SCHOOL ATTAINMENT

Academic and policy research has consistently reported that the overall educational status of Latinos is markedly inferior when compared to other groups.[59] Researchers unfailingly report grim findings about the educational achievements by Latinos. No matter what indicators are used; whether the percentage of adults over 25 years of age who have completed high school, dropout rates, or college entrance and college graduation rates, the results are disheartening. Marín and Marín, for instance, call attention to "the scandalously high rate of Hispanic adolescents who never finish high school (35.7 percent), a rate that is almost triple that of Whites and double that of Blacks."[60] By 1999, only 56 percent of Hispanics older than 25 were high school graduates compared to 84 percent of non-Hispanics (U.S. Census Bureau). The impact on employment opportunities is devastating. The majority of Latinos are employed in occupations such as operative, laborer, and clerical positions. In 1999, half of Hispanic households were living with less than $28,000; that is $12,000 below the U.S. median. The census of 2000 reported only 7 percent of Hispanic households reached a middle-class income level of $40,000 or more a year. In other words, despite specialized federal programs and a period of unprecedented prosperity of the Latino population is poor, an increase from 8 percent twenty years ago.

The societal consequences of lower educational attainment by Hispanics are evident if we keep in mind how they are transforming the United States' demographic landscape. About 40 percent are children under 19 years of age, compared to 28 percent for the general population. Formerly comprised of primarily Mexicans, Puerto Ricans and Cubans, today Latinos encompass persons tracing their origins to all the nationalities of Latin America. Perhaps most importantly, the census of 2000 reported a rapid influx of Hispanics in rural and small-town areas of the United States. This diaspora into heartland America from the cities and the traditional bastions of Latino culture and history in the Southwest and California means that educators are now confronted with a challenge that has become national and not merely regional. For the Catholic Church and its parochial schools, the Latino population represents an increasingly large segment of the United States' Catholic Church. In a certain measure, the future of the Church as the largest in the United States depends upon the Catholic convictions of Latinos.

## THE LATINO IN THE CATHOLIC SCHOOL

With dismal achievements in education, Latinos have joined in the rising tide of criticism of the public schools. In order to demonstrate that the generally poor performance in the public schools was not due to Latino culture or the inadequacy of the students, researchers turned to Latinos in Catholic schools for evidence that the educational system could produce better results. In fact, the enrollment of Latino children in Catholic schools has been rising since 1995. The Hispanic share of classroom seats now reaches 10 percent nationally, and 37 percent in a highly Hispanic city such as New York.[61] According to the New York State Department of Education, Hispanic participation has increased in both the public and Catholic schools of New York City. Hispanics were 13.8 percent of the Catholic school population in 1970, 29.1 percent in 1991,[62] but 37 percent in 2000.[63]

Reports on Catholic schools indicate that Hispanics benefit from attending such schools, as measured by the graduation rates they exhibit compared with

Latino children attending public schools. For instance, by 1996 the overall graduation rate from New York City Catholic high schools was 98 percent; of these, 89 percent went to college.[64]  On the other hand, only 50 percent of public high-school students graduate within the stipulated four years. Coleman and Hoffer concluded that "the greatest differences in Catholic and public school achievement are found when schools with the highest levels of minority composition are compared."[65]  For example, in schools where Latinos and African Americans are between 81 and 100 percent of the total, third-grade Catholic school children surpass their public school black and Latino counterparts in reading (10+ percent) and math (11+ percent). Fifth-graders in Catholic schools also hold an advantage in writing (6 percent). By the same token, Catholic school sixth-graders perform better than public school sixth-graders in reading (10%+) and math (11 percent).[66]

During the early 1980s, Benson and Yeager conducted a study of Catholic high schools in low income areas and found that "Hispanics appear[ed] to be particularly well-served" by such schools. From the ninth to the twelfth grades, on five of the ten outcomes they measured, the average Hispanic student appeared to gain more than the average white student. On the other five, Hispanics appeared to gain as much. They note that further research will be required to determine why Hispanics appeared to thrive in Catholic schools. Nonetheless, they reported that 16 percent of the ninth-grade sample and 12 percent of the twelfth-grade sample were Hispanic. The difference, according to them, suggested that some Hispanic students were dropping out before the twelfth grade, and cautioned that the apparent gains could be a product of the dropout phenomenon owing to the exit of struggling students[67]

A 1987 research project was conducted to probe the differences in quality regarding the schools Latinos attend. Using the "school file" from one of the most authoritative studies on education in the U.S. (i.e., Coleman's *High School and Beyond*), the researcher[68] compared 40 barrio schools (where Hispanics are 50 percent or more) and 198 white schools (where over 98 percent of the student body is white). Among some of her findings, which she projected to 171 barrio schools and 6,251 white schools in the U.S. public school sample, are: The two types of schools are similar in several areas, including spending per pupil, teacher salaries, physical equipment, and curriculum. The major differences appear in the areas of student discipline, including absenteeism and cutting classes (reported by 82 percent of barrio school administrators as a serious or moderate problem); student-teacher ratios (17:1 for barrio schools versus 14:1 for white schools); academic credentials of teachers (less likelihood for barrio school teachers to hold either an MA or a Ph.D. degree); teacher absenteeism and lack of motivation (only 10 percent of barrio school administrators reported no absenteeism problem compared to 36 percent of white school administrators). Notably also, 31 percent of barrio school administrators report "serious lack of parental interest" as compared to only seven percent of white-school administrators. So she concludes that, "the above figures point to the fact that students in the barrio schools are placed in larger classes and receive lower quality teaching than white-school students," even within the same school districts.[69] When Hispanic parents express their views, they give evidence of knowing not only about the circumstances constraining their choices, but also about conditions affecting urban schools, or particularly the schools in their neighborhoods. They also elaborate sophisticated arguments for choosing one particular type of school over another, not limiting themselves, for instance, to economic or religious factors. The anxiety over safety, standards, morality in the curriculum and the norms for student discipline have fostered a bit of a renaissance in Catholic education. Parochial school closings, though still high, have been leveling off.[70]

Research consistently finds that religiously-based schools, which make up about 80 percent of nonpublic schools, on the average educate the pupils in their charge better than public schools.[71] The New York State 1993 Blue Ribbon Panel on Catholic Schools states that "Catholic schools are effective learning environments. Their effectiveness is evident through analysis of standardized examination results, minimal dropout rate, and high college attendance rate. The success of Catholic schools is most dramatic in the education of students with at-risk characteristics."[72]

But even in religious schools, where Hispanics perform relatively well, they lag behind when compared with other groups, including blacks. In their study, Benson, Yeager and Guerra found that, "Catholic schools appear to retain white students with greater success than minority students. Fifty-nine percent of ninth graders are minority, falling to 52 percent in twelfth grade—with the greatest attrition occurring among Hispanics (16 percent in ninth, 12 percent in twelfth)."[73] Probably it is not only the quality of the school that makes a difference in whether Hispanic students can finish school successfully, but also the general conditions affecting their performance, such as their parents' socioeconomic status and involvement.

School authorities and commentators have been reported to accuse Hispanic parents of negligence concerning aspects of their children's schooling, such as their avoidance of interaction with schools.[74] Nevertheless, other research on Hispanics, especially one that is broad in its considerations of relevant variables, indicates that Hispanic parents face considerable obstacles in matching the response from higher-income Catholic-school parents. From this perspective, Hispanic parents exhibit a remarkable participation in the education of their children, in spite of the odds. For instance, the 1992 Latino National Political

Survey (LNPS) found that compared with any other government or public agency, schools are the institutions with which Latinos interact. According to the LNPS, "more than half of Mexican and Puerto Rican and 40 percent of Cuban respondents engaged in school-related activities. The most often mentioned activities were meeting with a teacher and attending PTA meetings. The least-frequently mentioned activity was attending a school board meeting."[75] Be that as it may with Hispanics in the public system, Latinos with children in Catholic schools generally envision a collaborative relationship with the schools their children attend. It is true that some have stories of close relationships with schools, whereas others report less warm ones. Nevertheless, most prefer to give schools the benefit of the doubt and are willing to share the responsibility in the educational enterprise. Parents' concern for their children's schooling and education is manifested in different degrees through initiatives as diverse as setting time apart for regular family dialogue, teaching children to use time efficiently, reading aloud to them and hiring tutors to supplement parents' efforts when they are short of ability or time.

## SYNERGY BETWEEN CATHOLIC SCHOOLS AND FAMILIES

Indeed, parental involvement becomes a major issue in contrasting Hispanics' performance in religious schools versus public schools. Nationwide studies and surveys conducted over the past 30 years have focused on the doctrinal and organizational factors contributing to make religiously-based schools effective educational organizations.[76] Although they have hinted at the importance of the family, their treatment of it has been peripheral. Convey, for example, citing Neuwien's pioneer study of 9,451 elementary and 2,075 secondary Catholic schools says that, "the vast majority (91 percent) of the [Catholic school] students rated their parents' interest in school as at least average, with 34 percent rating parents' interest as extremely strong." The influence of family was judged "most important" even in the area of religious development by 48.3 percent of students. The figure compares favorably with the 22.3 percent who said their school's religious instruction was "most important."[77] For his part, Andrew Greeley's, *Catholic High Schools and Minority Students* —one of the few studies involving Latinos— used a random sample of 14,000 students, 7,000 from Catholic schools and 7,000 from public schools, and found that 77 percent of blacks and 70 percent of Hispanics in Catholic schools said their parents expected them to graduate from college. Only slightly more than 40 percent of the public school students said the same.[78]

Researchers and practitioners insist that parental involvement weighs heavily among the variables that explain the positive results attained by students in Catholic schools. The ability to elicit or coax such involvement is one of Catholic teachers' and administrators' virtues. There is no consensus, though, as to what really motivates, influences, and informs parental behavior concerning, first, the selection of school and enrollment and, second, the follow-up and investment of considerable time and energy to assure their children's success. Latino parents exhibit awareness that a good education involves more than schooling. But Roman Catholics are little inclined to associate their concept of a good education with a religious inspiration. Though, when probed, all parents agree on the need to cultivate the moral dimension in their children.

In a recent study, Pantoja found that most Catholic parents respond to the question about what their definition of a good education is by going directly to its secular dimension.[79] The typical definition emphasizes exposing children to good schools so that they learn the basics well. From there, children who receive a good education are the ones who acquire ever more advanced and modern knowledge; later they must meet the test of being able to apply in real life their accumulated knowledge. Whether they refer to basic skills or to academic degrees, parents show awareness of the need to help their children to face the challenges of living in a modern society, such as the United States. Nonetheless, there are subtle differences among Catholics. These differences stem from the saliency that religion plays in some more than others.

It is possible to find interspersed in the literature adduced reasons for parents' preferences for parochial schools. Greeley, for instance, reports that "superior discipline in Catholic schools often comes up in conversations with black parents in inner cities as one of the reasons why they choose to send their children to Catholic schools even though they are not Catholics themselves."[80] Such assertions are corroborated in New York and other places where there exist schools whose students are up to 90 percent non-Catholic. It seems reasonable to suppose that such factors as discipline and safety also rank high among Latinos' priorities. There is evidence that excellence in academics is not the only goal parochial schools pursue. Or as principal Pat Kelly of Saint Angela Merici school in the South Bronx puts it, "We are here to educate and empower these kids, to do two things with them.[...] One is to make sure that they learn how to read, write and do math—every day. The other is to form their character. We believe in the divinity of being; we believe in the holiness of our existence. That infuses the culture we are in."[81] Researchers have found that the factors determining superior results in parochial schools are not restricted to such variables as socio-economic status or level of parental education;[82] much less are they solely dependent on per-pupil expenditures, location of schools, or staff salaries.

## CULTURAL EFFECTS OF CATHOLIC SCHOOLS ON LATINO CHILDREN

The "Americanization" of the progeny of waves of European immigrants is part and parcel of the historical experience of public and Catholic schools. We must now assess how schools are functioning regarding the socialization of Hispanic immigrants' children. In connection with this, we may also ask: Do Catholic schools contribute to Hispanic cultural preservation or even to a heightened sense of ethnic identity? Or on the contrary, do they weaken attachment to the students' particular ethnic culture? What are the mechanisms through which such results are effected? How do these cultural goals match the evangelizing concerns of inculturation?

Catholic school influence on Latino children is through instruction in English. Bilingual programs as defined by statute do not exist. But, even though the Spanish language is not utilized in most instruction, the faculty and staff of Catholic schools now include a growing number of Hispanics.[83] We might presume such teachers to be more sensitive than those who don't share their background—especially when compared with previous decades—to children whose primary language may be Spanish. Nowadays, teachers may "code-switch" when necessary, that is, move back and forth between languages in order to explain a task or a concept. Most children, however, start school already fluent in English. Moreover, even in classrooms where Hispanic children predominate, their preference for English is obvious; whether they are in the teacher's presence, the cafeteria or the schoolyard.[84] Thus, the lack of instruction in the Spanish language need not be interpreted as a lack of sensitivity to Latino culture and values.

Religious instruction is also imparted in the parochial school classroom. In so far as children interpret what they hear and read in class through the prism of their home teachings, their Catholicism is going to be colored by their traditions. All Catholic parents are encouraged to take their children to Mass on Sunday, but among Latinos, this implies attendance at the Spanish Mass. In this case as in others, compliance with a general norm reinforces a specific identity as Latinos. We should consider the teaching of prayers, the cultivation of devotional life and the formation of Catholic school children with a sense of liturgy as vital areas where Latino culture can be fostered with the aim of inculturation.

## CONCLUSIONS

In drawing conclusions from this socio-historical analysis of the Latino presence and the current challenges to Catholic school education, it seems the recommendations of the 1984 report, "Integral Education," are a departure point.

The call in that document that came from the NCEA for programs in cultural methodology, personal support that is culturally sensitive, and for language assistance where needed should be reiterated. But now that we are in the twenty-first century, circumstances require more attention to administrative policies along these lines. The recruitment and preparation of more Latinos as Catholic school teachers is a high priority in the effort to create a learning environment for more Hispanic students.

Clearly, the members of the NCEA are better qualified than social-science academics to design the implementation of such policies. But, as detailed in a recent presentation on the theme of Latino Catholic history, non-educational scholars can assist in outlining a specifically Latino Catholic content to the curriculum.[85] Unlike the European immigrants, who used Catholic schools to leave behind the old country and assimilate to the United States culture, Latinos have a heritage that was American and Catholic before the Declaration of Independence in 1776. Our Catholic schools need a curriculum of church history that revisits the pre-invasion past of native Catholicism.[86] Those achievements need to be better pictured as the enduring foundation of an inculturating faith so that Latinos/Hispanics accurately see themselves as partners in the shaping of Catholicism in the United States and not merely the beneficiaries of benevolence from Euro-American charity.

Latinos bring to contemporary U.S. Catholicism a different outlook on race. Eloquently explained in theological terms by the nationally recognized San Antonio priest, Virgilio Elizondo, these ideas also have pastoral and liturgical applications.[87] It would seem that Catholic schools should incorporate Latino customs such as reenactments of the life of Christ in morality plays.[88] The tradition of shrines, common throughout Catholicism although disparaged in some quarters, has a special importance to Latinos as a touchstone of identity.[89] The direction for Catholic education should be multiculturalism, seeking to present Latino experiences as integral parts of Catholicism in the United States. There are dangers in multiculturalism of course, but with a clearer notion about the ways in which religion and cultural expression relate to identity and politics the task is not an impossible one to persons who understand the pulse of the community.[90] Most importantly, the demographic increase of Latinos makes them an indispensable part of a future that needs to rethink its basic approaches to Latinos who are "no longer a minority."[91] The Hispanic Pastoral Encounter, held in Los Angeles in the Summer of 2000, shared the Latino experiences of how culture can animate the apostolate to a pastoral audience that included all the nationalities within the Church. These efforts should be added to the specialized approach to Latino educational needs as for instance in the Jesuit-run high schools for Latinos, such as Cristo Rey in Chicago.

We believe that the same processes can be injected into Catholic education nationwide. We would not presume that such curriculum revision has not already taken place in many local settings, both formally and informally. But it does seem to us that there is a need for a generally adopted text on United States church history, written for elementary and high school students, that elaborates this message. In revising current approaches to the transmission of the Catholic legacy, we will discover a new set of heroes and create a gallery of role models that reinforce the message that one can be Latino and Catholic without prejudice to either identity. Such an effort ought not to replace the Euro-American narrative of the immigrant-made-mainstream with the saga of Latino survival and resurgence. Rather, the integration of these two different journeys needs to be offered as the complete story of Catholicism in the United States.

## ENDNOTES

[1] Anthony M. Stevens-Arroyo and Ana María Díaz-Stevens, "Religious Faith and Institutions in the Forging of Latino Identities," in *Handbook for Hispanic Cultures in the United States,* ed. Felix Padilla (Houston: Arte Publico Press, 1993), 257–91.

[2] See Robert J. Yeager, Peter L. Benson, Michael J. Guerra, and Bruno V. Manno, *The Catholic High School: A National Portrait* (Washington, D.C.: National Catholic Educational Association, 1985).

[3] Diego Irarrával, *Inculturation: New Dawn of the Church in Latin America,* trans. Philip Berryman (Maryknoll: Orbis Books, 2000); originally published as *Inculturación: amanecer eclesial en América Latina* (Lima, Peru: Centro de Estudios y Publicaciones [CEP], 1998); and Suzanne Hall, SNDdeN, and Carleen Reck, SSND, eds., *Integral Education: A Response to the Hispanic Presence* (Washington, D.C.: National Catholic Educational Association, 1987).

[4] See Ruth Doyle, Olga Scarpetta, Thomas M. McDonald, and Norman Simmons, *Hispanics in New York: Religious, Cultural and Social Experiences,* 2 vols. (New York: Office of Pastoral Research, Roman Catholic Archdiocese of New York, 1982); and Ruth Doyle, John Kuzloski, Thomas M. McDonald, and Olga Scarpetta, *Church Related Hispanic Youth in New York: An Exploratory Study* (New York: Office of Pastoral Research, Archdiocese of New York, 1983).

[5] Juan González, *Harvest of Empire: A History of Latinos in America* (New York: Viking, 2000); Ana María Díaz-Stevens and Anthony M. Stevens-Arroyo, *Recognizing the Latino Resurgence in U.S. Religion: The Emmaus Paradigm* (Boulder, Co.: Westview Press, 1998).

[6] Joseph Burkholder Smith, *The Plot to Steal Florida: James Madison's Phony War* (New York: Arbor House, 1983).

[7] Rodolfo Acuña, *Occupied America* (San Francisco: Canfield Press, 1972); Jay P. Dolan and Gilberto M. Hinojosa, eds., *Mexican Americans and the Catholic Church, 1900–1965,* Hispanic Catholics in the United States, vol. 1 (Notre Dame, Ind.: University

[8] of Notre Dame Press, 1994).

Jay P. Dolan and Jaime R. Vidal, eds., *Puerto Rican and Cuban Catholics in the U.S., 1900–1965*, Hispanic Catholics in the United States, vol. 2 (Notre Dame, Ind.: University of Notre Dame Press, 1994).

[9] David F. Gómez, *Somos Chicanos: Strangers in Our Own Land* (Boston: Beacon Press, 1973).

[10] Sarah Deutsch, *No Separate Refuge: Culture, Class and Gender on an Anglo-Hispanic Frontier in the American Southwest, 1880–1940* (New York: Oxford University Press, 1987), 20n29.

[11] Díaz-Stevens and Stevens-Arroyo, *Recognizing the Latino Resurgence.*

[12] Acuña, *Occupied America.*

[13] Díaz-Stevens and Steven-Arroyo, *Recognizing the Latino Experience.*

[14] Claudio F. Benedi, "Visión Reformista de Félix Varela" *Americas* 29, no. 4 (April 1977): 9–12.

[15] Anthony M. Stevens-Arroyo, "The Latino Religious Resurgence," *Annals of the American Academy of Political and Social Science* 558 (July 1998): 163–77.

[16] See David Abalos, *Latinos in the United States: The Sacred and the Political* (Notre Dame, Ind.: University of Notre Dame Press, 1986); Gilbert R. Cadena, "Religious Ethnic Identity: A Socio-Religious Protrait of Latinos and Latinas in the Catholic Church," in *Old Masks, New Faces: Religion and Latino Identities,* ed. Anthony M. Stevens-Arroyo and Gilbert R. Cadena (New York: Bildner Center Books, 1995), 33–60; Ana María Díaz-Stevens, *Oxcart Catholicism on Fifth Avenue* (Notre Dame, Ind.: University of Notre Dame Press, 1993).

[17] Jay P. Dolan and Gilberto M. Hinojosa, eds., *Mexican Americans and the Catholic Church, 1900–1965*, Hispanic Catholics in the United States, vol. 1 (Notre Dame, Ind: University of Notre Dame Press, 1994); Jay P. Dolan and Jaime R. Vidal, eds., *Puerto Rican and Cuban Catholics in the U.S., 1900–1965*, Hispanic Catholics in the United States, vol. 2 (Notre Dame, Ind.: University of Notre Dame Press, 1994). Jay P. Dolan and Allan Figueroa Deck, S.J., eds., *Hispanic Catholic Culture in the U.S.: Issues and Concerns*, Hispanic Catholics in the United States, vol. 3 (Notre Dame, Ind.: University of Notre Dame Press, 1994).

[18] Moises Sandoval, ed., *Fronteras: A History of the Latin American Church in the USA Since 1513,* General History of the Church in Latin America, Commission on Studies for Church History in Latin America (CEHILA), vol. 10 (San Antonio, Tex.: Mexican American Cultural Center, 1983).

[19] Alberto López Pulido, "Searching for the Sacred: Conflict and Struggle for Mexican Catholics in the Roman Catholic Diocese of San Diego, 1936–1941," *Latino Studies Journal* 5, no. 3 (September 1994): 37–59; see also Otto A. Maduro, *Religion and Social Conflicts* (Maryknoll: Orbis Books, 1982).

[20] Juan Romero, with Moises Sandoval, *Reluctant Dawn* (San Antonio, Tex.: Mexican American Cultural Center, 1976).

[21] Alvin R Sunseri, *Seeds of Discord: New Mexico in the Aftermath of the American Conquest, 1846–1861* (Chicago: Nelson Hall, 1979).

[22] Dolan and Vidal, *Puerto Rican and Cuban Catholics.*

[23] Jay P. Dolan, *The American Catholic Experience* (Notre Dame, Ind.: University of Notre Dame Press, 1992).

[24] Allan Figueroa Deck, S.J., *The Second Wave* (Mahwah, N.J.: Paulist Press, 1989),

25    63–65; see also Dolan and Deck, *Hispanic Catholic Culture in the U.S.*

Charles J. Beirne, S.J., *The Problem of Americanization in the Catholic Schools of Puerto Rico* (Río Piedras: Editorial Universitaria de la Universidad de Puerto Rico, 1975).

26

Richard Griswold del Castillo, *The Los Angeles Barrio, 1850–1890: A Social History* (Berkeley: University of California Press, 1979).

27

David C. Bailey, *Viva Cristo Rey!* (Austin, Tex.: University of Texas Press, 1974); Jean Meyer, *La Cristiada,* 3 vols. (Mexico, D.F.: Siglo Veintiuno Editores, 1973).

28

Deck, *Second Wave,* 64–65n38.

29

Anthony M. Stevens-Arroyo, "Catholic Ethos as Politics: the Puerto Rican Nationalists," in *Twentieth Century World Religiou Movements in Neo-Weberian Perspective,* ed. William Swatos (Lewiston, N.Y.: Edwin Mellen Press, 1992), 175–93; Anthony M. Stevens-Arroyo, "Jaime Balmes Redux: Catholicism as Civilization in the Political Philosophy of Pedro Albizu Campos," in *Bridging the Atlantic: Iberian and Latin American Thought in Historical Perspective*, ed. Marina Pérez de Mendiola (Albany, N.Y.: SUNY Press, 1996), 129–51.

30

Stephen A. Privett, S.J., *The United States Catholic Church and Its Hispanic Members: The Pastoral Vision of Archbishop Robert E. Lucey* (San Antonio, Tex.: Trinity University Press, 1988).

31

Félix D. Almaráz, Jr., *Knight without Armor: Carlos Eduardo Castañeda, 1896–1958* (College Station, Tex.: Texas A&M University Press, 1999).

32

Mario T. García, *Mexican Americans: Leadership, Ideology and Identity, 1930–1960* (New Haven, Conn.: Yale University Press, 1989).

33

Virginia E. Sánchez-Korrol, *From Colonia to Community: The History of Puerto Ricans in New York City, 1917–1948* (Westport, Conn.: Greenwood Press, 1983).

34

Sunseri, *Seeds of Discord.*

35

Gómez, *Somos Chicanos;* cf. Phillip Gleason, *Keeping the Faith: American Catholicism, Past and Present* (Notre Dame, Ind.: University of Notre Dame Press, 1987).

36

See William M. Halsey, *The Survival of American Innocence: Catholics in an Era of Disillusionment, 1920–1940* (Notre Dame, Ind.:University of Notre Dame Press, 1980).

37

Deck, *Second Wave;* Díaz-Stevens, *Oxcart Catholicism.*

38

Moises Sandoval, *On the Move* (Maryknoll, N.Y.: Orbis Books, 1990); Díaz-Stevens and Stevens-Arroyo, *Recognizing the Latino Resrugence.*

39

Dolan and Vidal, *Puerto Rican and Cuban Catholics in the U.S.*

40

Yolanda Prieto, "Continuity or Change? Two Generations of Cuban American Women," *New Jersey History* 113, no. 1–2 (1995): 47–60.

41

See Dolan and Deck.

42

Felix Padilla, *Latino Ethnic Consciousness: The Case of Mexican Americans and Puerto Ricans in Chicago* (Notre Dame, Ind.: University of Notre Dame Press, 1985).

43

See Helen Rose Ebaugh and Janet Chafetz, eds., *Religion and the New Immigrants* (Walnut Creek, Calif.: Altamira Press, 2000).

44

Díaz-Stevens and Stevens-Arroyo, *Recognizing the Latino Resurgence.*

45

Acuña, *Occupied America.*

46

Díaz-Stevens and Stevens-Arroyo, *Recognizing the Latino Resurgence.*

47

Rudolfo González, "Corky," in *I Am Joaquín* (New York: Bantam Books, 1972). (Copyright of poem, 1967; reproduced with permission in Antonio M. Stevens-Arroyo, *Prophets Denied Honor* [Maryknoll, N.Y.: Orbis, 1980], 15–20).

48    See Dolan, *American Catholic Experience.*

49    Stevens-Arroyo, "Latino Religious Resurgence"; Díaz-Stevens and Stevens-Arroyo, *Recognizing the Latino Resurgence.*

50    Anthony M. Stevens-Arroyo, *Prophets Denied Honor* (Maryknoll, N.Y.: Orbis Books, 1980).

51    See Gilbert R. Cadena, "Chicano Clergy and the Emergence of Liberation Theology," *Hispanic Journal of Behavioral Sciences* 11 (May 1989): 2:107–21.; and Lara Medina, "Las Hermanas: Chicana/Latina Religious-Political Activism, 1971–1997" (Ph. D. Diss., Claremont Graduate University, 1998).

52    Díaz-Stevens and Stevens-Arroyo, *Recognizing the Latino Resurgence.*

53    Anthony M. Stevens-Arroyo and Ana María Díaz-Stevens, "Latino Church and Schools as Urban Battlegrounds" in *Urban Schooling in America*, ed. Stanley Rothstein (Westport, Conn.: Greenwood Press, 1993), 245–70.

54    Carmen Theresa Whalen, "Bridging Homeland and Barrio Politics: The Young Lords in Philadelphia," in *The Puerto Rican Movement: Voices from the Diaspora,* ed. Andrés Torres and José E. Velzquez (Philadelphia, Penn.: Temple University Press, 1998), 107–23; see also Anneris Goris, "Rites for a Rising Nationalism: Religious Meanaing and Dominican Community Identity in New York City," in *Old Masks, New Faces: Religion and Latino Identities*, ed. Anthony M. Stevens-Arroyo and Gilbert R. Cadena (New York: Bildner Center Books, 1995), 117–42.

55    Ana María Díaz-Stevens, "Latino Youth and the Church," in *Hispanic Catholic Culture in the U.S.: Issues and Concerns,* ed. Jay Dolan and Allan Figueroa Deck (Notre Dame, Ind.: University of Notre Dame Press, 1994), 278–307.

56    Mary Johnson, SND de N., "The Reweaving of Catholic Spiritual and Institutional Life," *The Annals of the American Academy of Political and Social Science* 558 (July 1998): 135–43; see also Vytautus Kavolis, "Contemporary Moral Cultures and the 'Return of the Sacred,'" *Sociological Analysis* 49, no. 3 (fall 1988): 203–16.

57    Edward Rivera, *Family Installments: Memories of Growing Up Hispanic* (New York: William Morrow & Company, 1982); Richard Rodriguez, *Hunger of Memory: The Education of Richard Rodriguez* (Boston: David R. Godine, 1982).

58    Judith Ortíz Cofer, *Silent Dancing: A Partial Remembrance of a Puerto Rican Childhood* (Houston, Tex.: Arte Público Press, 1990).

59    Lori Orum, *The Education of Hispanics: Status and Implications* (Washington, D.C., National Council of La Raza, 1986); Patria Marín, "Factors Contributing to High School Graduation among Hispanics" (Ph.D. diss., Yeshiva University, New York, 1989); Johnny Ramírez, "Religion, Education, and Success in the Leominster, MA., Puerto Rican Seventh-Day Adventist Church Community" (Doctor of Education Thesis, Harvard University, 1993).

60    Gerardo Marín and Barbara VanOss Marín, *Research with Hispanic Populations*, Applied Social Research Methods Series, vol. 23 (Newbury Park, Calif.: Sage Publications, 1990), vii.

61    Minorities are 64 percent of New York City's Catholic schools. 36 percent are Hispanic, 23 percent are African-American and 5 percent are Asian *Catholic New York,* (August 15 1996): 20.

62    Hugh Carey and Seymour P. Lachman, *Blue Ribbon Panel on Catholic Schools* (New York: New York State Department of Education, 1993*), 33.

63    "Growth Continues: Catholic Schools Start Third Century in New York Sept. 6 with

64   Higher Enrollment," *Catholic New York, (*17 August 2000): 19.

65   *Catholic New York,* 1996, p. 20

Based on data from the High School and Beyond study, Coleman and Hoffer compared the achievement growth of students from different racial-ethnic backgrounds between the sophomore and the senior year. They found that "the achievement benefits of Catholic school are considerably greater for black and Hispanic students than for non-Hispanic whites." For example, the Catholic advantage for black and Hispanic students is more than double the item increment for whites in verbal achievement (James S. Coleman and Thomas Hoffer, *Public and Private Schools: The Impact of Communities* [New York: Basic Books, Inc, 1987], 122).

66   New York State Education Department 1993:12. CK-No info in reference list on this.

67   Peter L. Benson, Robert J. Yeager, and Michael J. Guerra, *Catholic High Schools: Their Impact on Low-Income Students* (Washington, D.C.: National Catholic Educational Association, 1986), 162. Coleman and Hoffer also found that high school dropout rates are lower in Catholic and other private schools than in public schools for blacks, Hispanics and non-Hispanic whites. However, "the absolute size of the Catholic sector reduction, relative to public schools, is least for Hispanics and greatest for blacks." (Coleman and Hoffer, *Public and Private Schools,* 127). In addition, they found that "socioeconomic status is strongly related to dropping out in the public and private schools[...] Catholic school students in the lowest socioeconomic quartile are over four times as likely to drop out than those in the next lowest quartile" (127). On the other hand, the Catholic sector benefits are especially great for students from families with deficiencies, whether functional or structural. "The relation of dropout to deficient families is small or absent in Catholic schools [...] In contrast, the public sector and the other private sector show  strong relationships of dropout to family deficiencies" (129).

68   A. Y. So, "The Educational Aspirations of Hispanic Parents," *Educational Research Quarterly* 11 (1987): 47–53.

69   Ibid., 15.

70   For instance, during 1995-96 school year, 50 Catholic schools closed nationwide ("Catholic School Enrollment up for Fourth Year," *Brooklyn Tablet,* 20 April 1996, 10). Nevertheless, schools are being built and expanded in the south east and south west, areas of rapid demographic growth. On the other hand, there is indication that demand for Catholic education is on the rise. For instance, enrollment has been steadily increasing during the 1990s in the Archdiocese of New York. The number of students stood at 107,980 in 1996, and it rose to 113,450 in 2000. The national figure for the decade hovered around 2.6 million  ("Growth Continues," 19).

71   John J. Convey, *Catholic Schools Make a Difference: Twenty-Five Years of Research* (Washington, D.C.: National Catholic Educational Association, 1992).

72   Hugh L. Carey and Seymour P. Lachman, *Blue Ribbon Panel on Catholic Schools,* 5.

73   Benson and Yeager, *Catholic High Schools,* 68.

74   The 1980 and 1982 High School and Beyond principals' surveys found that "Principals of almost 20 percent of the Catholic school students believe that parental lack of interest in school matters is a problem, but even this relatively high rate is still less than half of the corresponding public school rate." (Coleman and Hoffer, *Public and Private Schools,* 53).

75 Rodolfo De La Garza et al., *Latino Voices: Mexican, Puerto Rican, and Cuban Perspectives on American Politics* (Boulder, Colo.: Westview Press, 1992), 117.

76 R. Neuwien, ed., *Catholic Schools in Action* (Notre Dame, Ind.: University of Notre Dame Press, 1966); Andrew Greeley, *Catholic High Schools and Minority Students* (New Brunswick, N.J.: Transaction Books, 1982); Benson and Yeager, *Catholic High Schools;* Anthony S. Bryk, Valerie E. Lee, and Peter B. Holland, *Catholic Schools and the Common Good* (Cambridge, Mass.: Harvard University Press, 1993).

77 Convey, *Catholic Schools Make a Difference,* 12.

78 Greeley, *Catholic High Schools and Minority Students,* 21.

79 Segundo Pantoja, "Religion and Parental Involvement in the Education of Hispanics" (Ph.D. diss., City University of New York, 1998).

80 Greeley, *Catholic High Schools and Minority Students,* 29.

81 Stern 1996, p. 93-94. CK: not listed in reference list.

82 In Pantoja's study, Catholics concur in rating the cost of religious schools as the number one reason for not sending their children to one of those schools ("Religion and Parental Involvement"). On the other hand, those parents who have chosen to use the services of a Catholic school are aware that such tuition is a significant amount in their budgets, but they generally reject the idea of calling this expense a "sacrifice." Rather, some parents see it as an investment, and others prefer to treat it as a fixed cost, comparable to the apartment rent or the cost of utilities. Similarly, in a recent national survey of Catholic school teachers, 64 percent agreed that "where Catholic schools are available, tuition is the main reason parents do not choose Catholic schools for their children" (National Catholic Education Association, *The People Who Work There: The Report of the Catholic Elementary School Teacher Survey* [Washington, D.C.: NCEA, 1995], 72).

83 "Most catholic school teachers who belong to a racial or ethnic minority population are Hispanic [...] In 1986, for example, Hispanics comprised approximately 3.4 percent of all teachers and 52 percent of all minority teachers in Catholic schools. [...] The probability of a typical teacher being Hispanic is about the same in Catholic schools as in public schools. [...] Finally, evidence from the Catholic High School: A National Portrait indicates that the percentage of minority teachers is directly related to, but considerably less than, the percentage of minority students in the school" (Convey, *Catholic Schools Make a Difference,* 115).

84 Alejandro Portes and Richard Schauffler, "Language Acquisition and Loss among Children of Immigrants," in *Origins and Destinies: Immigration, Race and Ethnicity in America,* ed. S. Pedraza and R. Rumbaut (Belmont, Calif.: Wadsworth Publishing Company, 1996), 432–43.

85 Anthony M. Stevens-Arroyo, "Discovering the Intellectual Components of Latino Catholicism" (Thirteenth Annual Bishop J. Flanagan Lecture, College of the Holy Cross, Worcester, Mass., 8 February 2001).

86 Ibid.

87 Virgil Elizondo, *The Future is Mestizo* (New York: Crossroad Publishing Company, 1992); see also Virgil Elizondo and Timothy Matovina, *San Fernando Cathedral: Soul of the City* (Maryknoll, N.Y.: Orbis Books, 1998).

88 Richard R. Flores, *Los Pastores: History and Performance in the Mexican Shepherd's Play of South Texas* (Washington, D.C.: Smithsonian Institution Press, 1995).

89 See Thomas A. Tweed, *Our Lady of the Exile: Diasporic Religion at a Cuban Catholic*

90  *Shrine in Miami*  (New York: Oxford University Press, 1997).
See Allan Figueroa Deck, S.J., "The Crisis of Hispanic Ministry: Multiculturalism as an Ideology," *America* 163, no. 2 (14–21 July 1990): 33–36; Rhys H. Williams, "Religion as Political Resource: Culture or Ideology?" *Journal for the Scientific Study of Religion* 35, no. 4 (December 1996): 368–78; and Anneris Goris, "Rites for a Rising Nationalism," 117–42.

91  David Hayes Bautista, *No Longer a Minority: Latinos and Social Policy in California* (Los Angeles: Chicano Studies Research Center, UCLA, 1992); see also William D'Antonio, James Davidson, Dean Hoge, and Ruth Wallace, *Laity American and Catholic: Transforming the Church* (Kansas City, Mo.: Sheed and Ward, 1996).

## CHAPTER 14

# 'NEVER TAKE SHAME IN YOUR MOTHER TONGUE…AND YOUR FATHERLAND IN AMERICA:' CATHOLIC SCHOOLS AND IMMIGRANTS

*Timothy J. Meagher*

In a recent article about contemporary immigration in the *New York Review of Books*, the noted sociologist, Christopher Jencks, invoked, as almost all such discussions of recent migrations do, past immigrants. More specifically, Jencks argued that the "assimilation [of immigrants at turn of the twentieth century]… proceeded quickly" because "urban schools were among the best in the nation …. big cities established free secondary schools well before most rural districts did [and]…attracted better educated teachers… ." Explicit in Jencks' contention was an assumption that immigrants at the turn of the century, largely from Poland, Italy, Russia, the Baltic States, the Balkans and Greece, assimilated quickly. Implicit was an assumption that not just education, but public education ("big cities established free secondary schools…") was a cause of this rapid assimilation, one of many, perhaps, but an important one. [1]

Yet as Jencks, one of the best known experts in America on the impact of schools on racial and ethnic inequality, well knows, and others might remind him if he forgot, hundreds of thousands, indeed, millions of immigrant children did not attend public schools. In 1910, the Senate's Immigration Commission found that parochial students made up almost 15% of all students in twenty four selected cities that included, Baltimore, Boston, Detroit, Los Angeles, New York, Philadelphia, and San Francisco. Jencks might well be forgiven, however, for in today's sometimes heated debates about contemporary immigrants and their success or failure in assimilating into American culture, invocations of the past roles of public schools are frequent, but references to parochial education are few. In large part, this springs from what Leslie Tentler has called "the continued marginality of American Catholic history" in the scholarly study of American history. [2]

Did parochial schools, like the public schools as Jencks contends, effect immigrant children's easy and rapid assimilation? Were they established to encourage the melting away of ethnic differences into an American mainstream, or did they have a different vision? Whatever their initial intention may have been, what were their concrete effects on immigrant children? Did they preserve home-land languages, customs or did they hasten the embrace of American culture?[3]

For most Americans in the nineteenth and twentieth centuries, the public school was, as Paula Fass states, "the great institution of assimilation. This was one of its primary purposes." Most school systems represented at best a broad, non-ethnic, non-religious consensus on what children should learn to become American; at worst, they represented only native stock, Protestant Americans and their old immigrant religious allies, intent on stripping immigrant children of inferior cultures and inculcating them with American values. Friend and foe alike, understood the public school as an agent of Americanization, benign or harsh, offered or imposed. Founders of the public school tradition were from the beginning, suspicious of infection of the schools by teachers of the wrong religion, stiffly resistant to sharing the public purse with Catholic schools. By the late nineteenth century, the public school had become a kind of totem for assimilationists so much so that American-Protective-Association nativists hauled a mock-up of the archetypal public school, the "Little Red Schoolhouse" through the streets of East Boston in a July 4th parade in1895, provoking a riot in that immigrant neighborhood that left one dead and four wounded. Faith in public education's essential role in Americanization and, conversely, the parochial school's dangerous foreignism, probably climaxed in the 1920s when the state of Oregon required all its children to attend them (effectively eliminating Catholic and other private schools). Advocates of the law argued: "That we recognize and proclaim our belief in the free and compulsory education of the children of our nation in public primary schools supported by public taxation, upon which all children shall attend and be instructed in the English language only without regard to race or creed as the only sure foundation for the perpetuation and preservation of our free institutions … ." [4]

Some public schools in the nineteenth and twentieth centuries might have been attentive or, at least, sensitive to ethnic cultures in towns or regions where such ethnic groups dominated. The local control of schools in the United States permitted such sensitivity in cities like Cincinnati with large German populations or even in Irish or other ethnic-dominated neighborhoods in New York when that city permitted ward-based committees extensive control of local schools. A predominance of teachers from a particular ethnic group like the Irish in Massachusetts could also assure public school respect for ethnic cultures. Such local control may have had even more effect on shaping curricula and the teaching corps in rural areas, where immigrants from a single foreign country or even a specific region or province within that country might dominate. As Jon Gjerde and others have documented such settlements of Germans, Swedes, Norwegians or other groups were common the late nineteenth century. [5]

In the end, however, there was little room within the public-school system for significant ethnic variation among schools. Usually teaching staffs lagged a generation behind their students in the ever shifting sources of immigrant waves. In many eastern cities, for example, native stock, or second-generation Irish or German teachers taught Jews, Italians and Poles, whose children, in turn, taught Puerto Ricans, Mexicans and Vietnamese. Over time, through the first half of the twentieth century, too, centralization of administration and standards at city or state levels allowed less and less deviation to meet the desires or needs of ethnically diverse residents for their neighborhood or local schools.

Catholic schools were, or could be, different. Parishes were often formed by laymen or priests and then only confirmed or denied by dioceses. Even when bishops or priests acting in their bishops' behalf played a role in creating parishes, they were still dependent on the congregations' finances. This is not to say that American bishops freely assented to the wishes of those congregations to perpetuate old-world cultures. Bitter conflicts between Americanizing bishops, largely Irish-born or of Irish descent, and lay or clerical immigrants of various nationalities broke out all over the country through the second half of the nineteenth and the first half of the twentieth centuries. From French Canadians in Maine to Germans in St. Louis and Cincinnati, to Poles in Chicago, the church's history in this era is a litany of ethnic battles. The very fact that the battles occurred, however, testified to the power of the ethnic laity and clergy and the weakness of the bishops, at least in controversies over preserving national traditions. In most cases, bishops acceded to national parishes – they had little choice – even if they maintained their ultimate right to control parish property and to select pastors. The Catholic Church, therefore, provided the cultural space for immigrant groups to create their own schools to preserve their culture in America. As Paula Fass contends, however much Irish American bishops might grumble, the Church provided the opportunity for a "significant alternative" to the public school's assimilation. The simple existence of national parochial schools testified to that.[6]

Yet if Catholic education provided all Catholic immigrant groups with the opportunity to preserve their cultures, not all groups chose to take advantage of that opportunity. French Canadians, Poles, and some other Slavic groups like Lithuanians and Slovaks, spent enormous sums of money and amounts of energy building their own schools, but Italians and some others such as the Portuguese, seemed indifferent to Catholic education, and Irish Americans ambivalent about parochial schools, at least in the Northeast. The causes for this variation are hard to untangle, but seemed to revolve around the differing linkages or relationships among Catholicism, nationalism and language in each group's culture and historical experience. The French Canadians and Poles both suffered conquest by a (or in the Poles case more than one) national, religious and linguistic others and that conquest seemed to encourage them to treat their own national identities, and Catholic and language loyalties as inseparable. Germans also believed that those three allegiances were linked, but less from a sense of oppression in the old country and more from a sense of superiority in the new. Southern-Italian immigrants, suspicious both of the church and the new Italian nationalism, conceived of their group loyalties more in terms of family and neighborhood than Catholic institutions or nationalist movements. Irish immigrants fiercely asserted the links between their nationalism and Catholic religion, but few saw the need to preserve the Irish language and customs through schools. For all these groups, roots of identities may have run deep in the old country, but often did not become articles of faith for the mass of immigrants until they were discussed and debated in the United States.

For French Canadians the national, religious and linguistic oppressors were the English. England did little to interfere with French-Canadian Catholic religious practice in Quebec but the Catholic Quebecois certainly felt that they had become second-class citizens in their own land when France ceded Canada to England in 1763. Over the next century, French-Canadian leaders hammered out a sense of national mission for French Canadians called *La Survivance*. According to this notion French Canadians were the vehicle for preserving Catholicism in North America, but the *Canadiens* could not save their Catholicism unless they preserved their language and held fast to their pastoral and pure life on the farmlands of their Quebec homeland. French Canadian leaders in New England and elsewhere insisted, as Gerard Brault has suggested, "that abandoning the French language was tantamount to abandoning the Catholic faith."[7]

The explosion of population on those Quebec farms, an increase nearly eightfold by the middle of the nineteenth century, and the lure of opportunities in burgeoning New England and northern New York mills eventually drew the French south off their farms. Yet if they abandoned the pristine agricultural setting *La Survivance* idealized, they did not abandon its linkage of faith and culture. French-Canadian commitment to the faith in their own language prompted conflicts with English-speaking bishops, largely Irish in background, throughout New England from Maine to Connecticut during the late nineteenth and early twentieth centuries. Rather than accelerating French-Canadian assimilation, however, the hierarchical crackdowns that produced these battles probably sharpened the *Canadien* sense of ethnic difference and boundaries and their own ethnic interests.

French Canadians thus labored hard to build their own French-language parishes and, because to preserve the faith of future generations meant to preserve their language, too, established their own French-language schools. Early French-Canadian communities opened such schools in church basements or private homes, employing lay women or men, but by the 1870s and 1880s French Canadian communities across new England from Rutland, Vermont, to Lewiston, Maine, to Worcester and Fall River, Massachusetts, were drawing orders of sisters from Quebec to run their schools. By 1870, for example, the Souers Des Saints Noms de Jesus et Marie were teaching in the school of Rutland's Immaculate Heart of Mary Parish, and by 1877 the Religeuses de Jesus Marie of Sillery at the Parish of Notre Dame de Lourdes in Fall River. By the end of the twentieth century's first decade, Rev. J.A.Burns claimed that 161 of 188 French Canadian parishes in the United States had their own French language schools. These schools, heavily concentrated in New England, educated over 60,000 students or about half of all the children of French-Canadian immigrants in the nation.[8]

Poland, like French Canada, suffered oppression, too, by two national, linguistic and religious "others," Orthodox Russian and Protestant Prussian as well as the Catholic, German-speaking Austrian "others." The trio of Prussia, Russia and Austria had carved up the old kingdom of Poland in three partitions in the late eighteenth century, but Poles did not submit easily to their conquerors. Poles revolted in 1830-31, 1846, 1848 and 1863 against one or more of their oppressors without success. As John Bukowcyk notes, like the French Canadians, Poles developed a mystical sense of mission in this struggle, likening the Polish nation to a suffering Christ who died and yet rose again. As Bukowcyk and others point out, nationalism seemed strongest among an emerging Polish middle class in the nineteenth century; it was weaker, or at least less clearly articulated , among the millions of peasants who came to the Untied States. Victor Greene and Bukowcyk argue that over the course of the nineteenth century's last two decades, debates in the United States between two associations, the clerical-dominated Polish Roman Catholic Union (PRCU) and the lay-middle-class Polish National Alliance (PNA), helped educate the once peasants - now immigrant industrial workers about what Poland should be and what being Polish meant. Partisans in local Polish American struggles over control of churches or local institutions frequently invoked the rhetoric of the PRCU or PNA to support their own local claims. Matthew Jacobson notes that the Polish immigrant press also helped fire that nationalist enthusiasm. Polish newspapers frequently fed its readers serialized versions of the novels of the great nationalist writer, Henryk Sienkiewicz, recalling Polish Catholic resistance to the Swedes and Cossacks in the seventeenth century, as well as verses from the Catholic, nationalist poet, Adam Mickiewicz."[9]

Polish immigrants thus developed an acute sense of a special national identity. That identity reinforced and was reinforced by their faithfulness to Catholicism. Like the *Canadiens* they were eager to establish churches and schools, but determined that those churches and schools should preserve their own language and customs. Again like the French Canadians, this determination led them into numerous battles with Americanizing bishops which probably enhanced their sense of separate identity. Indeed, in the Polish case, it led to a schism, the creation of a Polish National Catholic Church in 1904. By 1916, the schismatic church counted about thirty churches and thirty thousand parishioners. The vast majority of Poles remained within the Roman Catholic Church, however, and founded their parishes and schools within its fold. By 1921, Polish Americans had built 511 schools in their 762 parishes, teaching nearly 220,000 students. By that time Polish parish schools taught an astounding 60% of the children of Polish immigrants in both Chicago and Detroit.[10]

German immigrants came to America bearing memories of a different experience in the homeland than the Poles and French Canadians, but they too became strong partisans of national parochial schools. German immigrants came from all parts of what became a united Germany in 1871: Prussia, Westphalia, Bavaria, Wurtemberg and many other small states and provinces. Unlike the Poles or French Canadians, Catholicism was not tied to nationalism. Indeed, Catholics may have been a minority, a substantial minority, to be sure, but a minority nonetheless among German immigrants to America: Protestants, Liberal "Free Thinkers" and Jews, also came from Germany to America in large numbers. Moreover, though many German Catholics welcomed unification, Catholics in Germany would soon suffer from the new Protestant dominated German state's *kulturkampf.*[11]

Yet most Germans in America of whatever religious background - Free Thinkers, Lutherans and other Protestants, Jews and Catholics - seemed devoted to German culture and its perpetuation in American life. German Lutherans, in fact, were probably more intensely committed to establishing and maintaining German language schools than German Catholics. Kathleen Conzen and a host of other historians suggest that this German devotion to their national culture was born not out of the sting of oppression and a resulting sense of inferiority, but rather from a belief in German culture's superiority to Anglo-American arts, literature and customs and a nagging resentment that other Americans were not giving German culture due recognition. Conzen points out that most German-American leaders in the nineteenth century strongly endorsed the ideals of American republican government, but they were reluctant to agree that "American society was closed; its development essentially complete … its character set." They "saw much that was … crass, materialistic and hypocritical in America." They had, Conzen notes, an "instinctive" sense of German cultural superiority. Discussing one such German American intellectual, Conzen points out: "Like most new immigrants of his ilk … [Julius] Frobel could not bring himself to accept an America that had no place for what he regarded as superior German culture." Though many of the German intellectuals Conzen discusses were Free Thinkers, such ideas were nonetheless pervasive among Lutherans, Jews and Catholics. [12]

There were also special reasons why religious Germans wished to preserve their language. Some sects, the Amish, Mennonites and others, explicitly tied the German language to religion and managed to preserve both through radical isolation. Yet even many in mainstream German faiths believed, like the French Canadians, that faith and language were inseparable. As Frederick Luebke points out, German Lutherans of the Missouri Synod, were convinced that their faith could not be preserved in future generations unless those generations continued to be German speakers. [13]

German Catholics shared this belief and it was reinforced by their conflicts with the English-speaking Irish in a series of major intra-church battles in the 1880s and 1890s. In a memorial sent to Rome in 1886, German American Bishop Michael Heiss of Milawukee complained: "wherever that most sad dictum 'let them learn English' has prevailed or now prevails, there has been and there will be, a truly deplorable falling away from the church … experience teaches that the only means by which Catholic Germans (and other foreigners) shall be able to preserve their Catholic faith and morals is that they shall have their own priests, who shall instruct them in the language and traditions of their fatherland." No wonder, then that a guide for German Catholic immigrants written in 1869 by Boston Jesuit, Ernst Reiter, charged: "Finally, never take shame in your mother tongue, your nation and your fatherland in America. Pfui!" [14]

No wonder then, too, that German Catholics rivaled the Poles and French Canadians in their commitment to parochial education. Dolores Liptak records that there were over 700 German-Catholic churches in the United States in 1870 and 95% of them had schools. At one point in the 1890s, she notes, every German parish in America had its own school. School building was clearly so important to German Americans that it proceeded almost immediately after, or even at the same time, as a parish was being formed. One study comparing Irish and German parishes found that two-thirds of the German parishes established schools within two years of a parish's formation but less than 30% of the Irish parishes built schools that quickly. [15]

Unlike German, Polish or French Canadian Americans, Italian Americans had little use for parochial schools. Indeed, Italian immigrant indifference to Catholic education was legendary. At the end of the twentieth century's first decade Burns reported only 48 Italian parishes with schools educating but 13,838 students, or about one-sixth as many schools and one-ninth as many students as their fellow "new immigrant" Poles. In Chicago, James Sanders reports, an exasperated Archbishop Quigley wrote Rome in 1913 that "there are sufficient parochial schools for all the children of immigrants except the Italians ... ." His diocesan newspaper, the *New World*, thought they knew why: "experience has taught that the Italians will not send their children to parochial schools if they have to pay for them there ... ." Fearful of losses among the Italians to Protestants the Chicago Archdiocese subsidized a parish school in St. Philip Bonizi parish in the 1910s. Yet diocesan efforts hardly offset Italian immigrant indifference and the vast bulk of Italian-American children went to public school. Mary Elizabeth Brown contends "Italian parishes have a poor reputation regarding the establishment of such schools, and Italian parents have a poor reputation for supporting them, but this reputation is only partly borne out by statistics." She notes that twenty of forty-seven Italian-American parishes in New York city had their own schools by 1941. Nevertheless, if the Italian "reputation" for indifference or hostility to parochial education has been exaggerated, it still seems clear that Italian immigrants placed much less value on them than other immigrants like the Poles, French Canadians and Germans. [16]

Why this is true is harder to explain. At its most basic level Italian immigrant understandings of ethnic identity simply differed from Polish, French Canadian and German ones. The Italian nationalist movement was strongest in northern Italy. When the movement triumphed and "reunited" the peninsula, the north dominated the new nation and imposed a harsh regime of heavy taxes and coercion on the poor peasants of the south hardly encouraging their affection for the new nation. It was these southern Italian peasants who made up the vast bulk of the Italian immigrants to America in the 1890s and early 1900s. Neither nationalists, nor southern skeptics of nationalism, however, seemed to have much use for the institutional Church. To the nationalists the Church was an active opponent of reunification; to southern peasants it had long been linked to oppressive landowners and notables. Such peasants were not indifferent or hostile to religion – religious belief and ritual were critical to their lives – but they were suspicious of the clergy and the institutional church. There was no sense of immediate oppression by the religiously, linguistically and ethnically other as there was in French Canada or Poland. Instead of the broad basis for some sense of belonging to a broadly imagined nation as happened in Poland or French Canada, southern Italians developed thick, powerful bonds to their families and local communities and those loyalties defined critical boundaries between themselves and others. [17]

The emigration process reinforced these bonds and boundaries. Almost all immigrants to America made the journey to the United States through networks of family members and close friends, what have been called immigrant "chains," but for Italian immigrants these chains seemed particularly important. Friends and family members followed each other to America in long trails, emptying out villages in Italy and depositing them on clusters of streets in American cities, where they created tight colonies of migrants from particular regions and villages. The immigrants in such colonies often organized into their own small associations or clubs centering on feast-day celebrations of saints from their villages in Italy. In the urban American hothouse of ethnic rivalries and competition a broader Italian-American ethnic identification eventually evolved out of these narrower loyalties. As Peter D'Agostino has pointed out, Italian-American Catholic priests as well as the Italian government played important roles in fostering this new national pride. Yet even then, there was never the fusion of language, religion and nationalism that seemed to make parochial schools such a necessity for the Poles, French Canadians or even the Germans. Italian American group identities seemed tied to family and neighborhood. These two not only defined group boundaries but served as the social mechanisms for transmitting group culture and identity. The parochial school was simply irrelevant.[18]

Irish-American experiences with parochial schools present yet another pattern; and perhaps an instructive example of how the relations between nationalism, religion, and identity affected an immigrant people's attitudes about parochial schools. In the course of nearly two-hundred years of war in the sixteenth and seventeenth centuries, Irish nationalism seemed to fuse with Catholicism in opposition to Ireland's English and Protestant oppressor. Indeed, the Irish used the same term in the Irish language to denote both English and Protestant. There was a point in the eighteenth and nineteenth centuries when some Protestant and Catholic Irish crafted a non-sectarian Irish-Republican nationalism. Among Irish Catholic peasants, too, English suppressions of the church had helped erode understanding of, or commitment to, institutional Catholicism throughout that period. Most Irish in the western part of the island did not attend mass regularly or knew little of their faith because for a long time there were no chapels or priests to accommodate them. Yet when Irish-Catholic immigration began running at floodtide in the 1830s and 1840s and throughout the nineteenth century, Irish nationalism and Catholicism were powerfully and intimately linked. Non sectarian republican Irish nationalism suffered grievously after the 1798 rebellion degenerated into a religious bloodbath and Daniel O'Connell's rise in the 1810s and 1820s religion and nationalism were tightly connected. Moreover, a "devotional revolution" in Irish Catholicism had transformed tribal Catholic loyalties into a disciplined institutional fidelity. [19]

At the same time, however, the Irish language was rapidly declining and by the end of the nineteenth century, almost all Irish spoke English and the vast majority spoke it alone. The revival of the Irish language would become an article of faith for many late-nineteenth and early twentieth-century Irish nationalists and the new independent Ireland would make the language an integral part of elementary education in the twentieth century. Nevertheless, the decline of Irish as an everyday language had progressed too far. Thus, if most Irish immigrants thus came to America with some sense of the intimate link between religion and nationalism, few felt that preservation or revival of the Irish language was essential to the maintenance of their group identity. In this sense, the Irish differed radically from the French-Canadians, Germans and Poles.[20]

This complex Irish heritage translated into a complicated Irish-American pattern of support for parochial education. In some dioceses like Chicago, Irish Americans strongly supported Catholic education, but in Massachusetts, which had the highest concentration of Irish immigrants and their children in the nation, Irish pastors were very slow to build schools. Indeed, the Archdiocese of Boston and the Diocese of Springfield, which divided the state in the late-nineteenth century, were among the worst dioceses in the nation in the construction of parochial schools. [21]

For Irish Catholics, parochial schools were not critical vehicles for passing on a specifically national culture. Some schools taught Irish history but almost none taught the Irish language, and organizations like the Ancient Order of Hibernians believed that even the number that taught Irish history was woefully tiny. In the early twentieth century, the A.O.H. launched a campaign to convince parochial and public schools to include Irish history in their curricula but had little success with either. Irish Catholic schools thus became the English language or "American" schools that over time would draw in students from all ethnic groups. This did not trouble Irish-American bishops and clerics. Indeed, partly out of self-interest to justify their power in the American church and partly out of genuine enthusiasm for American culture, most second-or third-generation Irish as well as some Irish-born clerics and bishops were strong advocates of Americanization of all immigrants—as long as it was Catholic Americanization. Even conservative bishops in the Americanist controversies of the late nineteenth century, like Bernard McQuaid of Rochester, New York, staunchly insisted on Americanization of immigrants.[22]

The intention to preserve old-country culture and identity through parochial schools was only the beginning. Even groups like the Poles, French-Canadians, and Germans were willing to establish such schools but faced difficult obstacles in trying to make them effective means of cultural transmission and preservation. One of the most important obstacles was the difficulty in securing the appropriate teachers. Catholic schools, in general, relied heavily on women religious for teachers. Indeed, it seems clear that the Catholic school system would not have existed without legions of dedicated women religious who worked tirelessly for a pittance. Securing such sisters was always hard even after the number of American-born women religious began to rise in the late-nineteenth century. It could be especially difficult for pastors of national parishes to find women religious for their schools because they had to have sufficient language fluency to be able to teach it to their students: foreign-born sisters, who presumably would be fluent, would have to be brought from overseas; native-born sisters might be more easily accessible but less likely to be fluent.

Jo Ellen McNergny Vinyard's recent study of parochial schools in Detroit is the best work on immigrants and Catholic schools that discusses in rich detail the problems that women religious and pastors faced in staffing national parish schools. As Vinyard points out, some such schools, German-American parish schools in Detroit for example, relied not only on German orders but also ethnically diverse women religious congregations like the Sisters of Immaculate Heart of Mary to staff their schools. The IHMs, as they were called, attracted Irish, French-Canadian, and French as well as Germans to their ranks and as early as the 1860s were drawing heavily from American-born children or grandchildren of these immigrant groups. Nevertheless, as late as 1887, the order taught not only almost all of Detroit's-Irish children in Catholic schools but nearly half of the students in German American parish schools as well. The IHM sisters were well aware of the different nationalities in the schools where they served and were careful to match each teacher's background and skills to her assignment. Still it seems clear that the pan-ethnic Catholic IHMs likely had a different perspective on the German schools they taught in than many of the most intensely nationalistic parents who sent their children to those schools. The School Sisters of Notre Dame staffed many of the other German-American parish schools in Detroit. Though open to all nationalities the SSND sisters in Detroit were largely German. Their schools in German parishes, Vinyard reports, were "unmistakably German ... from writing on the blackboard to the decorations on the walls." Yet even the SSND sisters, Vinyard points out, did not make the German language a "centerpiece of the curriculum." They understood teaching the German language as a practical necessity to ease second generation entry into American society and soften conflicts with immigrant parents. [23]

Polish immigrants flooded Detroit in the late nineteenth and early twentieth centuries, and there, as elsewhere, they were steadfastly committed to erecting their own parishes and parish schools. Polish pastors in Detroit (and actually elsewhere through the United States) drew heavily on the Felician sisters to staff their schools. Father Daborwoski of that city had invited the Felicians to the United States, suggesting that they "understand the spirit and tradition of the nation," In 1874 five sisters answered his invitation, established a motherhouse for the order in Detroit, and began recruiting candidates from among American born Polish women to the order. Though they recruited over 300 sisters between 1875 and 1900—all but 15 born in America—the rapid multiplication of Polish national schools around the country put intense pressure on the Felicians to turn out new teachers quickly. By the early 1890s the Felicians were staffing 38 schools from Massachusetts to Wisconsin and desperate superiors felt compelled to speed young women through their training and into the classroom. If their training was often rushed, the Felicians were, nonetheless, devoted to the preservation of Polish culture. Vinyard reports that in Detroit, schools in Polish parishes taught catechism, bible history, poetry, church history, literature, Polish history, art and music in Polish; reading, spelling, composition, arithmetic and in later grades, geography and history in English. Even in some of the English classes, she notes, some sisters lapsed into Polish, because they felt more comfortable speaking it.[24]

How successful, then, were such schools in nourishing old-country language and culture among their charges? That is hard to answer, if for no other reason than because there are no historical studies that have attempted to answer it. That is understandable because it is difficult enough to decide what customs or values might be measured to reveal the persistence of ethnic culture and what sources might measure them, much less determine how to link that persistence to schooling. One possible measure might be whether the children or grandchildren of immigrants retained their ancestral language. Clearly, Polish immigrants, for example, believed that language was central to their identity and thus a critical element, perhaps the critical element, in their culture that they wished to pass on to younger generations. In 1940 United States Census samples reveal that about 1.4 million second-generation and 185,820 third-generation Polish Americans claimed Polish as their mother tongue. About twice as many American born Poles made such claims as immigrants that year. Italian Americans, by contrast, did not support parochial schools with anything near the same zeal as Polish Americans. It is also less clear, as well, whether Italians considered language an essential marker of ethnic identity. Burns claimed in 1912 that even when Italian parishes had schools, the teachers often taught largely or even exclusively in English. In 1940, about two million second-generation and 125,040 third-generation Italian Americans claimed Italian as a mother tongue. Together the two American-born generations made up only about 1.4 times the number of immigrants making that claim that year. It appears from this very rough comparison that the Polish investment in parochial schools "paid off" somewhat in preserving the language - at least through the second generation. Yet neither language seemed to survive the transition to the third generation. [25]

Such statistics are hardly conclusive evidence of the efficacy of national parish schools in preserving ethnic culture and identity. Such schools did not exist in a vacuum. As Roy Rosenzweig, Liz Cohen, James Barrett and a host of other historians have argued American popular culture was a powerful Americanizing force affecting immigrant and second generation workers in the early twentieth century, particularly as radios became more commonplace even in working class homes and movies popular even in the most densely settled ethnic neighborhoods. Economic exigencies, the need to use English in jobs, also worked to erode the persistence of old country languages. It is interesting that the mother tongue languages endured more easily in rural areas of the west and south than the urban east. Only 8.9 percent of the Polish third-generation in the Midwestern states like Ohio, Michigan or Illinois claimed Polish as a mother tongue but nearly 18% in the plains states further west, including Kansas, Nebraska and the Dakotas, did. Similarly, only 6.5 percent of the third-generation Poles living in cities claimed Polish as a mother tongue in 1940, but nearly 19 percent of the Polish generation's members living on farms did. Similar discrepancies appeared in the statistics for the French and Germans. Presumably, enough members of a group could concentrate in rural areas in some isolation from the demands of a complex economy or the unmediated power of popular culture to preserve the old country tongue. [26]

Yet it was not only popular culture or economic exigencies that pressed the children and grandchildren of immigrants to assimilate. The leaders of the Catholic Church itself, top heavy with bishops of Irish birth or descent, also pushed hard for Americanization. In the 1920s the National Catholic Welfare Conference, the recently formed national voice of the American bishops, launched its own Americanization campaign encouraging the teaching of civics in Catholic elementary schools. In dioceses, trends toward the centralization of Catholic school administration and the development of Catholic high schools over the course of the twentieth century, also seemed to lend new momentum to that push for Americanization. Cardinal Mundelein expanded the diocese's central education bureaucracy and extended its reach into school curriculum and teaching. Chicago imposed regular meetings of teachers from all its schools, common examinations and common English-language texts for basic subjects. Such changes sparked heated responses from a number of ethnic groups, particularly Polish Americans, and ethnic conflicts plagued the Chicago Archdiocesan school system throughout the 1920s. The development of Catholic high schools also "vastly expanded interethnic contacts which would eventually facilitate the assimilation forestalled by parish schools with single nationalities" because high schools were usually larger than elementary schools, more expansive, and thus almost always "translocal." Some ethnic groups thus resisted diocesan sponsored high schools. In Rhode Island in the late 1920s, for example, French Canadians, particularly in the heavily French town of Woonsocket, refused to support new diocesan high schools and the conflict became so bitter that Bishop Hickey excommunicated some of the high school program's opponents.

If resistance testified to the endurance of ethnic loyalties and the commitment of French Canadians, Poles and others to education in their own culture, diocesan efforts to mix Americanization with standardization and centralization as those trends gained momentum also reflected the hierarchy's persistent and ever more successful investment in assimilation. As Cardinal Gibbons suggested much earlier, for most leaders of the Church, national parish schools were not justified as a means of resistance to assimilation but as a particularly efficacious means of accomplishing it. Gibbons argued that "Our Catholic schools afford a much easier pathway for the foreigner to enter American life than the public school [teachers in Catholic schools] understand – their peculiar idioms of thought and speech ... [and can help their charges learn English] gradually, almost unconsciously." J.A. Burns stated it more pointedly in 1912: "There could be no clearer evidence of the thoroughness of the work of assimilation effected in the Catholic school than the fact that the German or Polish young man, removed by two – and sometimes by only one – generations from his immigrant ancestry has become the strongest advocate of the use of English in his children."[27]

The evolution of mutually reinforcing trends of centralization and Americanization in parochial education may have reached its peak in the establishment of the Commission of American Citizenship at Catholic University in 1938. Inspired by Pope Pius XI, the American hierarchy stated the commission's purposes: "our people from childhood to mature age [must] be instructed in the true nature of Christian democracy ... they must be held to the conviction that love of country is a virtue and that disloyalty is a sin." To carry out that charge the Commission fostered the founding of civics clubs in Catholic schools around the country and published a magazine, the *Young Catholic Messenger*, and a Catholic comic book series, *Treasure Chest*, for parochial school children.[28]

One of the commission's most significant efforts, however, was to publish a series of school readers, the "Faith and Freedom" series, that were used in nearly three-fifths of American Catholic elementary schools by the early 1960s. In the nineteenth century Catholic publishing houses like the Sadlier Company and Benziger Brothers had produced a number of texts for parochial schools. As Timothy Walch has pointed out: "The overwhelming majority of Catholic school books were in complete thematic agreement with public school texts." Walch points out, however, that "Catholic school books ... agreed that America was superior to other nations," but "these texts emphasized the continuing involvement and contributions of *Catholics* [italics added] in American history. Lesson after lesson recalled the exploits of American Catholic heroes from the obvious, such as Commodore John Barry and Bishop John Carroll, to the preposterous, such as Bishop Gorda, a missionary to Greenland."[29]

The commission's textbooks carried on this theme, emphasizing Catholic heroes from the nation's founding like Barry, Carroll, William Gaston of North Carolina, and Pere Marquette. Such heroes did more than impress their readers with the harmony of Catholicism and American patriotism; as Vladimir Nahirny suggests, they provided the new American Catholic group that was forming out of diverse immigrant peoples with an alternative line of descent, a new ancestry. The Knights of Columbus, by far the most popular Catholic fraternal organization at that time, did much the same thing in its lionization of Christopher Columbus, the first American Catholic. Of course, the "Faith and Freedom" readers celebrated contemporary American Catholic heroes as well. The series reader, *These Are Our Freedoms*, included a letter home from John J. Shea, who served in the Navy during World War II and died at the battle of the Coral Sea in 1942. In this letter to his young son shortly before his death, Shea stated succinctly the commission's principal article of faith: "Be a good Catholic and you can't help being a good American." [30]

Yet if the commission and the national Church organization seemed intent on inculcating American patriotism and respect for American values into American schoolchildren, they were not anti-immigrant or even necessarily opposed to ethnic pluralism. As Gary Gerstle has pointed out, nationalism in World War II, when the first edition of the "Faith and Freedom" readers were written, was "deployed against racial domination" espoused by the Nazis. It thus offered, in turn, a "celebration of American ethnic and racial diversity without precedent in the country's history." Gerstle notes that "the key image [of this new nationalism in popular culture] ... was the multicultural platoon" that usually included Midwestern or Yankee elite or southern white Protestants; Catholic ethnics of all varieties, Jews and even Filipinos and Mexicans. As Gerstle makes clear, there were limits to this new pluralism; blacks were usually excluded from the popular imagery, just as the government still rigidly segregated the armed services. Yet the incorporation of pluralism in American nationalism was a dramatic change from its earlier ethnicity and racially narrow versions.[31]

The Church's national educational organizations and the Commission on American Citizenship took up this new nationalist pluralism and in some ways moved beyond it. Though stoutly anti-communist and happy advocates of celebrations of American patriotism like "I am an American Day" for Catholic schoolchildren, the NCWC and the NCEA resolutely backed the rights of immigrants in America and opposed racially or ethnically discriminatory immigration laws. The NCWC had opposed the original Immigration Restriction Acts of 1924 that discriminated against southern and eastern European as well as Asian immigrants. In 1952, Senator Patrick McCarran, an Irish Catholic from Nevada, introduced new immigration "reform" legislation that, nonetheless, preserved the discriminatory quotas of the older acts. The National Catholic Welfare Conference opposed McCarran's bill because it was still "based upon arbitrary quotas which reflect national and religious prejudices." Monsignor Hochwalt, simultaneously head of NCWC's department of education and the National Catholic Educational Association, launched "an educational campaign for a Christian and democratic attitude toward emigration" in Catholic schools to combat the new bill. The campaign sought to raise "a doubt about our present immigration policies" and urged the adoption of a more "scientific" immigration legislation. The NCEA and NCWC began development of a new teacher's handbook on immigration and curriculum guides as part of the campaign as well, and Rev. Thomas Martin of the Commission for American Citizenship urged diocesan superintendents of schools to "include a talk by a diocesan resettlement director or some other competent person on the topic of immigration."[32]

The Commission on American Citizenship was the center of this campaign. The commission worked to mobilize Catholic civics clubs "to give friendly help to the children of Displaced Persons and other newcomers in the community." NCEA and NCWC staff members also suggested that the *Young Catholic Messenger* and other commission publications "feature stories on the topic of the Christian and democratic attitude toward immigration." Yet as Rev. Thomas Martin of the commission pointed out in a memorandum to Monsignor Tanner on March 11, 1952, the commission had already been doing just that. Martin cited hundreds of examples in the "Faith and Freedom" readers from grades one to eight that endorsed a pluralist vision of America, including *"Eddie Patterson's Friends* ... a story of interracial and international friendliness among children expressed at a birthday party [Eddie's friends included an African-American and Chinese boy] [and]... *Christmas Eve* [which] shows a Mexican family in Los Angeles." If Church educational leaders seemed intent on Americanizing immigrant children, then they also seemed sensitive to immigrant needs, opposed to the racist immigrant policies of their day, and in line with the burgeoning pluralism of their era, eager to educate students about American ethnic variety.[33]

In the 1960s the timid World War II and Cold War pluralism, bathed in American patriotism, gave way to a political, social and cultural revolution that completely transformed how Americans understand ethnicity and race in America.

The revolution vanquished the old WASP elite breaking forever its pretensions to cultural and social authority. African Americans led this assault, especially as the Civil Rights movement evolved into the Black Power movement. Though tiny in size, and, perhaps, limited in its impact on politics, Black Power, nonetheless, had a powerful effect on American culture by attacking the notion of assimilation and crusading for racial and ethnic pride. Black Power directly inspired Red Power movements among native Americans, Yellow Power among Asian Americans, and Brown Power among Mexican Americans. Those movements crystallized in protests in the late 1960s at San Francisco State for Asian Americans, for example, or Alcatraz Island for Native Americans. Interestingly, however, white ethnics, many of them Catholics, were also moved by this cultural revolution. Many white ethnic Irish, Italian, Poles and others reacted angrily to the claims of blacks and other minorities. Yet many also took up the assumptions and themes of ethnic cultural assertion trumpeted in Black Power rhetoric to inspire and justify their own "white ethnic revival," centered on a new ethnic pride.

Some Catholic leaders moved quickly to take part in the new multicultural revolution. Monsignor Geno Baroni, who had worked in both white-ethnic and African American parishes, hailed blacks for questioning "the melting-pot myth and the Americanization process that dictates everyone is to be the same." He created the National Center for Urban Ethnic Affairs to give voice to the ethnic concerns of Italian, Polish and other white ethnic Americans. Catholic educational leaders also joined the effort. In late 1971, an NCEA-sponsored meeting of Diocesan School Superintendents agreed to "develop a curriculum guide for a Catholic-value education that both embraces and supports a valid pluralism in life styles and cultural roots and insists upon the value of group cultural differences as portraying the genuine picture of American Society." Rev. C. Albert Koob, president of NCEA, was enthusiastic about the new cultural pluralism and worked hard through 1972 to organize a conference on "An Approach to Ethnic Studies in Parochial Education" but was frustrated by a lack of funding. In 1975, however, the NCEA, the Catholic Conference on Ethnic and Neighborhood Affairs and the National Center for Urban Ethnic Affairs sponsored a conference on "The Intercultural Dimension in Catholic Education." Baroni was the keynote speaker and sessions discussed the "Intercultural Dimension of Catholic Education," "Ethnic Studies as an Integral part of the Education Process," and "The Role of the Parish in Facilitating Education Models for Neighborhood and Community." The next year Rev. John Meyers, the new president of NCEA, William McCready of the National Opinion Research Center, and Monsignor Baroni announced the creation of a new Consortium on Research in Catholic Education that would focus on, among other things, "the relationship between ethnicity and Catholic schools." [34]

Nevertheless, the white-ethnic revival appeared to have little direct effect on Catholic schools and those schools little effect on the revival. Some historians and social scientists wonder whether there was much of an ethnic revival at all. They dismiss the white-ethnic revival as brief and shallow, enlisting few and seriously affecting less of the nation's millions of Italian, Polish, Irish Americans and other white ethnics. Yet even if the white ethnic revival is taken seriously, there is no evidence that Catholic schools played an important part in it. One reason was that partisans of the revival, even devout Catholic ones, believed that the Church's leadership and institutions had been part of the problem of forced assimilation and could hardly be counted on to be part of the new pluralist or multicultural solution. Many Italian, Polish and other eastern or southern European ethnics resented an Irish-dominated Church's efforts to force them to conform to Irish versions of American Catholicism. In December 1975, the National Conference of Catholic Bishops held hearings on "Race and Ethnicity" in Newark in preparation for the Bicentennial of 1976. Some witnesses praised the Church, but more criticized it. Baroni, the theologian Michael Novak, and local community activists, Gerard Muench and Thomas Michaski, noted that the Church had long seemed intent on making all immigrants, "in effect, become Irish Americans." Baroni jokingly charged that the Irish nuns in his parochial school tried to rename him "Kevin," and, in the same spirit, Novak claimed that he had to call himself "O'Novak" for many years. Muench, a Ukrainian-rite Catholic, was more sober and blunt: "The Church has never tried to solve the problem of preserving diversity." The reaction against the Church was not just against its past commitment to assimilation, however. It was part of a broader transformation of Catholicism in America that led thousands of priests and sisters to leave the religious life and hundreds of parochial schools to close. Indeed, the institutional Church's transformation was, in turn, just a part of an even broader revolt among Americans of every religion and ethnic background against American institutions claiming cultural authority. [35]

Older institutions and organization like schools and even fraternal or sororal societies thus played little part in the white-ethnic revival. Participants seeking to celebrate ethnic identity in the ethnic revival did so more often now through more informal, intimate, and what they considered, more authentic social and cultural entities such as families, tracing their roots or nourishing it with ethnic cuisine, or neighborhoods, marking off their historic sites or celebrating it with festivals. In Baltimore, for example, St. Leo's Italian parish became the focus of a revival of the city's Little Italy in the 1960s and 1970s. Yet at the very same time residents started a very successful neighborhood festival and created numerous new organizations centered on the Church during the revival, the parish school quietly closed down. [36]

There was another dimension to the sixties' revolution, however, that would prove more important for Catholic education. In 1965, Congress passed real immigration reform, eliminating the old national quotas favoring northwestern Europe over the rest of that continent as well as Asia and Africa. Despite the law's new provisions, no one at the time expected the global sources of immigration to America to change considerably. At the signing ceremony, President Lyndon Baines Johnson remarked: "The bill we sign today is not a revolutionary bill." And yet the law, and several other events and trends, such as America's defeat in Vietnam and the effects of globalization on Latin American economies, combined to transform the sources and volume of American immigration. The number of Mexican immigrants rose from 250,000 in the 1950s to 1.5 million by the 1980s and the Puerto Rican population climbed from 300,000 to more than two million over the same time period. Thousands, hundreds of thousands, more came from Cuba, Guatemala, the Dominican Republic and El Salvador. Meanwhile, Asian immigration from countries like Vietnam, Korea, Taiwan and mainland China rose 140 percent in the 1970s and another 100 percent in the 1980s.[37]

Many of these immigrants, not only Latinos from the Americas, but even some of the new Asian immigrants, were Catholics, but few appeared eager to establish their own schools. Because they had so few priests of their own, and because of the Church's continuing commitment to Americanization, Latinos, for example, rarely created their own parishes. In the Northeast, Midwest and Southeast most moved into older urban parishes, which they shared, sometimes uneasily, with the remnants of the churches' older white congregations. In some cities, dioceses created non-territorial missions for Latino immigrants. The Archdiocese of Miami, for example, established such missions to serve the vast influx of Cubans and other Latinos into its cities and towns in the 1960s. Later in Miami many parishes simply became Cuban by default, as the newcomers flooded old neighborhoods. Still, if the parishioners might be all or largely Cuban or members of another Latino immigrant group, the priests were not. Michael McNally points out that while about one quarter of Miami's parishes were principally Latino-dominated by the 1980s only about one-seventh of the archdiocese's priests were Latinos. Cubans in Miami did, however, create some of their own parishes that self consciously sought to maintain a Cuban-American identity. McNally cites St. John Bosco parish, founded in 1963, soon after the first big wave of Cuban immigrants. St. John Bosco soon boasted 5,000 families, a festival, a rich associational life, and a very active after-school-educational center, but not a full-time parochial school. For Asian Americans the patterns were often similar. Local studies suggest that even where Vietnamese or Korean Catholics created vibrant communities, for the Vietnamese in New Orleans, for example, and for Korean Catholics in Boston, such vitality did not mean the creation of a full-time parochial school, but rather educational or community centers offering Saturday or after-school programs. [38]

The vast majority of Catholic schools, then, even those serving the new immigrants, had no ethnic affiliation. Their teachers and school staff members, even in inner-city schools, remained overwhelmingly white. In an examination of the staffs of hundreds of inner-city secondary and elementary schools in 1995-1996, Joseph O'Keefe and Jessica Murphy discovered that even when whites averaged only a tenth to a quarter of the students in such schools, they made up two-thirds to nearly four-fifths of the teachers and over four-fifths of the principals. As the NCEA's interest in multicultural education and numerous efforts by individual schools and teachers testifies, many Catholic schools worked hard to make their minority students comfortable in these settings. Nevertheless, they could no longer claim to play a central role in the preservation of the immigrant child's ethnic culture as the old national parish schools did, or, at least, had attempted to do. As important, they now faced stiffer competition from public schools in accommodating immigrant children's cultural differences. What Stanley Lieberson said about public schools and African-American culture and identity was also true of public schools and the new immigrants: "The European groups attempted to provide their offspring with a background in the unique facets of their groups and sought to generate pride in their heritage. This was done almost entirely outside public institutions... The development of black pride is not basically different from the attitudes that motivated the new European groups in the past decades to create a variety of organizations devoted to maintaining their distinctive cultures. But now the expectation is that the public school systems will provide such an outlet ... black power to influence such events has finally been reached at a time when the schools are generally more susceptible to local, specialized pressures." Such efforts have embroiled public schools in controversies over bilingual education programs, history curricula and canons of literature, but those controversies, ranging from the fights over national history standards to a struggle over Black English "Ebonics" also testify to how much the multicultural revolution had affected American public education. Public schools were no longer starkly differ from parochial schools in their commitment to ethnic pluralism. [39]

If there are many reasons why immigrant children might not be attracted to Catholic schools, substantial numbers nonetheless go to them. As before, however, the proportions vary significantly from group to group. In a study of eighteen dioceses nationwide (including fifteen of the twenty largest dioceses) Stewart Lawrence found wide discrepancies among groups in the proportion of their children who attended parochial schools. At the high end were the Filipino Americans; at the low end Mexican-and Nicaraguan-Americans; other groups,

Haitians, Vietnamese, Puerto Ricans, Koreans ranged in between. In Los Angeles and San Jose California dioceses, about one-sixth of Filipino school-age children (16.2 percent and 15.4 percent respectively) were enrolled in Catholic schools. In the same dioceses only 4 percent and 3.2 percent respectively of Mexican American children went to parochial schools. Lawrence cites several possible reasons for these discrepancies: the size of the group in a diocese; the administrative efficiency and wealth of the diocesan school system; the immigrant group's prior experience with Catholic education; and its current socioeconomic status. Whatever the reasons, they do not seem to be the same as those that once distinguished Polish and Italian immigrants in earlier days. Catholic schools may work hard today to nourish their students' pride in their own cultures, but they are not explicitly designed as they once were to be vehicles of cultural preservation.[40]

If we can say that much at least, it is clear nonetheless that there is still much we do not know about the roles Catholic schools have played in helping immigrant children adjust to American life over the last century and half. Most research on contemporary Catholic schools and minorities, for example, focuses on their work with African Americans. Exciting, rich and significant as that literature is, there is a need for much more attention to the schools and immigrant children, Latinos and Asians in particular. We know even less, however, about the impact of the schools on immigrant children of the nineteenth, and early twentieth-centuries. We have attempted some crude measures here to suggest how well national parish schools performed in preserving national languages, but those measures are crude indeed and merely suggestive. More important, we know little about the broader impact of those schools on their charges. Jencks, for example, is convinced that public education helped early twentieth century immigration children to master the complexities of America's modern industrial economy and move up the occupational ladder. Did Catholic schools help their children as much or more? There is little evidence to answer that question and what does exists seems contradictory. Jo Ellen Vinyard notes, for example, that many middle-class Polish Americans in turn-of-the-century Detroit worried that their schools prepared their children poorly to succeed in the American economy. There is today a debate among historians of Polish Americans about that very issue. Josef Miaso argues that the buildings were overcrowded, the sisters hastily and often poorly trained, and that the Polish parochial schools thus lagged "far behind [public schools] in both their educational level and in the teaching methods."

Other historians of Polish America, like Anthony Kuzniewski, suggest that the public school alternatives were not likely to be much better than the parochial schools and the Polish parish schools buoyed Polish ethnic self esteem in an era of WASP forced assimilation. There are few historical studies tracing Polish-American students through the schools and into careers that might resolve such a debate. Joel Perlman did such a study of Irish Catholics and other groups in Providence, Rhode Island, at the turn of the twentieth century. He found no significant differences in occupational mobility rates between Irish children in parochial schools and those in public schools or even between Irish children in parochial schools and native stock Yankees in public schools. Perlman's is the only serious historical study linking career patterns and parochial school attendance to date, but surveys by Andrew Greeley and Peter and Alice Rossi from the 1950s on found that Catholic schools seemed to help mobility. At this point there is still simply too little evidence to know. [41]

Yet if there is much we do not know about Catholic schools and immigrants, it is important to acknowledge that we need to know much more. We need to move beyond the history of the establishment of the schools or the battles over them within the church and outside of it. We need to probe how the schools themselves worked and how they shaped and influenced their students. We need to know this because we will never fully understand the history of the American Catholic Church, the Church of the immigrants, unless we know more about the role Catholic schools played in the lives of immigrants and their children. Similarly, we will never fully understand the history of American immigration if we do not know more about that role. And, finally, we will never be able to understand fully how the history of parochial schools and immigrants might affect our policies for schools and immigrants in the present. If we continue to draw on history to inform our present understanding of immigration, as like Christopher Jencks and almost all who discuss contemporary immigration do, then we need to know that full story.

## ENDNOTES

1. Christopher Jencks, "Who Should Get In?" New York Review of Books Volume XLVIII, Number 19 (November 29, 2001), 57.

2. Immigration Commission, *The Children Of Immigrants in Schools*, Volume 34, (Washington: GPO, 1911) 151; Leslie Tentler, "On the Margins: The State of American Catholic History, " *American Quarterly*, Volume 45, no. 1 March:1993): 105.

3. Roger Daniels, *Coming to America: A History of Immigration and Ethnicity in American Life* (Harper: New York, 1990), 216; Rev. J.A. Burns CSC, *The Growth and Development of the Catholic School System in the United States* (New York: Benziger Borthers, 1912), 319.

[4]
Paula Fass, *Outsiders In: Minorities and the Transformation of American Education* (New York: Oxford University Press, 1989), 82; David B. Tyack, "The Perils of Pluralism: The Background of the Pierce Case," Volume 74 (October, 1968): 77; Robert H. Lord, John E. Sexton and Edward T. Harrington, *History of the Archdiocese of Boston*, Volume III (New York: Sheed and Ward, 1944), 153.

[5]
Rudolf Vecoli and Suzanne M. Sinke, *A Century of European Migrations, 1830-1930* (Urbana: University of Illinois Press, 1991).

[6]
Fass, *Outsiders In*, 190.

[7]
Gerard Brault, *The French-Canadian Heritage in New England* (Hanover : University Press of New England, 1986), 73.

[8]
Burns, *The Growth*, 307; Brault, *The French Canadian Heritage*, 74.

[9]
John Bukowcyk, And My Children Did Not Know Me: A History of the Polish-Americans (Bloomington, Indiana: Indiana University Press, 1987), 3-14, 34-51; Victor Greene, *For God and Country : The Rise of Polish and Lithuanian Ethnic Consciousness in America, 1860-1910* (Madison : State Historical Society of Wisconsin, 1975); Matthew Jacobson, *Special Sorrows: The Diasporic Imagination of Irish, Polish, and Jewish Immigrants in the United States* (Cambridge: Harvard University Press, 1995).

[10]
Daniels, *Coming To America*, 221-222.

[11]
Daniels, *Coming to America*, 145-159; Hans Trefousse, "The German-American Immigrants and the Newly Founded Reich," in Frank Trommler and Joseph McVeigh eds. *America and the Germans: An Assessment of Three Hundred Year History, Volume I, Immigration, Language and Ethnicity* (University of Pennsylvania Press, Philadelphia, 1985), 160-163.

[12]
Conzen, "German Americans and The Invention of Ethnicity" in Trommler and McVeigh eds., 135.

[13]
Frederick Luebke, *Germans in the New World: Essays in the History of Immigration* (Urbana: University of Illinois, 1990), 6-7.

[14]
Jeffrey M. Burns, Ellen Skerrett and Joseph M. White eds., *Keeping Faith: European and Asian Catholic Immigrants* (Orbis: New York, 2000), 64, 53.

[15]
Dolores Liptak, *Immigrants and Their Church* (MacMillan: New York, 1989), 99.

[16]
James W. Sanders, The Education of an Urban Minority: Catholics in Chicago, 1833-1965 (New York: Oxford University Press, 1977) 69, 70; Mary Elizabeth Brown, "Italian and Italian American Secular Clergy in New York, 1880-1950," *U.S. Catholic Historian*, Volume 6, number 4 (Fall: 1987): 296-298.

[17]
see for example Robert Orsi, The Madonna of 115th Street: faith and Community in Italian Harlem, 1880-1950 (New Haven: Yale University Press, 1985) .

[18]
Peter R. D'Agostino, "The Scalibrini Fathers, The Italian Emigrant Church and Ethnic Nationalism in America," *Religion and American Culture*, 7, (1997): 121-159.

[19]
S.J. Connolly, *Priest and People in Pre-Famine Ireland, 1780-1845* (Dublin: Gill and Macmillan, 1982).

[20]
Kerby Miller, *Emigrants and Exiles: Ireland and the Irish Exodus to North America* (New York: Oxford University Press, 1985), 119-122.

[21]
Sanders, Education of an Urban Minority, 14, 49; Timothy J. Meagher, Inventing Irish America: Generation, Class and Ethnic Identity in a New England City, 1880 –1928 (South bend: University of Notre Dame Press, 2001), 157-162.
Sanders 49.

[22] John O'Dea, *History of the Ancient Order of Hibernians and Ladies Auxilary*, Volume III (New York: National Board of the A.O.H., 1923), 1171, 1196, 1274, 1434-1437.Glen Janus, "Bishop Bernard McQuaid: On 'True' and 'False' Americanism," *U.S. Catholic Historian* Volum11, no. 3 (Summer, 1993): 59-65.

[23] Jo Ellen McNergney Vinyard, *For Faith and Fortune: The Education of Catholic Immigrants in Detroit, 1805-1925* (Urbana: University of Illinois Press, 1998), 69-82.

[24] Vinyard, *For Faith*, 117-127.

[25] Lowry Nelson, "Speaking of Tongues," *American Journal of Sociology*, Volume 54, no. 43 (November 1948): 203.

[26] Nelson, "Speaking of Tongues," 207-208.

[27] Fass, *Outsiders In*, 194; Burns, *The Growth*, 295; Gary Gerstle, *Working Class Americanism: The Politics of Labor in a Textile City, 1914-1960* (New York: Cambridge University Press, 1989).

[28] Timothy J. Meagher, "Reconciling Patriotism and Catholic Devotion: Catholic Children's Literature in Postwar America," in Colleen McDannell, *Religions of the United States in Practice* Volume II (Princeton, New Jersey: Princeton University Press, 2001), 161.

[29] Timothy Walch, *Parish School: American Catholic Parochial Education from Colonial Times to the Present* (New York: Crossroad Publishing, 1996) 74-75.

[30] Sister M. Charlotte RSM and Dr. Mary Synon, *These are Our Freedoms* (Washington DC: Ginn and Company for The Catholic University of America, 1944), 74.

[31] Gary Gerstle, *American Crucible: Race and Nation in the Twentieth Century* (Princeton: Princeton University Press, 2001), 195, 204.

[32] NCWC News Service, Editorial Information, October 30, 1952, Rev. Thomas Martin to Diocesan Directors, February 15, 1952; Rev. Thomas Martin to Superintendents, February15, 1952, Folder Immigration Act, NCWC, Department of Education Files; Memorandum: From Mr. Cummings to Monsignor Hochwalt, June 3, 1946, Folder I Am an American Day, NCWC, Department of Education files. Archives of the Catholic University of America, (hereafter ACUA)

[33] Rev. Thomas Martin to Rt. Rev Msgr. Paul Tanner, March 11, 1952, Folder Immigration Act, NCWC, Department of Education Files, ACUA.

[34] Gerstle, *American Crucible*, 333-335; National Conference of Catholic Bishops Committee for the Bicentennial, *Liberty and Justice for All*, "Ethnicity and Race," Newark Hearing, December 4-6, 1975, 3-5; Meyer to Francis Sussna, Dec 16, 1971, Folder, National Center for Urban Ethnic Affairs, Folder Multicultural Institute, November 1, 1975; Press Release, "New Organization Formed, " William Watman to Jack Myers, December 8, 1976, Folder National Center for Urban Ethnic Affairs, Rev. Albert Koob files, NCEA, ACUA.

[35] NCCB, "Ethnicity and Race," 7, 12, 13, 29.

[36] Jay Dolan ed. *The American Catholic Parish: A History from 1850 to the Present*, Volume I, Part I, Michael J. McNally, "A Peculiar Institution: A History of Catholic Parish Life in the Southeast (1850-1980)" 210-211; Marilyn Halter, *Shopping for Identity: The Marketing of Ethnicity* (New York: Schocken Books, 2000). Joseph Casino, "From Sanctuary to Involvement: A History of the catholic Parish in the Northeast".

[37] David Reimers, *Still the Golden Door: The Third World Comes To America* (New York:

[38] Columbia University Press, 1992).
McNally, "A Peculiar Institution," 212-215; Joseph Casino, "From Sanctuary to Involvement: A History of the Catholic Parish in the Northeast", 86-87.

[39] Joseph M. O'Keefe and Jessica Murphy, "Ethnically Diverse Catholic Schools: School Structure, Students, Staffing and Finance," in James Youniss and John Convey eds. *Catholic Schools at the Crossroads: Survival and Transformation* (New York: Teachers College Press, 2000), 122; Stanley Lieberson, *A Piece of the Pie: Blacks and White Immigrants Since 1880* (Los Angeles: UCLA Press, 1980), 114.

[40] Stewart Lawrence, "'New' Immigrants in the Catholic Schools: A Preliminary Assessment," in Youniss and Convey eds., *Catholic Schools*, 178-200.

[41] Anthony Kuzniewski, "Boot Straps and Book learning: Reflections on the Education of Polish Americans," *Polish American Studies*, 5-26; James Pula, *Polish Americans: An Ethnic Community* (New York: Twayne Publishers, 1995), 76-77; Joel Perlmann, *Ethnic Difference: Schooling and Social Structure Among the Irish, Italians, Jews, and Blacks in an American City, 1880-1935* (New York: Cambridge University Press, 1988), 73-82; Fass, *Outsiders In*, 223-224.

# AFTERWORD

>--~

*Michael J. Guerra*

## HISTORY LESSONS

The centennial of the National Catholic Educational Association provides both the rationale and support for this publication, a collection of diverse and fascinating essays examining the experiences of Catholic education in the United States over the past one hundred years. Several of the essays concentrate on NCEA's work on behalf of Catholic education at one or more levels (Augenstein, Wister, Mahoney, McBride). Other chapters describe the shifting historical, political and social contexts which shaped the work of Catholic education in the United States, and influenced NCEA's understanding of its priorities and responsibilities to its members.

I am not surprised to find many of the authors dipping into the nineteenth century to trace the sources of a number of Catholic education's twentieth century challenges. The deep-roots award goes to Thomas Groome, who chooses to begin his extraordinary analysis of a unique linkage between Catholic schooling and catechesis with Clement of Alexandria in the second century. Groome's reference to Tertullian's attempt to sever this connection ("Jerusalem has no need of Athens") suggests an early version of the debate reignited in the 1960s by Mary Perkins Ryan's book, "Are Parochial Schools the Answer?" Fortunately, neither Tertullian nor Ryan prevailed, or this would be a much shorter book, and a much poorer world.

The roots of Catholic education in the United States run deep. Catholic education's periods of growth and decline, and the struggles and successes of its past provide a dark glass in which we can see many of the challenges and opportunities of the future. A number of critical issues illustrate how strategic decisions and directions that will shape the future of Catholic education can be illuminated by reflections on our history. Many of the strongest challenges facing Catholic education today have been raised before. While our responses to these recurring questions need to account for substantial changes in context, there is much we can learn from the past.

If our future depends on our ability to prepare a new generation of educational and catechetical leaders, what lessons can we learn from the Sister Formation Movement of the 1950s?

If our future challenges us to provide an articulate, compassionate and faithful voice for Catholic values in the public square, what lessons can we learn from the powerful and unified Catholic response to the efforts to eliminate religious schools and privatize religious values in the 1920s?

If our future calls us to collaborate with others to improve education for all, especially the children of the poor, what lessons can we learn from involvement of Catholic educators in the coalitions that promoted the 1965 Elementary and Secondary Education Act, or the Milwaukee and Cleveland voucher programs in the 1990s?

If our future challenges us to keep our doors, our minds and our hearts open to all, especially those who are most likely to be excluded, what lessons can we learn from the past experiences of African Americans in our parishes and schools, and the role Catholic schools played in the earliest days of the civil rights movement?

Our history is not an unblemished record of successes. There are also important lessons to be learned from past struggles, from instances when Catholic leadership was weakened by premature pessimism and lack of courage, from political setbacks that punctured our Panglossian innocence, from our failures to support one another in the shortsighted and self-centered expectation that we could strengthen one ministry, or one institution, at the expense of another.

We can learn from our honest mistakes, our failure to anticipate the impact of changing patterns of religious vocations, and the consequent gross underestimation of the need for fair compensation for religious. We could take some small comfort from the fact that our country's Social Security system suffers from a similar actuarial myopia, but we need to do better. How will we meet the educational ministry's share of responsibility for religious congregations' unfunded retirements, while also providing appropriate compensation for our active lay and religious colleagues, so that we will not only recruit but also retain the committed teachers, catechists and administrators who will continue to breathe new life into Catholic education?

What can we learn from past efforts to expand lay involvement in governance? Depending on the reporter, lay trusteeship was a hopeful 19th century preview of the current trend toward broader lay participation in governance and leadership, or an early sign of tension between the laity and the hierarchy. Today lay participation in Catholic educational governance has helped many institutions pass through troubled times to emerge with greater strength and strong prospects for the future. But there have also been failures – some institutions were lost because they moved too slowly to expand their support base and were susceptible to the vagaries of changing demographics or new ministerial priorities on the part of their ecclesial sponsors; others were weakened by self-perpetuating governing bodies unable to prevent slippage in their understanding and commitment to mission.

One basic question is raised directly or implicitly in virtually every chapter. The question is answered in a variety of ways by the authors and those whose earlier work they chronicle. What does it mean to be a Catholic in America? To the nativists of the nineteenth century, an American Catholic was an oxymoron. They argued that young Catholics should be required to be educated in public schools to enhance their capacity for citizenship, and to privatize if not purge their allegiance to religious superstition and a foreign sovereign. Timothy Walch reminds us that more than fifty years ago John Courtney Murray challenged the opinion of a Supreme Court justice that would in effect "…forbid the child to be simultaneously a citizen and a child of God."

Our predecessors worked hard to disprove Nativist allegations. But, as Timothy Meagher points out, their enthusiasm for assimilation and recognition as good and patriotic citizens did not overwhelm their concern for human rights and the dignity of all God's children. Meagher offers interesting examples from the "Faith and Freedom" series that endorse a surprisingly strong pluralist vision of America.

A fair reading of our history will acknowledge an abundance of ambivalence as Catholic education continued to search for an appropriate balance between unity and diversity in its relationships with Jerusalem and Athens. But our predecessors raised the right questions, and their responses were often heroic and prophetic, if at times timid and superficial. We have much to learn from those who went before us, and much more to do before we turn the future over to those who will come after us. We will not provide final answers to questions that our successors will take up in their turn, but a centennial celebration that begins with a reflection on our history should remind all who are committed to the future of Catholic education that it is our turn to transform a faithful past into a faith-filled future.

# CONTRIBUTORS

JOHN J. AUGENSTEIN, is the Dean of the Marquette University School of Education. In his 42 years in education he has been an elementary and a high school teacher in Catholic and public schools, a superintendent, and a university professor. He has co-authored two books with Dr. M. William Konnert of Kent State University: *Superintendency for the Nineties: What Superintendents and Board Members Need to Know* (1990) and *The School Superintendency-Leading Education into the 21st Century* (1995). He has also authored a monograph, a national report, chapters in three books, and numerous articles. The National Catholic Educational Association published his third book, *Lighting the Way 1908-1935: The Early Years of Catholic School Superintendency, The history of the Chief Administrators of Catholic Education* (CACE). He's been a member of NCEA since 1965.

ANGELYN DRIES, OSF, taught junior and senior high school in Wisconsin and North Carolina for fifteen years, worked as a parish Director of Religious Education, and was novice director for the Sisters of St. Francis of Assisi, Milwaukee, Wisconsin. She completed her doctoral studies at the Graduate Theological Union, Berkeley, California. Dries is Associate Professor and Chair of the Religious Studies Department at Cardinal Stritch University, Milwaukee, Wisconsin, where she has taught since 1989. Her research interests encompass the U.S. Catholic mission movement, women's approaches to mission and the intersection of Catholicism and Asian religions. Her publications include *The Missionary Movement in American Catholic History* (1998) and, along with Joseph Chinnici, *Prayer and Practice in the American Catholic Community* (2000). She is associate editor of *Missiology*, the journal of the American Society of Missiology.

313

She also has been a pastoral presence in the Milwaukee Korean Catholic Community for ten years.

GERALD P. FOGARTY, SJ, is William R. Kenan, Jr., Professor of Religious Studies and History at the University of Virginia. He received his BA and MA from Fordham University, his Ph.D. in history at Yale, and then pursued theological studies at Woodstock College. He has taught at Woodstock College, Fordham, Boston College, and the Catholic University of America. Among his books are *The Vatican and the American Hierarchy from 1870 to 1965* and *Commonwealth Catholicism: A History of the Catholic Church in Virginia.*

THOMAS H. GROOME is a senior professor of Theology and Religious Education at Boston College. His most recent book is *What Makes Us Catholic: Eight Gifts for Life.* He is also the author of *Coming to Faith Religion Curriculum* (K to 8th grade), the most widely used catechetical series throughout American Catholic schools and parishes. He completed his doctorate in education and theology (EdD) at Columbia University Teacher's College and Union Theological Seminary, New York. He makes his home in Chestnut Hill, Massachusetts, with his spouse, Colleen Griffith, also a pastoral theologian at Boston College, and their son Ted.

MICHAEL J. GUERRA is the president of the National Catholic Educational Association. He had served as the executive director of the Secondary Schools Department at NCEA for 19 years and had a major role in the design and implementation of the *National Congress on Catholic Schools for the 21st Century.* He led several research projects, including *Belief and Values of Catholic Secondary School Teachers; The Heart of the Matter,* assessing school program effects on student beliefs, values and behaviors; and *CHS 2000:* a comprehensive study of the American Catholic high school. He also has authored many publications, including *Lighting New Fires: American Catholic Schooling 25 Years After Vatican II.* He contributed chapters to *Religion and Schooling in Contemporary America* and *Catholic School Leadership.* An outspoken advocate for school choice and educational reform, he has served as a member of the National Assessment Governing Board and as a consultant to the National Educational Goals Panel.

CHRISTOPHER J. KAUFFMAN occupies the Catholic Daughters of the Americas Chair at the Catholic University of America. He is the author of the histories of the Alexian Brothers, the Sulpicians, the Marianists, the Knights of Columbus, a biography of William Howard Bishop, the priest founder of the Glenmary Home Missioners, and a Religious History of Catholic Health Care in the United

States. He is the editor of the *U.S. Catholic Historian*, the general editor of the award-winning six volume history of the Catholic Community. Professor Kauffman is also general editor of a nine-volume set of documents, *American Catholic Identities*.

KAREN M. KENNELLY, CSJ, is a member of the Congregational Leadership Team of the Sisters of St. Joseph of Carondelet, a U.S.-based community with nearly 2,000 members with missions in South America and Asia. She assumed this position in 2002, following experience as province director for the St. Paul Province of her congregation, and as president of Mount St. Mary's College, Los Angeles. She is a co-founder of the Conference on the History of Women Religious (1988), and continues to serve as its Coordinator and newsletter editor. Her trusteeship experience includes positions on the boards of directors for the American Council on Education; the Association of Catholic Colleges and Universities; and the National Association of Independent Colleges and Univer-sities; as well as serving as a trustee for a number of Catholic colleges, seminaries, and hospitals in the Midwestern and Western regions. Kennelly's recent publi-cations include "Faculties and What They Taught," in *Catholic Women's Colleges in America; Gender Identities in American Catholicism;* and "Women Religious in American Catholic History" for *The Encyclopedia of American Catholic History*. An alumna of the College of St. Catherine, St. Paul, MN, she holds a master's degree in history from The Catholic University of America and a doctorate in history from the University of California, Berkeley. The recipient of many academic honors and awards, including Fulbright and American Council of Learned So-cieties fellowships, she is a member of Phi Beta Kappa and has received honorary doctorates from a number of colleges and universities.

KATHLEEN A. MAHONEY is a graduate of the University of Rochester where she studied the history of American education. She has held a number of academic appointments, including a postdoctoral fellowship from the National Academy of Education (1998). Most recently she was assistant professor in the higher education program at the Lynch School of Education at Boston College, where she was founding director of the Institute for Administrators in Catholic Higher Education. She is author of a number of articles and studies on religion and higher education, including *Catholic Higher Education in Protestant America* (Johns Hopkins University Press, 2003). Dr. Mahoney currently serves at the president of the Humanitas Foundation in New York City.

MARIA MAZZENGA works for National History Day, a program aimed at improving the teaching and learning of history in U.S. schools. She received a Ph.D. in

History from Catholic University of America. She has written and delivered papers on youth culture, education, ethnicity, and religion in the United States, and is currently working on a book tentatively titled "Junior Victory: Young Baltimoreans Fight World War Two." She has taught history at Catholic University, George Mason University, and Virginia Commonwealth.

LAWRENCE J. MCANDREWS is Associate Professor of History at St. Norbert College in DePere, WI, where he teaches History of the United States, Constitutional History of the United States, Diplomatic History of the United States, Social History of the United States, The Americas, and The Catholic Contribution to the United States. He is the author of *Broken Ground: John F. Kennedy And The Politics Of Education* as well as several articles on twentieth-century American political history in such journals as *The Catholic Historical Review, U.S. Catholic Historian, Records of the American Catholic Historical Society, Journal of Church and State, Journal of Negro History,* and *Presidential Studies Quarterly.*

ALFRED MCBRIDE, O.PRAEM, Philadelphia born, Father McBride is a Norbertine and a member of St. Norbert Abbey, De Pere, Wisconsin. Ordained to the priesthood in 1953, he has served as a parish priest, high school teacher, novice master and university professor. He holds a Diploma in catechetics from Lumen Vitae, Brussels, Belgium, 1963. He earned a doctorate in religious education from The Catholic University of America, Washington DC, 1971. He was the founder and executive director of the department of religious education at the National Catholic Educational Association, 1972-79. Our Sunday Visitor has published his four books on the Catechism: *Essentials of the Faith, Fr McBride's Teen Catechism; Father McBride's Family Catechism* and *Father McBride's College Catechism.* He has also published books with St. Anthony Messenger Press and Servant Books. He has done several thirteen-part programs with EWTN. Currently he is professor of Homiletics at Blessed John XXIII Seminary in Weston, MA.

TIMOTHY J. MEAGHER is curator of American Catholic History Collections and professor of Irish American and American Immigration History at The Catholic University of America. He received his BA from Georgetown University, MA from the University of Chicago, and Ph.D. from Brown University. Previous positions include Director of the Center for Irish Studies at CUA, Program Officer at the National Endowment for the Humanities and professor at Worcester Polytechnic Institute. He has written several essays and articles on Irish American and American-Catholic history as well as *Inventing Irish America: Generation, Class and Ethnic Identity in a New England City, 1880 to 1928,* edited *From Paddy to Studs: Irish American Communities at the Turn of the Century,* and co edited the collection, *The New York Irish*. The latter won the James Donnelly prize for the Best Book in Irish or Irish American history offered by the American Conference for Irish Studies in 1997. He is currently writing *A Guide to Irish American History* for Columbia University press.

CECILIA A. MOORE is on the faculty of the Department of Religious Studies at the University of. Dayton. Since 1998, she been a member of the faculty of the Institute for Black Catholic Studies at Xavier University of Louisiana. She received her doctorate in American Religious History from the University of Virginia in 1997. Her areas of specialization are African-American Catholic history, the history of Catholic education in the United States, United States Catholic history and African-American religious history. Her work has been published in *U.S. Catholic Historian, Catechist, Catholic Education: A Journal of Inquiry, Church History, Sacred Rock, and The North Star: A Journal of African-American Religious History*. Soon her encyclopedia essay on African-American Catholic women will be published in *The Encyclopedia of Women and Religion in North America*. But, most importantly, Dr. Moore is a proud graduate of Sacred Heart Catholic School in Danville, Virginia, class of 1981.

SEGUNDO PANTOJA is Coordinator of the Center for Ethnic Studies at the Borough of Manhattan Community College of the City University of New York. He is a Co-Investigator in the National Survey of Latino/a Parishes and Congregations conducted by the Office for Research in Society and Culture at Brooklyn College. Professor Pantoja is currently engaged in research on Catholic schools in Cuba. He received an MA in Latin American Studies from Queens College (CUNY)in 1991 and a Ph.D. in Sociology from The Graduate School of the City University of New York (1998).

ANTHONY M. STEVENS-ARROYO is Professor of Puerto Rican and Latino Studies at Brooklyn College and Distinguished Scholar of the City University of New York. Widely published both in English and Spanish, he has written more than 40 scholarly articles and authored nine books, including the four-volume PARAL series on religion among Latinos/as. His 1980 book, *Prophets Denied Honor*, is considered a "landmark of Catholic literature." With his spouse, Ana María Díaz-Stevens, he authored *Recognizing the Latino Religious Resurgence*, which was named an Outstanding Academic Book for 1998 by Choice Magazine. A spokesperson for civil and human rights, he has testified before the U.S. Congress and the United Nations and was named by President Jimmy Carter to the Advisory Board of the U.S. Commission of Civil Rights for two terms. Presently, he directs the Research Center for Religion In Society and Culture (RISC).

TIMOTHY WALCH is the director of the Herbert Hoover Presidential Library, one of ten presidential libraries administered by the National Archives and Records Administration. He also serves as an associate editor of the *U.S. Catholic Historian*, the award-winning quarterly of the U.S. Catholic Historical Society. Educated at the University of Notre Dame and Northwestern University, Dr. Walch is the author of dozens of books and articles on the history of American Catholicism in general and the history of Catholic education in particular. Of special note is his book, *Parish School: American Catholic Parochial Education from Colonial Times to the Present* (Crossroad/Herder, 1996), a work praised by the Reverend Andrew M. Greeley as "the best summary review of the history of Catholic education in the last half century."

ROBERT J. WISTER, a priest of the Archdiocese of Newark, is associate professor of Church History in Immaculate Conception Seminary School of Theology and Faculty Fellow of the John Whitehead School of Diplomacy and International Relations at Seton Hall University. He holds a Master of Sacred Theology degree from Union Theological Seminary and a Doctorate in Ecclesiastical History from the Gregorian University. He served as Executive Director of the Seminary Department of the National Catholic Educational Association in Washington, DC from 1988 to 1993. He has published articles and reviews in the *U.S. Catholic Historian, the Catholic Historical Review, Theological Studies, Theological Education, Thought,* and *Momentum.* He is editor of *Psychology, Counseling and the Seminarian* and *Priests: Identity and Mission* and the United States Bishops' *Program of Priestly Formation.* He has written extensively on theological education, contributing the extended article ""The Effects of Institutional Change on the Office of Rector and President in the Catholic Theological Seminaries – 1965-1994" to *Theological Education.* He serves as consultant to CBS News on matters concerning Catholicism and the Vatican, in particular, the next papal election.